Literary Afterlife

Literary Afterlife

*The Posthumous Continuations
of 325 Authors'
Fictional Characters*

Bernard A. Drew

McFarland & Company, Inc., Publishers
Jefferson, North Carolina, and London

LIBRARY OF CONGRESS CATALOGUING-IN-PUBLICATION DATA

Drew, Bernard A. (Bernard Alger), 1950–
    Literary afterlife : the posthumous continuations of 325 authors'
fictional characters / Bernard A. Drew.
        p.   cm.
    Includes bibliographical references and index.

    ISBN 978-0-7864-4179-2
    softcover : 50# alkaline paper ∞

    1. Fictitious characters.   2. Persona (Literature)   3. Influence
(Literary, artistic, etc.)   4. Characters and characteristics in
literature.   I. Title.
PN218.D74   2010
809'.927 — dc22   2009037844

British Library cataloguing data are available

Cover image ©2010 Photos.com

Manufactured in the United States of America

*McFarland & Company, Inc., Publishers
  Box 611, Jefferson, North Carolina 28640
  www.mcfarlandpub.com*

For the readers Donna, Jessie and Darcie

Table of Contents

Introduction

"First-time author sinks teeth into legend of Dracula," hailed *USA Today* in 2005, introducing a 700-page novel that took ten years to research.

"Bantam Pays $3.5 Million for 3 Dune Prequels," blared a headline in 1998, announcing Brian Herbert's contract to write three new books based on his father's classic science fiction tale.

"'Gone With Wind' Sequel An Astonishing Best Seller," *The New York Times* announced in October 1991—as if fifty-five years of pent-up interest and a huge promotional budget would have rendered anything *but* excitement for the release of Alexandra Ripley's *Scarlett*.

What is it about some writers' literary characters or plot situations that their popularity lives beyond their originators?

What is it about some writers that they feel compelled to carry on with characters or situations created by others? They are literary gravediggers — some with loving aspirations, some with mercenary motives.

Literary Afterlife: The Posthumous Continuations of 325 Authors' Fictional Characters is simple in concept. It is about the heroes and heroines of popular fiction who have lived on after their originators' deaths. Second chances. Literary mouth-to-mouth. Pastiches.

The term "pastiche" is used in this work to mean the writing of a fiction sequel or continuation of a book series by someone other than the originator. Pastiche has other literary meanings, of course, but as it is much simpler to identify books as pastiches than "works by other hands" or some other multiword label, the word pastiche will be used throughout.

Pastiches began at least two centuries ago and are still very much alive. Isabel Allende has given a feminist twist to Johnston McCulley's hero of the old Southwest, Zorro. Elizabeth Kostova has brought the vampire of legend, Bram Stoker's Dracula, creatively back from the dead. Mark Winegardner has uncovered more Mob crime to continue the saga of Mario Puzo's Godfather.

Some sequels grew from ideas of the authors. Others were instigated by

1

literary estates or publishing houses eager to keep a viable entity going a while longer. After mystery novelist Lawrence Sanders' death, his popular McNally series continued — written by someone else. The same happened with V.C. Andrews' gothic tales and Robert Ludlum's thrillers. Defense lawyer Perry Mason didn't die with Erle Stanley Gardner in 1970 — Thomas Chastain wrote new courtroom puzzlers featuring the battling lawyer in the early 1990s. Likewise, Robert Goldsborough continued Rex Stout's Nero Wolfe puzzlers. And dozens of writers have found more of Dr. Watson's cases in the old metal box.

Youthful readers are as avid devourers of neo-sequels as their elders. Gertrude Chandler Warner's warm series for middle readers, *The Boxcar Children*, ended with her death in 1979, after nineteen books. Then new hands took over, and there have been more than thirty-five sequels since 1991.

Pastiches exist in all genres. Louis L'Amour penned four Hopalong Cassidy novels in the early 1950s, carrying on Clarence E. Mulford's cowboy series, then gained enormous fame writing Westerns under his own name. Mulford was still alive, but didn't want to write any more books. In 2005, long after his death, two novice writers, Wild Ol' Dan Blasius and Susie Coffman, wrote yet newer Hoppy adventures for hardcover publication.

Modern-day writers have continued the works of Mark Twain and Jane Austen, Ray Bradbury and Louisa May Alcott, Edith Wharton and Dorothy L. Sayers, Owen Wister and Ian Fleming, Edgar Rice Burroughs and Charles Dickens, Robert Louis Stevenson and Laura Ingalls Wilder, J.M. Barrie and a slew of writers now forgotten.

David R. Slavitt in the *New York Times Book Review*, discussing new works featuring characters created by Arthur Conan Doyle, decried the "pastiche that is the product of calculatingly commercial writers and publishers — like these two attempts to squeeze further revenue out of Sherlock Holmes."

Andrew Delbanco in *The New Republic* termed Marion Mainwaring's completion of Edith Wharton's *The Buccaneers* "an exercise in literary necrophilia."

Are pastiche writers unoriginal hacks, coasting on the literary coattails of proven successes? "These are figures who have entered into the American cultural vocabulary," said Four Walls Eight Windows publisher John Oakes in justifying the issuance of a *Huckleberry Finn* sequel in 1992. "I don't think of it as lazy. I think of it as playful."

The list of pastiche writers includes four-star scribes Philip José Farmer, Louis L'Amour, Ray Bradbury, Lawrence Block, Robert B. Parker, Eric Lustbader and Joan Aiken — all successful with their own creations.

Some sequel writers are "motivated to tell us the 'real story' which lay behind the relatively brief appearances of characters such as the first Mrs. Rochester in *Jane Eyre* or Harry Flashman in *Tom Brown's Schooldays...*," defends David Pringle in *Million* for May–June 1992. "What greater testament to the enduring appeal of certain fictional works can there be than the fact that other authors are moving to write sequels to them?"

Literary Afterlife includes:

- Book series that have continued under a deceased writer's real or pen name — such as V.C. Andrews' thrillers;
- Undisguised offshoots issued under the new writer's real name — for example Eleanor Boylan's continuation of her late aunt Elizabeth Daly's Clara Gamadge mysteries or the many books featuring Dr. Watson, Irene Adler, Professor Moriarty, Mrs. Hudson, the Baker Street Irregulars or Inspector Lestrade, all based on characters from Arthur Conan Doyle's Sherlock Holmes mysteries;
- Posthumous collaborations, that is, unfinished manuscripts or story outlines completed by others, such as *Poodle Springs*, Robert B. Parker's version of Raymond Chandler's last Philip Marlowe mystery, Nancy Pickard's completion of Virginia Rich's last culinary mystery, or Desmond Bagley's last two thrillers, finished by his wife. With unfinished manuscripts by spymaster Donald Hamilton, Rumpole creator John Mortimer, Swedish crime novelist Stieg Larsson, mystery writers Kate Ross and Ellis Peters, Chilean author Roberto Bolano — not to mention Vladimir Nabokov — this subgenre has potential to grow;
- Unauthorized pastiches, such as stories about Edgar Rice Burroughs' Tarzan of the Apes or Japanese Harry Potter tales, for example;
- And "biographies" of literary characters (Horatio Hornblower, Miss Marple or Doc Savage) and cookbooks said to feature characters' favorite recipes (Nancy Drew, Nero Wolfe).

Generally omitted are books written under house names, or for which the original authors engaged substitutes during their lifetimes (assuming they held some literary control over the results). There are a few exceptions, just to show what's been going on.

Also left out are planned series issued under house names, often with multiple authors (Nancy Drew or Hardy Boys mysteries, for example). Exceptions include Kenneth Robeson's Doc Savage, a series that has seen new entries published after a forty-two-year gap.

Also disregarded are multiple-author novelizations, spin-offs, shared universes or planned series based on motion pictures or television programs, comic strip or comic book characters, unless they are derived from an original prose work (James Bond, for instance).

Parodies, or works in which the original character names are distorted for fun (Star Wreck, Hemlock Sholmes, essays by Max Beerbohm) are matter for another researcher, though a few have snuck in here. Authors included in this book are mostly serious in their interpretations.

The entries are largely limited to book publications (or collections of short stories).

Entries are organized alphabetically by author within several genre categories. Entries provide brief biographies of the creators, give overviews of their popular books or series and suggest reasons the series continued. The length of an entry only reflects upon the amount of interesting material available, not upon the literary merits of the original writers. Original books are listed, and pastiche works are provided in alphabetical fashion, by author.

Action and Adventure

Writers of popular adventure seem more susceptible to pastiche because their stories are more plot- than character-driven, and thus are easier to copy. Edgar Rice Burroughs, and later his heirs, were in lengthy battle to contain those who wanted to ape the apeman, as an example. The estate was cautious about allowing others to take up the story. Alistair MacLean's publisher attempted to wreak as much momentum from the writer's avid audience as it could, but interest soon waned. William W. Johnstone's family and publisher seem to be on a similar course, counting on old fans to pick up new works by another hand.

EDGAR RICE BURROUGHS

King of the Jungle

Chicago-born Edgar Rice Burroughs (1875–1950) had a vivid imagination and a creative hand. As a teen, during an influenza epidemic, he lived with his brothers George and Harry on a cattle ranch in Idaho. He graduated from Michigan Military Academy in 1895 and enlisted in the U.S. Army, serving with the Seventh Cavalry in Arizona Territory. He served as a railway policeman and door-to-door salesman, neither affording great potential. He rented a small office and began to write stories for the pulp fiction magazines of the day. He would soon shape adventure tales of the jungle (Lord Greystoke), Barsoom (John Carter) and Earth's core (David Innes). The first Tarzan story appeared in *All-Story Magazine* in October 1912 and earned him $700. It became the heart of the author's media empire in years to come.

"From this one novel sprang two dozen more, over forty movies, hundreds of comic books, radio shows, television programs, Tarzan toys, Tarzan gasoline, Tarzan underwear, Tarzan ice cream, Tarzan running shoes — the list is virtually endless. Edgar Rice Burroughs became one of the twentieth century's most popular authors, and Tarzan one of the world's best-known literary characters," according to the official Burroughs website.

The original works are in the public domain, but the name Tarzan is copyrighted. ERB Inc. routinely enforces its rights, as when it stifled five books by Barton Werper in 1964-65. The Fritz Leiber book *Tarzan and the Valley of Gold* was authorized. Philip José Farmer called his character, obviously based on Tarzan, "Lord Grandrith," except in the authorized novel *The Dark Heart of Time* (1999). John Coleman Burroughs, the author's son and an illustrator, wrote one Barsoom story. J.T. Edson's Bunduki is Tarzan in all but name. A number of authorized stories have appeared in the Tarzan syndicated newspaper comic strip and comic books.

Original Barsoom Works

A Princess of Mars (1917)
Gods of Mars (1918)
Warlord of Mars (1919)
Thuvia, Maid of Mars (1920)
Chessmen of Mars (1922)

Master Mind of Mars (1928)
Fighting Man of Mars (1931)
Swords of Mars (1936)
Synthetic Men of Mars (1940)
Llana of Gathol (1940) short stories

Barsoom Pastiches

John Coleman Burroughs, *John Carter of Mars* (1964) aka *John Carter and the Giant of Mars* short stories
Mike Resnick, *Forgotten Sea of Mars* (1965)

Original Pellucidar Works

At the Earth's Core (1922)
Pellucidar (1923)
Tanar of Pellucidar (1930)
Tarzan at the Earth's Core (1930)

Back to the Stone Age (1937)
Land of Terror (1944)
Savage Pellucidar (1963)

Pellucidar Pastiches

George Alec Effinger, *Maureen Birnbaum, Barbarian Swordsperson* (1993) includes "Maureen Birnbaum at the Earth's Core"
Allan Howard Gross, *Farewell Pellucidar* (1991)
John Eric Holmes, *Mahars of Pellucidar* (1976); *The Red Axe of Pellucidar* (1993)

Original Tarzan Works

Tarzan of the Apes (1914)
Return of Tarzan (1915)
Beasts of Tarzan (1916)
Son of Tarzan (1917)
Tarzan and the Jewels of Opar (1918)
Jungle Tales of Tarzan (1919) short stories
Tarzan the Untamed (1920)
Tarzan the Terrible (1921)
Tarzan and the Golden Lion (1923)
Tarzan and the Ant Men (1924)

Tarzan Twins (1927)
Tarzan, the Lord of the Jungle (1928)
Tarzan and the Lost Empire (1929)
Tarzan at the Earth's Core (1930)
Tarzan the Invincible (1931)
Tarzan Triumphant (1931)
Tarzan and the City of Gold (1933)
Tarzan and the Lion Man (1934)
Tarzan and the Leopard Men (1935)
Tarzan and the Tarzan Twins with Jad-Bal-Ja, the Golden Lion (1936)

Tarzan's Quest (1936)
Tarzan and the Forbidden City (1938)
Tarzan the Magnificent (1939) short
    stories

Tarzan and the Madman (1964)
Tarzan and the Castaways (1964) short
    stories
Tarzan, the Lost Adventures (1997)

Tarzan Pastiches

Anonymous, *Tarzan and the Lost Safari* (1966); *Greystoke: The Legend of Tarzan Lord of the Apes* (1983) movie novelization

Zdenck Burian, *Jungle Scenes of Tarzan* (1973)

J.T. Edson, *Bunduki* (1975); *Bunduki and Dawn* (1976); *Sacrifice for the Quagga God* (1976); *Fearless Master of the Jungle* (1980)

Philip José Farmer, *A Feast Unknown* (1969); *Lord of the Trees* (1970); *The Mad Goblin* (1970); *The Adventure of the Peerless Peer* (1974) aka *The Adventure of the Three Madmen in The Grand Adventure* (1984), with Tarzan exorcised; *Hadon of Ancient Opar* (1974); *Flight to Opar* (1976); *Time's Last Gift* (1985); *The Dark Heart of Time* (1999)

William Gilmore, *Tarzan and the Lightning Man* (1963)

Edward Hirschman, *Tarzan at Mars' Core* (1977)

Fritz Leiber, *Tarzan and the Valley of Gold* (1966)

Douglas Niles, *Tarzan and the Well of Slaves* (1985)

Richard Reinsmith, *Tarzan and the Tower of Diamonds* (1985)

R.A. Salvatore, *Tarzan: The Epic Adventures* (1996) based on teleplay by Burt Armus

Barton Werper, *Tarzan and the Silver Globe* (1964); *Tarzan and the Cave City* (1964); *Tarzan and the Snake People* (1964); *Tarzan and the Abominable Snowmen* (1965); *Tarzan and the Winged Invaders* (1965)

Fictional Biography

Philip José Farmer, *Tarzan Alive* (1972)

MICHAEL CRICHTON

Jurassic Parker

Chicago-born Michael Crichton (1942–2008) trained as a physician. When he started to write novels, he specialized in medical and techno thrillers. Crichton grew up on Long Island. He graduated from Harvard, taught for a few years then entered Harvard Medical School. His first novel, *Odds On*, came out in 1966 under the penname John Lange. Five books later, he used his own name for *The Andromeda Strain* (1969). That and *The Terminal Man* (1972), *The Great Train Robbery* (1975), *Jurassic Park* (1990), *Airframe* (1996) and other novels soared to the top of the bestseller lists. Many of the books were adapted as films, and Crichton himself directed *Pursuit* (1972) as a television movie, and wrote and directed *Westworld, Coma* and other theatrical films. He created the television series *ER* in 1994.

Upon his death from throat cancer, Crichton left a finished manuscript, *Pirate Latitudes*, which was quickly readied for print. He also left an incomplete manuscript that "will be finished once [the publisher] Harper, Crichton's agent Lynn Nesbit, and his widow, Sherri Crichton, chose a co-writer," according to SFScope's Ian Randal Strock. "'We want a high-level thriller writer, somebody who understands Michael's work,' [HarperCollins publisher Jonathan] Burnham said. 'From what I gather, there are notes and indications of which direction the novel was going, so the writer has material to work from apart from the actual material that was finished.'"

Posthumous Collaboration
Announced (2010)

C.S. FORESTER
Horatio Hornblower

A Hollywood scriptwriter and wartime newspaper correspondent, Cecil Scott Forester (1899–1966) created a popular hero of the sea, Horatio Hornblower, in a series of stories noteworthy for historical detail, deft characterization and gripping plots. The novels were frequently serialized in *The Saturday Evening Post*. Hornblower owed much to Admiral Horatio Nelson for his hero and setting. A film version of *Captain Horatio Hornblower* (1951) starred Gregory Peck and a 1998–2003 television series featured Ioan Gruffudd.

"Forester was a genuinely great storyteller who loved the creative, imaginative process that turned words into the illusion of a past reality," said Sanford Sternlicht in *Twentieth-Century Romance and Historical Writers* (1990), adding that Forester's books had sold eight million copies by his death.

Mr. Midshipman Hornblower, chronologically the first exploit, finds a young Hornblower fighting a duel and captured by the Spanish. The time is 1794–1798. In *Lieutenant Hornblower*, set in 1800–1803, the hero weds. In *Hornblower and the Hotspur*, 1803–1805, he becomes a father and captures a Spanish treasure. *Admiral Hornblower in the West Indies* takes place at the end of the hero's career, 1821–1823

Forester was born in Egypt, lived in Spain and France and attended school in England. He studied medicine but decided on writing as a career instead. His *Hornblower Companion* (1964) contained naval history, maps, chronology and a description of how Hornblower was created.

English-born Cyril Northcote Parkinson (1909–1993) wrote a Hornblower biography before going on to create his own fictional series about seagoing adventurer Richard Delancey. David Weber's Honor Harrington science fiction series is modeled very closely on the Horatio Hornblower books, though it is not a direct pastiche. Ditto Ben Jeapes' *Her Majesty's Starship* (1998) and David Feintuch's Nicholas Seafort tales such as *Midshipman's Hope* (1994). Likewise, L. Neil Smith's *Henry Martyn* (1989) is a swashbuckling tale that acknowledges Forester's seafaring sagas. Peter Cannon's short story, "Sherlock Holmes and the Loss of the British Barque Sophy Anderson," featured Lt. Richard Hornblower, great-grandson of Horatio H., in *Resurrected Holmes* (1996) edited by Marvin Kaye. Weber also wrote a short story, Captain Honario Harpplayer, R.N.," for the March 1963 issue of *Fantasy & Science Fiction*.

In the last book listed in Forester's originals, below, "Hornblower During the Crisis" was incomplete at the author's death but is published with notes. "Hornblower's Temptation" is also known as "Hornblower and the Widow McCool."

Original Horatio Hornblower Works

The Happy Return (1937) aka *Beat to Quarters* (1937)

A Ship of the Line (1938)

Flying Colours (1939)

The Commodore (1945) aka *Commodore Hornblower* (1945)

Lord Hornblower (1946)

Mr. Midshipman Hornblower (1950)

Lieutenant Hornblower (1952)

Hornblower and the Atropos (1953)

Hornblower in the West Indies (1958) aka *Admiral Hornblower in the West Indies* (1958)

Hornblower and the Hotspur (1962)

The Hornblower Companion (1964) includes short story "The Point and the Edge"

Hornblower During the Crisis and Two Stories: Hornblower's Temptation and the Last Encounter (1967)

Fictional Biography

C. Northcote Parkinson, *The Life and Times of Horatio Hornblower* (1970)

H. RIDER HAGGARD

She

H. Rider Haggard (1856–1925) wrote tales of high adventure in unusual places. Born in Norfolk, England, he worked as a colonial assistant in Natal, South Africa. He became court registrar in the Transvaal. When he returned to England, he began to write of the robust hero Allan Quatermain in *King Solomon's Mines* and of She Who Must Be Obeyed in *She*.

Sigfriour Skaldaspillir wrote a sequel to Haggard's Viking tale, and other writers added stories of She and Quatermain.

Original Allan Quatermain Works

King Solomon's Mines (1885)

Allan Quatermain (1887)

Allan's Wife (1887)
Maiwa's Revenge; or, The War of the Little Hand (1888)
Marie (1912)
Child of Storm (1913)
The Holy Flower (1915)
Finished (1917)
The Ivory Child (1916)

The Ancient Allan (1920)
She and Allan (1920)
Heu-heu-or, The Monster (1924)
The Treasure of the Lake (1926)
Allan and the Ice-gods (1927)
Hunter Quatermain's Story: The Uncollected Adventures of Allan Quatermain (2004)

Allan Quatermain Pastiches

Thomas Kent Miller, *The Great Detective at the Crucible of Life; or, The Adventure of the Rose of Fire* (1977/2005)

Original She Works

She (1886)
Ayesha: The Return of She (1905)
She and Allan (1920)

Wisdom's Daughter: The Life and Love Story of She-Who-Must-Be-Obeyed (1923)
Allan and the Ice-gods (1927)

She Pastiches

Sidney J. Marshall, *King of Kor; or, She's Promise Kept, a Continuation of the Great Story of She* (1903)
Thomas Kent Miller, *Sherlock Holmes on the Roof of the World; or, The Adventure of the Wayfaring God* (1987)
Richard Monaco, *Journey to the Flame* (1985)
Peter Tremayne, *The Vengeance of She* (1978)

Original Eric Work

Saga of Eric Brighteyes (1890) aka *Eric Brighteyes* (1891)

Eric Pastiche

Sigfriour Skaldaspillir, *Eric Brighteyes 2: A Witch's Welcome* (1979)

GARY JENNINGS

Aztec

Gary Jennings (1928–1999), a native of Virginia, wrote robust historical novels. He lived for more than a decade in Mexico, and thoroughly researched the background for his Aztec sagas.

Novelist and attorney Junius Podrug and Jennings' editor Robert Gleason continued the Aztec books, based on Jennings' notes.

Original Aztec Works

Aztec (1980)

Aztec Autumn (1998)

Aztec Pastiches

Junius Podrug and Robert Gleason, *Aztec Blood* (2002); *Aztec Rage* (2006); *Aztec Fire* (2008)

W. E. JOHNS

Biggles

Englishman William Earl Johns (1893–1968) wrote adventure stories, many about a flying ace named Biggles. Johns served in the British Army and was commissioned into the Royal Flying Corps during World War I. He was a flight instructor. Shot down while on a bombing run, he was a prisoner of war until the conflict ended. He began to write in 1922, and his first Biggles book (the hero's name is actually James Bigglesworth) came out ten years after that, under the penname Captain W.E. Johns. The character also appeared in comics and film.

John Pearson wrote a biography of the fictional character.

Original Biggles Works

The Camels Are Coming (1932)
The Cruise of the Condor (1933)
Biggles of the Camel Squadron (1934)
Biggles Flies Again (1934)
Biggles Learns to Fly (1935)
The Black Peril (1935)
Biggles Flies East (1935)
Biggles Hits the Trail (1935)
Biggles in France (1935)
Biggles & Co (1936)
Biggles in Africa (1936)
Biggles—Air Commodore (1937)
Biggles Flies West (1937)
Biggles Flies South (1938)
Biggles Goes to War (1938)
The Rescue Flight (1939)
Biggles in Spain (1939)
Biggles Flies North (1939)
Biggles—Secret Agent (1940)
Biggles in the Baltic (1940)
Biggles in the South Seas (1940)
Biggles Defies the Swastika (1941)
Biggles Sees It Through (1941)
Spitfire Parade (1941)
Biggles in the Jungle (1942)
Biggles Sweeps the Desert (1942)
Biggles—Charter Pilot (1943)

Biggles in Borneo (1943)
Biggles Fails to Return (1943)
Biggles in the Orient (1945)
Biggles Delivers the Goods (1946)
Sergeant Bigglesworth CID (1947)
Biggles' Second Case (1948)
Biggles Hunts Big Game (1948)
Biggles Takes a Holiday (1948)
Biggles Breaks the Silence (1949)
Biggles Gets His Men (1950)
Another Job For Biggles (1951)
Biggles Goes To School (1951)
Biggles Works It Out (1952)
Biggles Takes the Case (1952)
Biggles Follows On (1952)
Biggles—Air Detective (1952)
Biggles and the Black Raider (1953)
Biggles in the Blue (1953)
Biggles in the Gobi (1953)
Biggles of the Special Air Police (1953)
Biggles Cuts It Fine (1954)
Biggles and the Pirate Treasure (1954)
Biggles Foreign Legionnaire (1954)
Biggles Pioneer Air Fighter (1954)
Biggles in Australia (1955)
Biggles' Chinese Puzzle (1955)
Biggles of 266 (1956)

No Rest For Biggles (1956)
Biggles Takes Charge (1956)
Biggles Makes Ends Meet (1957)
Biggles of the Interpol (1957)
Biggles on the Home Front (1957)
Biggles Presses On (1958)
Biggles on Mystery Island (1958)
Biggles Buries a Hatchet (1958)
Biggles in Mexico (1959)
Biggles' Combined Operation (1959)
Biggles at the World's End (1959)
Biggles and the Leopards of Zinn (1960)
Biggles Goes Home (1960)
Biggles and the Poor Rich Boy (1960)
Biggles Forms a Syndicate (1961)
Biggles and the Missing Millionaire (1961)
Biggles Goes Alone (1962)
Orchids for Biggles (1962)
Biggles Sets a Trap (1962)
Biggles Takes It Rough (1963)
Biggles Takes a Hand (1963)
Biggles' Special Case (1963)
Biggles and the Plane That Disappeared (1963)

Biggles Flies to Work (1963)
Biggles and the Lost Sovereigns (1964)
Biggles and the Black Mask (1964)
Biggles Investigates (1964)
Biggles Looks Back (1965)
Biggles and the Plot That Failed (1965)
Biggles and the Blue Moon (1965)
Biggles Scores a Bull (1965)
Biggles in the Terai (1966)
Biggles and the Gun Runners (1966)
Biggles Sorts It Out (1967)
Biggles and the Dark Intruder (1967)
Biggles and the Penitent Thief (1967)
Biggles and the Deep Blue Sea (1967)
The Boy Biggles (1968)
Biggles in the Underworld (1968)
Comrades in Arms (1968)
Biggles and the Little Green God (1969)
Biggles and the Noble Lord (1969)
Biggles Sees Too Much (1970)
Biggles Does Some Homework (1997)
  incomplete
Biggles Air Ace: The Uncollected Stories (1999)

Fictional Biography

John Pearson, *Biggles—The Authorized Biography* (1978)

WILLIAM W. JOHNSTONE

Action series

Missouri-born William W. Johnstone (1938–2004) wrote Westerns, adventure, science fiction and horror novels. He was one of the last of the pulpish, gritty, action-at-all-costs authors agile in multiple series in several genres. He persevered when dozens of action, secret agent, cowboy, and weird villains who reigned in paperback originals in the 1960s and '70s succumbed to a more demanding audience.

The estate and publisher are continuing several series, at first under the "co-authorship" of Fred Austin, now under the house name "with J.A. Johnstone."

See Johnstone entry in "Westerns."

Original Blood Bond Series

Blood Bond (1989)   *Brotherhood of the Gun* (1990)

Gunsight Crossing (1991)
Gunsmoke and Gold (1992)
Devil Creek Crossfire (1992)
Shootout at Gold Creek (1993)

San Angelo Showdown (1994)
Death in Snake Creek (1994)
Slaughter Trail (2006)

Blood Bond Pastiches

J.A. Johnstone, *The Hanging Road* (2007); *Texas Gundown* (2008); *Ride for Vengeance* (2008); *Deadly Road to Yuma* (2009)

Original Dog Team Work

The Last of the Dog Team (1980)

Dog Team Pastiches

Fred Austin, *The Return of the Dog Team* (2005)
J.A. Johnstone, *Revenge of the Dog Team* (2009)

Original Eagles Series

Eyes of Eagles (1993)
Dreams of Eagles (1994)
Talons of Eagles (1996)
Screams of Eagles (1997)
Rage of Eagles (1998)

Song of Eagles (1999)
Cry of Eagles (1999)
Blood of Eagles (2000)
Destiny of Eagles (2004)
Revenge of Eagles (2005)

Eagles pastiches

J.A. Johnstone, *Pride of Eagles* (2006); *Crusade of Eagles* (2007); *Thunder of Eagles* (2008); *Bloodshed of Eagles* (2009)

Invasion USA series/pastiches

William W. Johnstone with Fred Austin, *Invasion USA* (2006)
William W. Johnstone with J.A. Johnstone, *Border War* (2006)

Sidewinders series/pastiches

William W. Johnstone with J.A. Johnstone, *Sidewinders* (2008); *Massacre at Whiskey Flats* (2009); *Cutthroat Canyon* (2009)

Town Called Fury series/pastiches

William W. Johnstone with Fred Austin, *A Town Called Fury* (2006)
William W. Johnstone with J.A. Johnstone, *Hard Country* (2007); *Judgement Day* (2007)

Non-series pastiches

William W. Johnstone with Fred Austin, *Black Ops: American Jihad* (2006)

JIM KJELGAARD

Prehistorical Stalker

James Arthur Kjelgaard (1910–1959) grew up on a farm in Potter County, New York. He attended Syracuse University. He worked as a surveyor's assistant, trapper and forester. His experiences inspired the book *Forest Patrol* (1941). He wrote numerous animal stories for young adult readers, including books about Big Red, Stormy and Snow Dog.

Science fiction and fantasy author David Drake (b. 1945) wrote a sequel to Kjelgaard's YA novel *Fire-Hunter,* at the request of publisher Jim Baen. The book is about a Paleolithic young man named Hawk who, expelled from his tribe, is forced to survive by his own devices. "*The Hunter Returns* didn't make me a lot of money in exchange for the amount of research it required; but heck, the research was fun and it's not like I was missing meals as a result of poverty. I like to do different things in my writing. This project was not only different, it was a lot of fun," Drake said on his website.

Original Work

Fire-Hunter (1951)

Pastiche

David Drake, *The Hunter Returns* (1991)

ALISTAIR MACLEAN

Eagles Dare

A Scotsman by birth, an adventure writer by trade, Alistair MacLean (1922–1987) wrote thrilling action tales of sea (*H.M.S. Ulysses*), wasteland (*Ice Station Zebra*) and mountain (*Where Eagles Dare*), several of which became popular motion pictures.

Born in Glasgow, the son of a minister, he spent his younger years in the Scottish Highlands. He joined the Royal Navy in 1941, and served most of the time on Russian convoy routes. He graduated from Glasgow University after the war and became an educator. Discovering a knack for writing, he sold his first novel based on his military service, *H.M.S. Ulysses*. He later lived in Switzerland.

At his death, MacLean left several plot outlines that became the basis for pastiches. Sam Llewellyn wrote two sequels to MacLean's *The Guns of Navarone*— the only book to which MacLean himself had written a sequel.

Original Navarone Works

The Guns of Navarone (1957)   *Force 10 from Navarone* (1968)

Force 10 From Navarone Pastiches

Sam Llewellyn, *Storm Force from Navarone* (1996); *Thunderbolt from Navarone* (1998)

Pastiches, some based on MacLean outlines

John Denis, *Hostage Tower* (1980); *Air Force 1 Is Down* (1981)

Simon Gandolfi, *Alistair MacLean's Golden Girl* (1992); *Alistair MacLean's Golden Girl: Golden Web* (1993); *Alistair MacLean's Golden Girl: Golden Vengeance* (1994)

Alastair MacNeill, *Alistair MacLean's Death Train* (1989); *Alistair MacLean's Night Watch* (1989); *Alistair MacLean's Red Alert* (1990); *Alistair MacLean's Time of the Assassins* (1991); *Alistair MacLean's Dead Halt* (1992); *Alistair MacLean's Code Breaker* (1993); *Alistair MacLean's Rendezvous* (1995)

Hugh Miller, *Alistair MacLean's UNACO Prime Target* (1997); *Alistair MacLean's UNACO Borrowed Time* (1998)

PATRICK O'BRIEN

Aubrey and Maturin at sea

Patrick O'Brien (1914–2000), born Richard Patrick Russ, set his Jack Aubrey and Stephen Maturin seagoing series — Aubrey is an English naval captain, Maturin is his friend, an Irish-Catalan physician — in the early 19th century. The richly textured books had a wide following. "It's impossible for writers of historical fiction to completely expunge modern sensibilities from their work," Brian Bethuen wrote in *Maclean's* (Nov. 24, 2003), "but O'Brien came closer than anyone else." *Master and Commander* was a motion picture in 2005.

So much food was discussed in the O'Brien novels that two fans created a cookbook.

Original Aubrey and Maturin Works

Master and Commander (1969)

Post Captain (1972)

HMS Surprise (1973)

The Mauritius Command (1977)

Desolation Island (1978)

The Fortune of War (1979)

The Surgeon's Mate (1980)

The Ionian Mission (1981)

Treason's Harbour (1983)

The Far Side of the World (1984)

The Reverse of the Medal (1986)

The Letter of Marque (1988)

The Thirteen-Gun Salute (1989)

The Nutmeg of Consolation (1991)

Clarissa Oakes (1992) aka *The Truelove*

The Wine-Dark Sea (1993)

The Commodore (1994)

The Yellow Admiral (1996)

The Hundred Days (1998)

Blue at the Mizzen (1999)

21: The Final Unfinished Voyage of Jack Aubrey (2004)

Cookbook

Anne Chotzinoff Grossman and Lisa Grossman Thomas, *Lobscouse and Spotted Dog* (2003)

BARONESS EMMUSKA ORCZY

The Scarlet Pimpernel

The turmoil of the French Revolution inspired a play by Emmuska Orczy (1865–1947), whose name is usually shortened to Baroness Orczy. It was called *The Scarlet Pimpernel.*

Born in Hungary, Emmuska studied music in Budapest, Brussels and Paris. In London, she attended art school. She married Englishman Montague MacLean Barstow and worked as a translator and illustrator. Her first novel was *The Emperor's Candlesticks* (1899). She and her husband wrote a play about an aristocratic Englishman, Sir Percy Blakeney, who worked for the cause of good during the French Revolution. The 1903 play ran four years, and the book version found a publisher. She wrote a dozen sequels, some about the League of the Scarlet Pimpernel. She also wrote stories of Lady Molly of Scotland Yard, without the same success.

John Montague Orczy-Barstow (1899–?), the only son of Baroness Orczy, wrote a biography of the Scarlet Pimpernel. C. Guy Clayton wrote very loose pastiches. Marguerite Blakeney and Lauren Willig, author of historical romances, wrote the Pink Carnation series about the Scarlet Pimpernel's associates.

Original Scarlet Pimpernel Works

The Scarlet Pimpernel (1905)
I Will Repay (1906)
The Elusive Pimpernel (1908)
Eldorado (1913)
The Laughing Cavalier (1913)
Lord Tony's Wife (1917)
The League of the Scarlet Pimpernel (1919)
The First Sir Percy (1920)
The Triumph of the Scarlet Pimpernel (1922)

Pimpernel and Rosemary (1924)
Sir Percy Hits Back (1927)
Adventures of the Scarlet Pimpernel (1929)
A Child of the Revolution (1932)
The Way of the Scarlet Pimpernel (1933)
The Scarlet Pimpernel Looks at the World (1933)
Sir Percy Leads the Band (1936)
Mam'zelle Guillotine (1940)

Scarlet Pimpernel Pastiches

C. Guy Clayton, *Daughter of the Revolution* (1984); *Such Mighty Rage* (1985); *Bordeaux Red* (1986)

Lauren Willig, *The Secret History of the Pink Carnation* (2005); *The Masque of the Black Tulip* (2005); *The Deception of the Emerald Ring* (2006); *The Seduction of the Crimson Rose* (2008); *The Temptation of the Night Jasmine* (announced)

Fictional Biography

John Montague Orczy-Barstow as John Blakeney, *The Life and Exploits of the Scarlet Pimpernel* (1938)

SAX ROHMER

Yellow Menace

Arthur Sarsfield Ward (1883–1959) used the name Sax Rohmer for a series of stories about an Oriental super-villain who was relentlessly pursued by Commissioner Nayland Smith and his associate, Dr. Petrie. The stories were often serialized in *Colliers* and were filmed several times.

Ward was the son of an Irish couple but was born in Birmingham, England. He favored in his writing the mystical, the magical, the exotic. The "yellow peril" theme was not his invention, but he exploited it in his tales of Fu Manchu. This is from *The Insidious Dr. Fu Manchu*: "Imagine a person, tall, lean and feline, high-shouldered, with a brow like Shakespeare and a face like Satan, a close-shaven skull, and long, magnetic eyes of the true cat-green. Invest him with all the cruel cunning of an entire Eastern race, accumulated in one giant intellect, with all the resources of science past and present, with all the resources, if you will, of a wealthy government — which, however, already has denied all knowledge of his existence. Imagine that awful being, and you have a mental picture of Dr. Fu-Manchu, the yellow peril incarnate in one man."

The series inspired several screen, radio and television adaptations.

Cay Van Ash, Rohmer's biographer, continued the print series with permission. Richard Jaccoma mildly disguised Fu Manchu as Dr. Chou en Shu in his novel. The David McDaniel book is based on the *Man from U.N.C.L.E.* television series and is about T.H.R.U.S.H. agents wooing Fu Manchu to their cause.

Original Fu Manchu Works

The Mystery of Dr. Fu Manchu (1913)
  aka *The Insidious Dr. Fu-Manchu*
  (1913)
The Devil Doctor (1916) aka *Return of
  Dr. Fu-Manchu* (1916)
The Si-Fan Mysteries (1917) aka *The
  Hand of Fu-Manchu* (1917)
The Golden Scorpion (1931)
Daughter of Fu Manchu (1931)
The Mask of Fu Manchu (1932)
Fu Manchu's Bride (1933) aka *The Bride
  of Fu Manchu* (1933)

The Trail of Fu Manchu (1934)
President Fu Manchu (1936)
The Drums of Fu Manchu (1938)
The Island of Fu Manchu (1941)
The Shadow of Fu Manchu (1948)
Re-Enter Fu Manchu (1957) aka *Re-
  Enter Dr. Fu Manchu* (1957)
Emperor Fu Manchu (1959)
*The Secret of Holm Peel and Other
  Strange Stories* (1970) short stories
*The Wrath of Fu Manchu and Other Sto-
  ries* (1973) short stories

Fu Manchu Pastiches

G.A. Effinger, "*Sherlock Holmes in Orbit* (1995) story "The Musgrave Version"
Richard Jaccoma, *Yellow Peril: The Adventures of Sir John Weymouth-Smythe* (1978)
William Patrick Maynard, *The Terror of Fu Manchu* (2009)
David McDaniel, *The Rainbow Affair* (1967)

Cay Van Ash with Elisabeth Sax Rohmer, *Ten Years Beyond Baker Street: Sherlock Holmes Matches Wits with the Diabolical Dr. Fu Manchu* (1984)
Cay Van Ash, *The Fires of Fu Manchu* (1987)

BARRY SADLER

Green Beret with pen

Barry Sadler (1940–1988) was born in Carlsbad, New Mexico. He enlisted with the Air Force in 1958. Returning to civilian life, he toured as a musician. He returned to service during the Vietnam War. While at Fort Benning's jump school, he wrote "Ballad of the Green Berets," which became a radio smash in 1966. It was his only hit. He turned to fiction and wrote *Casca: The Eternal Mercenary*, which grew into a popular action series. Sadler was shot while riding in a taxi-cab in Guatemala in 1988 and never recovered.

Sadler wrote the first twenty-two books about Casca Longinus, the historic figure who speared Jesus Christ on the cross, to end the Savior's torment. As a reward/curse, he was given eternal life.

Sadler's literary heirs engaged Paul Dengelegi, a Connecticut dentist, to write two books to continue the series, then Tony Roberts and Michael B. Goodwin picked up for the next in the series.

Original Casca series

The Eternal Mercenary (1979)
God of Death (1979)
The War Lord (1980)
The Panzer Soldier (1980)
The Barbarian (1981)
The Persian (1982)
The Damned (1982)
Soldier of Fortune (1983)
The Sentinel (1983)
The Conquistador (1984)
The Legionnaire (1984)

The African Mercenary (1984)
The Assassin (1985)
The Phoenix (1985)
The Pirate (1985)
Desert Mercenary (1986)
The Warrior (1987)
The Cursed (1987)
The Samurai (1988)
Soldier of Gideon (1988)
The Trench Soldier (1989)
The Mongol (1990)

Casca Pastiches

Paul Dengelegi, *The Liberator* (1999); *The Defiant* (2001)
Michael B. Goodwin, *Immortal Dragon* (2008)
Tony Roberts, *Halls of Montezuma* (2006); *Johnny Reb* (2007); *Casca the Confederate* (2008); *The Avenger* (2008); *Napoleon's Soldier* (2009)

SAPPER

"Bulldog" Drummond

Herman Cyril McNeile (1888–1937) usually went by H.C. McNeile, but was "Sapper" for his popular books. McNeile was born in England, educated at the Royal Military Academy and served in the Royal Engineers from 1907–19, retiring as a lieutenant colonel. In 1920 McNeile, as Sapper, wrote his first story of an adventurous British military man, Capt. Hugh "Bulldog" Drummond, discharged after the war and with nothing to do.

"For a period of some fifteen years, ('Bulldog' Drummond) was almost a household word...," said Donald McCormick in *Who's Who in Spy Fiction*. He noted the hero, "the 1920ish portrait of a 'clean-limbed young Englishman,' was out for adventure and always ready to check the fiendish plots of Carl Peterson and any other 'Hun,' 'Dago' or other foreigner. This was the language of 'Sapper': his characters spoke in stilted clichés, expressed right-wing views, frequently indulged in anti–Semitism and regarded all lovely young Englishwomen as purity personified."

The Drummond character achieved a wide audience in motion pictures, appearing in twenty-three films from 1922 to 1971. John Howard was featured in seven pictures in the 1930s. Dismissing the movies' quality, Robert Sampson in *Yesterday's Faces Vol. 6: Violent Lives* similarly found the prose "pleasantly ugly. Frequently he gets tight. If someone needs killing, Drummond will obligingly kill him.... First and always, he is a man of action. Not complex. Not subtle at all...."

London-born Gerald Fairlie (1899–1983) was a close friend of McNeile's and apparently served as the model for Drummond. McNeile and Gerald du Maurier collaborated on the play *Bulldog Drummond* in 1925. Fairlie collaborated with McNeile on the 1937 stage drama *Bulldog Drummond Hits Out*. Fairlie wrote screenplays for many years for British and American film studios, among them *Calling Bulldog Drummond* (1951) with Howard Emmett Rogers and Arthur Wimperis and filmed with Walter Pigeon in the title role. According to McCormick, "When McNeile was dying, he and Fairlie discussed the last 'Bulldog' Drummond story plotted by 'Sapper' and finally Fairlie agreed to write the book." Fairlie re-introduced earlier characters such as villainess Irma Peterson. He crafted a more likeable hero and treated women characters more sympathetically. Henry Reymond's book is based on a later motion picture.

Original Bulldog Drummond Works

Bull-Dog Drummond: The Adventures of a Demobilized Officer Who Found Peace Dull (1920)
The Black Gang (1922)
The Third Round (1924) aka *Bulldog Drummond's Third Round* (1924)

The Final Count (1926)
The Female of the Species (1928) aka *Bulldog Drummond Meets the Female of the Species* (1943) aka *Bulldog Drummond Meets a Murderess*
Temple Tower (1929)

Tiny Carteret (1930)

The Return of Bull-Dog Drummond (1932) aka *Bulldog Drummond Returns* (1932)

Knock-Out (1933) aka *Bulldog Drummond Strikes Back* (1933)

Bulldog Drummond at Bay (1935)

The Challenge (1937)

Pastiches

Gerald Fairlie, *Bulldog Drummond on Dartmoor* (1938); *Bulldog Drummond Attacks* (1939); *Captain Bulldog Drummond* (1945); *Bulldog Drummond Stands Fast* (1947); *Hands Off Bulldog Drummond* (1949); *Calling Bulldog Drummond* (1951); *The Return of the Black Gang* (1954)

Henry Reymond, *Deadlier Than the Male* (1966) based on a story by Jimmy Sangster; *Some Girls Do* (1969) based on a script by David Osborn and Liz Charles-Williams

Jack Smithers, *Combined Forces: Being the Latter-Day Adventures of Maj. Gen. Sir Richard Hannay, Captain Hugh (Bulldog) Drummond, and Berry & Co.* (1983)

RUSSELL THORNDIKE

Doctor Syn

Most remember Doctor Syn as the character in a three-part *World of Disney* program in 1963 with Patrick McGoohan as the Scarecrow of Romney Marsh. British writer Russell Thorndike wrote the stories that inspired the episodes.

The vicar of Dymchurch, in the late 1700s, was once the notorious pirate Christopher Syn. He has retired to a pious life until an oppressive government inspires him to recruit helpers and illegally import the goods necessary to keep his community alive. Something of a British Zorro, Doctor Syn was twice earlier rendered on film, in 1937 and 1938 movies featuring George Arliss.

Thorndike (1885–1972) originally killed off his hero in the first book, thought better of it, and resurrected him for later volumes. Recovered from wounds suffered during World War I, Thorndike joined a theatrical company with his sister, Sybil Thorndike, and toured. He once even played his own character, Doctor Syn, on stage. He appeared in a few early silent films.

The Disney show's popularity prompted Vic Crume's episode. Crume also wrote *Partridge Family* and other TV-oriented novels. William Buchanan, an American writer, anticipated the Disney program's popularity with his own adaptation of Thorndike's tale. It is his story, in fact, that Disney optioned for its show.

Original Stories

Doctor Syn (1915)

Doctor Syn Returns (1935) aka *Scarecrow Rides* (1935)

Further Adventures of Doctor Syn (1936)

Doctor Syn on the High Seas (1936)

Amazing Quest of Doctor Syn (1938)

The Courageous Exploits of Doctor Syn (1939)

The Shadow of Doctor Syn (1944)

Pastiches

William Buchanan, *Christopher Syn* (1960)
Vic Crume, *Doctor Syn Alias the Scarecrow* (1975)

EDGAR WALLACE

Sanders of the River

Edgar Wallace (1875–1932), co-creator of *King Kong*, was a master of the thriller. The British writer's 175 books include mysteries, detective stories and outright adventure.

Adopted by a London fisherman and his wife, Wallace never finished school. He joined the Royal West Kent Regiment from 1893–1896, and served with the Medical Staff Corps in South Africa. He became a news correspondent, covered the Russo-Japanese War, and learned of the clandestine world of spies. His first novel, *The Four Just Men* (1905), was about a quartet of vigilantes. *Sanders of the River* (1911), about a British Foreign Office commissioner, gave Wallace firm footing as a writer. The movie *Sanders of the River* came out in 1935. Wallace also wrote detective stories featuring J.G. Reeder.

Of the pastiche writers listed below, Francis Gerard (1905–?) wrote Sanders sequels, and books featuring the occult detective Sir John Meredith. British writer J.T. Edson (b. 1928) wrote Mr. Reeder into two of his "Picadilly" Western yarns.

Original Mr. Reeder Works

Room Thirteen (1923)
Mind of Mister J.G. Reeder (1925) aka
   Murder Book of Mister J.G. Reeder
Terror Keep (1927)

Red Aces (1929)
Guv'nor, and Other Stories (1932)
Mister J.G. Reeder Returns (1932)

Mr. Reeder Pastiches

J.T. Edson, *Cap Fog, Texas Ranger, Meet Mr. J.G. Reeder* (1977); *The Return of Rapido Clint and Mr. J.G. Reeder* (1984)

Original Sanders Works

Sanders of the River (1911)
People of the River (1912)
Bosambo of the River (1914)
Bones (1915)
Keepers of the King's Peace (1917)
Lieutenant Bones (1918)

Bones in London (1921)
Bones of the River (1923)
Sanders (1926) aka *Mister Commissioner Sanders*
Against Sanders (1928)
Sandi, the Kingmaker (1922)

Sanders Pastiches

Francis Gerard, *The Return of Sanders of the River* (1938) short stories; *Law of the River* (1939) short stories; *Justice of Sanders* (1951) short stories

JOHANN DAVID WYSS
Tree house

Clergyman Johann David Wyss (1743–1818) wrote the castaway adventures of *The Swiss Family Robinson* after having enjoyed Daniel Defoe's *Robinson Crusoe.* His novel tells of six people shipwrecked in the East Indies and their resourcefulness in surviving.

The author was born in Bern, Switzerland. He became a clergyman and, like his fictional hero, had four sons. One son, Johann Rudolf Wyss (1782–1830), a philosophy professor and creator of the Swiss national anthem, edited the book for publication and another son, Johann Emmanuel Wyss, illustrated it.

The *Robinsons* book invited some interesting pastiches.

Original Work

Swiss Family Robinson: or, The Adven-   *Uninhabited Isle Near New Guinea*
    tures of a Shipwrecked Family on an   (1812)

Pastiches

Paul Adrian, *Willis the Pilot* (1855)
Jules Verne, *Their Island Home* (1900); *Castaways of the Flag* (1900)
Owen Wister, *New Swiss Family Robinson* (1882)

DORNFORD YATES
Jonah Mansel

Cecil William Mercer (1885–1960) was best known under his penname Dornford Yates. The native of Kent, England, was a cousin of the writer H.H. Munro (Saki). After service during World War I, the writer abandoned a career in the law for one in words. He lived in France and South Rhodesia. He wrote books in several series, including ones about Berry and Chandos and the gentleman adventure seeker Jonah Mansel.

Jack Smithers included Bulldog Drummond and Richard Hannay in his pastiche, improbably working together on a case.

Original Jonah Mansel Works

Jonah and Co. (1922)

Blind Corner (1927)

Perishable Goods (1928)

She Fell Among Thieves (1935)

Gale Warning (1939)

Shoal Water (1940)

An Eye for a Tooth (1943)

Red in the Morning (1946)

Cost Price (1949)

Pastiche

Jack Smithers, *Combined Forces: Being the Latter-Day Adventures of Maj. Gen. Sir Richard Hannay, Captain Hugh (Bulldog) Drummond, and Berry & Co.* (1983)

Classics
(18th Century and Earlier)

This section includes some of the earliest writers in English and a few other languages, up through the 18th century. We see immediately that none of our literature was immune to replay at other hands—from an Old English epic that could have been written as early as the 8th century to 9th-century Homer and 11th-century Murasaki Shikibu to 14th-century Chaucer and 16th-century Shakespeare. Parke Godwin's reinterpretation of *Beowulf* is, of course, a modern exercise, as are the several *Odyssey* sequels. But Miguel Cervantes faced an unauthorized rival's use of his characters within a decade of the publication of *Don Quixote*. His solution, in those pre-copyright times, was to write his own sequel. Samuel Richardson had the same experience—Henry Fielding, no less, swiped his character Pamela—and he responded with his own follow-up novel. Jonathan Swift's Gulliver was so innovative that other writers couldn't wait to issue variations. Murasaki Shikibu's *The Tale of Genji* was such an inexorably long serial, one wonders why Ryuutei Teanehiko felt the need to add to it.

ANONYMOUS

Beowulf

"Now Beowulf bode in the burg of the Scyldings, leader beloved, and long he ruled in fame with all folk...." Unknown hands crafted the Old English story of Beowulf well more than a thousand years ago. It is the oldest epic in British literature. There has been considerable debate as to whether it was written down after having survived in oral tradition, or was shaped brand-new. It is set in early Denmark and Sweden. In the course of his adventure Beowulf confronts Grendel, Grendel's mother and a dragon.

Parke Godwin (b. 1929), who also reinterpreted Robin Hood, wove a historical fantasy around the Beowulf saga.

Original Work

Anonymous, *Beowulf* (ca. 1100)

Pastiche

Parke Godwin, *The Tower of Beowulf* (1996)
Caitlin R. Kiernan, *Beowulf* (2007) film novelization

MIGUEL CERVANTES
Sancho Panza tags along

Spanish novelist, playwright and poet Miguel de Cervantes Saavedra (1547–1616) wrote the sprawling *Don Quixote* (1605) about a questing, dreaming elder Spaniard. Don Quixote is ever optimistic, ever idealistic, and enormously chivalric as he tilts at windmills. He adores his beloved lady Dulcinea, rides a tired horse named Rocinante and is attended by the faithful and pudgy Sancho Panza. Several pirated editions came out, and an annoying pastiche. The musical *Man from La Mancha* includes the song "Dream the Impossible Dream."

Alonso Fernandez de Avellaneda's false sequel spurred Cervantes to hasten his own second volume, which appeared in 1615. Many consider it a stronger work than the original. Editions today combine the two Cervantes manuscripts. Satirist Henry Fielding couldn't resist his own version of Don Quixote.

Original Works

Don Quixote (1605)   *Segunda Parte* (1615)

Pastiches

Julian Branston, *Tilting at Windmills: A Novel of Cervantes and the Errant Knight* (2005)
Alonso Fernandez de Avellaneda, *Second Volume of the Ingenious Gentleman Don Quixote of La Mancha* (1614)
Henry Fielding, *Don Quixote in England* (1734)

GEOFFREY CHAUCER
Troilus and Criseyde

Geoffrey Chaucer (ca. 1340–1400), best known for his rousing and ribald *Canterbury Tales*, also wrote a great romantic poem, *Troilus and Criseyde*, set against a background of war-torn Troy. Troilus is a Trojan knight who falls in love with the widow Criseyde.

Details of Chaucer's early life are sketchy. He likely was born in London and may have attended school at St. Paul's Cathedral. He became a page in the Countess of Ulster's household, and later served in her husband Prince Lionel's retinue. One of his first works was a memorial poem to Queen Philippa. Chaucer called his poetic *Troilus and Criseyde* a tragedy (the hero dies on the field of battle). It appeared some time between 1380 and 1387. Chaucer gained stature as a philosopher and diplomat. He went on to compile the first of his Canterbury Tales beginning in 1387, but died before they were all put to paper.

Scottish poet Robert Henryson (ca. 1425–1506) wrote *The Testament of Cresseid* as a sequel, finishing rather harshly the story of the heroine.

The Canterbury Tales didn't elude apers. British historical novelist Maurice Hewlett (1861–1923), author of *Richard Yea-and-Nay* and *The Forest Lovers* and novels based on *Greenland* and other sagas, offered his own tales (which saw original publication in *Collier's, Harper's* and other periodicals) of a scrivener and a prioress and others in 1901.

Original Work

The Canterbury Tales (14th century)

Pastiche

Maurice Hewlett, *New Canterbury Tales* (1901)

Original Work

Troilus and Criseyde (1380s)

Pastiche

Robert Henryson, *The Testament of Cresseid* (1400s)

JOHN CLELAND

Fanny

John Cleland (1709–1789) minced few words in describing the sexual exploits of his heroine, Fanny Hill. It's no surprise the book was long banned.

The son of an army officer, Cleland was born in Kingston Upon Thames, Surrey, and grew up in London. He worked for British East India Company and was a soldier in India. In debt, he wrote *Memoirs of a Woman of Pleasure* and published it in two volumes in 1748 and 1749. He disavowed the book when taken to court. Marketed underground, the unexpurgated book didn't appear in print legitimately in England until 1970.

The author of a centuries-later sequel didn't take credit for his or her work.

Original Work

Fanny Hill: Memoirs of a Woman of Pleasure (1748/1749)

Pastiches

Anonymous, *Fanny Hill's Daughter* (1985)

DANIEL DEFOE

Robin and Moll

British writer Daniel Defoe (1660–1731), born Daniel Foe, popularized the novel form — in fact, he wrote several hundred novels, along with pamphlets and journal essays. He grew up as the child of Presbyterian dissenters during troubled times in London during years beset by plague and catastrophic fire. An unsuccessful merchant, he went to prison at various times for debt or political activism.

He wrote his best-known works, including *Robinson Crusoe* and *Moll Flanders*, in the years 1719 to 1724. The former book is apparently based on the true story of Alexander Selkirk. Shipwrecked Crusoe meets mutineers and fierce natives in his 28 years on an island somewhere near Venezuela. Tim Severin in the non-fiction *Seeking Robinson Crusoe* (2002) pursued many historical threads of the novel about the island castaway and his man Friday.

Moll Flanders was born in Newgate Prison, where her mother was an inmate. She enters servitude, has affairs with two sons in the family, marries one, is widowed and struggles toward redemption.

Both Defoe works inspired motion picture versions, and centuries-later prose sequels.

Original Robinson Crusoe Works

The Life and Strange Surprizing Adventures of Robinson Crusoe of York, Mariner: Who lived Eight and Twenty Years, all alone in an un-inhabited Island on the coast of America, near the Mouth of the Great River of Oroonoque; Having been cast on Shore by Shipwreck, where-in all the Men perished but himself. With An Account how he was at last as strangely deliver'd by Pyrates. Written by Himself (1719) aka *Robinson Crusoe*

The Farther Adventures of Robinson Crusoe (1719)

Robinson Crusoe Pastiches

Thomas Berger, *Robert Crews* (1994)
J.M. Coetzee, *Foe* (2003)
Bill Ford, *Lt. Robin Crusoe, USN* (1966)
Tracy Sinclair, *Miss Robinson Crusoe* (1990)

Michel Tournier, *Friday* (1967)
Henry Treece, *Return of Robinson Crusoe* (1958)
David A. Wells, *The Remarkable Financial Fortunes and Misfortunes of a Remote Island* (1876)

Original Moll Flanders Work

The Fortunes and Misfortunes of the Famous Moll Flanders, Etc. Who Was Born in Newgate, and During a Life of Continu'd Variety for Threescore Years, Besides Her Childhood, Was Twelve Years a Whore, Five Times a Wife [Whereof Once to Her Own Brother], Twelve Years a Thief, Eight Years a Transported Felon in Virginia, at Last Grew Rich, Liv'd Honest, and Died a Penitent (1722) aka *Moll Flanders*

Moll Flanders Pastiche

Marcia McEwan, *Confessions of Moll Flanders* (1965)

HENRY FIELDING

Tom Jones

Henry Fielding (1707–1754) wrote the sprawling, humorous, lusty tale of Tom Jones. Taken in by wealthy Squire Allworthy, youthful Jones falls in love with a neighbor's daughter, Sophia Western, but is discouraged from wedding her because of his illegitimacy.

Aside from his writing, Fielding is known for having created the legendary Bow Street Runners police force in London. Fielding was a playwright and journalist. He and Samuel Richardson are credited with having brought realism to English literature. Born in Somerset to a prominent family, he attended Eton College, where he studied the literature of the Greeks and Romans. His early play, *Love in Several Masques*, was performed in 1728 in London. He developed a knack for satire, and government figures were a frequent target.

Bob Coleman added to the Jones cannon. And it's only fitting, since Fielding himself knocked off pastiches of *Don Quixote* and *Pamela Andrews*.

Original Work

The History of Tom Jones, a Foundling (1749) aka *Tom Jones*

Pastiche

Bob Coleman, *The Later Adventures of Tom Jones* (1986)

HOMER

Odyssey

The Greek poet Homer is believed to have written the epic poems the *Iliad* and the *Odyssey* some time in the late 9th century. *Iliad* is about the Greek siege of Troy. *Odyssesy* is about Odysseus's travels to Ithaca after Troy has fallen.

Adventure writer H. Rider Haggard and historian Andrew Lang produced a centuries-later sequel, relating Odysseus's last quest. Margaret Atwood related the tale from the point of view of Odysseus's wife, Penelope. Nikos Kazantzakis employed the hexameter verse form for his continuation of Odysseus's adventures once he returns to Ithaca.

Original Works

Iliad (late 9th century)   *Odyssey* (late 9th century)

Pastiches

Margaret Atwood, *The Penelopiad* (2005)
H. Rider Haggard and Andrew Lang, *The World's Desire* (1890)
Nikos Kazantzakis, *The Odyssey: A Modern Sequel* (1958)

ALAIN-RENÉ LESAGE

Devil on Two Sticks

Alain-René Lesage (1668–1747) was born in France, attended a Jesuit college, practiced law, translated Spanish literature and wrote plays. He gained attention with a prose farce, *Crispin Rival de Son Maître* (1707). Others of his better known works include *Gil Blas* and *Le Diable Boiteux*, the latter a satire of human folly based somewhat on the work of Luis Velez de Guevara.

Le Diable Boiteux inspired a pastiche by British writer William Combe (1741–1823).

Original Work

Le Diable Boiteux (1707) aka *The Devil Upon Crutches* aka *The Devil Upon Two Sticks* aka *Devil on Two Sticks*   aka *Asmodeus: Or, The Devil Upon Two Sticks*

Pastiche

William Combe, *Devil Upon Two Sticks in England: Being a Continuation of Le Diable Boiteux of Lesage* (1790)

MATTHEW LEWIS

Gothic in spades

Matthew Lewis (1775–1818) was famed for his gothic romances. A London native, he was schooled at Oxford. He served in the British diplomatic force in the Hague, during which time he wrote *Ambrosio; or, the Monk*, published in 1795. It was a popular work, though the author excised some sensitive material from a second edition. The story is about the failure of a Spanish monk who lusts for one of his students, Matilda, and then pursues another student, and on.

The French writer Antonin Artaud (1896–1948) reworked the same plot, sharpening the controversial aspects, in *The Monk* (1931), said to be a "loose translation." Science fiction writer Thomas M. Disch (1840–2008) loosely patterned his *The Priest* on *The Monk* on Lewis's original, using a Minneapolis setting for his story of Father Pat Bryce of St. Bernadine, a pedophile.

Original Work

Ambrosio; or, the Monk (1795)

Pastiche

Antonin Artaud, *The Monk* (1931)
Thomas M. Disch, *The Priest: A Gothic Romance* (1995)

CHRISTOPHER MARLOWE

Hero and Leander

Christopher Marlowe (1564–1593) was an Elizabethan playwright and poet. Some theorize he wrote plays credited to William Shakespeare. At his death, Marlowe left a fragmentary poem, "Hero and Leander," the story of two lovers. Hero is the priestess of Aphrodite and Leander is a young man from across the river. Leander swims the Abydos each night to be with Hero. Hero lights a lamp in the tower in Sestos so Leander can find her.

Two versions of the poem appeared in 1598: Marlowe's original 818 lines alone and with more lines added by English playwright George Chapman (ca. 1560–1634).

Posthumous Collaboration with George Chapman

Hero and Leander (1598)

MURASAKI SHIKIBU

Genji

The Tale of Genji, which fills some 50-plus volumes, is considered by many to be the first great novel of literature. The Japanese noblewoman Murasaki Shikibu (b. circa 978) wrote the work in 54 volumes. The copy held in the Library of Congress identifies supplemental volumes including volume 59, "Yamaji no tsuyu," or a sequel to the work by a later author. There have been several translations of the novel into English, the first by Suematsu Kencho. Royall Tyler's 2001 translation is widely recommended.

The story is about Hikaru Genji, the son of an emperor and his beloved concubine, and his various trials and love affairs. It was written serially. It relates the activities of at least 400 characters, most of whom are simply identified by occupation. "It contains no military adventures nor epic journeys," said a writer in *The Economist* in 2008. "Yet 'The Tale of Genji' is in every way Japan's equivalent of Hilmer's 'Iliad.'"

The text was apparently completed by 1021. And yet, it ends in mid-sentence, leaving some to question whether it was finished to the author's satisfaction, or might have gone on. Some suggest the author's daughter, Daini no Sanmi, took a hand in writing the tale after chapter 34; others say an anonymous editor shaped parts of the book. Colin Graham wrote a libretto for an opera based on the work for the Opera Theater of St. Louis in 2000.

There reportedly have been several Genji pastiches. One is cited.

Original Work

The Tale of Genji (11th century)

Genji Pastiche

Ryuutei Teanehiko, *Nise murasaki inaka genji* (early 19th century)

SAMUEL RICHARDSON

Pamela

Samuel Richardson (1689–1761) was born in Derbyshire, England, a carpenter's son. He became a printer, and eventually a writer and contemporary of Henry Fielding. His epistolary novel *Pamela, or Virtue Rewarded*, came out in two volumes in 1740, to great success. *Clarissa Harlowe* (1742) is considered his masterwork.

When Henry Fielding published spurious sequels that mocked the spiciness in *Pamela*, Richardson retorted with his own sequel in 1742.

Original Works

Pamela; or Virtue Rewarded (1740)   *Pamela in Her Exalted Condition* (1742)

Pastiches

Henry Fielding, *An Apology for the Life of Mrs. Shamela Andrews* (1741); *The History of the Adventures of Joseph Andrews* (1742)

WILLIAM SHAKESPEARE

All the world's a stage

Playwright and poet William Shakespeare (ca. 1564–1616) of Stratford-upon-Avon, England, is one of the most highly regarded writers in the English language. His thirty-eight surviving stage comedies, tragedies and histories are widely performed, and some 154 sonnets and other poems are widely translated.

For one so famous, there's a dearth of factual material about Shakespeare's life. He was the son of glovemaker and merchant John Shakespeare and his wife Mary Arden. He probably attended the King's New Grammar School in Stratford. At age eighteen he married Anne Hathaway, eight years his senior. They had three children. There are lost years in Shakespeare's life. He had ended up in London by 1592, where he probably was an actor and playwright. His first poem, "Venus and Adonis," was registered in 1593. He appeared as an actor in a performance for Queen Elizabeth in 1594. He became financially comfortable through real estate dealings, enabling him time to shape his stage plays. The First Folio of his plays came out in 1623 and sold for one pound.

Pastiches abound, beginning with William Painter (ca. 1540–1594), a former ordnance clerk at the Tower of London. John Reed, who was born in 1969 in New York City, assembled *All the World's a Grave: A New Play by William Shakespeare* (2008) from lines in Shakespeare plays reassembled into a new work.

Original *King Lear*

King Lear (between 1603 and 1606)

***King Lear* Pastiche**

Christopher Moore, *Fool* (2009)
Jane Smiley, *A Thousand Acres* (1991)

Original *Macbeth*

Macbeth (between 1603 and 1606)

***Macbeth* Pastiches**

Caroline Cooney, *Enter Three Witches* (2007)
Bonnie Copeland, *Lady of Moray* (1979)

Dorothy Dunnet, *King Hereafter* (1998)
Susan Fraser King, *Lady Macbeth* (2008)
Michael Leigh, *He Couldn't Say Amen* (1951)
Rebecca Reisert, *The Third Witch* (2002)

Original *Merchant of Venice*

The Merchant of Venice (between 1596 and 1598)

Merchant of Venice Pastiches

Erica Jong, *Shylock's Daughter: A Novel of Love in Venice* (2004)
Miriam Pressler, *Shylock's Daughter* (2001)
Miriam Schwartz, *Shylock and His Daughter: A Play Based on a Hebrew Novel* (1947)
Grace Tiffany, *The Turquoise Ring* (2006)

Original *Romeo and Juliet*

Romeo and Juliet (between 1591 and 1595)

Romeo and Juliet Pastiches

Larry Baker, *Flamingo Rising* (1997)
Lisa Fiedler, *Romeo's Ex: Rosalind's Story* (2006)
James Edwards, *Romeo and Juliet: A Modern Day Sequel* (2007)

Original *Tempest*

The Tempest (between 1610 and 1611)

Tempest Pastiches

Grace Tiffany, *Ariel* (2005)
Tad Williams, *Caliban's Hour* (1995)

Original *Much Ado About Nothing*

Much Ado About Nothing (ca. 1612–1613)

Much Ado About Nothing Pastiche

St. John Hankin, *Mr. Punch's Dramatic Sequels* (1901)

Other Selected Original Works

Hamlet (between 1599 and 1601)   *Twelfth Night, or What You Will* (ca. 1601)

Pastiches

Anne Perry, editor, *Much Ado About Murder* (2003)
Mike Ashley, editor, *Shakespearean Whodunits: Murders and Mysteries Based on Shakespeare's Plays* (2000)
John Reed, *All the World's a Grave: A New Play by William Shakespeare* (2008)

JONATHAN SWIFT
Lilliput

Dublin-born Jonathan Swift (1667–1745), essayist, poet and satirist, created worlds gargantuan and miniscule in his classic *Gulliver's Travels* in 1726. At the same time a parody of social mores and a takeoff on travel literature, the novel embellished our language with Lilliputians and Brobdingnagians and Yahoos.

Swift graduated from Dublin University in 1686 with a bachelor's degree and fled to England during political troubles. He became secretary and personal assistant to Sir William Temple, an English diplomat. He contracted Meniere's disease but was able to complete his studies for a master's degree at Hertford College, Oxford University, in 1692. He was ordained a priest in the Church of Ireland, with an undistinguished parish in County Antrim. His first satire, *The Battle of the Books*, came out in 1704. Swift earned a Doctor of Divinity degree, continued his writing and became politically active in Ireland and England.

Travels invited pastiches from writers French (Pierre Desfontaine), Hungarian (Frigyes Karinthy), Ukrainian (Vladimir Savchenko), English (John Myers Myers) and American (T.H. White).

Original Gulliver Work

Gulliver's Travels (1726) aka *Travels into Several Remote Nations of the World*   *Memoirs of the Court of Lilliput* (1727)

Pastiches

Anonymous, *Cursory View of the History of Lilliput for These Last Forty Three Years* (1727)

John Arbuthnot, *Account of the State of Learning in the Empire of Lilliput* (1728)

John Paul Brady, *Voyage to Inshneefa* (1987)

Pierre Desfontaine, *Le Nouveau Gulliver ou Voyages de Jean Gulliver, fils du captitaine Lemuel Gulliver* (1730) aka *The New Gulliver; or, the Travels of John Gulliver, Son of Captain Lemuel Gulliver* (1931)

Esme Dodderidge, *New Gulliver* (1979)

Wendell Phillips Garrison, *New Gulliver* (1898)

Lemuel Gulliver, Jr., *Lilliput* (1796)

Willis Hall and Rowan Barnes-Murphy, *The Return of the Antelope* (1986); *The Antelope Company at Large* (1987)

Louis Herman, *In the Sealed Cave* (1935)

Matthew Hodgart, *New Voyage to the Country of the Houhnhnms* (1969)

Frigyes Karinthy, *Utazas Faremidoba* (1916) aka *Voyage to Faremido*; *Capillaria* (1921)

John Myers Myers, *Silverlock* (1949)

Elbert Perce, *Gulliver Joi* (1851)

Adam Roberts, *Swiftly* (2008)

Vladimir Savchenko, *Gulliver's Fifth Travel—The Travel of Lemuel Gulliver, First a Surgeon, and Then a Captain of Several Ships to the Land of Tikitaks*

T.H. White, *Mistress Masham's Repose* (1946)
David Wilson, *Modern Lilliput* (1924)
Henry Winterfield, *Castaways in Lilliput* (1958)

CAO XUEQIN

The Story of the Stone

Cao Xueqin is believed to have written *Dream of the Red Chamber*, also known as *The Story of the Stone*, during the Qing Dynasty, in the mid 1700s. The novel, which has a huge cast and brims with details of life in the Chinese aristocracy, was first published anonymously in hand-copied versions. Gao E and Cheng Weiyuan published a print version in 1791 as *Dream of the Red Chamber*. This version had 40 chapters beyond Cao's 80, and in a second edition, in 1792, the authors explained they extended the story based on the author's manuscripts. Many believe the two either made up the material, or were deluded by someone who sold them a false manuscript.

Though it may not have come into print, at least one individual, Hu Nan, is known to have completed a 108-chapter online sequel, *A Dream of Red Mansions* (2006). (This is not to be confused with *The Dream of the Red Chamber*, a 1958 translation, or *A Dream of Red Mansions*, a 1978–1980 translation.) Among the many writers who have written endings for the book, Hu Nan is the youngest. "Because of her age, she can better understand the feelings of the characters in the book and write down their destinies," commented a writer in *Beijing Review*.

Posthumous Collaboration

Gao E and Cheng Weiyuan, *Dream of the Red Chamber* (1792)

Classics (19th Century)

That *Flatland*, of all books, should engender so many pastiches! Louisa May Alcott's romping *Little Women*, we can understand, given a generally young (and not necessarily mathematical) readership. Likewise Alexandre Dumas' boisterous Musketeers. Charles Dickens' *A Christmas Carol* is a story that can't be bettered — but better isn't always the motive for sequelizers. The same author's unfinished Edwin Drood puzzler has invited more than a dozen completionists due to its dangling resolution.

EDWIN A. ABBOTT

Flatland

Edwin Abbott Abbott (1838–1926) during his tenure as headmaster at City of London School wrote *Flatland: A Romance in Many Directions*, a literary oddity that mixed mathematics and philosophy. He published it under the penname "A Square" and illustrated it himself. His other works included *Shakespearian Grammar* (1870) and a trilogy of religious romances. *Flatland*, with its two-dimensional characters roaming a two-dimensional universe, had an unusual resilience.

British mathematician C.H. Hinton wrote imaginative books about the fourth dimension, but remained with three dimensions for his *Flatland* tribute — his characters lived on a spherical world. Dionys Burger wrote the story of A Square's grandson, A Hexagon, as he encounters geometry. Canadian mathematician A.K. Dewdney offered a modern technological take on Abbott's theme, *The Planiverse*. British mathematics professor Ian Stewart inserted more comedic elements in his story of Vikki Line, A Square's great-great-granddaughter, in *Flatterland*. Rudy Rucker ventured into the bizarre in his tale of Joe Cube (latter-day A Cube from Abbott's original) thrust into a fourth-dimension skirmish. It all adds up.

Original work

Flatland: A Romance in Many Directions (1884)

Pastiches

Dionys Burger, *Sphereland: A Fantasy About Curved Spaces and an Expanding Universe* (1965)
A.K. Dewdney, *Planiverse: Computer Contact with a Two-Dimensional World* (1984)
Charles Howard Hinton, *Episode of Flatland: Or, How Plain Folk Discovered the Third Dimension* (1907)
Rudy Rucker, *Message Found in a Copy of Flatland* (1983); *Spaceland: A Novel of the Fourth Dimension* (2002)
Ian Stewart, *Flatterland: Like Flatland, Only More So* (2002)

LOUISA MAY ALCOTT
Little Women

Louisa May Alcott (1832–1888) lived most of her life in Concord, Massachusetts, with a bright-cum-buffoon educator father, Amos Bronson Alcott, and a long-suffering mother, Abigail May Alcott. Her literary neighbors included Nathaniel and Sophia Hawthorne, Ralph Waldo Emerson and Margaret Fuller. She visited Henry David Thoreau at his Walden Pond cottage. She served as a Union nurse in Washington, D.C., during the Civil War, and became a long-toiling writer of potboiler romances under pennames such as A.M. Barnard. *Flower Fables* in 1854 was her first book. Her childhood experiences with three sisters provided the focus for *Little Women* and its several sequels.

Australian Geraldine Brooks (b. 1955) in her novel *March* follows the story of the March girls' father, a Concord idealist who becomes a Union Army chaplain and later a teacher on a Southern plantation. It won a Pulitzer Prize in fiction in 2006. Susan Beth Pfeffer (b. 1948), a prolific writer of girls' fiction, modernized the language, if not the stories. A Broadway musical, *Little Women*, with libretto by Allan Knee and music by Jason Howland and lyrics by Mindi Dickstein, had a run in 2005.

Original Little Women Works

Little Women (1868)
Good Wives (1869)
Little Men: Life at Plumfield with Jo's Boys (1871)

Jo's Boys, and How They Turned Out (1886)

Pastiches

Geraldine Brooks, *March* (2005)

Susan Beth Pfeffer, *Amy's Story* (1997); *Jo's Story* (1997); *Beth's Story* (1997); *Meg's Story* (1997); *Amy Makes a Friend* (1998); *Beth Makes a Friend* (1998); *Jo Makes a Friend* (1998); *Meg Makes a Friend* (1998); *A Gift for Amy* (1999); *A Gift for Beth* (1999); *A Gift for Jo* (1999); *A Gift for Meg* (1999); *Birthday Wishes* (2000); *Christmas Dreams* (2000); *Ghostly Tales* (2000)

Cookbooks

Sean Brand, *Literary Feasts: Inspired Eating from Classic Fiction* (2006)

Shaunda Kennedy Wenger and Janet Kay Jensen, *The Book Lover's Cookbook: Recipes Inspired by Celebrated Works of Literature and the Passages That Feature Them* (2005)

EDWARD BULWER-LYTTON
Zanoni

Edward Bulwer-Lytton (1803–1873) grew up in a well-to-do household and published his first novel, *Ismael: An Oriental Tale, with Other Poems*, in 1820. He became very popular in his day and was friends with Charles Dickens, among others.

The author crafted the immortal literary sentence, "It was a dark and stormy night," for his novel *Paul Clifford* (1830), words that inspired an annual bad-story writing contest. Few today read the rest of the sentence: "the rain fell in torrents — except at occasional intervals, when it was checked by a violent gust of wind which swept up the streets (for it is in London that our scene lies), rattling along the housetops, and fiercely agitating the scanty flame of the lamps that struggled against the darkness."

It is Bulwer-Lytton's novel of the French Revolution, *Zanoni*, however, that inspired a decades-later sequel by Michael Willey, *Ojisan Zanoni*. Zanoni died by guillotine in the original. Willey carries on the story through the eyes of new characters Christopher and Ayami, who had become friends of Zanoni in earlier days.

Original Work

Zanoni (1842)

Pastiche

Michael Willey, *Ojisan Zanoni* (2006)

ANTON CHEKHOV
Uncle Vanya

Russian-born Anton Pavlovich Chekhov (1860–1904) was highly regarded for his short stories and his plays. He at various times worked as a physician, an educator and an editor. A frequent theme in his works of a loss of home came from real-life experience. His father's business failed and the family lost its house, thanks to the wrangling of a bureaucrat.

Chekhov's first writings were for humor publications in the 1880s, one of the few markets at the time in Russia. Limited print space in the periodicals obliged Chekhov to hone his short story style. In the United States, small immigrant groups put on his dramas for their own enjoyment well before the works drew wide public and critical interest. Once translated into English, Chekhov's plays such as *The Bear* (1915) and *The Seagull* (1916) were given fully staged productions.

Brian Friel (b. 1929) is from Northern Ireland. Stephen Dietz (b. 1958) is from Colorado. Neil Simon (b. 1927) is from the Bronx. All three took Chekhov's works in new directions.

Original Work

The Seagull (1895)   *Three Sisters* (1900)
Uncle Vanya (1899)

Pastiches

Brian Friel, *Three Plays After* (2002) includes *The Yalta Game,* based on Chekhov's "The Lady with the Lapdog," and *Afterplay* with characters from *Uncle Vanya* and *Three Sisters*
Stephen Dietz, *Nina Variations* (1996) based on *The Seagull*
Neil Simon, *The Good Doctor* (1980) based on several Chekhov plays and several of his stories

JAMES FENIMORE COOPER
Leatherstocking

America's rugged eastern forests of New York state figure in the Leatherstocking Tales of James Fenimore Cooper (1789–1851). Cooper was born in New Jersey and later lived in New York and Europe. His hero Nathaniel "Natty" Bumppo, also known as Hawkeye or Deerslayer or Leatherstocking or The Longue Carabine, stalks the menacing wilderness during the times of the French and Indian Wars. *The Last of the Mohicans* has been filmed several times. It is the story of Bumppo, his Mohican friend Chingachgook and Chingachgook's son Uncas as they escort the Munro sisters to reunite with their father at Fort William Henry. Hurons kidnap the women, and Uncas shows his enormous bravery in undertaking their rescue. Cooper's works with their strong hero and supportive sidekick of another race became a blueprint for myriad cowboy and private detective writers of later generations.

Paul Block in his sequel wrote of the days after Uncas's death. Sara Donati wrote of Nathaniel Bonner, son of Natty and Cora.

Original Hawkeye Works

Deerslayer (1841)   *Prairie* (1827)
Last of the Mohicans (1826)   *Pathfinder* (1840)
Pioneers (1823)

Pastiches

Paul Block, *Song of the Mohicans* (1995)
Sara Donati, *Into the Wilderness* (1998)

CHARLES DICKENS
Bah!

Charles Dickens (1812–1870) dominated English literature in the Victorian age, the latest installments of his serialized fiction avidly grabbed up by his faithful readers. The son of an impoverished naval clerk, he was born in Portsmouth, Hampshire, England. He worked as a youth in a bootblack factory near Charring Cross in London. The experience, of which he seldom spoke, spurred his future creativity and provided a ready theme for several of his works. He became a law clerk and court stenographer, and still later, a journalist. He married Maria Beadnell, the daughter of a banker. After that marriage ended, he wed Catherine Hogarth.

His first published work appeared in 1834, and he began to use the name "Boz" for some of his sketches. His first novel, *The Pickwick Papers*, came out in 1836, followed by *Oliver Twist* (1837), *Nicholas Nickleby* (1838), *Bleak House* and others. Dickens by now was a full-time author in comfortable circumstance. His final novel, *The Mystery of Edwin Drood*, was unfinished at his death.

Among Dickens copycats, Sir Harry Johnston (1858–1927) was perhaps the least likely. He was a British explorer and colonial officer in Cameroon, Nayasaland and Katanga.

Original Scrooge Work

A Christmas Carol (1843)

Christmas Carol Pastiches

Louis Bayard, *Mr. Timothy* (2003)
Bruce Bueno De Mesquita, *The Trial of Ebenezer Scrooge* (2001)
Andrew Angus Dalrymple, *God Bless Us Every One!: Being an Imagined Sequel to A Christmas Carol* (1985)
Marvin Kaye, *The Last Christmas of Ebenezer Scrooge* (2003)
Mark Hasard Osmun, *Marley's Ghost* (2000)
Dale Powell, *Timothy Cratchit's Christmas Carol 1917* (1998)

Original *Dombey and Son* Work
Dombey and Son (1848)

***Dombey and Son* Pastiche**
Harry Johnson, *The Gay-Dombeys* (1919)

Original Edwin Drood Work
The Mystery of Edwin Drood (1870) unfinished

Posthumous Drood Collaborations and Pastiches
Ruth Alexander, *The Mystery of Edwin Drood* (1935)
Percy Theodore Carden, *Murder of Edwin Drood, Recounted by John Jasper* (1920)
Walter E. Crisp, *The Mystery of Edwin Drood* (1914)
Charles Forsyte, *The Decoding of Edwin Drood* (1980)
Carlo Fruttero and Franco Lucentini, *The D. Case: Or, the Truth about the Mystery of Edwin Drood* (1993)
Leon Garfield, *The Mystery of Edwin Drood* (1980)
Elwin Harris, *John Jasper's Gatehouse* (1931)
Thomas James, *The Mystery of Edwin Drood, Complete* (1873)
Mary Kavanagh, *New Solution of the Mystery of Edwin Drood* (1919)
Loyal Dickensian, *Dickens' Mystery of Edwin Drood* (1927)
Henry Morford, *John Jasper's Secret: A Narrative of Certain Events Following and Explaining* The Mystery of Edwin Drood (1872)
Dan Simmons, *Drood: A Novel* (2009); *John Jasper's Secret* (1871)
Gillan Vase, *Great Mystery Solved* (1878)
J. Cuming Walters, *The Complete Mystery of Edwin Drood, the History, Continuations and Solutions, 1870–1912* (1912)
Michael West, *The Mystery of Edwin Drood, Completed and Abridged* (1952)

Original *Great Expectations* Work
Great Expectations (1860)

***Great Expectations* Pastiches**
Peter Carey, *Jack Maggs* (1998)
Alanna Knight, *Estella* (1986)
Michael Noonan, *Magwitch* (1982)

Original Oliver Twist Work
Oliver Twist (1837)

Oliver Twist Pastiche
Joanne Mattern, *Oliver Twist* (1996) Wishbone series

Original *Our Mutual Friend* Work
Our Mutual Friend (1865)

Our Mutual Friend Pastiche
Harry Johnson, *The Veneerings* (1922)

Original *Tale of Two Cities* Work
A Tale of Two Cities (1859)

Tale of Two Cities Pastiches
Susanne Alleyn, *A Far Better Rest* (2000)
Diana Mayer, *Evremonde* (2006)

Other Pastiches
Mike Ashley, editor, Hilary Bonner, Anne Perry, Charles Todd, Kate Ellis, Alanna
    Knight, Martin Edwards, Gillian Linscott and others, *The Mammoth Book of Dickensian Whodunits* (2007)
Anne Perry, Peter Tremayne, Carole Nelson Douglas, Brendan DuBois, Lillian Stewart Carl, Bill Crider, P.N. Elrod, Martin Edwards, Carolyn Wheat, Marcia Talley,
    Gillian Linscott, *Death by Dickens* (2004)

FYODOR DOSTOYEVSKY
Porfiry Petrovich

Russian novelist Fyodor Dostoyevsky (1821–1881) is known for the psychological insights in his novels *The Brothers Karamazov* (1880) and *Crime and Punishment*. The latter is a crime tale featuring Porfiry Petrovich, a detective who must solve the murder of Rodion Romanovich Raskolnikov.

Born in Moscow, the son of an abusive doctor, Dostoyevsky served in the Russian Army in 1843-1844 and again from 1854–1859. He studied to be a military engineer but soon turned to journalism and fiction writing. His first book was *Poor Folk* (*Bednye Lyudi*) in 1846. He was married twice and had three children. He joined the radical Petrashevsky Circle of socialists 1847–1849 and was a political prisoner in a labor camp from 1850–1854.

Longtime collaborators Carlo Fruttero (b. 1926) and Franco Lucentini (1920–2002) resurrected Petrovich, and other series detectives, for their 1983 novel. R.N. Morris brought Petrovich back to solve a bizarre double murder in St. Petersburg in *The Gentle Axe*.

Original Work
Crime and Punishment (1866)

Pastiches
Carlo Fruttero and Franco Lucentini, *The Palio of the Dead Quarters* (1993)
R.N. Morris, *The Gentle Axe* (2008)

ALEXANDRE DUMAS

One for all, and all for one

The French author Alexandre Dumas père (1802–1870) excelled in historical adventure novels from *The Count of Monte Cristo* to *The Three Musketeers*.

Dumas was one-quarter black Haitian descent. Although there had been wealth in the Dumas family, it did not reach his generation. Dumas was obliged to take up the pen. He wrote essays and dramas, and in the 1830s he turned out *Le Capitaine Paul*, the first of his long serial novels. His lifetime production encompassed several hundred plays, novels and stories. He rewrote E.T.A. Hoffman's story of "The Nutcracker" and Pyotr Ilyich Tchaikovsky used the variation for his ballet of the same name. The author made no claim to historical accuracy, rather, he was a storyteller of great gift. He frequently employed ghostwriters, among them Auguste Maquet, who assisted with *The Count of Monte Cristo* and *The Black Tulip*. Dumas became something of a celebrity after 1844 and took up a rich lifestyle, though he was as often as not in debt. His illegitimate son, Alexandre Dumas fils (1824–1895), supported him in his last years.

Several writers continued the D'Artagnan romances. Claude Schopp assembled texts from a serialized novel, unfinished at Dumas's death, and wrote the final two and a half chapters.

Original Musketeer Works

The Three Musketeers (1844) also in two volumes *Les Trois Mousquetaires* and *Les Quatre Mousquetaires*
Twenty Years After (1845) aka *Vingt Ans Après*

The Vicomte de Bragelonne (1847) also in separate volumes *Ten Years Later, Le Vicomte de Bragelonne, Louise de la Valière* and *The Man in the Iron Mask*

Three Musketeers Pastiches

John Adams, *The Three Musketeers* (1935) film novelization
Frank L. Beals and Bernadine Bailey, *The Story of the Three Musketeers* (1947)
H. Bedford-Jones, *D'Artagnan* (1928); *The King's Passport* (1928); *D'Artagnan's Letter* (1931)
Stephen Brust, *The Phoenix Guards* (1991); *Viscount of Adrilankha* (2002)
Cami, *Pour Lire sous la Douche* (1912) includes "Le Fils des Trois Mousquetaires"
François Ceresa, *Les Trois Hussards* (1999)
Sarah D'Almeida, *Death of a Musketeer* (2006); *The Musketeer's Seamstress* (2007); *The Musketeer's Apprentice* (2007); *Dying by the Sword: A Musketeers Mystery* (2008); *A Death in Gascony: A Musketeers Mystery* (2008)
Jean Demais, *L'Enfant des Mousquetaires* (1929); *Les Chevaliers du Gai* (1935); *Le Voyage Inoui de M. Rikiki* (1938)
Maurice Coriem, *Les Aventures de D'Artagnan* (1938)
Bill Crider and Rick Duffield, *Muttketeer!* (1997) Wishbone series

Jean-Loup Dabadie, *D'Artagnan* (1989)

Xavier de L'Ange, *Les Quatre Mousquetaires: L'Éminence Rouge* (1946)

Jean-Luc Dejean, *Le Cousin de Porthos* (1981)

Emile Desbeaux, *Les Trois Petits Mousquetaires* (1882/1919)

Jean-Pierre Dufreigne, *Le Dernier Amour d'Aramis* (1993)

Michel Duino, *D'Artagnan, Capitaine-Lieutenant des Mousquetaires du Roi* (1961)

Gabriel Fersen, *La Protégée de D'Artagnan* (1945)

Paul Feval fils, *Le Fils de d'Artagnan* (1924); *Le Vieillesse d'Athos* (1925); *D'Artagnan Contre Cyrano de Bergerac* (1925); *D'Artagnan et Cyrano Réconciliés* (1928)

Maurice-Ch. Fox, *Contes du Val-de-Saire* (1955) includes "D'Artagnan et la Russet-Red Dame"

Michael Jan Friedman, *The Mutt in the Iron Muzzle* (1997)

Robert and Jean Grimey, *Le Triomphe de Richelieu* (1949)

Michael Hardwick, *The Four Musketeers* (1974) film novelization

Rudyard Kipling, *The Three Musketeers* (1888)

Maxime la Tour, *L'Enfant des Mousquetaires* (1953)

Jehan Lebas, *Sang de D'Artagnan* (1952)

Arsene Lefort, *Le Grand Secret de D'Artagnan* (1955)

Voldemar Lestienne, *Furioso* (1971); *Fracasso* (1973)

Paul Mahalin, *Le Fils de Porthos, Le Mort d'Aramis* (1883); *Le Villeul d'Aramis* (1896)

Albert Maurin, *Les Véritable Mémoires de D'Artagnan le Mousquetaire* (1874)

Hubert Monteilhet, *De Plume et d'Épée: Roman Louis XIII* (1999)

Roger Nimier, *Les Indes Galandes* (1952) includes "Frederic, D'Artagnan and La Petite Chinoise"; *D'Artagnan Amoreux* (1962)

Lucien Pemjean, *Le Jeunesse de D'Artagnan* (1930); *Le Capitaine D'Artagnan* (1931)

Arturo Perez-Reverte, *Club Dumas* (1993)

Ch. Quinel and A. de Montgon, *Le Beau D'Artagnan et Son Époque* (1930)

Yak Rivais, *Milady, Mon Amour; Une Femme dans la Tourmente 1627–1628* (1986)

Joel Rosenberg, *Not Exactly the Three Musketeers* (1999)

Paul-Yves Sebillot, *Les Deux Mousquetaires* (1954)

Paul Segonzac, *Les Amours de d'Artagnan* (1924)

Paul-Loup Sulitzer, *Les Nouveau Trois Mousquetaires* (1999) anthology

Paco Ignacio Taibo II, *Le Rendezvous des Heros* (1987)

Tiffany Thayer, *Three Musketeers* (1939); *Three Musketeers and a Lady* (1939)

Emile Watin, *Les Trois Pages de Monsieur D'Artagnan* (1905)

Henry Llewellyn Williams, *D'Artagnan, The King-Maker* (1901); *D'Artagnan's Exploit* (1904)

Chelsea Quinn Yarbro, *A Dandle for D'Artagnan* (1989)

Posthumous Collaborations

Alexandre Dumas fils, *Joseph Balsano* (1870)

Claude Schopp, *Le Chevalier de Sainte-Hermine* (2005) aka *The Knight of Saint Hermine*

GEORGE DU MAURIER
Trilby

George du Maurier (1834–1896), grandfather of novelist Daphne du Maurier, was born in France but lived in Great Britain after he married Emma Wightwick. He was on the illustration staff of *Punch*, the humor magazine. Eyesight problems forced him to take up writing. His second book, *Trilby* (1894), a gothic horror tale, is about impoverished Trilby O'Ferrall, who posed "in the altogether" for Bohemian Parisian artists Little Billee, the Laird and Taffy to earn a few centimes. Little Billee is in love with Trilby, but she rejects him when, under the spell of the roguish Svengali, she turns into a singing sensation. *Trilby* was a popular seller. Trilby felt hats came into fashion. The Svengali figure became widely recognized. The story became a stage play, written by Paul M. Potter and first performed in 1895. It also inspired *The Studio Girl* in 1927.

Trilby inspired such diverse writers as Lucy Maud Montgomery (who was intrigued with the main character as she set about to write *Anne of Green Gables*) and Gaston LeRoux (who wrote *The Phantom of the Opera* in 1910, an indirect pastiche). Poet Mary Kyle Dallas (ca. 1837–1897) reversed the genders in her novel *Billtry*. *Literary News* in 1895 noted, "Mary Kyle Dallas has had the wisdom to assure her readers that she is making fun in a kindly spirit of a book of which she is an ardent and sincere admirer. She says: 'Though without the great, beautiful "Trilby" this absurd little "Billtry" would never have been. It is simply the reverse of the question — "the other side of the shield" — the *"what might have been"* — had the bachelor artists of the Parisian studios been bachelor girls of Gotham, and their model masculine, instead of feminine — Billtry, in fact, instead of Trilby — and even of this I did not take thought until the morsel was written." Billtry has beautiful feet, images of which are reproduced in promotions for soap and candy.

Original Work
Trilby (1894)

Pastiche
Mary Kyle Dallas, *Billtry* (1895)

GEORGE ELIOT
Daniel Deronda

It was a male-dominated literary world into which Mary Anne Evans (1819–1880) boldly strode when she wrote *The Mill on the Floss* (1860).

Born in Warwickshire, England, Evans grew up on an estate where her father was head farmer. She was allowed to read books in the estate's library, and developed an interest in becoming a writer. She worked for several years as a housekeeper and tutor, and got her break when she helped edit *The Westminster Review* for publisher John Chapman. She gained a wide following with *Adam Bede* (1859), *Middlemarch* (1871-72) and *Silas Marner* (1861)—all published under the name George Eliot.

Her last novel, *Daniel Deronda,* contained passages in support of Jewish Zionism, which is why it prompted a pastiche.

Original Work
Daniel Deronda (1876)

Pastiche
Anonymous, *Gwendolen* (1878)

THOMAS HARDY
Tess

Thomas Hardy (1840–1928) was a writer and poet of the naturalist movement. Among his works are *Mayor of Casterbridge* (1886) and *Tess of the d'Urbervilles* (1891).

Born in Dorset, England, the son of a building contractor, Hardy apprenticed to an architect whose specialty was church restorations. He enrolled at King's College in London. He returned to Dorset, where he began to write poetry. His first novel, *The Poor Man and the Lady*, never saw print. The success of *Far from the Madding Crowd* (1874) allowed him to abandon his architectural work. He married Emma Lavinia Gifford in 1874. Many of his stories are set in the imagined Wessex. Ever a pessimist, Hardy made human travails vastly entertaining. *The Return of the Native* (1878) and *Jude the Obscure* (1895) found ready audiences, though the latter was controversial because of its carnal depictions. He eventually quit writing fiction and returned to poetry. After his wife's death in 1912, Hardy married his secretary, Florence Emily Dugdale. He wrote a two-volume autobiography, though in publication it was purported to be by Florence Hardy.

London-born novelist Emma Tennant (b. 1937) wrote a *Tess* sequel a century after the original appeared.

Original Work
Tess of the d'Urbervilles (1891)

Pastiche
Emma Tennant, *Tess* (1993)

NATHANIEL HAWTHORNE
Scarlet Letter

Hester Prynne struggles against shame and indignity when, unwed, she gives birth to a daughter, in Nathaniel Hawthorne's novel *The Scarlet Letter.*

Hawthorne (1804–1864), a pillar of 19th century American literature, was born in Salem, Massachusetts, and lived for many years in Concord, though this novel appeared the year he and his family lived in Stockbridge, Massachusetts. Others of his well-known works include *The House of the Seven Gables* (1851) and *Twice-Told Tales* (1837).

Hawthorne left three unfinished romances at his death, and ordered their destruction. The family instead took them to a publisher, as edited by son Julian Hawthorne (1846–1934). Gothic and young adult novelist Deborah Noyes in her sequel follows the life of Pearl, Hester Prynne's illegitimate daughter, as she matures and marries. The British educator Christopher Bigsby did the same in *Pearl*. His earlier *Hester* zooms in on Ms. Prynne.

Original Work
The Scarlet Letter (1850)

Pastiches
Christopher Bigsby, *Hester* (1990); *Pearl* (1995)
Deborah Noyes, *Angel and Apostle* (2005)

Posthumous Collaboration
Julian Hawthorne, *Doctor Grimshawe's Secret* (1883)

E.T.A. HOFFMAN
Nutcracker

Ernst Theodor Wilhelm Hoffman (1776–1822) was a German Romantic writer of horror and fantasy tales, as well as an artist and composer. He used the penname E.T.A. Hoffman.

The son of a Prussian barrister, Hoffman grew up in a split household, living with his mother and his siblings. He worked as a clerk while struggling to find an audience for his compositions. He eventually received a posting in Warsaw, Poland. He began to sell fiction with *Ritter Gluck* in 1809. In a tumultuous professional life, Hoffman eventually settled in Berlin, where Berlin Theatre staged his opera *Undine*. He later accepted governmental appointment. He died in Berlin in 1822.

Marius Petipa and Lev Ivanov choreographed "The Nutcracker" ballet for the Imperial Theatre in Russia in 1892 with music by composer Pyotr Ilyich Tchaikovsky and based on Hoffman's 1816 story "The Nutcracker and the King of Mice." That is, it is based on Alexandre Dumas père's version of Hoffman's story of a young German girl who dreams of a Christmas nutcracker who turns into a handsome prince and engages in a fierce duel with the seven-headed Mouse King. Dumas rewrote the story to appeal to children, and Petipa found the version more suited to stage.

Original Work
"The Nutcracker and the King of Mice" (1816)

Pastiche
Alexandre Dumas père, "The Nutcracker of Nuremberg" (1844)

THOMAS HUGHES
Tom Brown

British lawyer and author Thomas Hughes (1822–1896) wrote two books about students and their antics at Rugby School, which he had attended. Schoolboy tales enjoyed a wide audience in the late 19th century.

Hughes was born in Uffington, Berkshire, and attended Twyford School until age eleven, when he transferred to Rugby School. He adored the headmaster, Thomas Arnold, and idealized him in his novels. Hughes did better at cricket than literature. He graduated from Oriel College, Oxford, in 1845, became Queen's Counsel in 1869. He accepted a county judgeship in 1882. He twice served in Parliament and was known as a social reformer. He fostered establishment of a utopian settlement in Rugby, Tennessee, intended for the young sons of Englishmen. It failed. He married Frances Ford in 1848 and while the two lived in Wimbledon, he wrote his tale of Brown's educational misadventures of Brown, Scud East, Diggs and Flashman. Hughes based the main character on his brother, George Hughes.

George MacDonald Fraser (1925–2008) appropriated the villain from Hughes' books, Harry Flashman, for his own heavily researched series of "sea and saber" tales. (Fraser's Flashman, interestingly, inspired Raymond M. Saunders to write several novels featuring a like character, Fenwick "Fenny" Travers.)

Original Works
Tom Brown's School Days (1857)   *Tom Brown at Oxford* (1861)

Pastiches
George MacDonald Fraser, *Flashman* (1969); *Royal Flash* (1970); *Flash for Freedom*

(1971); *Flashman at the Charge* (1973); *Flashman in the Great Game* (1975); *Flashman's Lady* (1978); *Flashman and the Redskins* (1982); *Flashman and the Dragon* (1985); *Flashman and the Mountain of Light* (1990); *Flashman and the Angel of the Lord* (1994); *Flashman and the Tiger* (1999); *Flashman on the March* (2005)

VICTOR HUGO

Jean Valjean

French writer Victor Hugo (1802–1885) penned poetry and drama, but is best known for the novels *The Hunchback of Notre Dame* (1831) and *Les Misérables*. The second title relates how former convict Jean Valjean established himself anew, against the formidable opposition of Inspector Javert. The work was been made into some forty-five films as well as plays and a musical.

The author's great-great-grandson Pierre Hugo fought unsuccessfully against publication of François Ceresa's *Cosette, or the Time of Illusions* in 2001, seeking 425,000 pounds for alleged violation of intellectual property rights and the damage to Victor Hugo's reputation. He particularly objected to a change in the original ending of *Les Misérables*. A court decision in 2007 found in favor of Ceresa and his publisher Plon.

Original Work

Les Miserables (1862)

Pastiches

François Ceresa, *Cosette, ou Le temps des illusions* (2001) aka *Cosette, or the Time of Illusions*; *Marius ou le fugitif* (2002) aka *Marius; or the Fugitive*
Laura Kalpakian, *Cosette* (1995)

HENRIK IBSEN

A Doll's House

Henrik Ibsen (1828–1906), a Norwegian playwright, wrote such realistic works as *Peer Gynt* (1867) and *Ghosts* (1881). His *A Doll's House* (1879) created a stir with its grim depiction of marriage. Some directors who stage the work use an alternative, more upbeat ending.

Besides works listed below, dramatist M. Fabre produced *La Maison d'Argile* in 1907. Ednah D. Cheney wrote a short story, "Nora's Return: A Sequel to A Doll's House of Henrik Ibsen." And Walter Besant did the same, "The Doll's House — And After."

Original *Doll's House* Work
A Doll's House (1879)

***A Doll's House* Pastiche**
Tormod Skagestad, *Nora Helmer*

Original Gabler Work
Hedda Gabler (1891)

Hedda Gabler Pastiche
J.M. Barrie, *Ibsen's Ghost* (1891)

Original Lady Work
The Lady from the Sea (1888)

***The Lady from the Sea* Pastiche**
St. John Hankin, *Mr. Punch's Dramatic Sequels* (ca1901)

HENRY JAMES
What Maisie Knew

Henry James (1843–1916) was born in the United States but lived mostly in England. He helped establish a school of realistic fiction through such novels as *Daisy Miller* (1878), *Portrait of a Lady* (1881), *The Bostonians* (1886) and *The Europeans* (1878).

A New York City native, James studied traveled widely as a youth and was taught largely by tutors, though he did take classes at Harvard Law School. His first short story, "A Tragedy of Errors," came out in 1864. He became a regular author for *Nation*, *Atlantic Monthly* and *New York Tribune*. He often wrote of Americans living or traveling abroad.

Geoffrey Wolff spun off James' story of a dysfunctional family, *What Maisie Knew*, for a new novel. Hilary Bailey and Toby Litt wrote new takes on James' ghost story, *The Turn of the Screw*. Litt had previously edited James' last completed novel, *The Outcry*, for Penguin.

Original Maisie Work
What Maisie Knew (1897)

***What Maisie Knew* Pastiche**
Geoffrey Wolff, *The Age of Consent* (1995)

Original *Turn of the Screw* Work

The Turn of the Screw (1898)

The Turn of the Screw Pastiche

Hilary Bailey, *Miles and Flora: A Sequel to Henry James' The Turn of the Screw* (1998)
Toby Litt, *Ghost Story* (2004)

Posthumous Collaboration

Toby Litt, *The Outcry* (2001)

CHARLES KINGSLEY

Advocate for laborers

Born in Holne, Devon, England, Charles Kingsley (1819–1875) was an educator, social reformer and novelist whose writings sometimes depicted the West. Kingsley studied at Kings' College in London, the University of Cambridge and Magdalene College in Cambridge. He married Frances Grenfell in 1844. He abandoned his work in the law in favor of the ministry. While serving as a church rector, he also taught modern history at the University of Cambridge. He tutored the Prince of Wales, later to become King Edward VIII. His first novel was *Alton Locke* (1849). He was a Christian Socialist and amateur naturalist. He advocated for agrarians and laborers in the novel *Yeast* (1849). The *Water Babies*, which first appeared as a Macmillan's magazine serial in 1862-1863, was a children's book about a youthful chimney sweep, made into an animated film in 1978.

Mary St. Legere Harrison, whose prose appeared under the penname Lucas Malet, explained in a prefatory note that after her mother's death in 1892, she received some of her father's papers including an unknown manuscript. "But I also found about a hundred and fifty foolscap pages of another novel, entitled 'The Tutor's Story,' which was entirely new to me. I never remember hearing my father speak of it, nor do I find any allusion to it in 'The Letters of Charles Kingsley and Memories of his Life.' The fact that the Yorkshire scenery, along with various names of persons and places is common to 'The Tutor's Story' and the opening chapters of 'The Water Babies' leads me to suppose it was written before and, probably, put aside in favor of the latter book, which appeared in 1863... The manuscript... offers a puzzle of which a good many pieces either are lost or have never existed since it was my father's habit to put down a scene, description, or dialogue just as it occurred to him, leaving all linking up and filling in to a final rewriting of his book... I have developed the characters, disentangled the plot, and completed the story to the best of my understanding and ability, and have doubled the length of the original manuscript in the process...."

Posthumous collaboration
Lucas Malet (Mary St. Legere Harrison), *The Tutor* (1916)

RUDYARD KIPLING
Kim

Rudyard Kipling (1865–1936) was born in Bombay. After attending United Services College in England, he became a journalist in India. He also wrote short stories and poetry, much of it glorifying the British Empire and particularly its military heroes. *Kim*, one of Kipling's most popular works, tells of the orphaned son of an Irish soldier who becomes friends with a lama. It was serialized in *McClure's* magazine in the United States and *Cassell's* Magazine in England, before it appeared as a book.

In his first sequel, Timeri Murari's Kim is older but remains torn between his allegiance to the British Raj and his love of India.

Original Work
Kim (1901)

Pastiches
Laurie R. King, *The Game* (2004)
Timeri Murari, *The Imperial Agent* (1987); *The Last Victory* (1988)

D. H. LAWRENCE
A gamekeeper's lady

D.H. Lawrence (1885–1930) wrote a spicy (and frequently banned) novel, *Lady Chatterley's Lover*, in 1928. The writer grew up in a British mining town in Nottinghamshire, won a scholarship and attended Nottingham High School. He eventually received a teaching certificate from University College Nottingham in 1908, by which time he had begun to write fiction. His first novel was *The White Peacock* (1910). He later penned *Sons and Lovers* (1913) and *Women in Love* (1920). Lady Constance Chatterley's lover, in the novel of the same name, was a working-class man, a gamekeeper named Oliver Mellors — which, along with the spicy sex scenes, limited the book's circulation for many years. The publisher Penguin was brought to trial for obscenity when it issued the book in Great Britain in 1960. The publisher was able to demonstrate literary merit.

Besides the sequel writers listed, Spike Milligan wrote two parodic books about Lady Chatterley.

Original Works

Lady Chatterley's Lover (1928)

The Second Lady Chatterley's Lover
(2007) more explicit earlier draft

Pastiches

Jehanne D'Orliac, Lady Chatterley's Second Husband (1935)
Anthony Gudaitis, as Anonymous, Lady Chatterley's Husbands (1931)
Patricia Robins, Lady Chatterley's Daughter (1961)
Clement Wood, Lady Chatterley's Friends (1932)

GASTON LEROUX

Aria

Gaston Leroux's gothic thriller The Phantom of the Opera was serialized in Le Gaulois in 1909-1910, but did not sell very well as a book. An English translation came out in 1911, and it has several times been adapted to stage and screen. Set in the Paris theatre Opera Garnier, it is purported to be based on a true story of a deformed musical genius. Leroux (1868–1927) was a journalist and writer of detective fiction (his detective was Joseph Rouletabille) — after having squandered a huge inheritance.

Thriller writer Frederick Forsyth envisioned Erik surviving Leroux's work and starting fresh in New York City. Andrew Lloyd-Webber reportedly plans a musical sequel, and intends to work with its storyline with Forsyth. Susan Kay re-envisioned the story for young adult readers.

Original Work

Le Fantôme de l'Opéra (1911) aka The Phantom of the Opera

Pastiches

Peter Bregman, The Trap-Door Maker: A Prequel to the Phantom of the Opera, Book 1 (2005); The Trap-Door Maker: A Prequel to the Phantom of the Opera, Book 2 (2006); The Trap-Door Maker: A Prequel to the Phantom of the Opera, Book 3 (2007)
Stephanie Cole, The Phantom Returns (2007)
Etienne de Mendes, The Return of the Phantom: Le Coeur Loyal (2007)
Lucille Epps, Phantom's Legacy (2008)
Frederick Forsyth, The Phantom of Manhattan (1999)
Colette Gale, Unmasked: An Erotic Novel of The Phantom of the Opera (2007)
Carrie Hernandez, Angel of Music: Tales of the Phantom of the Opera (2006)
Kae D. Jacobs, Beyond the Masque: The Untold Story of Erik and Christine (2007)
Susan Kay, Phantom (2006)
Jodi Leisure Minton, Darkness Brings the Dawn: Erik's Story (2006)

Sadie Montgomery, *Out of the Darkness: The Phantom's Journey* (2007); *The Phoenix of the Opera* (2007); *The Phantom's Opera* (2007); *Phantom Death* (2008)
Sam Siciliano, *Angel of the Opera: Sherlock Holmes Meets the Phantom of the Opera* (1994)
J.C. Sillesen, *No Return: A Contemporary Phantom Tale* (2007)
An Wallace, *Letters to Erik: The Ghost's Love Story* (2008)
Debra P. Whitehead, *Into the Light: A Phantom of the Opera Story* (2006)
Shirley Yoshinaka, *Deception: A Phantom of the Opera Novel* (2006)

CHARLES MATURIN
Melmoth's pact

Irish dramatist and novelist Charles Robert Maturin (1782–1824) attended Trinity College in Dublin and became a curate. He had writing success with the novels issued pseudonymously as by Dennis Jasper Murphy — *The Fatal Revenge* (1807) and *The Wild Irish Boy* (1808). His prose came to the favorable attention of Sir Walter Scott and Honore de Balzac.

Balzac wrote a sequel to Maturin's gothic novel *Melmoth the Wanderer*. The hero, John Melmoth, sells his soul to the devil for 150 extra years of life. He then spends his days seeking someone to assume his compact.

Original Work
Melmoth the Wanderer (1820)

Pastiche
Honore de Balzac, *Melmoth Réconcilié à l'Eglise* (1835) aka *Melmoth Reconciled*

HERMAN MELVILLE
Quest for the whale

Born in New York City, Herman Melville (1819–1891) spent years at sea on the whaler *Acushnet* and other ships, gathering material for his South Seas adventure tales *Typee* (1846) and *Omoo* (1847) and his classic, *Moby-Dick* (1851), the dark tale of Ahab's relentless pursuit of the great white whale. Melville crafted the book from his study at Arrowhead, a country farmhouse in Pittsfield, Massachusetts. Melville's writing brought him insufficient income, and from 1866 to 1885 he returned to New York to work as a customs inspector at the docks.

Recent sequels have centered on the travails of the sea captain's wife. Kentucky resident Sena Jeter Naslund, a professor at the University of Louisville, created the story of Una Spenser, who besides being wed to Ahab makes the acquaintance of real-life Margaret Fuller and Ralph Waldo Emerson. Louise M. Gouge, a writer of Christian romances and historicals, saw her first novel published in 1994, when she was fifty. She wrote the trilogy Ahab's Legacy about the sea captain's wife Hannah Rose and their son, Timothy Jacobs. Bruce Sterling gave a cyberpunk turn to the classic.

Original Work
Moby-Dick, or The Whale (1851)

Pastiches
Philip José Farmer, *The Wind Whales of Ishmael* (1971)
Louise M. Gouge, *Ahab's Bride* (2004); *Hannah Rose* (2005); *Son of Perdition* (2006)
Sena Jeter Naslund, *Ahab's Wife; or, The Stargazer* (1999)
Bruce Sterling, *Involution Ocean* (1977)

EDGAR ALLAN POE
Fear

American master of the macabre Edgar Allan Poe (1809–1849) introduced thoughtful investigation to the crime novel with his C. August Dupin stories. A Boston native, Poe was orphaned at a young age and taken in by a Richmond, Va., merchant's family. He lived in England for a time, served in the army, and began to write. *Tamerlane and Other Poems* (1827) was his first book. *The Narrative of Arthur Gordon Pym of Nantucket* is about a stowaway on a whaling ship whose adventures with mutiny and cannibalism become increasingly bizarre. Poe's story of Roderick Usher takes place in a dark and foreboding castle.

Jules Verne (1828–1905), in admiration of Poe, wrote a Pym sequel about the crew of the ship *Halbrane* in its search for the youth's fate. Robert Poe reportedly used his ancestor's notes for his sequels, which feature as a character John Charles Poe. Robert Bloch finished Poe's incomplete manuscript, *The Lighthouse*.

Original Mystery Works
Tales of the Grotesque and Arabesque (1839) includes "The Fall of the House of Usher"
Monsieur Dupin (1904) includes "The Murders in the Rue Morgue" (1841), "The Mystery of Marie Roget" (1942) and "The Purloined Letter" (1844)

Dupin Pastiches
Avi, *The Man Who Was Poe* (1989)
Mario Brelich, *Work of Betrayal* (1989)

Michael Harrison, *The Exploits of Chevalier Dupin* (1968) aka *Murder in the Rue Royale*
George Egon Hatvary, *The Murder of Edgar Allan Poe* (1997)
Jean-Marc Lofficier & Randy Lofficier, *Edgar Allan Poe on Mars* (2007)
Matthew Pearl, *The Poe Shadow* (2006)

House of Usher Pastiches

Marie Kiraly, *Madeline: After the Fall of Usher* (1996)
Robert M. McCammon, *Usher's Passing* (1984)
Robert Poe, *Return to the House of Usher* (1996)

Original Gordon Pym Work

Narrative of Arthur Gordon Pym of Nantucket (1838) aka *Arthur Gordon Pym* aka *Wonderful Adventures of Arthur Gordon Pym*

Pym Pastiche

Jules Verne, *The Sphinx of the Ice Fields* (1897) aka *Le Sphinx des Glaces* aka *Antarctic Mystery* (1897) based on *Narrative of Arthur Gordon Pym of Nantucket*

Original Lighthouse Work

Edward Woodberry, editor, *Life of Poe* (1909) fragment "The Lighthouse"

Posthumous Collaborations

Christopher Conlon, editor, *The Lighthouse* (2007) with completed versions by Robert Bloch, William F. Nolan and others

Other Pastiches

Stuart M. Kaminsky, editor, *On a Raven's Wing* (2009)
Robert Poe, *The Black Cat* (1997)
Kim Newman, John Langan, Delia Sherman, Pat Cadigan, Laird Barron, Sharyn McCrumb, Suzy McKee Charnas, Lucius Shepard and others, *Poe: 19 New Tales Inspired by Edgar Allan Poe*, edited by Ellen Datlow (2009)

GEORGE SAND

Duped

Amandine Aurore Lucile Dupin, Baroness Dudevant (1804–1876) was a feminist — it must have grated on her to have to use the pseudonym George Sand for her fiction. She often wore men's clothing, smoked and apparently had a lesbian affair. She collaborated with Jules Sandeau on her first novel, *Rose et Blanche* (1831). Among her better-known works are *Consuelo* (1842) and its sequel, *La Comtesse de Rudolstady* (1843).

Lew Vanderpoole claimed to be her nephew and in 1887 sold purported Sand stories to periodicals. *Publishers' Weekly* for Sept. 24, 1887, called Vanderpoole "a writer of some notoriety," and reported that he was arrested and charged with obtaining money under false pretenses for offering *Cosmopolitan* magazine and Schlicht-Field Company the unpublished "Princess Nourmahal," "which was one of 127 stories that he had to dispose of. Challenged as to the manuscript's authenticity, he admitted he had no copy and "he had read the story and had such a good memory that he rewrote it."

The New York Times in its review of *Princess Nourmahal* scoffed at the possibility that it was by George Sand: "The only interest attaching to 'Nourmahal' is the question how any one could be deceived into supposing that its hysterical, labored love-transports, its cheap villain, its false Orientalism and its musty mysteries could have come from the authoress of 'Consuelo.' Yet it was accepted by a monthly magazine on one occasion, and, though it never came to publication, is now a full-fledged book. Somebody is the victim of a cruel falsification."

Pastiche

Lew Vanderpoole, translator, *Princess Nourmahal* (1888)

SIR WALTER SCOTT

Ivanhoe

The Scottish poet and novelist Sir Walter Scott (1771–1832) wrote a long list of novels, among them the 12th-century adventure *Ivanhoe*. The hero is in love with the Lady Rowena. This displeases his father, Cedric of Rotherwood, as does Ivanhoe's allegiance to King Richard I. Robin Hood and his Merry Men appear in the tale.

Scott was born in Edinburgh. His father was a solicitor. Scott studied arts and law at Edinburgh University and entered the bar in 1792, seven years later accepting appointment as sheriff in County of Selkirk. Keenly interested in old border tales and ballads, it's no surprise his first major works were *Minstrelsy of the Scottish Border* (1802) and *The Lady of the Last Minstrel* (1805). His vigorous output of novels included *The Lady in the Lake* (1810), *Waverly* (1814), and *Rob Roy* (1817). Scott was designated a baronet in 1820, and soon after established the Bannatyne Club.

Of the handful of sequels by other hands, William Makepeace Thackeray's is early and in a mock-heroic vein. Simon Hawke's is the first in his TimeWars time travel series. Christopher Vogler's features Brian de Bois Guilbert, the villain in *Ivanhoe*. Scott's robust novel about the Scottish outlaw Rob Roy Macgregor prompted two sequels by Nigel Godwin Tranter.

Original Ivanhoe Work

Ivanhoe (1819)

Ivanhoe Pastiches

Simon Hawke, *The Ivanhoe Gambit* (1999)
William Makepeace Thackeray, *Rebecca and Rowena* (1850)
Christopher Vogler, *Ravenskull* (2006)

Original Rob Roy Work

Rob Roy (1817)

Rob Roy Pastiches

Nigel Godwin Tranter, *Macgregor's Gathering* (1957); *Clansman* (1959)

GEORGE BERNARD SHAW
Shocking

George Bernard Shaw (1856–1950), an Irish playwright known for *Major Barbara* (1905) and *Pygmalion* (1912), in *Mrs. Warren's Profession* wrote of the relationship between a prostitute and her daughter Vivie, who is horrified at her mother's profession. British officials initially banned the play, but it was performed in London in 1902, though a 1905 performance in New York City resulted in the performers being arrested.

Shaw was a freethinking advocate of women's rights and social economic equality. He grew up in mild poverty, the son of a grain wholesaler. After the family fractured, he was raised largely by hired help. Much of Shaw's education came from his own inquiries at the British Museum. He disdained meat, tobacco and alcohol. He was active with the socialist Fabian Society. His marriage to Charlotte Payne-Townshend brought him financial security.

Sir Harry Johnston (1858–1927) also wrote sequels to Dickens novels.

Original Work

Mrs. Warren's Profession (1893)

Pastiche

Harry Johnston, *Mrs. Warren's Daughter: A Story of the Woman's Movement* (1920)

MARY SHELLEY
Creature

Wife of Romantic poet Percy Bysshe Shelley, Mary Wollstonecraft Shelley (1797–1851), the British essayist, biographer, travel writer and novelist, crafted her gothic masterpiece *Frankenstein* in 1818. It was published anonymously; her name appeared on the book only in 1831. Dr. Victor Frankenstein dances too close to the secrets of life in the course of the novel, assembling a powerful Creature from body parts. The story was made into films again and again.

Several writers have regenerated the monster in years-later sequels.

Original Work

Frankenstein: or, The Modern Prometheus (1818)

Pastiches

Brian Aldiss, *Frankenstein Unbound* (1973)
Brian Aldiss, Isaac Asimov, Kurt Vonnegut, Loren D. Estleman and Charles deLint, *The Ultimate Frankenstein* (2003)
C. Dean Andersson, *I Am Frankenstein* (1996)
Don W. Baranowski, *Sherlock Holmes: The Adventures of the Frankenstein Monster* (2006)
Michael Burgen, *Frankenstein* (1996) Wishbone series
Jean-Claude Carrièrre, writing as Benoît Becker, *La Tour de Frankenstein* (1957) aka *The Tower of Frankenstein*; *Le Pas de Frankenstein* (1957) aka *The Step of Frankenstein*; *La Nuit de Frankenstein* (1957) aka *The Night of Frankenstein*; *Le Sceau de Frankenstein* (1957) aka *The Seal of Frankenstein*; *Frankenstein Rode* (1958) aka *Frankenstein Prowls*; *La Cave de Frankenstein* (1959) aka *The Cellar of Frankenstein*
Joseph Covino, Jr., *Frankenstein Resurrected* (2005)
Timothy Basil Ering and Roscoe Cooper, *Diary of Victor Frankenstein* (1997)
Elizabeth Hand, *The Bride of Frankenstein* (2007)
Dean Koontz, *Dead and Alive* (2009)
Dean Koontz with Kevin J. Anderson, *Prodigal Son* (2004)
Dean Koontz with Ed Gorman, *City of Night* (2005)
Allan Rune Pettersson, *Frankenstein's Aunt* (1978); *Frankenstein's Aunt Returns* (1989)
Stefan Petrucha, *The Shadow of Frankenstein* (2006)
Richard Pierce, *Creation* (1994) Frankenstein's Children series; *Revenge* (1994) Frankenstein's Children series; *Curse* (1995) Frankenstein's Children series
Theodore Roszak, *The Memoirs of Elizabeth Frankenstein* (1996)
Fred Saberhagen, *The Frankenstein Papers* (1986)

ROBERT LOUIS STEVENSON

Long John Silver

Argh, maties, *Treasure Island* is the gold standard of boys' pirate adventures. Scotsman Robert Louis Stevenson (1850–1894) was a travel writer and he knew how to weave exotic locales into his fiction. He abandoned Great Britain for health reasons and lived for a time in the New York Adirondacks before heading for California, then the Samoan Islands.

Stevenson's Jekyll/Hyde tale of a split personality became a classic, to be often replicated.

Stevenson originally meant to call his pirate tale of island treasure "The Sea Cook"—for peg-legged Long John Silver, who is quartermaster under Captain Flint—but his editors had a better idea. *Kidnapped*, set in 18th century Scotland, is about David Balfour's experiences in the foreboding House of Shaws and his mysterious Uncle Ebenezer Balfour.

Jim Hawkins, Ben Gunn, Flint—all these characters had second lives in pastiche sequels. Philip José Farmer wrote the most far-out variant, about Greatheart Silver, descendant of Long John, in a science fiction novel. Arthur Quiller-Couch (1863–1944), who often published under the penname Q, completed an unfinished Stevenson manuscript, *St. Ives*.

Original Jekyll/Hyde Work
The Strange Case of Dr. Jekyll and Mr. Hyde (1886)

Dr. Jekyll and Mr. Hyde Pastiches
Robert Bloch and Andre Norton, *The Jekyll Legacy* (1990)
Loren D. Estleman, *Dr. Jekyll and Mr. Holmes* (2001)
James Gelsey, *Scooby-Doo and You: The Case of Dr. Jenkins and Mr. Hyde* (2001)
Willis Hall, *Doctor Jekyll and Mr. Hollins* (1988)
Frances Little, *Untold Sequel to the Strange Case of Doctor Jekyll and Mister Hyde* (1890)
Valerie Martin, *Mary Reilly: The Untold Story of Doctor Jekyll and Mr. Hyde* (1990)
Donald Thomas, *Jekyll, Alias Hyde* (1988)
Joanne Mattern, Ed Parker and Kathryn Yingling, *Wishbone: The Strange Case of Dr. Jekyll and Mr. Hyde* (1996)
C.W. Meisterfeld and Darlene Perez, *Jelly Bean versus Dr. Jekyll and Mr. Hyde* (1989)
Emma Tennant, *Two Women of London* (1989)

Original *Kidnapped* Works
Kidnapped (1886)   *Catriona* (1893) sequel to *Kidnapped*

Kidnapped Pastiches
A.D. Howden Smith, *Alan Breck Again* (1934)

Original *Treasure Island* Work
Treasure Island (1883)

Treasure Island Pastiches
Kathryn Acker, *Pussy King of the Pirates* (1996)
Francis Bryan (Frank Delaney), *Jim Hawkins and the Curse of Treasure Island* (2001)
Harold Augustin Calahan, *Back to Treasure Island* (1936)
Edward Chupack, *Silver: My Own Tale as Written by Me with a Goodly Amount of Murder* (2008)
John Connell, *The Return of Long John Silver* (1949)

R.F. Delderfield, *The Adventures of Ben Gunn* (1956)
Philip José Farmer, *Greatheart Silver* (1982)
Roger L. Johnson, *Dead Man's Chest: The Sequel to Treasure Island* (2001)
Denis Judd, *Return to Treasure Island* (1978)
Bjorn Larsson, *Long John Silver* (1999)
Sam Llewellyn, *Last Will and Testament of Robert Louis Stevenson* (1981)
Justin Scott, *Treasure Island: A Modern Novel* (1994)
A.D. Howden Smith, *Porto Bello Gold* (1924)
Leonard Wibberley, *Flint's Island* (1972)

Posthumous Collaboration

Arthur Quiller-Couch, *St. Ives: Being the Adventures of a French Prisoner in England* (1897)

HARRIET BEECHER STOWE
Uncle Tom's Cabin

The little lady that started a war, President Abraham Lincoln called Harriet Beecher Stowe (1811–1896). A daughter of Protestant minister Lyman Beecher and sibling of abolitionist and theologian Henry Ward Beecher, Stowe's first book, *The Mayflower*, came out in 1834. *Uncle Tom's Cabin* first appeared in the anti-slavery weekly, *National Era*, and it drew attention to the treatment of slaves in the South. It sold more copies than any other novel in the 19th century. Stowe, who lived most of her life in Connecticut, was spurred to write the story after passage of the Fugitive Slave Law in 1850. In Hartford, her next-door neighbor was Samuel Clemens.

Stowe's book, and the myriad stage productions (written without permission by others) that toured the country, spurred numerous anti–Tom books. The works listed here are in that last category, but are more directly tied to Stowe's novel. Mary Henderson Eastman's *Aunt Phillis's Cabin* probably sold the most copies — barely a tenth of Stowe's sales.

Original Work

Uncle Tom's Cabin; or, Life Among the Lowly (1852)

Selected Pastiches

Mary Henderson Eastman, *Aunt Phillis's Cabin; or, Southern Life As It Is* (1852)
Adolphus M. Hart, *Uncle Tom in Paris; or, Views of Slavery Outside the Cabin* (1854)
J.W. Page, *Uncle Robin in His Cabin in Virginia, and Tom Without One in Boston* (1853)
W.L.G. Smith, *Life at the South; or, Uncle Tom's Cabin As It Is: Being Narratives, Scenes, and Incidents in the Real "Life of the Lowly"* (1852)
C.H. Wiley, *Life in the South, a Companion to Uncle Tom's Cabin* (1852)

AUGUST STRINDBERG

Miss Julie

August Strindberg (1849–1912) was a Swedish playwright with fifty-eight dramas to his credit. Born in Stockholm, the author grew up in a middle-class family with a dozen children. Strindberg dropped out of the University of Uppsala in 1867 and worked briefly for the Royal Dramatic Theatre. He returned to his studies, became a journalist and wrote a historical drama, *Master Olof.* He was assistant librarian at the Royal Library from 1874 to 1882. He married into money: Baroness Siri von Essen. Persecuted for perceived anti–Semitism in his writings, Strindberg had an emotional breakdown. Nevertheless, he soon had his greatest successes with *Miss Julie* (1888) and other plays and novels.

Patrick Marber (b. 1964) is an English actor, comedian, playwright and screenwriter. Olov Enquist (b. 1934) is a native of Sweden.

Original Work
Miss Julie (1888)

Pastiches
Patrick Marber, *After Miss Julie* (1995)
Olov Enquist, *Night of the Tribades: A Play from 1889* (1975)

WILLIAM MAKEPEACE THACKERAY

Barry Lyndon

English novelist William Makepeace Thackeray (1811–1863) wrote several satirical novels including *Vanity Fair* (1848), which featured the prickly miss, Becky Sharp.

Born in Calcutta, India, where his father worked for the British East India Company, Thackeray wrote humorous pieces for *Fraser's Magazine* and *Punch.* "The Luck of Barry Lyndon" first appeared as a magazine serial in 1844 (revised for book issue) and tells of an Irish gentryman scheming to enter the British aristocracy.

Christopher Wood's novel came out a year after Stanley Kubrick's successful motion picture *Barry Lyndon.*

Original Work
The Memoirs of Barry Lyndon, Esq. (1844)

Pastiche
Christopher Wood, *The Further Adventures of Barry Lyndon, By Himself* (1976) based
  on a screenplay

LEO TOLSTOY
War and Peace

Two novels by Leo Tolstoy (1828–1910) stand at the acme of Russian realist literature: *War and Peace* (1865) and *Anna Karenina* (1873). Born in Central Russia, Tolstoy came from aristocracy. He was orphaned by age nine, but nevertheless studied law and Oriental languages at Kazan University. He joined the artillery and served in Chechnya. His first novel, *Childhood*, came out in 1852.

Anna Karenina has inspired a pastiche in Croatian, reportedly, and *War and Peace* inspired a spicy followup. Readers found the 1996 two-volume pastiche *Pierre and Natasha* racier than expected, given the original work. The book generates a romance between Natasha Rostova and Pierre Bezukhov. It was inspired, according to editors of the publishing firm Vagrius, by the *Scarlett* followup to *Gone with the Wind*. "For Russians, *War and Peace* is *Gone with the Wind*," Vagrius senior editor Gleb Uspensky told *The New York Times* in 1996. The new book's two authors were not immediately revealed.

Original Work
War and Peace (1865)

War and Peace Pastiche
Staroy, *Pierre and Natasha* (2008)

ANTHONY TROLLOPE
Framley Parsonage

Anthony Trollope (1815–1882), was a Victorian writer best known for his *Chronicles of Barsetshire*, which includes *Framley Parsonage*, originally serialized in *Cornhill Magazine* in 1860.

A contemporary of Dickens, Trollope was a prolific and widely read novelist. The son of a barrister-turned-farmer, he was born in London, attended Harrow School and enrolled in Winchester College, both miserable experiences. Trollope worked for the British Post Office, and was assigned to work in Ireland until 1859. He began to write while making long train rides as part of his job. When he returned to England, still with the Post Office, he introduced the red mailbox that became ubiquitous throughout Great Britain. *The Warden* (1855) was his first literary success. He wrote four dozen novels, all told, as well as short stories and travelogues.

Jo Walton (b. 1964), a native of Wales who won the John W. Campbell Award for Best New Writer in 2002, wrote a science fiction/Victorian romance with dragons, a takeoff on *Framley Parsonage*, and garnered the World Fantasy Award in 2004. Angela Thirkell (1890–1961) set a series of novels in Trollope's Barsetshire.

Original Barsetshire Novels

The Warden (1855)
Barchester Towers (1857)
Doctor Thorne (1858)

Framley Parsonage (1861)
The Small House at Allington (1864)
The Last Chronicle of Barset (1867)

Pastiches

Angela Thirkell, *High Rising* (1933); *The Demon in the House* (1934); *Wild Strawberries* (1934); *August Folly* (1936); *Summer Half* (1937); *Pomfret Towers* (1938); *Before Lunch* (1939); *The Brandons* (1939); *Cheerfulness Breaks In* (1940); *Northbridge Rectory* (1941); *Marling Hall* (1942); *Growing Up* (1943); *The Headmistress* (1944); *Miss Bunting* (1945); *Peace Breaks Out* (1946); *Private Enterprise* (1947); *Love Among the Ruins* (1948); *The Old Bank House* (1949); *County Chronicle* (1950); *The Duke's Daughter* (1951); *Happy Return* (1952); *Jutland Cottage* (1953); *What Did It Mean?* (1954); *Enter Sir Robert* (1955); *Never Too Late* (1956); *A Double Affair* (1957); *Close Quarters* (1958); *Love at All Ages* (1959); *Three Score and Ten* (1962)

Other Pastiche

Jo Walton, *Tooth and Claw* (2003)

IVAN TURGENEV

First Love

Russian novelist Ivan Turgenev (1818–1883) is best known for *Fathers and Sons*. But a shorter work, *First Love*, inspired a modern pastiche. The novella relies heavily on Turgenev's memories of his childhood as the son of an Imperial Russian cavalryman and his heiress wife. Turgenev as a child had heard the poetry of Mikhail Kheraskov read aloud by a family servant. He was a friend of Gustave Flaubert and exchanged darts with Fyodor Dostoyesky and Leo Tolstoy.

Novelist Charles Simmons said he retold Turgenev's *First Love* because in his own four earlier books he had exhausted what he wanted to say about himself. His most difficult task, he said in an interview with Powells, was invention. "I can invent fantastic episodes by the dozen, but to invent everyday occurrences that are not taken from my experience, are not literary clichés, and yet are exactly right for the story I find very difficult. I have to try out ten to get one good one."

Original Work

First Love (1860)

Pastiche
Charles Simmons, *Salt Water* (1998)

MARK TWAIN

Huck Finn

A steamboatman turned writer, Missouri-born Samuel Langhorne Clemens (1835–1910), alias "Mark Twain," worked as a printer's apprentice and typesetter before taking to the river. He later worked for the government in Nevada, and mined and reported for a newspaper. Once established as a successful fiction writer and humorist, Clemens traveled and lectured.

Clemens created two enduring youthful literary adventurers. His *The Adventures of Tom Sawyer* is set in a small Mississippi River town. Playful Tom, who with his serious brother Sid lives with Aunt Polly, quarrels with his sweetheart Becky Thatcher then runs off with Huckleberry Finn on a nighttime adventure. They watch Injun Joe stab the town doctor. More adventures ensue; Tom and Huck hide on an island. They watch the town hold a funeral for them. After the two wanderers return to town, Tom and Becky become lost in a cave and stumble upon Injun Joe's hiding place. Great rough and tumble fun for young readers.

Clemens took most of the characters and situations from his own childhood. "Most of the adventures recorded in this book really occurred; one or two were experiences of my own, the rest those of boys who were schoolmates of mine. Huck Finn is drawn from life; Tom Sawyer also, but not from an individual — he is a combination of the characteristics of three boys whom I knew, and therefore belongs to the composite order of architecture," he said in his *Autobiography*.

Considered a picaresque classic is the companion *The Adventures of Huckleberry Finn*, which James D. Hart in *The Oxford Companion to American Literature* said "is on the whole a keener realistic portrayal of regional character and frontier experience on the Mississippi." Huck, displeased with life with the Widow Douglas, strikes off down the river on a raft with runaway slave Jim. They witness a murder, help settle a legal claim and consort with a variety of rascals.

Finn suffered censorship. *Century Magazine* when publishing the novel in 1884-1885 excised parts it considered "too lurid for the refined readers of the times," according to Jerry Allen in *The Adventures of Mark Twain* (1954). "...Huck was not allowed to be 'in a sweat,' or go naked on the raft; people could not blow their noses, chaw tobacco, or recognize 'the signs of a dead cat being around'...." The book was banned at libraries such as one in Concord, Massachusetts — purportedly because Huck used the curse word "Hell."

Clemens took it all in stride. In a letter reproduced in his *Autobiography* (1924), he (with tongue in cheek) thoroughly agreed "the mind that becomes soiled in youth can never again be washed clean; I know this by my own experience, and to this day I cherish an unappeasable bitterness against the unfaithful guardians of my young life, who not only permitted but compelled me to read an unexpurgated Bible through before I was 15 years old...."

With the rediscovery of Twain's original manuscript, missing sections and chapters were restored for a 1996 edition of *Huckleberry Finn*.

John Seelye (b. 1931), an English professor and editor, amplified Twain's tale of Finn, which "was mostly by Mr. Mark Twain, only there was some things, which he stretched and some which he left out," said Huck in the original, adding in the pastiche, "so I went to work and done the best I could to fix it up...." The book exhibited rougher language and a stronger hint of sex, and had a less upbeat ending—Jim drowns in this version.

Australia-born Greg Matthews (b. 1949), a freight loader, office cleaner and parcel wrapper before turning writer, moved to the United States in 1981. His first novel continued the Finn story beginning with the false accusation of Huck for the murder of Judge Thatcher.

Richard White (b. 1931), a teacher, journalist and writer of historical fiction, was a third recent writer to extend the saga. He introduced an older Huck—after years of cowboying, buffalo hunting and trapping, he's become sheriff in Wind River, Wyoming. The story centers on Charlie Prescott, a twelve-year-old who gets in trouble for a prank that results in the school teacher making a hasty escape. Josiah Grey, a black man with a Harvard education, is the new teacher who helps Charlie out of further scrapes in this coming-of-age story.

There were eighteen film and television versions of Sawyer's and/or Finn's adventures, beginning with the silent *Tom Sawyer* (1917) through the 1985 American Playhouse production of *The Adventures of Huckleberry Finn*.

Jon Clinch resurrected Twain's characters with a dark view in *Finn: A Novel*, an examination of Huck's feckless father. *School Library Journal* said, "Many fans of Twain's masterpiece will want to read Clinch's inspired interpretation of pap, but some might find it too gruesome, and too void of hope...."

Lee Nelson read Twain's unfinished Huck sequel when it appeared in *Life* magazine. He explained in a foreword to his 2002 collaborative effort: "Early in 2002, while watching a documentary on Mark Twain on a local PBS station, I remembered reading the *Among the Indians* story in the barbershop. By this time I had published a dozen historical novels with settings on the American frontier, and realized I was probably as qualified as any other living author to finish the work begun by Twain. A little research on the web led me to those who controlled the copyright—The Mark Twain Foundation and the University of California Press. Contact was made, approval was granted, a contract was drawn up, and the following story is the result. I have no idea how Twain intended to finish the story, and I reason that he didn't know either, or he would have done it. I just hope that wherever he is, he enjoys my conclusion as much as I enjoyed his beginning."

California poet and educator Stephen Stewart, author of the nonfiction *Meet*

Mark Twain (1999), in 2002 added twenty-one chapters to Twain's unfinished nine for another sequel.

Albert Bigelow Paine, Twain's biographer, published a "complete" version of *The Mysterious Stranger*, a work Twain struggled with for years and never found a satisfactory ending for. Paine presumably wrote the ending.

Original Tom Sawyer and Huck Finn stories

The Adventures of Tom Sawyer (1878)
The Adventures of Huckleberry Finn (1884)
Tom Sawyer Abroad (1894)

Tom Sawyer, Detective (1896)
Huck Finn and Tom Sawyer Among the Indians and Other Unfinished Stories (1989)

Posthumous collaborations

Lee Nelson, *Huck Finn and Tom Sawyer Among the Indians* (2003)
Stephen Stewart, *Huck Finn & Tom Sawyer, Collaboration: The Sequel to Adventures of Huckleberry Finn* (2002)

Pastiches

Jon Clinch, *Finn: A Novel* (2007)
W. Bill Czolgosz, *Adventures of Huckleberry Finn and Zombie Jim* (2009)
Clare "Dwig" Dwiggins, *The Adventures of Huckleberry Finn* (1990) comic strips
Greg Matthews, *The Further Adventures of Huckleberry Finn* (1983)
Nancy Rawles, *Mr. Jim* (2004)
John Seelye, *The True Adventures of Huckleberry Finn* (1970)
Richard White, *Mister Grey, or The Further Adventures of Huckleberry Finn* (1992)

Posthumous Restoration

Victor Doyno, editor, *Adventures of Huckleberry Finn: The Only Comprehensive Edition* (1996)

Other Posthumous Collaboration

Albert Bigelow Paine, *The Mysterious Stranger: A Romance* (1916)

LEW WALLACE

Charioteer

A Union general in the Civil War, Lewis Wallace (1827–1905) led a colorful life as a lawyer, statesman and writer of historical fiction. Born in Indiana, where his father was for a time governor, he fought in the Mexican War and during Civil War service saw action at Fort Henry, Fort Donaldson and Shiloh. Wallace was governor of New Mexico Territory from 1878 to 1881, during which time his novel *Ben-Hur* appeared under the Harper & Brothers imprint in 1880. The book outsold Harriet Beecher Stowe's *Uncle Tom's Cabin* (1852). It was in turn bested by Margaret Mitchell's *Gone with the Wind* (1939). *Ben Hur* was four times filmed, the 1959 version featuring Charlton Heston.

A prose sequel showed up a century after the original.

Original Work
Ben-Hur: A Tale of the Christ (1880)

Pastiche
Karl Tunberg and Owen Walford, *The Quest of Ben-Hur* (1981)

EDITH WHARTON
Buccaneers

Edith (Newbold Jones) Wharton was the first woman to win distinguished literary awards such as the Gold Medal of the National Institute of Arts and Letters and an honorary degree from Yale. Well-known are her *Ethan Frome* (1911) and *The Age of Innocence* (1920), both of which were made into major films released in 1993.

New York-born Wharton (1862–1937), in the view of Wendy Steiner in *The New York Times Book Review* for 17 October 1993, "chronicled early-20th-century New York with the acid wit of Jane Austen and a Jamesian genius for innuendo."

The Buccaneers was first published, incomplete, in 1938. "...To the astonishment of the literary world, it then appeared that Edith Wharton, who had not written anything first-rate since 1920, was half-delivered of another masterpiece," wrote Olivia Coolidge in *Edith Wharton 1862–1937* (1964). "Perhaps in truth *The Buccaneers* would never actually have turned out as well as it promised. But it proved that in spite of the ill-digested outpourings of the twenties, Edith Wharton had still been an authoress of powers, and that she had grown." The book was re-issued in 1993 together with Wharton's first novel, written when she was in her teens.

The story takes place in the 1870s. Nan St. George is the teenaged heroine who eventually flees a distasteful marriage — braving a scandalous divorce — to the arms of a man she loves, creating the social conflict that is at the work's root. "Ms. Mainwaring's conclusion devotes much space to the injustices of the old divorce laws and the intolerance of even the kindest citizens toward those who violate their nuptial vows," wrote Steiner.

Marion Mainwaring received her Ph.D from Radcliffe College in 1949. She taught, edited, and corresponded for newspapers before becoming foreign editor for the Adams Papers for Harvard University and the Massachusetts Historical

Commission in 1964-65. Elizabeth Cooke retold Ethan Frome's story from Zeena's perspective.

Original Work

Fast and Loose and the Buccaneers edited and with an introduction by Viola Hopkins Winner (1993)

Posthumous Collaboration

Marion Mainwaring, *The Buccaneers* (1993) from an incomplete manuscript and brief synopsis

Original Ethan Frome Work

Ethan Frome (1911)

Pastiche

Elizabeth Cooke, *Zeena* (1996)

OSCAR WILDE

Fading Picture

Irish poet and playwright Oscar Wilde (1854–1900) is best remembered for his raucous courtship play *The Importance of Being Earnest* (1895).

The son of a poet-journalist mother and physician-writer father, Wilde became an outspoken aesthete and advocate for art. He lectured in Great Britain, France, Canada and the United States. Though he married and had children, in later life he fell in love with Lord Alfred Douglas. His only novel is *The Picture of Dorian Gray*, a story of temptation and tragedy.

Dorian Gray inspired two pastiches.

Original Work

The Picture of Dorian Gray (1891)

Pastiches

Jeremy Reed, *Dorian* (1996)
Will Self, *Dorian, An Imitation* (2002)

Classics (20th Century)

In the 20th century, we see a number of novels completed by friendly hands following an author's death — the last works of Alex Haley, for example, Malcolm Lowry and Horace McCoy. We see a few authors' creations turned into motion pictures, and new novelizations emerging as a result (Max Brand, Peter Benchley). We see a few heavily revised works (such as William Faulkner's *Flags in the Dust*) restored by new editors. We find the great demand sequels — to Margaret Mitchell's *Gone with the Wind* or Boris Pasternak's *Doctor Zhivago*— and the lesser demand ones — to Grace Metalious's *Peyton Place*.

JAMES AGEE
Death

James Agee (1909–1955) wrote poetry, prose, screenplays and film reviews. Born in Knoxville, Tennessee, he worked for *Fortune* and *Time* magazines before he became a critic for *The Nation*, and, later, *Time*. He scripted such films as *The African Queen* (1951) and *The Night of the Hunter* (1955). His books included *Let Us Now Praise Famous Men* (1941).

Agee worked on it for seven years, but never finished *A Death in the Family*. Editor David McDowell prepared the manuscript for publication, and the book won the Pulitzer Prize for Fiction. A half-century later, Michael Lofaro used the original manuscript and notes and brought to publication a version that he claims is closer to Agee's original plan.

Posthumous Collaboration

David McDowell, editor, *A Death in the Family* (1957)

Posthumous Restoration

Michael Lofaro, editor, *A Death in the Family: A Restoration of the Author's Text* (2007)

JAMES ROBERT BAKER
Rebel

James Robert Baker (1946–1997), a native Californian, grew up a liberal in a conservative household. He graduated from UCLA and worked as a screenwriter with little success. He fared better with his gay-themed novels, including *Adrenaline* (1985), about two men harassed by a homophobic policeman, also *Boy Wonder* (1988) and *Tim and Pete* (1993). As his later books met with controversy, his opportunities for publication diminished. He committed suicide. His partner Ron Robertson ushered several manuscripts into posthumous print, including *Testosterone* (2000).

Editor Scott Brassart revised Baker's manuscript for *Anarchy*.

Posthumous Collaboration

Scott Brassart, *Anarchy* (2002)

SAMUEL BECKETT
Godot

Irish dramatist Samuel Beckett (1906–1989), of the minimalist school, received the Nobel Prize in Literature in 1969. Born near Dublin to a middle-class, Protestant family, he apparently was never happy, neither as a child nor as an adult. In Paris, he became friends with James Joyce. He began to write. He moved frequently, to England, to Germany, to Ireland. He returned to Paris in 1937 and was active with the resistance movement during World War II. He had great success with *Waiting for Godot*, which made its premiere in January 1953. It is a play rich in character, but in which nothing seems to happen.

Yugoslavian Miodrag Bulatovic (1930–1991) wrote an unauthorized sequel to Beckett's best-known work; *Godot Arrived* appeared in its original Serbian and also German and French translations. Daniel Curzon's takeoff won the Southwest Theatre Association's 1999 National New Play Contest.

Original Work

Waiting for Godot (1952)

Pastiches

Miodrag Bulatovic, *Godot Arrived* (1966)
Daniel Curzon, *Godot Arrives* (1999)

HENRY BELLAMANN
Agricultural drama

Henry Bellamann (1882–1946) was a music teacher and journalist (he taught at the Juilliard School and Vassar College) and was a member of the New York Academy of Science, his specialty psychology. *Petenera's Daughter*, his first novel, centered around Pennsylvania Dutch farm families in Missouri. After his death from a heart attack, his widow, Katherine Jones Bellamann (1877–1956), also a novelist, completed *Parris Mitchell of Kings Row*, a sequel to his popular *Kings Row*.

Original Work

Kings Row (1940)

Posthumous Collaboration

Katherine Jones Bellamann, *Parriss Mitchell of Kings Row* (1948)

MAX BRAND
Doctor Kildare

While he is most associated with Westerns (see his entry in that section), prolific Max Brand was comfortable in several genres, including medical romances. Seattle native Frederick Schiller Faust (1892–1944) in his 30-million-word career wrote as Max Brand, Evan Evans, David Manning, Frederick Frost, John Schoolcraft and George Owen Baxter.

Faust attended the University of California at Berkeley, though he did not graduate. Shunned by the Ambulance Corps during World War I, dissatisfied as a ranch hand, he floundered briefly as an aspiring poet in New York City before he met *Munsey's* editor Robert Hobart Davis, who accepted his stories for *All-Story Weekly*. The writer's third story bore the Max Brand byline, in part because of anti–German feelings of the time and the obviously Germanic name Faust.

Brand's first Western novel was *The Untamed* (1919). One of his best-known novels was *Destry Rides Again* (1930). Brand went to work for MGM, the studio that had brought his first Doctor James Kildare story "Interns Can't Take Money" (from *Cosmopolitan* for March 1936), to the screen featuring Lew Ayres as the hero and Lionel Barrymore as Dr. Leonard Gillespie. Brand's career was cut short when, as a war correspondent for *Harper's*, he was killed in Italy during World War II.

Kildare also appeared on radio but emerged as a popular television series from 1961 to 1965, as portrayed by Richard Chamberlain (Raymond Masey was

Gillespie). This series prompted several new books by veteran writers of books based on TV shows.

Original Dr. Kildare Works

The Secret of Doctor Kildare (1940)
Calling Doctor Kildare (1940)
Young Doctor Kildare (1941
Doctor Kildare Takes Charge (1941)
Doctor Kildare's Crisis (1942)
Doctor Kildare's Trail (1942)

Doctor Kildare's Search (1943)
The Collected Stories of Max Brand (1994) includes the first Doctor Kildare story, "Interns Can't Take Money"

Dr. Kildare Pastiches

Robert Charles Ackworth, *Doctor Kildare* (1962); *Doctor Kildare Assigned to Trouble* (1963)
Norman A. Daniels, *Doctor Kildare's Secret Romance* (1962)
William Johnston, *Heart Has an Answer* (1963); *Faces of Love* (1963); *Magic Key* (1964)

ALBERT CAMUS

Numero uno

Author Albert Camus (1913–1960) was born in Algeria, where he associated with intellectual revolutionaries. He went to France at age twenty-five, was active with the resistance movement during World War II and became a columnist for the newspaper *Combat*.

Meursault, the main character in his play *L'Étranger* (*The Stranger*, 1942), is a desperate man without hope. Camus disdained the label existentialist, though it was frequently attached to his name. He opposed nihilism. He founded the Group for International Liaisons in the Revolutionary Union Movement. He received the Nobel Prize for Literature in 1957. Camus died in a car accident. A partial manuscript for a novel was found in the vehicle.

Catherine Camus, literary executor for her father, edited *Le Premier Homme* for publication in 1994.

Posthumous Collaboration

Catherine Camus, *Le Premier Homme* (1995) aka *The First Man*

RAYMOND CARVER

Shorter stories

Oregon native Raymond Carver (1938–1988) thrived on the short story form. He won the O. Henry Award posthumously in 1999. The son of a sawmill worker, he took a creative writing course with John Gardner. Living in California and working as a night custodian at a hospital, he published a book of poems, *Near Klamath* (1968). He wrote stories, taught at the Iowa Writers' Workshop and married poet Tess Gallagher (b. 1943). His first short story was "The Furious Seasons" (1960). *Will You Please Be Quiet, Please?*, his first collection, came out in 1976.

Carver was known for his minimalist style. His widow, Tess Gallagher, charged in 2007 that Carver's Knopf editor, Gordon Lish, drastically edited Carver's stories in his breakthrough collection, *What We Talk About When We Talk About Love* (1981). She sought to publish them as originally written. "'I just think it's so important for Ray's book, which has been a kind of secret, to appear,' Ms. Gallagher said.... But, she added, 'I would never want to take *What We Talk About* out of publication.' Those versions of the stories, she said, 'are now part of the history,'" Motoko Rich said in the *New York Times* in 2007. Gallagher sought a publisher for a posthumous uncollaboration.

Posthumous Restoration

Carver: *Collected Stories* (2009), unedited version of stories in *What We Talk About When We Talk About Love* and other stories not previously published

WILLIAM FREND DE MORGAN
Whimsy

William Frend de Morgan (1839–1917) was born in London and was educated at University College and the Royal Academy. He studied stained glass and ceramics and gained a reputation as an artist for his De Morgan titles. He wrote novels beginning with *Joseph Vance* in 1906. Some compared him to Dickens. He had an inventive mind, and gave himself the task of assisting his country in the early days of World War I. He died of virulent influenza.

De Morgan was married to Emily Pickering. Following his death, she completed his last two novels.

Posthumous Collaborations

E.P. De Morgan, *The Old Madhouse* (1919); *The Old Man's Youth* (1921)

DAPHNE DU MAURIER
Rebecca

Daphne Du Maurier (1907–1989) wrote plays, novels and short stories, several of which were made into films.

Born in London, she married Sir Frederick "Boy" Browning. She was living in Egypt when she wrote her singular work, *Rebecca*. "Last night I dreamt I went to Manderley again," begins the story of the new Mrs. De Winter, who quickly finds herself living in the shadow of Rebecca, Maxim de Winter's first wife, thanks to constant reminders from the housekeeper, Mrs. Danvers.

Several writers have pursued other angles of the story.

Original Work
Rebecca (1938)

Pastiches
Sally Beauman, *Rebecca's Tale* (2001)
Maureen Freely, *The Other Rebecca* (1996)
Susan Hill, *Mrs. De Winter* (1993)

RALPH ELLISON
Juneteenth

Ralph Ellison (1913–1994), an Oklahoman, won the National Book Award in 1953 for his novel *Invisible Man*. But while he wrote essays and other short pieces, he was unable to finish another novel. It wasn't for lack of trying; at his death, he left incomplete drafts of *Juneteenth*— some 2,000 pages worth.

Ellison's widow, Fanny McConnell, asked John F. Callahan, Ellison's literary executor, to pull the material together for the 358-page *Juneteenth*. The edition *Three Days Before the Shooting* incorporates more of Ellison's material.

Posthumous Collaboration with John F. Callahan
Juneteenth (2008) expanded as *Three Days Before the Shooting* (2008)

WILLIAM FAULKNER
Dust

William Faulkner (1897–1962) received the Nobel Prize in Literature in 1949. A chronicler of life in his native Mississippi, he was a leader of a Southern literary movement. He spent a few years in Hollywood writing scripts for *The Big Sleep* and *To Have and Have Not*. His novels included *The Sound and the Fury* (1929).

Houghton Mifflin's 1929 edition of the Yoknapatawpha County novel *Sartoris* was 40,000 words shorter than Faulkner's manuscript. Editor Douglas Day oversaw restoration of both the material and the author's original title, *Flags in the Dust*, in 1973. The restoration is now considered the definitive edition.

Posthumous Restoration

Douglas Day, editor, *Flags in the Dust* (1973)

F. SCOTT FITZGERALD
The Last Tycoon

F. Scott Fitzgerald (1896–1940) wrote short stories and novels of the Jazz Age. Born in St. Paul, Minnesota, he was named for a relative, Francis Scott Key. At Princeton University, he became friends with Edmund Wilson, who would also become a writer and critic. Fitzgerald's novel of the uninhibited 1920s, *The Great Gatsby* (1925), is his most-esteemed work.

Fitzgerald at his death left an incomplete manuscript for *The Love of the Last Tycoon*. Reportedly he asked his friend Nathaniel West (1903–1940), author of *Day of the Locust* (1939), to complete the work. But West and his wife died in a car accident the day after Fitzgerald died. Another friend, Edmund Wilson (1895–1972), took up the task and completed the book from Fitzgerald's notes. Fitzgerald scholar Matthew J. Bruccoli reassembled the seventeen chapters, about half of what Fitzgerald had planned, and included many of the author's notes and letters.

Posthumous Collaboration with Edmund Wilson

The Last Tycoon (1941) aka *The Love of the Last Tycoon* (1994)

Posthumous Restoration

Matthew J. Bruccoli, *The Love of the Last Tycoon: A Western* (1993)

ALEX HALEY
Black heritage

Alex Haley (1921–1992) was born in Ithaca, New York, but grew up in Henning, Tennessee. After college, Haley joined the United States Coast Guard. His enlistment up, he became a staff writer with *Reader's Digest*. Working for *Playboy* magazine, he inaugurated the periodical's extended interview feature.

Recalling stories his maternal grandmother had related about his ancestors including a slave named Toby, Haley began to research African customs and his own family origins. He uncovered the story of Kunta Kinte, a sixteen-year-old who went searching for wood to make a drum and was snatched from the forest by slavers and shipped to the United States in the 1760s. From freedom-yearning Kunta Kinte through his daughter Kizzy through her son Chicken George and George's son Tom down to Cynthia, Haley followed the line through his grandmother who married Will Palmer in Henning. Haley's novel *Roots: The Saga of an American Family* (1976) and the Emmy Award-winning 1977 television series sparked a widespread fascination with genealogy.

At the time of his death, the author was working on *Queen*, a book about his Haley family experience. David Stevens completed the manuscript.

Posthumous Collaborations

David Stevens, *Alex Haley's Queen: The Story of an American Family* (1993); *Mama Flora's Family* (1998)

ERNEST HEMINGWAY

Nick Adams

Illinois-born Ernest Hemingway (1898–1961) served with an American ambulance corps in France during World War I and became a newspaper correspondent in Europe. His fiction writing found a growing audience and he won the Nobel Prize for Literature in 1954. The citation for that prize noted his "manly love of danger and adventure," but his writing was also noteworthy for its economical prose, outdoor settings, skilled dialogue and narrative methods.

Hemingway wrote several near-autobiographical short stories featuring the character Nick Adams. Philip Young in *Ernest Hemingway* (1952) categorizes the stories among the writer's "hurt hero" tales: "The hero is a twentieth-century American, born, raised and hurt in the Middle West, who like all of us, has been going through life with the marks his experiences have made on him...." All fifteen Adams stories were collected, along with another eight segments, after the author's death. Richard Beymer appeared as Adams in the motion picture *Hemingway's Adventures of a Young Man* (1962).

As for the pastiches, we have to back up for a moment. Jose Luis Castillo-Puche in the biography *Hemingway in Spain* (1974) offers this chronology entry for 1922: "(November) A disaster befalls the Hemingways. As [the writer's wife] Hadley is leaving Paris to join Ernest in Lausanne for the International Peace Conference, in the Gare de Lyon she loses a suitcase containing all his manuscripts. Ernest is thoroughly disgusted and angry with her." Enter writer MacDonald Harris, whose fourteenth novel, *Hemingway's Suitcase*, builds on this above-reported incident. It tells of a dilettante, Nils-Frederik Glas, who returns from Europe with a suitcase containing what appears to be work by Hemingway, including five Nick Adams stories. The stories are reprinted within the novel. Harris is a penname for Donald (William) Heiney (b. 1921), who has also written a number of non-fiction works under his own name. His "Harris" book *The Balloonist* was nominated for a National Book Award.

Charles Scribner's Sons released Hemingway's unfinished *The Garden of Eden*, omitting some two-thirds of the original manuscript. The publisher edited and released Hemingway's *Islands in the Stream* in 1970.

Patrick Hemingway edited his father's notes for a "fictional memoir," *True at First Light*, based on a safari in Africa in 1953. The younger Hemingway had been on the jungle trek. Three excerpts had been published in *Sports Illustrated* in 1971 and 1972. Patrick Hemingway in a BookPage interview in July 1999 said, "It was essentially to keep as strong a story line as the original manuscript would allow. I had identified what I felt were the two principal story lines; one is a lion hunt, the second is a leopard hunt. Then there is a more complex story line that involves sexual politics and the triangle between a husband and wife and another woman. I wanted to make them as strong as possible and as integrated as possible. My tool was cutting, not making up material or inventing transitional passages. Just cutting. We ended up taking out about a quarter to a third of the manuscript." Robert W. Lewis and Robert E. Fleming re-edited and left more material in their version, which appeared as *Under Kilimanjaro*.

Original Nick Adams Works

Nick Adams Stories (1972) includes eight not-before-published stories or fragments

Nick Adams Pastiches

Donald Heiney writing as MacDonald Harris, *Hemingway's Suitcase* (1990)
Joe Haldeman, *The Hemingway Hoax* (1990) based on *Nick Adams Stories*

Original Francis Macomber Work

The Short Happy Life of Francis Macomber and Other Stories (1963)

Francis Macomber Pastiche

Warren Adler, *Private Lives* (1992)

Posthumous Collaborations

Charles Scribner, Jr., and Mary Hemingway, *Islands in the Stream* (1972); *The Garden of Eden* (1986)
Patrick Hemingway, *True at First Light* (1999)
Robert W. Lewis and Robert E. Fleming, *Under Kilimanjaro* (2005)

JAMES HILTON
Shangri-La

James Hilton (1900–1954) dreamed of a mythical Eden called Shangri-La in his 1933 novel *Lost Horizon*. Residents of the land high on a Tibetan mountaintop enjoy long lives and peaceful existences.

Hilton was born in Lancashire, England. His father was a school headmaster. Hilton began to write while attending college. His first novel, *Catherine Herself*, came out in 1920. *Goodbye, Mr. Chips* appeared initially in the *British Weekly* in 1934 and was reprinted in *Atlantic Monthly*. Derived from his own schoolboy experiences, it inspired a popular motion picture, as did *Random Harvest* and *Lost Horizon*. Hilton was twice married. He died in California, where he had settled in the mid–1930s to write screenplays. His *Mrs. Miniver* script, based on a novel by Jan Struther, won an Academy Award in 1942.

Frank DeMarco (b. 1946) wrote a sequel to *Lost Horizon*, as did Leslie Halliwell (1929–1989).

Original Work
Lost Horizon (1933)

Pastiches
Frank DeMarco, *Messenger: A Sequel to Lost Horizon, a Story of Shangri-La* (1994)
Leslie Halliwell, *Return to Shangri-La* (1987)

FRANZ KAFKA
Nightmares

Franz Kafka (1883–1924) was born in Prague. He became well known (and was highly influential) for his "Kafka-esque" worlds of extremely troubled characters afflicted with horrid nightmares and impossible personal tangles. He grew up in a middle class family, the oldest of six children — two of whom died at very young ages. He earned a law degree at Charles Ferdinand University in 1906 and went to work in the insurance industry, and later managed an asbestos factory. He never married, though was more than once infatuated with young women. He was intrigued with Yiddish theater. His first book was Meditation, a collection of stories, in 1913.

Max Brod ignored his close friend's plea to destroy his manuscripts after his death (to tuberculosis). Brod instead edited and shaped several of Kafka's manuscripts and nurtured them into print. The works were later published in their original, incomplete forms, through the efforts of editor Malcolm Pasley.

Posthumous Collaborations

Max Brod, editor, *The Trial* (1925); *The Castle* (1926); *Amerika* (1927)

Posthumous Restorations

Malcolm Pasley, editor, *The Castle* (1982); *The Trial* (1990)
Jost Schillemeit, editor, *Amerika* (1983)

BERNARD KATZ
Lucy Terry Prince

Bernard Katz (1901–1970), author of *The Social Implication of Early Negro Music in the United States* (1969), struggled with a dearth of information about 18th-century black poet Lucy Terry Prince (1730–1821). He ultimately decided to write a fictionalized account of her life.

Katz died before the book's completion and his son Jonathan (b. 1938) revised and completed the manuscript.

Posthumous Collaboration

Jonathan Katz, *Black Woman: A Fictionalized Biography of Lucy Terry Prince* (1973)

JACK KEROUAC
On the Road Again

Jack Kerouac (1922–1969) was a leading voice of the Beat Generation. Best known is his autobiographical *On the Road*, written in 1951 and published in 1957. Kerouac appears in the book as Sal Paradise. *On the Road* influenced a range of people, from gonzo journalist Hunter S. Thompson to bluesy singer Tom Waits.

All the original story of a drug-fueled road trip across the United States was restored for a 2007 anniversary edition, though not in Kerouac's original format: a single 120-foot roll of paper, single-spaced, no paragraphing. Real names (Allen Ginsberg, Neal Cassady, William S. Burroughs) are used again (instead of fake names Carlo Marx, Dean Moriarty, Old Bull Lee), and the spicy parts are intact.

Posthumous Restoration

On the Road: 50th Anniversary Edition (2007)

JACK LONDON
Killers

Jack London (1876–1916) is well remembered for *The Call of the Wild,* originally published in *The Saturday Evening Post* in 1903. London was born possibly out of wedlock in San Francisco and reared by an ex-slave nanny, Virginia Prentiss. His mother, Flora Wellman, later married John London, a Civil War veteran. As a youth, the author worked as a laborer at a cannery and as a seaman on a schooner. He took part in the Klondike gold rush in 1897. He saw his first story, "To the Man on the Trail," published in *The Overland Monthly. White Fang, The Sea-Wolf* and *Martin Eden* followed.

Mystery writer Robert Fish wrote the second half of *The Assassination Bureau,* the story of Ivan Dragomiloff's frantic defense against a secret agency he established. It was based on an idea London purchased from Sinclair Lewis. Fish worked from London's notes and an outline by his wife, Charmian London.

Posthumous Collaboration
Robert Fish, *The Assassination Bureau Ltd.* (1963)

MALCOLM LOWRY
Gabriola

English poet and novelist Malcolm Lowry (1909–1957), who attended The Leys School and St. Catharine's College in Cambridge, traveled widely and lived in France, New York and Hollywood, Mexico and Canada. His *Under the Volcano* came out in 1947.

Several Lowry works appeared after his suicide, including two completed by his widow, Margerie, and biographer Douglas Day (1932–2004.)

Posthumous Collaborations
Margerie Lowry and Douglas Day, *Dark as the Grave Wherein My Friend Is Laid* (1968); *October Ferry to Gabriola* (1970)

THOMAS MANN
Magic Mountain

Thomas Mann (1875–1955), a short story writer and essayist, was born in Germany, where he lived most of his life. He worked for an insurance company briefly before he launched a career as a writer. He received the Nobel Prize in Literature in 1929 for *Buddenbrooks* (1901). *The Magic Mountain*, an influential work, is a novel of ideologies and passion.

Curtis White teaches English at Illinois State University.

Original Work

The Magic Mountain (1924)

Pastiche

Curtis White, *America's Magic Mountain* (2004)

HORACE MCCOY

Horses

Horace McCoy (1897–1955) depicted the grim side of the Great Depression in novels such as *They Shoot Horses, Don't They?* (1935).

A Tennessee native, McCoy served in the Army Air Corps during World War I and earned France's Croix de Guerre for heroism. He was a sports editor for the *Dallas Journal* in the 1920s and began to sell stories to pulp fiction magazines. He moved to Hollywood and wrote scripts for movie studios, mostly crime thrillers and Westerns. McCoy published five novels.

After McCoy's death, editors pieced together manuscript fragments and parts of a movie scenario for a sixth book.

Posthumous Collaboration

Dell editors, *Corruption City* (1959)

AMANDA MCKITTRICK

Helen Huddleston

Amanda McKittrick Ros (1860–1939), born in County Down, Ireland, was a novelist and poet of eccentric writing style and modest reputation. She self-published her first book, *Irene Iddesleigh* (1898). Jack Loudon's biography *O Rare Amanda!: The Life of Amanda McKittrick Ros* came out in 1954.

Loudon completed McKittrick's last novel.

Posthumous Collaboration

Jack Loudon, *Helen Huddleston* (1969)

GRACE METALIOUS

Peyton Place

Marie Grace de Repentiguy (1924–1964), better known under her penname Grace Metalious, was a New Hampshire native She came to fame with her saucy soap opera novel, *Peyton Place*. Its success put her uncomfortably into the national spotlight, and she began to drink heavily. She continued to write intermittently.

After her death, *Peyton Place* became a nighttime television soap opera, and generated new sequels by Don Tracy (1905–1976), who also wrote Giff Speer mysteries. Barbara Delinsky recreated the Peyton Place situation, taking her main character back to New Hampshire.

Original Works

Peyton Place (1956)   *Return to Peyton Place* (1959)

Pastiches

Barbara Delinsky, *Looking for Peyton Place* (2005)
Don Tracy writing as Roger Fuller, *Again in Peyton Place* (1967); *Pleasures of Peyton Place* (1968); *Secrets of Peyton Place* (1968); *Evils of Peyton Place* (1969); *Hero in Peyton Place* (1969); *Thrills of Peyton Place* (1969); *The Nice Girl from Peyton Place* (1970); *Temptations of Peyton Place* (1970)

MARGARET MITCHELL

Scarlett and Rhett

"I'll think of it all tomorrow, at Tara. I can stand it then. Tomorrow, I'll think of some way to get him back. After all, tomorrow is another day," says Scarlett O'Hara on the final page of *Gone with the Wind*.

Georgia-born Margaret Munnerlyn Mitchell (1900–1949) was a newspaper columnist and feature writer before writing her best-selling and Pulitzer Prize-winning epic. The novel sold a record one million copies in six months and still disappears from bookstore shelves at the rate of a quarter million copies a year.

Fiery Scarlett O'Hara, spurned by Ashley Wilkes, marries second choice Charles Hamilton though she doesn't care for him. Her husband dies during the Civil War. Northerners occupy Atlanta. Scarlett, impoverished, struggles for her family and for the plantation Tara. She marries again, for money. After Frank Kennedy is killed in a duel, avenging her honor, she weds Rhett Butler, an unscrupulous but strong and shrewd profiteer. But theirs is not a comfortable union. Not until it is too late, and Rhett leaves, does Scarlett realize her love for him.

"Although much of the action of *Gone with the Wind* (1936) concerns Scarlett O'Hara's experiences during the Civil War and Reconstruction, the underlying value structure of the novel is prescribed by Scarlett's relationships with men" observed Kay Mussell in *Handbook of American Popular Literature*. The book's plot carries the assumption, she said, "unquestioned and unexamined except in a few books — that the necessary, preordained, and basic goal of any woman is to achieve a satisfying, mature, and all-fulfilling marriage...."

"Mitchell's pacing, her use of a solidly limiting past, and her characters' consequential choices set *Gone with the Wind* apart from other historical romances, making it more like *War and Peace* than like genre fiction," asserted Nancy Regan in *Twentieth-Century Romance & Historical Writers*.

"Whether or not *Gone with the Wind* is a masterpiece has always been a matter of controversy," said Anne Edwards in *The Road to Tara: The Life of Margaret Mitchell*. "It is, perhaps, the most compulsively readable novel in the English language, a book that, despite its length — it is as long as *War and Peace*— has been read by people over and over again, and each time with great suspense, as though, somehow, *this time* the story might end differently...."

The story was filmed in 1939 with Vivien Leigh as the heroine, Clark Gable as Butler. "The most popular picture of all time," Danny Peary calls it in his *Guide for the Film Fanatic*. "Margaret Mitchell's epic novel of the Old South was given grandiose treatment by producer David O. Selznick. It's a gorgeous film — it's exciting just to watch characters in their lavish costumes, or the fiery red skies that often serve as the backgrounds, or shots of the Tara plantation. Picture has wonderful period detail and a fine assortment of characters, white and black.... Vivien Leigh is the beautiful, slim-waisted, high-spirited, emotional, spoiled, indomitable, manipulative southern belle Scarlett O'Hara...."

Mitchell once said a sequel was out of the question. It took her estate until 1991 to authorize continuation of the Scarlett and Rhett Story. Warner Books paid $4.94 million for the rights to publish it. The Mitchell heirs made two stipulations: No miscegenation or graphic sex. Writer Alexandra Ripley (1934–2004) was handed a $160,000 advance to write the new book. Born in South Carolina, Ripley had previously written historical novels including *Charlestown* (1981) and *New Orleans Legacy* (1987).

Scarlett picks up within days of *Wind*'s 1873 ending, at the funeral of Melanie Wilkes. Author Ripley told *The New York Times*' Eleanor Blau in 1991 that she recognized early on that Mitchell fans would have her "pilloried" if Scarlett and Rhett did not get together again. And we soon find them living a marriage for appearances' sake.

Extensively researching the period, Ripley said she was intrigued with the tumultuous times in Ireland in 1873, and elected to send the heroine to that country. Ripley reportedly read *Wind* four times "and wrote out in longhand 350 pages of the original to get a feel for Mitchell's style," said Deidre Donahue in *USA Today* in 1991.

As might be expected, the new book had both its fans and its detractors.

"During the course of a stunningly uneventful 823-page holding action, Ms. Ripley dares to turn the swashbuckling Rhett Butler into a mama's boy and Scarlett O'Hara into a fatuous socialite with a near-pathological love of parties and shopping," said Janet Maslin in *The New York Times* in 1991. Two years later, it was announced that British actress Joanne Whalley-Kilmer would portray Scarlett in the inevitable CBS-TV miniseries sequel. The publisher rejected a manuscript by Emma Tennant, *Tara*, as too British. Novelist Pat Conroy couldn't reach an agreement because he felt too constricted — he couldn't kill off Butler, for example.

A second sequel to the Mitchell classic came out in 2007: *Rhett Butler's People* by Donald McCaig. A former advertising copywriter, McCaig had become a novelist of Civil War books as well as a sheep farmer in Virginia. The book, suggested Motoko Rich in *The New York Times* in 2007, was something of an attempt at redemption after the critical drubbing of Ripley's book and the ill will after an attempt to block issue of what the author called a parody, *The Wind Done Gone*, by Alice Randall in 2001. This book told the story from a slave's perspective.

McCaig said it took him six years to research and write his book. "There were a lot of people involved and a lot of different needs," he told journalist Rich. "It's a much more complex environment than most novels are written in."

Russian readers, meanwhile, have had a string of unauthorized sequels to read, thanks to Russia's snubbing of international copyright laws.

Original Story

Gone with the Wind (1936)

Pastiches

Yuliya Hilpatrik, *We Call Her Scarlett; The Secret of Scarlett O'Hara; Rhett Butler; The Secret of Rhett Butler; The Last Love of Scarlett*
Donald McCaig, *Rhett Butler's People* (2007)
Alice Randall, *The Wind Done Gone* (2001)
Alexandra Ripley, *Scarlett: The Sequel to Margaret Mitchell's* Gone with the Wind (1991)

VLADIMIR NABOKOV

Lolita

Humbert Humbert is obsessed with a twelve-year-old girl, Dolores Haze, in Vladimir Nabokov's now-classic 1955 novel *Lolita*.

Nabokov (1899–1977) was born in Saint Petersburg, Russia, and wrote his first novels in Russian. The family left Russia at the time of the revolution in 1917. Nabokov attended Trinity College, Cambridge. As he became established, he began to write in English. *Lolita* was written in English and later translated into Russian. By the time he wrote *Lolita*, Nabokov was living in the United States, where he was a lecturer at Wellesley College beginning in 1941. Nabokov later moved to Europe.

Pia Pera retold the story from Lolita's perspective. Dmitri Nabokov filed suit in a Manhattan court to block Farrar, Straus & Giroux from publishing the book in 1998. The publisher successfully argued fair use. Nabokov hemmed and hawed over following his father's directive to destroy the fifty notecards that are the beginning of one last novel, *The Original of Laura*. He finally engaged novelist Martin Amis to complete the work.

Original Work

Lolita (1955)

Posthumous Collaboration

Martin Amis, *The Original of Laura* (2008)

Pastiches

Kim Morrissey, *Poems for Men Who Dream of Lolita* (1992)
Pia Pera, *Lo's Diary* (2001)

JOHN O'BRIEN
Leaving

The novel *Leaving Las Vegas* by Ohio-born John O'Brien (1960–1994) was the basis of a 1995 film of the same name. It turned out to be the writer's only work published in his lifetime. He committed suicide within days of learning of the movie deal. A second novel, *Stripper Lessons* (1997), came out after his death, as did *The Assault on Tony's* (1996), both incomplete manuscripts finished by his sister, Erin O'Brien (b. 1965). O'Brien is a journalist and nonfiction writer. Her first independent novel, *Harvey and Eck*, came out in 2005.

Posthumous collaboration

Erin O'Brien, *The Assault on Tony's* (1996); *Stripper Lessons* (1997)

KYLE ONSTOTT
Plantation novels

Illinois native Kyle Onstott (1887–1966) established a subgenre of novels set in the South before the Civil War. "One of the paperback publishing sensations of the 1970s was the enormously successful 'plantation' novel," Christopher D. Geist wrote in *Paperback Quarterly*. "Loosely descended from *Uncle Tom's Cabin*, the works of Thomas Nelson Page, *Gone with the Wind* and the bosom and bravado historicals of Frank Yerby, the genre is part of a general resurgence of paperback historical romances."

After Onstott's death, Lance Horner (1902–1973), a native of New York state, continued the series, with even stronger emphasis on sex and violence. Ashley Carter carried on the Falconhurst tales after Horner. Ashley Carter was really Harry Whittington (1915–1990), a Floridian by birth. Carter added the Blackoaks books.

Original Works

Mandigo (1957)   *Master of Falconhurst* (1964)
Drum (1962)

Posthumous Collaborations

Lance Horner, *Falconhurst Fancy* (1966)
Harry Whittington, *Strange Harvest* (1986)

Pastiches

Ashley Carter (Harry Whittington), *Master of Blackoaks* (1976); *Sword of the Golden Stud* (1977) sequel to *The Golden Stud*; *Secret of Black Oaks* (1978); *Panama* (1978); *Taproots of Falconhurst* (1978); *Scandal of Falconhurst* (1980); *Heritage of Blackoaks* (1981); *Against All Gods* (1982); *Rogue of Falconhurst* (1983); *Road to Falconhurst* (1983); *A Farewell to Blackoaks* (1984); *The Outlanders* (1983); *A Darkling Moon* (1985); *Embrace the Wind* (1985); *Falconhurst Fugitive* (1985); *Miz Lucretia of Falconhurst* (1985); *Mandingo Mansa* (1986)

Lance Horner, *The Street of the Sun* (1956); *The Tattooed Rood* (1962) aka *Santiago Road* (1967); *Child of the Sun* (1966); *The Black Sun* (1967); *The Mustee* (1967); *Heir to Falconhurst* (1968); *The Mahound* (1969); *Flight to Falconhurst* (1971); *Mistress of Falconhurst* (1973); *Golden Stud* (1975) aka *Six-Fingered Stud* (1975); *Miz Lucretia of Falconhurst* (1986); *Falconhurst Fugitive* (1988)

Posthumous Collaboration

Lance Horner with Harry Whittington, *The Golden Stud* (1975)

BORIS PASTERNAK

Russia

Moscow-born Boris Leonovich Pasternak (1890–1960) was the son of an artist and a painter. He studied musical composition at the University of Moscow and took courses in philosophy at the University of Marburg in Germany. He began to write books of verse in 1922. His only novel, *Doktor Zhivago*, came out in 1957 in Russian and Italian. It won the Nobel Prize for Literature in 1958, though Pasternak declined the honor. The book, considered by many to be one of the great literary works of the 20th century, was banned in the Soviet Union, though it appeared in sixteen other languages. The story was turned into a popular motion picture in 1965 with Omar Sharif and Julie Christie.

The pseudonymous Alexander Mollin wrote a sequel. The publisher Feltrinelli, which had brought into print a smuggled copy of Pasternak's work in Italy, sued in 1992 to block publication of the new book to protect its sales of the original work.

Original work

Doctor Zhivago (1958)

Pastiche

Alexander Mollin, *Lara's Child* (1994)

RICHARD POWELL
The Philadelphian

Richard Powell (1908–1999) had a bestseller with the publication by Charles Scribner's Sons of *The Philadelphian* in 1957. The family saga begins with the story of an Irish immigrant girl in 1857 and ends a century later. Powell, a former *Philadelphia Evening Ledger* reporter and later an advertising and public relations executive, wrote eighteen other novels.

The book had been out of print for three decades when the author's daughter, Dorothy Powell Quigley, persuaded Plexus Publishing to issue a commemorative expanded edition. "If there was one book my father really wanted to write, it was *The Philadelphian*— it was his dream come true," Quigley is quoted as saying in a *Philly Future* story in 2006. "To see his favorite book restored 50 years later is a dream come true for me."

Original Work

The Philadelphian (1957)

Posthumous Restoration

The Philadelphian (2007)

MARIO PUZO
The Godfather

Mario Puzo (1920–1999) told us more than we ever expected to know about the Mafia with his novel *The Godfather* in 1969. Born in Hell's Kitchen in New York City, Puzo graduated from City College, served in the Air Force during World War II and wrote his first book in 1955. *The Godfather* inspired a threesome of motion pictures directed by Francis Ford Coppola.

At Puzo's request, Carol Gino completed a sprawling story of the 15th-century Borgia clan from the author's partial manuscript. Floridian Mark Winegardner wrote a sequel that takes place in the years 1955 to 1962, juggling plot elements of the original book and the movies.

Original Work
The Godfather (1960)

Pastiches
Carol Gino, *The Family* (2001)
Mark Winegardner, *The Godfather Returns* (2006)

HAROLD ROBBINS
Carpetbagger

New York native Harold Rubin (1916–1997), of Russian and Polish ancestry, later changed his name to Robbins. He established himself financially as a sugar wholesaler. When he turned to writing, he gained immediate notoriety with his first book, *Never Love a Stranger* (1948), because of its sensuality. He depicted Hollywood behind the scenes in *The Dream Merchants* (1949) and his *The Carpetbaggers* (1961) was based on the life of Howard Hughes.

Several novels have come out since Robbins' death. Junius Podrug, at the request of Jann Robbins, Harold Robbins' widow, completed manuscripts Robbins left behind or shaped new manuscripts.

Posthumous Collaborations or Pastiches
Junius Podrug, *Sin City* (2002); *Heat of Passion* (2003); *The Betrayers* (2004); *Blood Royal* (2005); *The Devil to Pay* (2006); *The Looters* (2007); *The Deceivers* (2008); *The Shroud* (2009)

J.D. SALINGER
The Catcher in the Rye

J.D. Salinger is known internationally for his 1951 coming-of-age novel *The Catcher in the Rye*. Born Jerome David Salinger in Manhattan in 1919, the son of a Jewish importer and his Scots-Irish wife, the author grew up in the Bronx. Salinger attended Ursinus College and New York University, and took a writing class at Columbia University with Whit Burnett, editor of *Story Magazine*. He sold a few short stories before entering the U.S. Army, with which he saw action at the Battle of the Bulge. After the war, *The New Yorker* magazine published his story "A Perfect Day for Bananafish" (1948) to critical notice, and most of his later short works appeared in that periodical. Salinger's novel *Rye*, the story of teen Holden Caulfield at loose ends in New York City after being expelled from a Pennsylvania prep school, enjoyed enormous success and has been included on many high school and college English class reading lists. Caulfield encounters a prostitute and drinks too much. And, as some critics have noted, by novel's end, Holden hasn't matured at all. An estimated 65 million copies were in print by 2009. But Salinger didn't enjoy the fame, and retreated to a New Hampshire homestead from which little of his writing has emerged since the 1960s.

Salinger, protective of his privacy and his work, emerged to bring suit in 2009 against American publication of *60 Years Later: Coming Through the Rye*. The work by J.D. California had already been printed by Windupbird Publishing for readers in Sweden and England. The book on its copyright page says it is "An Unauthorized Fictional Examination of the Relationship Between J.D. Salinger and His Most Famous Character." Salinger brought suit and in July 2009 prevailed, a federal judge banning its publication in the United States. The author, really Swedish writer Fredrik Colting, claimed the work was a parody and commentary and did not infringe on Salinger's rights. Salinger, through his lawyers, called it a rip-off. Colting and his publisher appealed, claiming no "shred of evidence of harm to the Plaintiff," adding, "Had this commentary and criticism been published as an essay, a dissertation or an academic article, there is no doubt that it never would have been enjoined."

Original Work
The Catcher in the Rye (1951)

Pastiche
J.D. California (Fredrik Colting), *60 Years Later: Coming Through the Rye* (2009)

MICHAEL SHAARA
The Civil War

Michael Shaara (1928–1988) wrote the Pulitzer Prize-winning Civil War novel *The Killer Angels*, which became the basis of the 1993 motion picture *Gettysburg*. *The Killer Angels* is about four men including Robert E. Lee and the days leading up to the war's bloodiest days.

Shaara was a New Jersey native who attended Rutgers University. He wrote science fiction and later mainstream stories for *The Saturday Evening Post, Cosmopolitan* and other periodicals. He taught creative writing at Florida State University.

The author's son, Jeff Shaara, wrote bookend novels to create a trilogy.

Original Work
The Killer Angels (1974)

Pastiches
Jeff Shaara, *Gods and Generals* (1996); *The Last Full Measure* (1998)

ROBERT NEILSON STEPHENS
Valley Forge

Robert Neilson Stephens (1867–1906), born in New Bloomfield, Pennsylvania, wrote drama and historical fiction. He was a journalist with the Philadelphia Press. He became a theatrical agent. One of his better-known books is *An Enemy of the King* (1897).

G.E. Theodore Roberts, author of *Comrades of the Trails*, completed Stephens' next-to-last novel. Herman Nickerson turned an unfinished swashbuckling manuscript into the last novel, *The Sword of Bussy*.

Posthumous Collaborations
G.E. Theodore Roberts, *A Soldier of Valley Forge: A Romance of the American Revolution* (1911)

Herman Nickerson, *The Sword of Bussy: or, the Word of a Gentleman. A Romance of the Time of Henry III* (1912)

JACQUELINE SUSANN

Valley of the Dolls

Philadelphia native Jacqueline Susann (1918–1974) wrote a torrid novel of the private lives of the rich, drug-reliant and often dysfunctional. It sold more than 30 million copies and was made into a 1967 motion picture and television mini-series. The author had pursued an acting career before she turned to writing. Her play *Lovely Me* ran on Broadway for 37 performances. Her first novel, *Every Night, Josephine!* (1963), was about her poodle.

The author's friend Rex Reed helped complete her last novel. Rae Lawrence, author of *Satisfaction* (1987), created a *Valley* sequel from Susann's notes.

Original Work
The Valley of the Dolls (1966)

Posthumous Collaborations
Rae Lawrence, *Shadow of the Dolls* (2001)
Rex Reed, *Dolores* (1976)

ANGELA THIRKELL

Barsetshire

Angela Thirkell (1890–1961) began writing when she settled in Australia with her second husband, George Lancelot Thirkell. Born Angela Margaret Mackail, the daughter of a civil servant, she was educated in London and Paris. She used the setting of Anthony Trollope's Barsetshire tales for her chronicles of Barsetshire. In her first book in the series, *High Rising* (1933), widowed Laura Morland writes books and dodges a suitor. Children in the household include Tony, who has a motor mouth and plays with motorized toy railroads. He comes to center in the next book, *The Demon in the House* (1934).

Following Thirkell's death, Caroline Alice Lejeune completed the last book from notes, and managed to tie together threads from the entire thirty-book series.

Original Barsetshire Works

High Rising (1933)	*Cheerfulness Breaks In* (1940)
The Demon in the House (1934)	*Northbridge Rectory* (1941)
Wild Strawberries (1934)	*Marling Hall* (1942)
August Folly (1936)	*Growing Up* (1943)
Summer Half (1937)	*The Headmistress* (1944)
Pomfret Towers (1938)	*Miss Bunting* (1945)
Before Lunch (1939)	*Peace Breaks Out* (1946)
The Brandons (1939)	*Private Enterprise* (1947)

Love Among the Ruins (1948)
The Old Bank House (1949)
County Chronicle (1950)
The Duke's Daughter (1951)
Happy Return (1952)
Jutland Cottage (1953)

What Did It Mean? (1954)
Enter Sir Robert (1955)
Never Too Late (1956)
A Double Affair (1957)
Close Quarters (1958)
Love at All Ages (1959)

Posthumous Collaboration

C.A. Lejeune, *Three Score and Ten* (1961)

WALTER C. UTT
Conflict

Walter C. Utt (1921–1985), a native Californian, taught at Pacific Union College in Angwin, California, from 1951 until his death. He became chairman of the history department in 1956. The school established an endowment in Utt's name.

Helen Godfrey Pyke combined Utt's *The Wrath of the King* (1966) and *Home to Our Valleys* (1977) and an unfinished Utt manuscript, added some material of her own and shaped two new books, *No Peace for a Soldier* and *No Sacrifice but Conscience*. Pyke teaches at Southern Adventist University. The stories are set during the reign of France's Louis XIV. "I enjoyed this project, but it was probably the most difficult writing I've ever done because I was doing it in the name of a writer whose work I have always respected but whose style and approach are quite different from my own. I'm glad Utt's family and friends are pleased with the results," Pyke said in a Pacific Union College interview. Reporter Lainey S. Croke said, "Her [Pyke's] work with the material involved 'incorporating some of Utt's dialogue and action, organizing the flow of the story to match historical events, and deciding how all this should be connected with the earlier work,' she says."

Original Works

The Wrath of the King (1966)   *Home to Our Valleys!* (1977)

Posthumous Collaboration

Helen Godfrey Pyke, *No Peace for a Soldier* (2008); *No Sacrifice but Conscience* (2008)

HELEN VAN SLYKE
Public Smiles

Helen Van Slyke (1919–1979) was the author of *A Necessary Woman* (1979), *Sisters and Strangers* (1978) and seven other novels. She was a former editor and had worked in advertising, cosmetics and fashion.

Van Slyke died before she could complete her tenth book and her publisher, Harper & Row, sought a writer to complete the manuscript from her outline. "It was a book that was very close to Helen, very autobiographical," Lawrence P. Ashmead told *The New York Times* in 1982. The publisher engaged Chicago native James Edward (1929–1996), the writer of several pseudonymous gothic novels and one mystery, for the task. *Public Smiles, Private Tears* is about a woman rising through the hierarchy of the fashion world. The book was on the bestseller list for fourteen weeks.

Posthumous Collaboration

James Edward, *Public Smiles, Private Tears* (1982)

DAVID FOSTER WALLACE
Third and last

A novel by David Foster Wallace (1962–2008), *Infinite Jest*, showed up on *Time* magazine's list of All-Time 100 Greatest Novels. An innovative writer, the Ithaca, New York, native grew up in Illinois, attended Amherst College and won the Gail Kennedy Memorial Prize for his senior philosophy thesis. His senior English thesis became his first novel, the critically acclaimed *The Broom of the System* (1987). He received a master of fine arts degree in creative writing from the University of Arizona. He taught English at Illinois State University and wrote short fiction. His second, sprawling novel, *Infinite Jest*, came out in 1996. The next year he received the MacArthur Foundation Genius Grant. Married to painter Karen L. Green since 2004, Wallace took a position teaching creative writing at Pomona College. The writer suffered from depression and committed suicide in 2008.

Wallace left a third novel unfinished. An excerpt appeared in *The New Yorker* in 2009 and Little, Brown publisher/editor Michael Pietsch said he would assemble *The Pale King* from Wallace's partial draft, outline and notes. Pietsch said in *Entertainment Weekly* it was a thrill "to watch an idea turning into a chapter into an entire section of the book."

Posthumous Collaboration

Michael Pietsch, *The Pale King* (announced)

ROBERT PENN WARREN
Willie Stark

Kentucky-born poet, novelist and literary critic Robert Penn Warren (1905–1989) wrote a bestselling political tale, *All the King's Men*, in 1946. It won the Pulitzer

Prize for Fiction the next year. The story derives from real-life Louisiana Gov. Huey "The Kingfisher" Long.

Warren's original name for Willie Stark was Willie Talos. That's only one of the changes obvious in the restored edition of the author's classic novel. At the time of re-publication, Joyce Carole Oates argued the 1946 edition should be given preference, as Warren himself was aware of editorial changes and sanctioned them with a preface for a 1963 commemorative edition.

Posthumous Restoration
Noel Polk, editor, *All the King's Men Restored Edition* (2002)

EVELYN WAUGH

Brideshead arises

British writer Evelyn Waugh (1903–1966) had a wicked sense of humor that shone in his novels such as *A Handful of Dust* and *Vile Bodies*, which make great fun of high society. Waugh was the son of editor and publisher Arthur Waugh. His brother, Alec, became a writer. Evelyn attended Hertford College, Oxford, but left without fulfilling degree requirements. He was a woodworker and journalist before his first novel, *Decline and Fall*, came out in 1928. Years later, while serving with the Royal Horse Guards, and newly converted to Catholicism, he wrote *Brideshead Revisited*, a more sober panorama of pre-war England that found a large audience. It was adapted for television and cinema.

The Waugh family bridled at *Brideshead Regained*, the further adventures of Sebastian Flyte and Charles Ryder, Michael Johnston's unauthorized 2003 sequel. The estate brought suit. Waugh's work does not go out of copyright until 2016. Johnston, an exuberant fan of the original novel, agreed to sell copies of his book only online, and not through bookstores.

Original Work
Brideshead Revisited: The Sacred and Profane Memories of Captain Charles Ryder (1945)

Pastiche
Michael Johnston, *Brideshead Regained* (2003)

THOMAS WOLFE

Homeward

Thomas Wolfe (1900–1938) was born in North Carolina. His mother was a real estate investor. His father was a monument carver. Wolfe grew up in a middle-class resort community and received a master's degree in playwriting at Harvard University. He taught at New York University. After a trip to Europe, he met Aline Bernstein, twenty years his senior, and had a passionate love affair, and through her financial and emotional support, completed his first novel, *Look Homeward, Angel*.

Wolfe was heavily edited by his Scribner's editor, Maxwell Perkins, and the same continued with Harper's, Wolfe's publisher for his last three books, which were released posthumously. Edward Aswell shaped three novels from a Wolfe manuscript called "October Fair."

Posthumous Collaborations

Edward Aswell, *The Web and the Rock* (1939); *You Can't Go Home Again* (1940); *The Hills Beyond* (1941)

Posthumous Restoration

O Lost (2000) version of *Look Homeward, Angel* with more Wolfe material

Crime and Mystery

Of the categories, mysteries have invited the most pastiches. Sherlock Holmes alone accounts for a windfall of new treatments. That so few Baker Street clones succeed points to the deceptively straightforward prose of Arthur Conan Doyle, and to the keen sense of place that permeates the originals. Private eyes and amateur investigators from Lou Largo to Charlie Chan to Hildegarde Withers have withstood the deaths of their creators. Police characters, excepting "Bony" Bonaparte and Charlie Chan and Inspector McCarthy and a few others, are in lesser supply. A handful of roguish or criminal heroes, such as The Saint or Parker, have invited marginal replay.

CLEVE F. ADAMS

Private Eyes

Cleve F. Adams (1895–1949) wrote robust crime novels about oil company troubleshooter William Rye, private detective John J. Shannon and wisecracking insurance investigator Rex McBride. His books came out under his own name and as John Spain. With Robert Leslie Bellem, he wrote one book under the joint pseudonym Franklin Charles.

After Adams' death, Bellem (ca. 1902–1968), creator of the outrageously pulpish Dan Turner, Hollywood Detective, series, completed some of his manuscripts.

Original Rex McBride Works

And Sudden Death (1940)

Sabotage (1940) aka Death Before Breakfast (1940) aka Death at the Dam (1946)

Decoy (1941)

Up Jumped the Devil (1943) aka Murder All Over (1950)

The Crooked Finger (1944)

Posthumous Rex McBride Collaboration

Robert Leslie Bellem, *Shady Lady* (1955)

Original John J. Shannon Work
The Private Eye (1942)

Posthumous John J. Shannon Collaboration
Robert Leslie Bellem, *No Wings on a Cop* (1950)

Posthumous Collaboration
Robert Leslie Bellem, *Contraband* (1950) aka *Borderline Cases*

MARGERY ALLINGHAM
Albert Campion

English mystery writer Margery Allingham (1904–1966) grew up in a literary family. She began her writing career contributing Sexton Blake stories to *The New London Journal* and published her first novel, *Blackkerchief Dick*, in 1923. She introduced her long-running, eccentric detective Albert Campion in *The Crime at Black Dudley* in 1929.

"At first, Allingham's novels edged toward the pure thriller, with plenty of action provoked by international criminal conspiracies and the like," said William L. DeAndrea in *Encyclopedia Mysteriosa*. "Later, some of Campion's eccentricities were downplayed, character was emphasized and detection came more to the fore."

Allingham's husband, artist and editor Philip Youngman Carter (1904–1970), completed Allingham's last Campion manuscript and wrote two more entries in the series.

Original Works

The Crime at Black Dudley (1929) aka *The Black Dudley Murder* (1929)
Mystery Mile (1930)
Look to the Lady (1931) aka *The Gyrth Chalice Mystery* (1931)
Police at the Funeral (1931)
Sweet Danger (1933) aka *Kingdom of Death* (1933)
Death of a Ghost (1934)
Flowers for the Judge (1936)
Mr. Campion: Criminologist (1937) aka *Case of the Late Pig* (1937)
Dancers In Mourning (1937)
The Fashion in Shrouds (1938)
Mr. Campion and Others (1939)

Black Plumes (1940)
Traitor's Purse (1941)
Coroner's Pidgin (1941) aka *Pearls Before Swine* (1941)
The Case Book of Mr. Campion (1947)
More Work for the Undertaker (1948)
The Tiger in the Smoke (1952)
The Beckoning Lady (1955) aka *The Estate of the Beckoning Lady* (1955)
Hide My Eyes (1958) aka *Tether's End* (1958)
The China Governess (1962)
The Mysterious Mr. Campion (1963)
The Mind Readers (1965)
Mr. Campion's Lady (1965)

Mr. Campion's Clowns (1967) with a
    memoir by Philip Youngman Carter
The Allingham Casebook (1969)

The Allingham Minibus (1973)
The Return of Mr. Campion (1989)

Posthumous Mr. Campion Collaboration

Philip Youngman Carter, *Cargo of Eagles* (1968)

Mr. Campion Pastiches

Philip Youngman Carter, *Mr. Campion's Farthing* (1969); *Mr. Campion's Falcon* (1970)

WILLIAM ARD

Lou Largo

William Ard (1922–1960) was "one of the top private eye writers in the business," in the opinion of Francis M. Nevins, Jr., in *The Armchair Detective*. Ard shunned the violent Mickey Spillane-style detective then in vogue, preferring in his series about detective Timothy Dane to follow the standard of Dashiell Hammett and Raymond Chandler — or perhaps in the case of Lou Largo, of Richard S. Prather's Shell Scott. Ard died only two books into the Largo series.

"After Ard's death, Monarch editor Charles Heckelmann made a deal with the Scott Meredith Literary Agency for ghost writers who would continue the Lou Largo series under the Ard byline...," said Nevins. "This arrangement quickly transformed Largo into a super-stud caricature.... Of the four posthumous Largos, the final three were written by John Jakes, whose Kent Family Chronicles series netted him more fame and money than Ard saw in his lifetime."

Jakes (b. 1932 in Chicago) has written in several genres including fantasy and Western but as Nevins noted, his most popular books are historical sagas. Lawrence Block (b. 1938 in New York), wrote one Largo before Jakes took over. An award-winning mystery writer, Block's recent series include Bernie Rhodenbarr, the professional burglar; Matthew Scudder, the ex-cop and recovering alcoholic; and Keller, the hit man.

Original Lou Largo Works

All I Can Get (1959)

Like Ice She Was (1960)

Pastiches published as by William Ard

Lawrence Block, *Babe in the Woods* (1960)
John Jakes, *Make Mine Mavis* (1960); *And So to Bed* (1961); *Give Me This Woman* (1962)

H.C. BAILEY

Reggie Fortune

British writer Henry Christopher Bailey (1878–1961) wrote short stories and a few novels about Dr. Reggie Fortune, a foppish yet persistent and talented hero in the vein of Dorothy L. Sayers' Lord Peter Wimsey. The quirky lawyer Josiah Clunk shows up in several of the tales.

Bailey was considered one of the more important mystery writers of the Golden Age, and his works were widely popular in Great Britain in the 1920s and '30s. Years later, Carlo Fruttero and Franco Lucentini included Fortune in their solution to the Edwin Drood puzzle.

Original Reggie Fortune Works

Call Mr. Fortune (1920)
Mr. Fortune's Practice (1923)
Mr. Fortune's Trials (1925)
Mr. Fortune, Please (1928)
Mr. Fortune Speaking (1929)
Mr. Fortune Explains (1930)
Case for Mr. Fortune (1932)
The Man in the Cape (1933)
Mr. Fortune Wonders (1933)
Shadow on the Wall (1934)
Mr. Fortune Objects (1935)
A Clue for Mr. Fortune (1936)
Black Land, White Land (1937)
Clunk's Claimant (1937) aka The Twittering Bird Mystery

This Is Mr. Fortune (1938)
The Great Game (1939)
The Veron Mystery (1939) aka Mr. Clunk's Text
Mr. Fortune Here (1940)
The Bishop's Crime (1940)
No Murder (1942) aka The Apprehensive Dog
Mr. Fortune Finds a Pig (1943)
Dead Man's Effects (1945) aka The Cat's Whisker
The Life Sentence (1946)
Honour Among Thieves (1947)
Saving a Rope (1948) aka Save a Rope

Pastiches

Carlo Fruttero and Franco Lucentini, The D Case: Or, The Truth About the Mystery of Edwin Drood (1993)

EARL DERR BIGGERS

Charlie Chan

Ohio-born Earl Derr Biggers (1884–1933) created a Honolulu police detective of Chinese ancestry, Charlie Chan, for a series of novels in the 1920s and early '30s. Biggers wrote other books, but Chan, thanks to a radio show, a syndicated comic strip and a series of B-budget movies, established his reputation. Several actors played Chan and his Number One Son in the black-and-white pictures, considered by many to be at least demeaning, if not racist, in their depictions of Orientals and Blacks. Biggers also wrote plays and screenplays and the novel *Seven Keys to Baldpate* (1913).

Two pastiches were based on screenplays. The Michael Collins book originally appeared in *Charlie Chan Mystery Magazine* under the house name Robert Hart Davis in 1974. The Pronzini and Wallman book had a similar origin.

Original Charlie Chan Mysteries

House Without a Key (1925)
Chinese Parrot (1926)
Behind the Curtain (1928)

Black Camel (1929)
Charlie Chan Carries On (1930)
Keeper of the Keys (1932)

Charlie Chan Pastiches

Michael Avallone, *Charlie Chan and the Curse of the Dragon Queen* (1981) based on a screenplay
John L. Breen, *Hair of the Sleuthhound* (1982)
Michael Collins, *Charlie Chan in the Temple of the Golden Horde* (2004)
Carlo Fruttero and Franco Lucentini, *The D Case: Or, The Truth About the Mystery of Edwin Drood* (1993)
Dennis Lynds, *Charlie Chan Returns* (1974) based on a teleplay
Bill Pronzini and Jeffrey M. Wallman, *Charlie Chan in the Pawns of Death* (2003)

JOHN G. BRANDON

Crime

John Gordon Brandon (1879–1941), an Australian transplant to England, wrote some 120 crime novels including many entries in the Inspector Patrick Aloysius McCarthy of Scotland Yard series. His aristocratic character Arthur Stukeley Pennington, along with his reformed crook manservant "Flash" Wibley and driver Big Bill Withers, first appeared in Brandon's Sexton Blake cases, then spun out into his own.

Gordon Brandon continued his father's series.

Original Inspector Patrick Aloysius McCarthy and Arthur Stukeley Pennington* (or Pennington alone**) Works

Red Altars (1930) aka *Secret Brotherhood*
Black Joss (1931)
West End (1933)*
Murder in Mayfair (1934)*
One-Minute Murder (1936)*
Riverside Mystery (1935)*
Pawnshop Murder (1936)*

Snatch Game (1936)*
Case of the Withered Hand (1936)
Death Tolls the Gong (1936)*
Dragnet (1936)
McCarthy, C.I.D. (1936)
Murder at the Yard (1936)
Bond Street Murder (1937)*

Death in Downing Street (1937)*
Hand of Seeta (1937)
Mail-Van Mystery (1937)
Murder in Soho (1937)
Night Club Murder (1938)
Regent Street Raid (1938)*
Bonus for Murder (1938)
Cork Street Crime (1938)*
Fifty Pound Marriage Case (1938) aka
    Two Hundred and Fifty Pound
    Marriage Case
Frame-up (1938)
Mark of the Tong (1938)
Fingerprints Never Lie (1938)
Crooked Five (1939)
Death on Delivery (1939)
Mister Pennington Comes Through
    (1939)*
Scream in Soho (1940)
Yellow Gods (1940)
Death in the Ditch (1940)**
Mister Pennington Goes Nap (1940)*

Death in the Quarry (1941)
Mister Pennington Barges In (1941)*
Transport Murder (1942)
Blueprint Murders (1942)
Death Comes Swiftly (1942)
Mister Pennington Sees Red (1942)*
Death in Jermyn Street (1942)*
Death in D Division (1943)*
Death in Duplicate (1945)
Candidate for a Coffin (1946)
M for Murder (1949)
Corpse of the Would-Be Widow (1950)**
Corpse Rode On (1951)*
Murderer's Stand-in (1953)*
Call-girl Murders (1954)*
Death of a Greek (1955)*
Murder on the Beam (1956)*
Death of a Socialite (1957)*
Murder in Pimlico (1958)*
Corpse from the City (1958)*
Death Stalks in Soho (1959)*
Espionage Killings (1959)

Pastiches

Gordon Brandon, *Murder Comes Smiling* (1959)*; *Death of a Mermaid* (1960)*

HERON CARVIC

Miss Emily Seeton

British actor and writer Heron Carvic (d. 1980) voiced Gandalf in a BBC Radio version of J.R.R. Tolkien's *The Hobbit* and appeared in episodes of *The Avengers* and *Police Surgeon*. He wrote five cozy mystery novels about retired art teacher Emily Seeton, who, though occasionally absent-minded, assists Inspector Delphic in solving crimes.

Two writers continued the cases. Roy Peter Martin was born in London in 1931, studied at Birkbeck College and served in the Royal Air Force. He later worked in education and cultural diplomacy.

Original Works

Picture Miss Seeton (1968)
Miss Seeton Draws the Line (1969)
Miss Seeton, Bewitched (1971) aka
    Witch Miss Seeton

Miss Seeton Sings (1973)
Odds on Miss Seeton (1975)

Miss Seeton Pastiches

Roy Peter Martin writing as Hampton Charles, *Advantage Miss Seeton* (1990); *Miss Seeton at the Helm* (1990); *Miss Seeton, by Appointment* (1990)

Sarah J. Mason writing as Hamilton Crane, *Miss Seeton Cracks the Case* (1991); *Miss Seeton Paints the Town* (1991); *Miss Seeton Rocks the Cradle* (1992); *Hands Up, Miss Seeton* (1992); *Miss Seeton by Moonlight* (1992); *Miss Seeton Plants Suspicion* (1993); *Miss Seeton Goes to Bat* (1993); *Starring Miss Seeton* (1994); *Miss Seeton Undercover* (1994); *Miss Seeton Rules* (1994); *Sold to Miss Seeton* (1995); *Sweet Miss Seeton* (1996); *Bonjour, Miss Seeton* (1997); *Miss Seeton's Finest Hour* (1999)

WILLIAM J. CAUNITZ
Cops

William J. Caunitz (1933–1996) wrote police procedurals from experience, and readers appreciated it. He was a member of the New York City Police Department for three decades, rising through the ranks to detective squad commander. His *One Police Plaza* became a television movie.

Christopher Newman, creator of the Joe Dante novels, completed Caunitz's final manuscript after the author's death. According to Tomas Kellner on Forbes.com, Adam Rice, a full-time investor from Brooklyn, NY, "sued Penguin Putnam last year after discovering that William J. Caunitz wasn't the sole author of cop potboiler *Chains of Command* (right there on the copyright page the book also names Christopher Newman, who picked up Caunitz's half-written manuscript and finished it after Caunitz died in 1996), claiming the publisher defrauded him by running a "classic bait-and-switch scheme." A New York State appeals court threw out the suit.

Posthumous Collaboration

Christopher Newman, *Chains of Command* (1999)

RAYMOND CHANDLER
Philip Marlowe

"It is difficult to imagine what the modern private-eye story would be like if a forty-five-year-old ex–oil company executive named Raymond Chandler had not begun writing fiction for *Black Mask* in 1933...," wrote Bill Pronzini in *1001 Midnights: The Aficionado's Guide to Mystery and Detective Fiction*. "Chandler took the hard-boiled prototype established by Dashiell Hammett, reshaped it to fit his own particular vision ... smoothed off its rough edges, and made of it something more than a tale of realism and violence; he broadened it into a vehicle for social commentary, refined it with prose at once cynical and poetic, and elevated the character of the private eye to a mythical status."

Chandler's hero Philip Marlowe was a modern-day knight searching for hidden truth, as Chandler described him in the essay "The Simple Art of Murder" in *The Atlantic Monthly* for December 1944. "Down these mean streets a man must go who is not himself mean, who is neither tarnished nor afraid."

The Marlowe stories exhibit all the trappings associated with private eye fiction: a loner detective; a small, shabby office; bare-bones living; a gruff hero who, as William Kittredge and Steven M. Krauzer describe him in *The Great American Detective* (1978), "is an idealist, willing to face arrest, physical abuse, even death, to protect or apprehend a murderer."

Chicago-born Raymond Chandler (1888–1959) moved to England as a boy and was educated in London. He served in the Canadian Army and Royal Air Force during the first World War. He worked for the government, as a reporter, as a ranch hand and bookkeeper and in a bank. He became a full-time writer in 1933. Several of his short stories for the pulp fiction magazines were later cannibalized for novels featuring Marlowe. Actor Humphrey Bogart played the character in the classic version of *The Big Sleep* (1946). There were other film versions of Chandler novels, as well as radio (starring Van Heflin, 1947–50) and television (with Philip Carey, 1959–60) series.

"Few 20th century writers have been as widely influential and imitated as Raymond Chandler," wrote Kim Newman in "The Return of Philip Marlowe" in *Million*. "Quite apart from the undoubted and enormous effect his prose style has had outside his field — many have learned from Chandler never to use a commonplace when it can be personalized and made distinctive — he has become a touchstone of the private-eye story, with Dashiell Hammett standing behind him and Ross MacDonald in front. He dominates the genre even thirty years after his death."

On the centenary of Chandler's birth, Byron Preiss enlisted "approximately twenty-five contemporary authors of the mystery story to celebrate Chandler's work, with the consent of his estate, by writing new Philip Marlowe stories." In a foreword, Preiss described how he searched through Chandler's papers hoping to find words which would give some "validation" to his project. He never quite found them, but published the book regardless.

Mystery writer Robert B. Parker (b. 1932 in Massachusetts) read Chandler stories as a youth growing up in New Bedford. An Army veteran, he worked as a technical writer and copywriter and in advertising before becoming a college professor. With the popularity of his Spenser series of private detective mysteries, Parker became a full-time fiction writer. His doctoral dissertation was on Hammett and Chandler. Marlowe, Parker told his students at Northeastern University, "is honest, likeable, a (Sam) Spade with empathy, Huck (Finn) smartened up, in the city to test the code" — his personal code. Parker completed a Chandler fragment in *Poodle Springs*, and incorporated sections of *The Big Sleep* into *Perchance to Dream*. "I don't want to make a career of writing some other guy's books," Parker told interviewer Tom Auer. "But I wanted to do this, because it seemed like a good thing to do."

Original Philip Marlowe series

The Big Sleep (1939)
Farewell, My Lovely (1940)
The High Window (1942)
The Lady in the Lake (1943)
The Little Sister (1949) aka *Marlowe* (1969)

The Long Goodbye (1953)
Playback (1958)
Raymond Chandler Speaking (1962)
    included unfinished "Poodle Springs"

Posthumous Collaboration

Robert B. Parker, *Poodle Springs* (1989)

Pastiches

Robert B. Parker, *Perchance to Dream* (1991) incorporating as flashbacks some material from *The Big Sleep*

Byron Preiss, editor, *Raymond Chandler's Philip Marlowe: A Centennial Celebration* (1988) introduced by Frank MacShane and containing one original story, "The Pencil" by Chandler, and pastiches by Simon Brett, Robert Campbell, Max Allan Collins, Robert Crais, Loren D. Estleman, James Grady, Ed Gorman, Joyce Harrington, Jeremiah Healy, Edward D. Hoch, Stuart M. Kaminsky, Dick Lochte, Eric Van Lustbader, John Lutz, Francis M. Nevins, Jr., Sara Paretsky, W.R. Philbrick, Robert J. Randisi, Benjamin M. Schutz, Roger L. Simon, Julie Smith, Paco Ignacio Taibo II and Jonathan Valin.

Julian Symons, *The Great Detectives: Seven Criminal Investigations* (1981)

LESLIE CHARTERIS

The Saint

Leslie Charteris (1907–1993), of Chinese-English ancestry, created the fictional globetrotting rogue/crime solver Simon Templar in his third novel, *Meet—The Tiger*, in 1928. The character evolved as Charteris settled in for a long series. The popularity of the Roger Moore television series eased the workload for Charteris, who allowed his publisher to commission new novels or reprint stories written by others for *The Saint Mystery Magazine*.

The pastiches are a film novelization and a novel published by the Saint Club, a fan organization Charteris started in the 1930s. Writer Burl Barer (b. 1947) also wrote the Edgar Award-winning nonfiction *The Saint: A Complete History in Print, Radio, Television and Film* (1992).

Original Saint Works

Meet—The Tiger! (1928)
Enter the Saint (1930)
The Last Hero (1930)
Knight Templar (1930)
Featuring the Saint (1931)
Alias the Saint (1931)
Wanted for Murder (1931)
She Was a Lady (1931)
The Holy Terror (1932)
Getaway (1932)
Once More the Saint (1933)
The Brighter Buccaneer (1933)
The Misfortunes of Mr. Teal (1934)
Boodle (1934)
The Saint Goes On (1934)
The Saint in New York (1935)
Saint Overboard (1936)
The Ace of Knaves (1937)
Thieves' Picnic (1937)

Prelude for War (1938)
Follow the Saint (1938)
The Happy Highwayman (1939)
The Saint in Miami (1940)
The Saint Goes West (1942)
The Saint Steps In (1942)
The Saint on Guard (1944)
The Saint Sees it Through (1946)
Call for the Saint (1948)
Saint Errant (1948)
The Saint in Europe (1953)
The Saint on the Spanish Main (1955)
The Saint Around the World (1956)
Thanks to the Saint (1957)
Señor Saint (1958)
The Saint to the Rescue (1959)
Trust the Saint (1962)
The Saint in the Sun (1963)

Collaborations

Vendetta for the Saint (1964) with Harry Harrison
The Saint on TV (1968) with Fleming Lee
The Saint Returns (1968) with Fleming Lee
The Saint and the Fiction Makers (1968) with Fleming Lee
The Saint Abroad (1969) with Fleming Lee
The Saint in Pursuit (1970)
The Saint and the People Importers (1971) with Fleming Lee
Catch the Saint (1975)
The Saint and the Hapsburg Necklace (1976) with Christopher Short
Send for the Saint (1977)
The Saint in Trouble (1978) with Graham Weaver
The Saint and the Templar Treasure (1979) with Graham Weaver
Count on the Saint (1980)
Salvage for the Saint (1983)
The Fantastic Saint (1982)

Pastiches

Burl Barer, The Saint (1997) film novelization; Capture the Saint (1997)

G. K. CHESTERTON
Father Brown

London-born Gilbert Keith Chesterton (1874–1936) wrote philosophical, poetical and biographical works as well as criminous ones featuring his delightful priest-detective Father Brown, featured in fifty-two short stories.

Chesterton was a substantial man in girth (he stood 6 feet 4 inches and weighed 300 pounds) and intellect. American Chesterton Society president Dale Ahlquist minces no words: "G.K. Chesterton was the best writer of the 20th century. He said something about everything and he said it better than anybody else. But he was no mere wordsmith. He was very good at expressing himself, but more importantly, he had something very good to express. The reason he was the greatest writer of the 20th century was because he was also the greatest thinker of the 20th century."

So of course Father Brown has invited copy. Carlo Fruttero and Franco Lucentini included Brown in their solution to the Edwin Drood puzzle. Stephen Kendrick paired the padre with the sleuth of Baker Street while David Langford took him into a futuristic realm.

Original Father Brown Works

The Innocence of Father Brown (1911)
The Wisdom of Father Brown (1914)
The Incredulity of Father Brown (1926)
The Secret of Father Brown (1927)
The Scandal of Father Brown (1935)
G.K. Chesterton Crime Omnibus (1987)
includes an uncollected story and an uncollected collaboration
The Collected Works of G.K. Chesterton, Vol. 14: Short Stories, Fairy Tales, Mystery Stories—Illustrations (1993) includes uncollected story

Pastiches

Carlo Fruttero and Franco Lucentini, *The D Case: or, The Truth About the Mystery of Edwin Drood* (1993)
Stephen Kendrick, *Night Watch: A Long Lost Adventure in Which Sherlock Holmes Meets Father Brown* (2003)
David Langford, *He Do the Time Police in Different Voices* (1996) includes "The Spear of the Sun"

AGATHA CHRISTIE
Marple and Poirot

Agatha Christie (1890–1976), the "Queen of Crime," had two eminent detectives, the spinster Jane Marple and the consulting detective Hercule Poirot.

Born in Devon, England, to an American stockbroker father and English mother, Christie published her first mystery novel, *The Mysterious Affair at Styles*, in 1920. Her play *Mousetrap* (1952) had remarkable longevity on the London stage, having begun its run in London's West End in 1952. Dame Agatha cleverly left at her passing two manuscripts intended to be the last cases of her creations, *Curtain* and *Sleeping Murder*.

That did not prevent the appearance of fictional biographies, however, and one novelization of three plays from 1930, 1958 and 1954.

Original Hercule Poirot Works

The Mysterious Affair at Styles (1920)
Murder on the Links (1923)
Poirot Investigates (1924) short stories
The Murder of Roger Ackroyd (1926)
The Big Four (1927)
The Mystery of the Blue Train (1928)
Black Coffee (1930) play
Peril at End House (1932)
Thirteen at Dinner (1933) aka *Lord Edgware Dies*
Murder on the Orient Express (1934) aka *Murder in the Calais Coach*
Murder in Three Acts (1935) aka *Three Act Tragedy*
Death in Air (1935) aka *Death in the Clouds*
The A.B.C. Murders (1936) aka *Alphabet murders*
Murder in Mesopotamia (1936)
Cards on the Table (1936)
Death on the Nile (1937)
Poirot Loses a Client (1937) aka *Dumb Witness*
Murder in the Mews (1937) short stories, aka *Dead Man's Mirror*
Appointment with Death (1938)
Murder for Christmas (1939) aka *Hercule Poirot's Christmas* aka *A Holiday for Murder*
The Regatta Mystery (1939)
Sad Cypress (1940)
Patriotic Murders (1940) aka *One, Two, Buckle My Shoe* and *Overdose of Death*
Evil Under the Sun (1941)
Murder in Retrospect (1942) aka *Five Little Pigs*
Poirot Knows the Murderer (1946) short stories

Poirot Lends a Hand (1946) short stories
Murder After Hours (1946) aka *The Hollow*
The Labours of Hercules (1947) short stories
Taken at the Flood (1948) aka *There Is a Tide*
Witness for the Prosecution (1948) short stories
Three Blind Mice (1950) short stories
The Under Dog and Other Stories (1951) short stories
Mrs. McGinty's Dead (1952) aka *Blood will Tell*
After the Funeral (1953) aka *Funerals Are Fatal*
Hickory Dickory Dock (1955) aka *Hickory Dickory Death*
Dead Man's Folly (1956)
Cat Among the Pigeons (1959)
The Adventure of the Christmas Pudding (1960) short stories
Double Sin and Other Stories (1961) short stories
13 for Luck! (1924) short stories
The Clocks (1963)
Third Girl (1966)
Hallowe'en Party (1969)
Elephants Can Remember (1972)
Poirot's Early Cases (1974) short stories
Curtain (1975) aka *Problem at Pollensa Bay and Other Stories* (1991) short stories
While the Light Lasts and Other Stories (1997) short stories
The Harlequin Tea Set (1997) short stories

Posthumous Hercule Poirot Collaborations

Charles Osborne, *Black Coffee* (1998) based on a play; *The Unexpected Guest* (1999); *Spider's Web* (2000)

Hercule Poirot Pastiche

Julian Symons, *The Great Detectives: Seven Criminal Investigations* (1981)

Original Miss Marple Works

The Murder at the Vicarage (1930)
The Body in the Library (1942)
The Moving Finger (1943)
A Murder Is Announced (1950)
They Do It with Mirrors (1952) aka
  Murder with Mirrors
A Pocket Full of Rye (1953)
4.50 from Paddington (1957) aka *What
  Mrs. McGillicuddy Saw!*

The Mirror Crack'd from Side to Side
  (1962) aka *The Mirror Crack'd*
A Caribbean Mystery (1964)
At Bertram's Hotel (1965)
Nemesis (1971)
Sleeping Murder (1976)

Miss Marple Pastiche

Julian Symons, *The Great Detectives: Seven Criminal Investigations* (1981)

Fictional Biographies

Anne Hart, *The Life and Times of Miss Jane Marple* (1989); *The Life and Times of Hercule Poirot* (1990)

WILKIE COLLINS

She wore white

English novelist and playwright Wilkie Collins produced some fifty short stories, twenty-seven novels and fifteen stage works, plus uncounted essays and other nonfiction. Born in London, he was the son of landscape artist William Collins. He grew up in Italy, apprenticed to a tea merchant and studied law. His first book was about his father. His first novel, *Antonia*, came out in 1850 and set him on a course as a fiction writer who specialized in "sensational" novels. He became a close friend of Charles Dickens. Opium, with which the author was familiar, relying on it to relieve him of the pain of his gout, figured in his popular novel *The Moonstone*. Though never married, Collins nevertheless fathered three children.

Collins' novel *The Woman in White*, which first was serialized in *All the Year Round* (England) and *Harper's* (United States), is recognized as one of the earliest mystery novels. It is about an artist, Walter Hartright, who falls in love with one of his students, Laura, and comes to her aid years later when her vile husband seeks to drive her insane, so he may have her wealth. The novel has inspired television series and an Andrew Lloyd Webber musical.

British writer James Wilson (b. 1948) wrote a sequel about Hartright accepting a commission to write the biography of painter Joseph M.W. Turner. American writers Douglas Preston (b. 1956) and Lincoln Child (b. 1957) recast the whole story in a modern setting and feature FBI Special Agent Aloysius Pendergast.

Original Work

The Woman in White (1859)

Pastiches

Douglas Preston and Lincoln Child, *Brimstone* (2004)
James Wilson, *The Dark Clue* (2001)

ARTHUR CONAN DOYLE

Sherlock Holmes and Dr. Watson

Sir Arthur Conan Doyle (1858–1930) was a physician, spiritualist, historical novelist and mystery writer. Doyle's master consulting detective Sherlock Holmes, along with his companion Dr. John Watson, have an enormous following to this day. Born in Edinburgh, Scotland, Doyle as a boy heard stories of his Irish ancestors. Doyle attended Jesuit schools before enrolling in the University of Edinburgh. While a student, he began to write stories for publication. He received his medical degree in 1885. He shaped his Holmes character around Dr. Joseph Bell, a diagnostician with whom he had taken classes. *A Study in Scarlet* came into print in 1887 in *Beeton's Christmas Annual*. Fifty-six short stories and another three novels followed. (Editor Peter Haining later collected miscellaneous Holmes scraps.)

The Doyle estate for many years kept a tight rein on Holmes pastiches. The character, meanwhile, appeared in popular motion pictures featuring Basil Rathbone, and a television series with Jeremy Brett. The range of 221B Baker Street prose tales in other hands is very wide. Some center on secondary characters, Professor Moriaty or Irene Adler or Mycroft Holmes, Inspector Lestrade or Mrs. Hudson or the Baker Street Irregulars or Dr. Watson. Ultimately, no one does it better than Doyle.

This listing omits dramas and parodies, and books/series that are obvious tributes, such as Robert L. Fish's Schlock Homes books and August Derleth's Solar Pons cases. (Derleth has his own entry.)

Original Sherlock Holmes Works

A Study in Scarlet (1887)   *The Sign of the Four* (1989)

The Adventures of Sherlock Holmes (1892)
The Memoirs of Sherlock Holmes (1894)
The Hound of the Baskervilles (1901)
The Return of Sherlock Holmes (1905)

The Valley of Fear (1915)
His Last Bow (1917)
The Case Book of Sherlock Holmes (1927)
The Final Adventures of Sherlock Holmes (1981) edited by Peter Haining

Pastiches

Charlton Andrews, *The Bound of the Astorbilts: A Modern Detective Story* (1902); *The Resources of Mycroft Holmes* (1973)

Val Andrews, *Beekeeper* (1983); *Carriage Clock* (1983); *Fair* (1983); *Fowlhaven Werewolf* (1983); *Last Reunion* (1983); *Sherlock Holmes and the Eminent Thespian* (1988); *Sherlock Holmes and the Brighton Pavilion Mystery* (1989); *Sherlock Holmes and the Egyptian Hall Adventure* (1993); *Sherlock Holmes and the Houdini Birthright* (1995); *Sherlock Holmes and Greyfriars School Mystery* (1996); *Sherlock Holmes and the Man Who Lost Himself* (1996); *Sherlock Holmes and the Secret Seven* (2001); *Sherlock Holmes: The Ghost of Baker Street* (2008)

Val Andrews and H. Penn, *Sherlock Holmes and the Arthritic Clergyman* (1980); *Case of the Chief Rabbi's Problem* (1980); *Mystery in the Sealed Room* (1980); *Sherlock Holmes and a Theatrical Mystery* (1980)

Alan Arnold, *Young Sherlock Holmes* (1985) based on screenplay by Chris Columbus

Mike Ashley, editor, *The Mammoth Book of New Sherlock Holmes Adventures* (1997)

Isaac Asimov, Martin H. Greenberg and Charles Waugh, editors, *Sherlock Holmes Through Time and Space* (1984)

Edmund Aubrey, *Sherlock Holmes in Dallas* (1980)

Hilary Bailey, *Strange Adventures of Charlotte Holmes* (1994)

Brian Ball, *The Baker Street Boys* (1983) based on teleplay by Anthony Read

John Kendrick Bangs, *R. Holmes & Co.; Being the Remarkable Adventures of Raffles Holmes, Esq., Detective and Amateur Cracksman by Birth* (1906)

Don W. Baranowski, *Sherlock Holmes: The Adventures of the Frankenstein Monster* (2006)

Sam Benady, *Sherlock Holmes in Gibraltar* (1991)

D.R. Bensen, *Sherlock Holmes in New York* (1976) based on screenplay by Alvin Sapinsley

Lloyd Biggle, Jr., *The Quallsford Inheritance* (1986); *The Glendower Conspiracy* (1990)

Matthew Booth, *Sherlock Holmes and the Giant's Hand* (2008)

Anthony Boucher, *The Case of the Baker Street Irregulars* (1940)

Craig Bowlsby, *The Hound of London* (1988)

Richard Boyer, *The Giant Rat of Sumatra* (1974)

Clive Brooks, *The Memoirs of Professor Moriarty* (1990); *Sherlock Holmes Revisited* (1990)

Russell A. Brown, *Sherlock Holmes and the Mysterious Friend of Oscar Wilde* (1988)

Colin Bruce, *The Strange Case of Mrs. Hudson's Cat, and Other Science Mysteries Solved by Sherlock Holmes* (1997)

Jacob Brussel, *Sherlock Holmes vs. Arsene Lupin: The Case of the Golden Blonde* (1946) aka *Arsene Lupin Conter Herlock Sholmes*

Carole Bugge, *The Star of India* (1998); *The Haunting of Torre Abbey* (2000)

Jeff Campbell and Charle Prepolec, editors, *Gaslight Grimoire: Dark Tales of Sherlock Holmes* (2008)

P.H. Cannon, *Pulptime* (1984)

Michael Capuzzo, *The Murder Room: The Heirs of Sherlock Holmes Gather to Solve the World's Most Perplexing Cold Cases* (2005)

Caleb Carr, *The Italian Secretary* (2005)

Philip J. Carraher, *Sherlock Holmes: The Adventure of the Dead Rabbits Society* (2001); *Sherlock Holmes in New York: The Adventure of the New York Ripper* (2005)

Michael Chabon, *The Final Solution* (2005)

Ian Alfred Charnock, *Watson's Last Case* (2000)

Ronan Coghlan, *Sherlock Holmes and the Heir of Albion* (2007)

Randall Collins, *Case of the Philosopher's Ring* (1978)

J. Storer Clouston, *The Truthful Lady* (1984)

Arthur Byron Cover, *An East Wind Coming* (1979)

Milton Creighton, *The Dynamiters* (1988); *The Royal Flush* (1988)

Mitch Cullin, *A Slight Trick of the Mind* (2005)

Marcel d'Agneau, *The Curse of the Nibelung: Being the Last Case of Lord Holmes of Baker Street and Sir John Watson* (1981)

David Stuart Davies, *Sherlock Holmes and the Hentzau Affair* (2007); *Sherlock Holmes: The Game's Afoot* (2008)

Martin Davies, *Mrs. Hudson and the Spirits' Curse* (2004); *Mrs. Hudson and the Malabar Rose* (2005)

Barry Day, *Sherlock Holmes and the Shakespeare Globe Murders* (1997); *Sherlock Holmes and the Alice in Wonderland Murders* (2001)

Dan Day and Arthur Conan Doyle, *Cases of Sherlock Holmes* (1989) graphic novel

Noel De Souza, *The Tibetan Affair* (1987)

Michael Dibden, *The Last Sherlock Holmes Story* (1978)

Charles Dickens, Carlo Fruttero and Franco Lucentini, *The D Case; Or, the Truth About the Mystery of Edwin Drood* (1992)

Terrence Dicks, *The Case of the Fagin File* (1978); *The Case of the Missing Masterpiece* (1978)

June Dixon and Donald Monat, *The Merchant of Death* (2008)

Carole Nelson Douglas, *Good Night, Mr. Holmes* (1990); *Good Morning, Irene* (1990); *Irene at Large* (1992); *Irene's Last Waltz* (1994)

Noel Downing, *Doctor Watson and the Invisible Man* (1992)

Adrian Conan Doyle and John Dickson Carr, *The Exploits of Sherlock Holmes* (1952)

William E. Dudley, *The Untold Sherlock Holmes* (1983)

David Dvorkin, *Time for Sherlock Holmes* (1983)

Ira Bernard Dworkin, *Sherlock Holmes in Modern Times* (1980)

David Eastman, *The Adventure of the Empty House* (2002)

Miles Elward, *Sherlock Holmes in Canterbury* (1995)

Loren D. Estleman, *Sherlock Holmes vs. Dracula: The Adventure of the Sanguinary Count* (1978); *Dr. Jekyll and Mr. Holmes* (1979)

Philip José Farmer, *Adventure of the Peerless Peer* (1974)

Chelsea Quinn Yarbro writing as Quinn Fawcett, *Against the Brotherhood* (1997); *Embassy Row* (1998); *The Flying Scotsman* (1999); *The Scottish Ploy* (2001)

Lewis Feuer, *The Revolutionist's Daughter: Sherlock Holmes Meets Karl Marx* (1983)

Charles Fisher, *Some Unaccountable Exploits of Sherlock Holmes* (1956)

Cindy Fisher, *The Adventure of the Copper Beeches* (1978)
John S. Fitzpatrick, *Sherlock Holmes: The Montana Chronicles* (2008)
Berkley Forsythe, *Expo '98: Sherlock Holmes in Omaha* (1987)
Brian Freemantle, *The Holmes Inheritance* (2004); *The Holmes Factor* (2005)
Esther Friesner, *Druid's Blood* (1989)
Gerald Frow, *Young Sherlock: The Mystery of the Manor House* (1984); *Young Sherlock: The Adventure at Ferryman's Creek* (1984)
Emanuel E. Garcia, Roger Jaynes and Edie Maguire, *Sherlock Holmes and the Three Poisoned Pawns* (2008)
John E. Gardner, *The Return of Moriarty* (1974); *The Revenge of Moriarty* (1975)
James Goldman, *They Might Be Giants* (1970) screenplay
Glenn Gravatt, *The Adventure of the Mysterious Lodger* (1979)
Richard Lancelyn Green, editor, *The Further Adventures of Sherlock Holmes* (1985)
Martin H. Greenberg, editor, *The Resurrected Holmes: New Cases from the Notes of John H. Watson, M.D.* (1996); *Ghosts in Baker Street* (2006)
Martin H. Greenberg, Jon L. Lellenberg and Carol-Lynn Waugh, editors, *Holmes for the Holidays* (1996); *More Holmes for the Holidays* (1999); *Murder in Baker Street: New Tales of Sherlock Holmes* (2002); *Murder, My Dear Watson: New Tales of Sherlock Holmes* (2002)
Martin H. Greenberg and Jon L. Lellenberg, editors, *The Ghosts in Baker Street: New Tales of Sherlock Holmes* (2005)
Martin H. Greenberg and Carol-Lynn Waugh, editors, *The New Adventure of Sherlock Holmes* (1987)
Ken Greenwald, *The Lost Adventures of Sherlock Holmes: Based on the Original Radio Plays by Dennis Green and Anthony Boucher* (1989)
L.B. Greenwood, *Sherlock Holmes and the Case of the Raleigh Legacy* (1986); *Sherlock Holmes and the Case of Sabina Hall* (1988); *Sherlock Holmes and the Thistle of Scotland* (1989)
John Hall, *Sherlock Holmes and the Telephone Murder Mystery* (1999)
Robert Lee Hall, *Exit Sherlock Holmes* (1977); *The King Edward Plot* (1987)
Leslie Halliwell, *The Ghost of Sherlock Holmes* (1984)
David L. Hammer, *The Twenty-Second Man; or, Re Sherlock Holmes, German Agent* (1989)
Edward B. Hanna, *The Whitechapel Horrors* (1992)
Michael Hardwick, *Prisoner of the Devil* (1979); *The Private Life of Dr. Watson* (1985); *The Revenge of the Hound* (1987)
Michael Hardwick and Mollie Hardwick, *The Private Life of Sherlock Holmes* (1970) based on a screenplay by Billy Wilder and I.A.L. Diamond
Claire Hartman, *Shirlee Holmes* (2001)
Thomas Bruce Haughy, *The Case of the Maltese Treasure* (1979)
H.F. Heard, *A Taste for Honey* (1941); *Reply Paid* (1944); *The Notched Hairpin* (1949)
Paul E. Heusinger, *The Secret Adventures of Sherlock Holmes* (2006)
M.P. Hodel and S.M. Wright, *Enter the Lion* (1979)
John C. Hogan, *Sherlock Holmes in Hongkong* (1969)
G. Randolph Holms, *The Hounds of the Vatican* (1986)
Sydney Hosier, *Elementary, Mrs. Hudson* (1996); *Murder, Mrs. Hudson* (1997); *Most Baffling, Mrs. Hudson* (1998); *The Game's Afoot, Mrs. Hudson* (1998)

Lois W. Hubbell writing as Ned Hubell, *The Adventure of Creighton Holmes* (1979)

James C. Iraldi, *The Problem of the Purple Maculas* (1968)

Mary Jaffee and Irving Jaffee, *Beyond Baker Street* (1973)

L. Frank James, *An Opened Grave: Sherlock Holmes Investigates His Ultimate Case* (2006)

Anita Janda, *The Secret Diary of Dr. Watson: Death at the Reichenbach Falls* (2001)

Roger Jaynes, *Sherlock Holmes: A Duel with the Devil* (2003); *Sherlock Holmes and the Chilford Ripper* (2006)

H. Paul Jeffers, *The Adventure of the Stalwart Companions* (1978)

Magda Jozsa, *Sherlock Holmes on the Wild Frontier* (2005)

Marvin Kaye, *The Incredible Umbrella* (1979)

Marvin Kaye, editor, *The Resurrected Holmes: New Cases from the Notes of John H. Watson, M.D.* (1997); *The Confidential Casebook of Sherlock Holmes* (1998); *The Game is Afoot: Parodies, Pastiche and Ponderings of Sherlock Holmes* (1994)

Stephen Kendrick, *Night Watch: A Long-Lost Adventure in Which Sherlock Holmes Meets Father Brown* (2001)

John R. King, *The Shadow of Reichenbach Falls* (2008)

Laurie R. King, *The Beekeeper's Apprentice* (1994); *A Monstrous Regiment of Women* (1995); *A Letter of Mary* (1996); *The Moor* (1998); *O Jerusalem!* (1999); *Justice Hall* (2002); *The Game* (2004); *Locked Rooms* (2005); *The Language of Bees* (2009)

Stephen King, *The Doctor's Case* (1987)

Hugh Kingsmill, *The Ruby of Khitmandu* (1932)

Michael Kurland, *The Infernal Device* (1978); *Death by Gaslight* (1982); *The Great Game: A Professor Moriarty Novel* (2001); *My Sherlock Holmes: Untold Stories of the Great Detective* (2003); *Sherlock Holmes: The Hidden Years* (2004)

W. Lane, *Sherlock Holmes and the Wood Green Empire Mystery* (1985)

Maurice Leblanc, *The Case of the Golden Blonde* (1946)

John Lellenberg, *Nova Fifty Seven Minor* (1995)

John Lellenberg, Daniel Stashower and Martin H. Greenberg, editors, *Murder, My Dear Watson: New Tales of Sherlock Holmes* (2002)

Christopher Leppek, *The Surrogate Assassin* (1998)

John T. Lescroart, *Son of Holmes* (1986); *Rasputin's Revenge* (1987)

Arthur H. Lewis, *Copper Beeches* (1971)

Gerald Lientz, *Murder at the Diogenes Club* (1987); *Death at Appledore Towers* (1987); *Crown vs. Doctor Watson* (1988); *Honour of the Yorkshire Light Artillery* (1988); *The Lost Heir* (1988)

Herman A. Litzinger, *Traveling with Sherlock Holmes and Doctor Watson* (1988)

J. Lovisi, *The Grey Nun Legacy* (1992)

Angus Maclaren, editor, *My Dear Watson: Being the Annals of Sherlock Holmes* (1995)

Seppo Makinen and Amartin Powell, *Sherlock Holmes: A Case of Blind Fear* (1996)

Michael Mallory, *The Exploits of the Second Mrs. Watson* (2008)

Lee A. Matthias, *Sherlock Holmes and Harry Houdini in the Adventure of the Pandora Plague* (1981)

Edith Meiser and Frank Giacoia, *Sherlock Holmes* (1988) graphic novel/newspaper comic strips

Ken Methold, *Sherlock Holmes in Australia* (1991)

Nicholas Meyer, *The Seven-Percent Solution* (1974); *The West-End Horror* (1976); *The Canary Trainer* (1993)

Rosemary Michaud, *Sherlock Holmes and the Somerset Hunt* (1992)

Thos. Kent Miller, *Sherlock Holmes: The Great Detective on the Roof of the World* (2008)

Larry Millett, *Sherlock Holmes and the Red Demon* (1996); *Sherlock Holmes and the Ice Palace Murders* (1998); *Sherlock Holmes and the Rune Stone Mystery* (1999); *Sherlock Holmes and the Secret Alliance* (2001); *The Disappearance of Sherlock Holmes* (2002)

Gladys Mitchell, *Watson's Choice* (1955)

Austin Mitchelson and Nicholas Utechin, *The Earthquake Machine* (1976); *The Hellbirds* (1976)

Roberts Morgan, *Spotlight on a Simple Case; or, Wiggins, Who Was That Horse I Saw with You Last Night?* (1959)

Carl Muusmann, *Sherlock Holmes at Elsinore* (1956)

Sena Jeter Naslund, *Sherlock in Love* (1993)

Robert Newman, *The Case of the Baker Street Irregular* (1981)

Jamyang Norbu, *Sherlock Holmes: The Missing Years* (1999); *The Mandala of Sherlock Holmes* (2003)

John North, *Sherlock Holmes and the Arabian Princess* (1990); *Sherlock Holmes and the German Nanny* (1990)

Keith Oatley, *The Case of Emily V* (1993)

Stuart Palmer, *The Adventure of the Marked Man, and One Other* (1973)

Jeremy Paul, *The Secret of Sherlock Holmes* (1989)

Shane Peacock, *Eye of the Crow: The Boy Sherlock Holmes, His First Case* (2007); *Death in the Air: The Boy Sherlock Holmes, His Second Case* (2008)

Gilbert Pearlman, *The Adventure of Sherlock Holmes's Smarter Brother* (1975) based on screenplay

Edmund Pearson, *Sherlock Holmes and the Drood Mystery* (1973)

Glen Petrie, *The Dorking Gap Mystery* (1989); *The Monstrous Regiment* (1990); *The Hampstead Poisonings* (1995)

Rohase Piercy, *My Dearest Holmes* (1988)

David Pine, *The Patient's Eyes: The Dark Beginnings of Sherlock Holmes* (2001)

Byron Preiss, *Son of Sherlock Holmes* (1977) graphic novel

Ellery Queen, *A Study in Terror* (1966) aka *Sherlock Holmes and Jack the Ripper* (1967) based on screenplay by Donald and Derek Ford

Ellery Queen, editor, *The Misadventure of Sherlock Holmes* (1944)

Michael Reaves and John Pelian, *Shadows Over Baker Street* (2003)

Mike Resnick and Martin H. Greenberg, *Sherlock Holmes in Orbit* (1997)

Theodore Riccardi, *The Oriental Casebook of Sherlock Holmes* (2003)

Frank Richardson, *Secret Kingdom* (1905)

Robert Richardson, *The Attwater Firewitch* (1989)

Jerry 'B-P' Riggs, *The Unusual Sherlock Holmes* (2007)

Barrie Roberts, *Sherlock Holmes and the Railway Maniac* (1994); *Sherlock Holmes and the Devil's Grail* (1995); *Sherlock Holmes and the Man from Hell* (1997); *Sherlock Holmes and the Royal Flush* (1998); *Sherlock Holmes and the Harvest of Death* (1999); *Sherlock Holmes and the Crosby Murder* (2002); *Sherlock Holmes and the Rule of Nine* (2004); *Sherlock Holmes and the King's Governess* (2005); *Sherlock Holmes and the American Angels* (2007)

E.C. Roberts, *The Strange Case of the Megatherium Thefts* (1945)

Lora Roberts, *The Affair of the Incognito Tenant: A Mystery with Sherlock Holmes* (2004)

S.C. Roberts, *Christmas Eve* (1936)

Peter Rowland, *The Disappearance of Edwin Drood* (1991)

Peter Ryan, *Black River Emerald* (1987)

Alvin Rymsha, *Sherlock Holmes: The Lost Cases* (2006)

Fred Saberhagen, *The Holmes-Dracula File* (1978) aka *Séance for a Vampire* (1994)

Robert Saffron, *The Demon Device* (1981)

William Seil, *Sherlock Holmes and the Titanic Tragedy* (1996)

Stephen Seitz, *Sherlock Holmes and the Plague of Dracula* (2007)

Allen Sharp, *The Unsolved Case of Sherlock Holmes* (1984); *The Meyringen Papers* (1986); *The Case of the Dancing Bees* (1987); *The Case of the Baffled Policeman* (1989); *The Case of the Devil's Hoofmarks* (1989); *The Case of the Frightened Heiress* (1989); *The Case of the Gentle Conspirators* (1989); *The Case of the Buchanan Curse* (1990); *The Case of the Howling Dog* (1990); *The Case of the Man Who Followed Himself* (1990); *The Case of the Silent Canary* (1990)

Stanley Shaw, *Sherlock Holmes at the 1902 Fifth Test* (1985); *Sherlock Holmes Meets Annie Oakley* (1986)

Floyd Sherrod, *The Secret Adventure of the Thoroughbred Ghost* (1972)

P.C. Shumway, *Sherlock Holmes and the Kiss of Death* (2005)

Sam Siciliano, *The Angel of the Opera: Sherlock Holmes Meets the Phantom of the Opera* (1994)

Dennis O. Smith, *The Adventure of the Purple Hand* (1982); *The Adventure of the Unseen Traveler* (1983); *The Adventure of the Zodiac Plate* (1984); *The Adventure of the Christmas Visitor* (1985); *The Secret of Shoreswood Hall* (1985)

George H. Smith, *The Second War of Worlds* (1978)

Raymond M. Smullyan, *The Chess Mysteries of Sherlock Holmes: Fifty Tantalizing Problems of Chess Detection* (1994)

Jo Soares, *A Samba for Sherlock* (1997)

Brett Spencer, *Sherlock Holmes Draco Draconis* (1996)

Nancy Spinger, *Enola Holmes: The Case of the Missing Marquess* (2007); *Enola Holmes: The Case of the Peculiar Pink Fan* (2008); *Enola Holmes: The Case of the Left-Handed Lady* (2008); *Enola Holmes: The Case of the Bizarre Bouquets* (2008)

Keith Spore, *Death of a Scavenger* (1980)

Vincent Starrett, *The Adventure of the Unique Hamlet* (1920)

Daniel Stashower, *Adventure of the Ectoplasmic Man* (1985)

Arthur M. Stokes, *Checkmate! Goldscheider* (1980)

Richard Stone, *Mysteries Suspended* (1993)

Alan Strockwell, *The Singular Adventures of Sherlock Holmes* (2006)

Julian Symons, *A Three-Pipe Problem* (1975); *How a Hermit Was Disturbed in His Retirement* (1981); *The Kentish Manor Murders* (1988)

John Robert Taylor, *Unopened Casebook of Sherlock Holmes* (1993)

David Thomas, *Sherlock Holmes and the Voice from the Crypt* (2001)

Donald Thomas, *The Secret Cases of Sherlock Holmes* (1998); *Sherlock Holmes and the Running Noose* (2002); *The Execution of Sherlock Holmes: New Adventures of the Great Detective* (2007)

Frank Thomas, *Sherlock Holmes Bridge Detective* (1978); *Sherlock Holmes Bridge Detective Returns* (1978); *Sherlock Holmes and the Golden Bird* (1979); *Sherlock Holmes and the Sacred Sword* (1980); *Sherlock Holmes and the Treasure Train* (1986); *Sherlock*

Holmes and the Masquerade Murders (1986); *The Secret Files of Sherlock Holmes* (2002); *Sherlock Holmes and the Panamanian Girls* (2004); *Sherlock Holmes and the Bizarre Alibi* (2004)

June Thomson, *The Secret Chronicles of Sherlock Holmes* (1990); *Secret Journals of Sherlock Holmes* (1993); *Holmes and Watson* (1995); *Secret Notebooks of Sherlock Holmes* (1997)

Lawrence Toppman and Steven Garland writing as Lawrence Garland, *The Affair of the Unprincipled Publisher* (1983)

Larry Townsend writing as J. Watson, *The Sexual Adventures of Sherlock Holmes* (1971)

M.J. Trow, *The Adventures of Inspector Lestrade* (1985); *Brigade: Further Adventures of Lestrade* (1986); *Lestrade and the Hallowed House* (1987); *Lestrade and the Leviathon* (1988); *Lestrade and the Deadly Game* (1990); *Lestrade and the Ripper* (1988); *Lestrade and the Brother of Death* (1988); *Lestrade and the Guardian Angel* (1990); *Lestrade and the Gift of the Prince* (1991); *Lestrade and the Dead Man's Hand* (2000); *Lestrade and the Mirror of Murder* (2001); *Lestrade and the Devil's Own* (2001); *Lestrade and the Kiss of Horus* (2001)

Mark Twain, *A Double-Barreled Detective Story* (1902)

Nicholas Utechin, *Sherlock Holmes at Oxford* (1977)

Cay van Ash, *Ten Years Beyond Baker Street* (1984)

Alan Vanneman, *Sherlock Holmes and the Giant Rat of Sumatra* (2002)

Ralph E. Vaughan, *Sherlock Holmes in the Adventure of the Ancient Gods* (1990); *The Dreaming Detective* (1991)

Daniel D. Victor, *The Seventh Bullet: A Holmes & Watson American Adventure* (1992)

Ian Walker, *The Singular Case of the Duplicate Holmes* (1994)

Ray Walsh, *The Mycroft Memoranda* (1985)

Alfred C. Ward, *Sherlock Holmes vs. John Thorndyke and Reginald Fortune* (1982)

William Watson, *Watson's Sampler: The Lost Casebook of Sherlock Holmes* (2007)

Manly Wade Wellman and Wade Wellman, *Sherlock Holmes's War of the Worlds* (1975)

Robert Weverka, *Murder by Decree* (1979) based on screenplay by John Hopkins

Ronald C. Weyman, *Sherlock Holmes and the Mark of the Beast* (1989); *Sherlock Holmes Travels in the Canadian West* (1991)

Gerard Williams, *Dr. Mortimer and the Aldgate Mystery* (2001); *Dr. Mortimer and the Barking Man* (2001)

Richard Wincor, *Sherlock Holmes in Tibet* (1968)

Sebastian Wolfe, editor, *The Misadventures of Sherlock Holmes* (1991)

Wayne Worcester, *The Monster of St. Marylebone* (1999); *The Jewel of Covent Garden* (2000)

Cheng Ziaoqinq, *Sherlock in Shanghai: Stories of Crime and Detection* (2006)

Biography

William Baring-Gould, *Sherlock Holmes of Baker Street* (1995)

Michael Hardwick, *Sherlock Holmes: My Life in Crime* (1986)

Michael Harrison, *I, Sherlock Holmes* (1977)

CYRIL CONNOLLY
Drawing Room Mystery

English writer and critic Cyril Connolly (1903–1974) attended St. Cyprian's School with George Orwell and Cecil Beaton. On the staff of *New Statesman,* he traveled, wrote one novel and turned out numerous essays and an autobiography. He was married three times.

Poet and archaeologist Peter Levi (1931–2000) completed Connolly's last fiction manuscript.

Posthumous Collaboration

Peter Levi, *Shade Those Laurels* (1991)

JOHN CREASEY
A Dandy

John Creasey (1908–1973) wrote some sixty adventures of Richard Rollison, an upper-class detective known as The Toff, and his gentleman's gentleman, Rolly. Creasey also wrote as J. (as in John) J. (as in his wife, Joan) Mar (as in son Martin) ric (as in son Richard). The hero was police Superintendent George Gideon. Creasey also wrote Department Z stories and The Baron stories, romances and Westerns and more. He produced a whopping 562 novels under twenty-eight names in a career that lasted forty years.

For those who still couldn't get enough of Creasey's characters, William Vivian Butler completed one Creasey Toff manuscript and added a handful of Gideon books to the canon.

Original Gideon Works as by J.J. Marric

Gideon's Day (1955)
Gideon's Week (1956)
Gideon's Night (1957)
Gideon's Month (1958)
Gideon's Staff (1959)
Gideon's Risk (1960)
Gideon's Fire (1961)
Gideon's March (1962)
Gideon's Ride (1963)
Gideon's Vote (1964)
Gideon's Lot (1965)

Gideon's Badge (1966)
Gideon's Wrath (1967)
Gideon's River (1968)
Gideon's Power (1969)
Gideon's Sport (1970)
Gideon's Art (1971)
Gideon's Men (1972)
Gideon's Press (1973)
Gideon's Fog (1975)
Gideon's Drive (1976)

Gideon Pastiches

William Vivian Butler, *Gideon's Force* (1978); *Gideon's Law* (1981); *Gideon's Way* (1983); *Gideon's Raid* (1986); *Gideon's Fear* (1990)

Original Toff Works as by John Creasey

Introducing the Toff (1938)
The Toff Steps Out (1939)
Here Comes the Toff! (1940)
The Toff Breaks In (1940)
Salute the Toff (1941)
The Toff Proceeds (1941)
The Toff Goes to Market (1942)
The Toff Is Back (1942)
The Toff Among the Millions (1943)
Accuse the Toff (1943)
The Toff and the Curate (1944)
The Toff and the Great Illusion (1944)
Feathers for the Toff (1945)
The Toff and the Lady (1946)
The Toff on Ice (1946) aka *Poison for the Toff* (1965)
Hammer the Toff (1947)
The Toff in Town (1948)
The Toff Takes Shares (1948)
The Toff and Old Harry (1949)
The Toff on Board (1949)
Fool the Toff (1950)
Kill the Toff (1950)
A Knife for the Toff (1951)
The Toff Goes Gay (1951)
The Toff Down Under (1953)
The Toff at Butlin's (1954)
The Toff at the Fair (1954)

A Six for the Toff (1955)
The Toff and the Deep Blue Sea (1955)
Make-Up for the Toff (1956)
The Toff in New York (1956)
Model for the Toff (1957)
The Toff on Fire (1957)
The Toff and the Stolen Tresses (1958)
The Toff on the Farm (1958)
Double for the Toff (1959)
The Toff and the Runaway Bride (1959)
The Rocket for the Toff (1960)
The Toff and the Kidnapped Child (1960)
Follow the Toff (1961)
The Toff and the Teds (1961) aka *The Toff and the Toughs*
A Doll for the Toff (1963)
Leave It to the Toff (1963)
The Toff and the Spider (1965)
The Toff in Wax (1966)
A Bundle for the Toff (1967)
Stars for the Toff (1968)
The Toff and the Golden Boy (1969)
The Toff and the Fallen Angels (1970)
Vote for the Toff (1971)
The Toff and the Trip-Trip-Triplets (1972)
The Toff and the Terrified Taxman (1973)
The Toff and the Sleepy Cowboy (1974)
The Toff and the Crooked Copper (1977)

Posthumous Toff Collaboration

William Vivian Butler, *The Toff and the Dead Man's Finger* (1978)

ELIZABETH DALY

Henry and Clara Gamadge

Elizabeth Daly (1878–1967) wrote cozy mysteries featuring bibliophile Henry Gamadge and, peripherally, his wife, Clara. The daughter of a New York Supreme Court justice, the author had a master's degree from Columbia University and tutored French and English at Bryn Mawr College. She published her first novel when she was sixty-two, and received an Edgar Award from the Mystery Writers of America.

The author's niece, Eleanor Boylan, a longtime Massachusetts resident and experienced short story writer, picked up the series but featured Clara Gamadge. Her first book was nominated for an Agatha Award for Best First Novel.

Original Works

Unexpected Night (1940)
Deadly Nightshade (1940)
Murders in Volume 2 (1941)
The House Without the Door (1942)
Nothing Can Rescue Me (1943)
Evidence of Things Seen (1943)
Arrow Pointing Nowhere (1944)
The Book of the Dead (1944)

Any Shape or Form (1945)
Somewhere in the House (1946)
The Wrong Way Down (1946)
Night Walk (1947)
The Book of the Lion (1948)
And Dangerous to Know (1949)
Death and Letters (1950)
The Book of the Crime (1951)

Pastiches

Eleanor Boylan, *Working Murder* (1989); *Murder Observed* (1990); *Murder Machree* (1992); *Pushing Murder* (1993); *Murder Crossed* (1996)

AUGUST DERLETH

Solar Pons

Wisconsinite August Derleth (1909–1971) created an obvious takeoff on Sherlock Holmes with his series character Solar Pons of Praed Street. Pons with his chronicler Doctor Lyndon Parker solved crimes in and around London.

Derleth wrote historical fiction in a variety of genres, including fantasy and horror. He was also a publisher; with Donald Wandrei he established Arkham House. Derleth was responsible for bringing a lot of H.P. Lovecraft's work into print. Derleth, in fact, energetically expanded and contributed to Lovecraft's shared universe, the Cthulhu Mythos.

Basil Copper (b. 1924), English journalist and writer of fantasy and horror, continued the Solar Pons series through an arrangement with Derleth's estate.

Original Works

In Re: Sherlock Holmes (1945) aka *Regarding Sherlock Holmes* aka *The Adventures of Solar Pons*, short stories
Three Problems for Solar Pons (1952) short stories

Return of Solar Pons (1958) short stories
Reminiscences of Solar Pons (1961)
The Casebook of Solar Pons (1965) short stories
Praed Street Papers (1965) short stories
Mr. Fairlie's Final Journey (1968)

Adventure of the Unique Dickensians (1968) short stories
Praed Street Dossier (1968) short stories
Chronicles of Solar Pons (1973) short stories

Adventures of the Orient Express (1965) aka *The Chronicles of Solar Pons* (1973) short stories
The Memoirs of Solar Pons (1951) short stories

Solar Pons Pastiches

Basil Copper, *The Dossier of Solar Pons* (1979) short stories; *Further Adventures of Solar Pons* (1979) short stories; *Secret Files of Solar Pons* (1979) short stories; *The Uncollected Cases of Solar Pons* (1980) short stories; *Recollections of Solar Pons* (1995) short stories; *Solar Pons and the Devil's Claw* (2004) aka *Solar Pons versus the Devil's Claw*; *The Final Cases of Solar Pons* (2005) short stories

R. AUSTIN FREEMAN
Doctor Thorndyke

London-born R. Austin Freeman (1862–1943) created the fictional forensics detective John Thorndyke. As he tackles a variety of crimes, Thorndyke is often assisted by his narror, Christopher Jervis, and his laboratory technician, Nathaniel Polton.

Freeman studied medicine at Middlesex Hospital. He was known for his skill with the inverted detective story in which the criminal is known and the case is largely about the pursuit. Freeman was in Colonial Service in Accra, Gold Coast (now Ghana), until disabled by blackwater fever. He turned to writing and sold his first story, *The Red Thumb Mark*, in 1907.

Four writers contributed later pastiches.

Original Doctor Thorndyke Works

The Red Thumb Mark (1907)
The Eye of Osiris (1911)
The Mystery of 31, New Inn (1912)
A Silent Witness (1914)
Helen Vardon's Confession (1922)
The Cat's Eye (1923)
The Mystery of Angelina Frood (1924)
The Shadow of the Wolf (1925)
The D'Arblay Mystery (1926)
A Certain Dr. Thorndyke (1927)
As a Thief in the Night (1928)

Mr. Pottermack's Oversight (1930)
Pontifex, Son and Thorndyke (1931)
When Rogues Fall Out (1932)
Dr. Thorndyke Intervenes (1933)
For the Defence: Dr. Thorndyke (1934)
The Penrose Mystery (1936)
Felo de se? (1937)
The Stoneware Monkey (1938)
Mr. Polton Explains (1940)
The Jacob Street Mystery (1942)

Doctor Thorndyke Pastiches

John H. Dircks, *Doctor Thorndyke's Dilemma* (1974)
Norman Donaldson, *Goodbye, Doctor Thorndyke* (1972)
Carlo Fruttero and Franco Lucentini, *The D Case: Or, The Truth About the Mystery of Edwin Drood* (1993)

EMILE GABORIAU

Monsieur Lecoq

French author Emile Gaboriau (1832–1873) was a pioneer of the amateur detective novel, and particularly of the detail-oriented, serious crime solver. His character Monsieur Lecoq, who first appeared in *L'Affaire Lerouge* (1866), was based on a real-life criminal turned-policeman. Lecoq was analytical to the extreme, able to describe a man from the shoeprints he left in the snow. The son of a public official, Gaboriau served with the Fifth Regiment as an infantryman from 1851 to 1853. He was a journalist and columnist in Paris. As secretary and assistant, he ghost wrote material for Paul Feval, a newspaper editor, dramatists and author of criminal romances.

Fortune Du Boisgobey (1821–1891) and others added to the series.

Original Works

L'Affaire Lerouge (1866) aka *The Lerouge Case*

Le Crime d'Orcival (1867) aka *The Mystery of Orcival* aka *Crime at Orcival*

Le Dossier No. 113 (1867) aka *File No. 113, Dossier No. 113* aka *The Blackmailers*

Les Esclaves des Paris (1868) aka *The Slaves of Paris*

Monsieur Lecoq (1869)

Le Petit Vieux des Batingoles (1876) includes "Une Disparition," aka *The Little Old Man of Batignole*, includes "A Disappearance"

Monsieur Lecoq Pastiches

Fortune du Boisgobey, *La Vieillesse de Monsieur Lecoq* (1878) aka *The Old Age of Monsieur Lecoq*

William Busnach and Henri Chabrillat, *La Fille de M. Lecoq* (1886) aka *The Daughter of Monsieur Lecoq*

J. Kéry, *Le Dernier Dossier de M. Lecoq* (1952) aka *Monsieur Lecoq's Last File*

Ernest A. Young, *File No. 114* (1886)

ERLE STANLEY GARDNER

Perry Mason

Erle Stanley Gardner (1889–1970) wrote for the pulp fiction magazines under a variety of pseudonyms. His first Perry Mason mystery, *The Case of the Velvet Claws*, is very much in the hardboiled tradition. While he had other successful book series, including the Donald Lam and Bertha Cool books written as A.A. Fair, Mason became Gardner's most popular hero, and appeared in *The Saturday Evening Post* serials, motion pictures, radio, comic books, comic strips and television (featuring Raymond Burr).

Born in Malden, Mass., Gardner's mining engineer/farmer father moved the family to Oregon and later to California. A somewhat rebellious youth, Gardner mellowed and read law and was admitted to the California bar in 1911. His practice was not immediately successful, so he began in the 1920s to write stories for *Black Mask* and other fiction magazines, developing running characters such as Sidney Zoom and Lester Leith. Gardner wrote remarkably quickly, more so with the later Mason courtroom thrillers, which he dictated to a secretary. Gardner once said of his lawyer-hero, "The character I am trying to create for him is that of a fighter who is possessed of infinite patience."

Canada-born Thomas Chastain (1921–1994), who created his own J.T. Spanner detective series and *Who Killed the Robins Family?*, wrote two Mason sequels.

Original Mysteries

The Case of the Velvet Claws (1933)
The Case of the Sulky Girl (1934)
The Case of the Lucky Legs (1934)
The Case of the Howling Dog (1934)
The Case of the Curious Bride (1934)
The Case of the Counterfeit Eye (1935)
The Case of the Caretaker's Cat (1936)
The Case of the Sleepwalker's Niece (1936)
The Case of the Stuttering Bishop (1937)
The Case of the Dangerous Dowager (1937)
The Case of the Lame Canary (1937)
The Case of the Substitute Face (1938)
The Case of the Shoplifter's Shoe (1938)
The Case of the Perjured Parrot (1939)
The Case of the Rolling Bones (1939)
The Case of the Baited Hook (1940)
The Case of the Silent Partner (1941)
The Case of the Haunted Husband (1941)
The Case of the Empty Tin (1941)
The Case of the Drowning Duck (1942)
The Case of the Careless Kitten (1942)
The Case of the Buried Clock (1943)
The Case of the Drowsy Mosquito (1943)
The Case of the Crooked Candle (1944)
The Case of the Black-Eyed Blonde (1944)
The Case of the Golddigger's Purse (1945)
The Case of the Half-Wakened Wife (1945)
The Case of the Borrowed Brunette (1946)
The Case of the Fan Dancer's Horse (1947)
The Case of the Lazy Lover (1947)
The Case of the Lonely Heiress (1948)
The Case of the Vagabond Virgin (1948)
Case of the Dubious Bridegroom (1949)

The Case of the Cautious Coquette (1949)
The Case of the Negligent Nymph (1950)
The Case of the One-Eyed Witness (1950)
The Case of the Fiery Fingers (1951)
The Case of the Angry Mourner (1951)
The Case of the Moth-Eaten Mink (1952)
The Case of the Grinning Gorilla (1952)
The Case of the Hesitant Hostess (1953)
The Case of the Green-Eyed Sister (1953)
The Case of the Fugitive Nurse (1954)
The Case of the Runaway Corpse (1954)
The Case of the Restless Redhead (1954)
The Case of the Glamorous Ghost (1955)
The Case of the Sun Bather's Diary (1955)
The Case of the Nervous Accomplice (1955)
The Case of the Terrified Typist (1956)
The Case of the Demure Defendant (1956)
 aka *The Case of the Missing Poison*
The Case of the Gilded Lily (1956)
The Case of the Lucky Loser (1957)
The Case of the Screaming Woman (1957)
The Case of the Daring Decoy (1957)
The Case of the Long-Legged Models
 (1958) aka *The Case of the Dead Man's Daughters*
The Case of the Foot-Loose Doll (1958)
The Case of the Calendar Girl (1958)
The Case of the Deadly Toy (1959) aka
 The Case of the Greedy Grandpa
The Case of the Mythical Monkeys (1959)
The Case of the Singing Skirt (1959)
The Case of the Waylaid Wolf (1960)
The Case of the Duplicate Daughter (1960)

The Case of the Shapely Shadow (1960)
The Case of the Spurious Spinster (1961)
The Case of the Bigamous Spouse (1961)
The Case of the Reluctant Model (1962)
The Case of the Blonde Bonanza (1962)
The Case of the Ice-Cold Hands (1962)
The Case of the Mischievous Doll (1963)
The Case of the Stepdaughter's Secret (1963)
The Case of the Amorous Aunt (1963)
The Case of the Daring Divorcee (1964)
The Case of the Phantom Fortune (1964)

The Case of the Horrified Heirs (1964)
The Case of the Troubled Trustee (1965)
The Case of the Beautiful Beggar (1965)
The Case of the Worried Waitress (1966)
The Case of the Queenly Contestant (1967)
The Case of the Careless Cupid (1968)
The Case of the Fabulous Fake (1969)
The Case of the Fenced-In Woman (1972)
The Case of the Postponed Murder (1973)
Four Cases of Murder (1989) comic strips

Perry Mason Pastiches

Thomas Chastain, *The Case of the Burning Bequest* (1989); *The Case of Too Many Murders* (1990)

BRUCE GRAEME

Blackshirt

The gentleman crook Blackshirt first appeared in a short story in *Thriller Weekly*. Blackshirt is really Richard Verrell, a best-selling crime writer. Police often ask his help in dealing with rampant crime.

British writer Graham M. Jeffries (1900–1982) created the series, using the penname Bruce Graeme. Early short stories formed the book *Blackshirt* (1925). Some subsequent books were about Blackshirt's son, Lord Blackshirt. Blackshirt appeared in illustrated form in *Super Detective Library* in the 1950s. Stories of Monsieur Blackshirt, Blackshirt's 16th century ancestor, came out under the byline David Graeme, purportedly a cousin of Bruce, but actually Graham Jeffries still. Jeffries had several other pennames and crime or detective series.

Graeme's son Roderic Jeffries (b. 1926 in London), a seaman and lawyer who settled in Mallorca, took over the writing in 1952, under the name Roderick Graeme.

Original Blackshirt Works by Bruce Graeme

Blackshirt (1925)
The Return of Blackshirt (1927)
Blackshirt Again (1929) aka *Adventure of Blackshirt*
Alias Blackshirt (1932)
Blackshirt the Audacious (1935)
Blackshirt the Adventurer (1936)
Blackshirt Takes a Hand (1937)

Blackshirt, Counter-Spy (1938)
Blackshirt Interferes (1939)
Blackshirt Strikes Back (1940)
Son of Blackshirt (1941)
Lord Blackshirt: The Son of Blackshirt Carries On (1942)
Calling Lord Blackshirt (1943)

Original Monsieur Blackshirt Works by David Graeme

Monsieur Blackshirt (1933)
Vengeance of Monsieur Blackshirt (1934)
Sword of Monsieur Blackshirt (1936)

Inn of Thirteen Swords (1938)
The Drum Beats Red (1963)

Blackshirt Pastiches by Roderic Graeme

Concerning Blackshirt (1952)
Blackshirt Wins the Trick (1953)
Blackshirt Passes By (1953)
Salute to Blackshirt (1954)
Amazing Mister Blackshirt (1955)
Blackshirt Meets the Lady (1956)
Blackshirt Helps Himself (1958)
Double for Blackshirt (1958)
Blackshirt Sets the Pace (1959)
Blackshirt Sees It Through (1960)
Blackshirt Finds Trouble (1961)
Blackshirt Takes the Trail (1962)
Call for Blackshirt (1963)
Blackshirt on the Spot (1963)
Blackshirt Saves the Day (1964)
Danger for Blackshirt (1965)
Blackshirt at Large (1966)
Blackshirt in Peril (1967)
Blackshirt Stirs Things Up (1969)

PATRICK HAMILTON

Gorse

Director Alfred Hitchcock turned stories by Patrick Hamilton (1904–1962) into the successful films *Gaslight* (1940) and *Rope* (1948). Hamilton's trio of books about Ernest Ralph Gorse depict a ruthless swindler.

The follow-up by Allan Prior (1922–2006), founding writer of the BBC-TV series *Z Cars*, is based on a BBC production derived from Hamilton's second book.

Original Gorse Works

The West Pier (1952)
Mr. Stimpson and Mr. Gorse (1953)

Unknown Assailant (1955)

Gorse Pastiche

Allan Prior, *The Charmer* (1987)

DASHIELL HAMMETT

Op

Samuel Dashiell Hammett (1894–1961) created Sam Spade, the Continental Op and Nick and Nora Charles — icons of American hardboiled detective fiction. He wrote for *Black Mask* and other pulp fiction magazines before he turned to novels. The iconic Sam Spade appeared in the novel *The Maltese Falcon* and in three short stories ("A Man Called Spade," *American Magazine*, July 1932; "Too Many Have Lived," *American Magazine*, October 1932; and "They Can Only Hang You Once," *Collier's*, Nov. 19, 1932) and is forever remembered in Humphrey Bogart's depiction in the 1941 motion picture directed by John Huston.

Born in rural Maryland, Hammett grew up in Philadelphia and Baltimore. He was an operative for Pinkerton's from 1915 to 1921, with a break for World War I service in the Ambulance Corps. He spent most of the war in the hospital, suffering from flu and tuberculosis. During the end of his life, in the company of playwright Lillian Hellman, he was a political activist for leftist causes. He again joined the ambulance corps for World War II duty. He was blacklisted during the McCarthy era.

Hammett or his editors often reshaped the author's original pulp magazine texts for later book publication. His original manuscripts were used for Library of America's 2001 collection, *Crime Stories and Other Writings*, ditto Vince Emery's *Lost Stories*.

Multi-Edgar winning crime writer Joe Gores (b. 1931), creator of the Daniel Kearney Associates series and author of numerous screenplays, wrote a *Maltese Falcon* pastiche in cooperation with Hammett heirs. "Gores slots his prequel directly into the original by having Spade set up his own shop after resigning from the Continental Detective Agency upon finishing the 'Flitcraft case' — a case Spade mentions in the early pages of *Falcon*. There are many such nuggets of connection and homage to Falcon in here," wrote Roger K. Miller in the *National Post*. Gores explained to reporter Nathalie Atkinson in the same publication that he was taken by Hammett biographer Rick Layman's suggestion that *The Maltese Falcon* was one of the first existential novels to be published in the United States. "These people come from nowhere: You read the book, you know who they are at that moment. I wanted to know more about them. How did Sam Spade come to the point where when the Fat Man shows up, he could say, 'You have to deal with me now, because this is my town.' How did San Francisco get to be Sam Spade's town?" Thus the new book.

"'I had a different style to write in,' Gores says over a club sandwich and an order of well-done fries. 'My own style is looser, more adjectives, more action. And I figured the only way the book would work would be if I could match Hammett's writing style,'" according to *San Francisco Chronicle* staff writer Edward Guthmann.

Gores had earlier written a novel, *Hammett* (1975), based on the crime writer himself.

Posthumous Restorations

Vince Emery, editor, *Lost Stories* (2005)

Steven Marcus, editor, *Crime Stories and Other Writings* (2001)

Original Sam Spade Works

The Maltese Falcon (1930)   *A Man Called Spade* (1944)

Pastiche

Joe Gores, *Spade & Archer: The Prequel to Dashiell Hammett's The Maltese Falcon* (2009)

THOMAS W. HANSHEW

Man of Forty Faces

Thomas W. Hanshew (1857–1914), a transplanted American living in England, wrote dime novel adventures for *All-Story Weekly* and other periodicals. The character Cleek was a bold criminal with royal blood. He often gave notice to the police of his criminal plans — generating his own suspense. Cleek ends his bad ways when he meets Ailsa Lorne. He reforms, thanks to the generosity of Superintendent Maverick Narokom, and becomes a consulting detective. Dollops the Cockney lad often helps.

After Hanshew's death, his wife Mary and daughter Hazel wrote more Hamilton Cleek stories.

Original Cleek Works

Man of the Forty Faces (1910) aka *Cleek, the Master Detective* aka *Cleek, the Man of Forty Faces* short stories
Cleek of Scotland Yard (1914) aka *The Affair of the Man Who Vanished* short stories
Cleek's Greatest Riddles (1916) aka *Cleek's Government Cases* short stories

Cleek Pastiches

Mary E. Hanshew and Hazel Phillips Hanshew, *The Riddle of the Night: Being the Record of a Singular Adventure of That Remarkable Detective Genius, Hamilton Cleek, the Man of the Forty Faces, Once Known to the Police as the Vanishing Cracksman* (1915); *Riddle of the Purple Emperor* (1916)

Hazel Phillips Hanshew writing as Mary E. Henshew, *Frozen Flame* (1920) aka *Riddle of the Frozen Flame*; *Riddle of the Mysterious Light* (1921); *House of Discord* (1922) aka *Riddle of the Spinning Wheel*; *Amber Junk* (1924) aka *Riddle of the Amber Ship*; *House of the Seven Keys* (1925)

Hazel Phillips Hanshew, *Riddle of the Winged Death* (1931); *Murder in the Hotel* (1932)

CHESTER HIMES
The Harlem beat

Missouri-born Chester Himes (1909–1984) was an African-American writer known for his Harlem novels featuring two police detectives, Coffin Ed Johnson and Gravedigger Jones. His writing career began inauspiciously while he was in Ohio Penitentiary, convicted of armed robbery. His short stories appeared in national magazines including Esquire. Released from prison in 1936, he lived in Los Angeles and France by the 1950s, where he received the Grand Prix de Litterature Policière in 1958.

Yesterday Will Make You Cry restores Himes material cut or rearranged for the original publication, under the title *Cast the First Stone* (1952). The novel is based on an actual 1930 prison fire at Ohio Penitentiary.

Posthumous Restoration
Yesterday Will Make You Cry (1999)

EDWARD D. HOCH
Nick Velvet

Breaking a self-stated rule for this book, one short story author must be included, for the sheer enormity of his output (nearly 950 stories), not to mention its quality. Edward D. Hoch (1930–2008), a native of Rochester, New York, began writing in 1955. He mastered the short form. His work impressed Frederick Dannay, half the Ellery Queen trio and editor of *Ellery Queen Mystery Magazine*, who began to purchase Hoch stories. Hoch wrote for every issue of the magazine from May 1973 until his death (announced in its June 2008 issue), and until the March/April 2009 issue (which carried a reprint). His stories featured many series characters. Nick Velvet, to mention one continuing hero, stole on assignment — but only if the object was worthless. Several collections of Hoch stories appeared over the years.

Hoch left a story unfinished at his death. *EQMM*'s columnist and mystery writer Jon L. Breen completed the tale.

Posthumous Collaboration with Jon L. Breen
"Handel and Gretel," *Ellery Queen Mystery Magazine*, November 2008.

E.W. HORNUNG

The Amateur Cracksman

Ernest William Hornung (1866–1921) was married to Constance Doyle, sister of Sir Arthur Conan Doyle. Hornung's first story of the gentleman thief and master of disguise appeared in *Cassell's Magazine* in 1898. Raffles' close friend and accomplice Bunny Manders narrates the stories.

Barry Perowne (actually Philip Atkey) (1908–1985) wrote the most sequels. John Kendrick Bangs (1862–1922) introduced Raffles' grandson and Sherlock Holmes's son (by way of Raffles' daughter Marjorie), Raffle Holmes. Graham Greene, Charles Sansom and Eugene W. Presbrey wrote Raffles plays, which are not listed.

Original Raffles Works

The Amateur Cracksman (1899) aka Raffles, *The Amateur Cracksman* (1906) short stories
The Black Mask (1901) aka *Raffles: Further Adventures of the Amateur Cracksman* (1901) short stories

A Thief in the Night (1905)
Mr. Justice Raffles (1909)
The Complete Short Stories of Raffles, The Amateur Cracksman (1984)

Raffles Pastiches

John Kendrick Bangs, *Mrs. Raffles* (1905) short stories; *R. Raffles & Company* (1906)
Philip Atkey as Barry Perowne, *Raffles After Dark* (1933) aka *The Return of Raffles* (1933) short stories; *Raffles in Pursuit* (1934) short stories; *Raffles Under Sentence* (1936) short stories; *She Married Raffles* (1936); *Raffles' Crime in Gibraltar* (1937) aka *They Hang Them in Gibraltar* (1939); *The A.R.P. Mystery* (1939); *Raffles and the Key Man* (1940); *Raffles Revisited* (1974) short stories; *Raffles of the Albany* (1976); *Raffles of the M.C.C.* (1979) short stories
Dolan F. Barber as David Fletcher, *Raffles* (1977)
Adam Corres, *Raffles and the Match-Fixing Syndicate* (2008)
Hugh Kingsmith, *The Ruby of Khitmandu* (1932)
Peter Tremayne, *The Return of Raffles* (1981)

DELFRIED KAUFMANN

Jerry Cotton's mouthpiece

Delfried Kaufmann's name won't be found on a library or bookstore shelf. While an employee of a German company that made laundry detergent, he wrote a crime novel featuring FBI agent Jerry Cotton. That was in 1954, for the publisher Bastei-Lübbe. It was titled *Ich suchte den Gangster-Chef* (*I Was Looking for the Gangster-*

Boss), part of the Bastei Kriminalroman series. Jerry Cotton was identified as author with *Ich jagte den Dimanten-Hai* (*I Hunted Down the Diamond-Shark*) in 1956.

"These books became immensely popular around the world — so popular, that after Kaufmann grew tired of working on the series, no fewer than 65 other authors were enlisted (anonymously) to continue Cotton's adventures through short stories and scripts for both the movies and television," according to George M. Demko.

The crime stories were translated into nineteen languages. They sold some 800 million copies. There were Jerry Cotton motion pictures in the 1960s, made for a German audience. There have been some 2,500 stories and many novelettes.

The German Perry Rhodan science fiction series has had a similarly long life. However, its creators, K.H. Scheer and Clark Darlton, from the start intended to engage outside writers.

ROSS MACDONALD

Lew Archer

Born in California, Kenneth Millar (1915–1983) grew up in Kitchener, Ontario, Canada. A graduate of the University of Michigan with a Ph.D. in literature, Millar wrote his first novel, *Dark Tunnel*, in 1944. His wife, Margaret Millar, was also a mystery writer. Millar used the name John Macdonald to create his own literary identity, changed it to John Ross Macdonald and, finally, Ross Macdonald, so as not to be confused with another popular writer, John D. MacDonald. His private eye series character, Lew Archer, appeared steadily until the writer's death.

Two Italian writers included Archer in their 1993 novel.

Original Lew Archer Works

The Moving Target (1949)
The Drowning Pool (1950)
The Way Some People Die (1951)
The Ivory Grin (1952) aka *Marked for Murder*
Find a Victim (1954)
The Barbarous Coast (1956)
The Doomsters (1958)
The Galton Case (1959)
The Wycherly Woman (1961)
The Zebra-Striped Hearse (1962)
The Chill (1964)
The Far Side of the Dollar (1965)
Black Money (1966)

The Instant Enemy (1968)
The Goodbye Look (1969)
The Underground Man (1971)
Sleeping Beauty (1973)
The Blue Hammer (1976)
The Name is Archer (1977) short stories
Strangers in Town: Three Newly Discovered Mysteries (2001) including "Strangers in Town" and "The Angry Man"
The Archer Files: The Complete Short Stories of Lew Archer, Private Investigator (2007)

Pastiche

Carlo Fruttero and Franco Lucentini, *The D Case: or, The Truth About the Mystery of Edwin Drood* (1993)

STUART PALMER

Miss Withers

Mystery writer Stuart Palmer (1905–1968), born in Wisconsin, wrote screenplays as well as mystery novels featuring Hildegarde Withers, an unmarried schoolteacher. Palmer wrote one book with Craig Rice, feathering together their respective series characters.

Following Palmer's death, Fletcher Flora completed the last novel.

Original Miss Withers Works

The Penguin Pool Murder (1931)
Murder on the Blackboard (1932)
The Puzzle of the Pepper Tree (1934)
The Puzzle of the Silver Persian (1934)
The Puzzle of the Red Stallion (1935)
The Puzzle of the Blue Banderilla (1937)
Miss Withers Regrets (1941)
The Puzzle of the Happy Hooligan (1941)

The Riddles of Hildegarde Withers (1947)
    short stories
Four Lost Ladies (1949)
The Green Ace (1950)
The Monkey Murder (1951)
Nipped in the Bud (1951)
Cold Poison (1954)
The People Vs. Withers and Malone (1963)
    written with Craig Rice

Posthumous Collaboration

Fletcher Flora, *Hildegarde Withers Makes the Scene* (1969)

ELLERY QUEEN

Ellery Queen

Cousins Frederic Dannay (1905–1982) and Manfred Lee (1905–1971) wrote mysteries featuring Ellery Queen, and used the Ellery Queen byline on the short stories and books. They co-founded the venerable *Ellery Queen's Mystery Magazine* and through various anthologies and essays did considerable work to promote the mystery genre. They hired ghost writers for later books.

Short story writers Norma Schier (she wrote pastiches of several classic detectives) and Julian Symons wrote new Ellery Queen short stories during Dannay's lifetime, and James Holding's blatant Ellery Queen, Jr., takeoffs first appeared in *EQMM*.

Original Ellery Queen Works

The Roman Hat Mystery (1929)
The French Powder Mystery (1930)
The Dutch Shoe Mystery (1931)
The Greek Coffin Mystery (1932)
The Egyptian Cross Mystery (1932)
The American Gun Mystery (1933)
The Siamese Twin Mystery (1933)
The Chinese Orange Mystery (1934)
The Adventures of Ellery Queen (1934) short stories
The Spanish Cape Mystery (1935)
Halfway House (1936)
The Door Between (1937)
The Devil to Pay (1938)
The Four of Hearts (1938)
The Dragon's Teeth (1939) aka *The Virgin Heiresses*
The New Adventures of Ellery Queen (1940) short stories
Calamity Town (1942)
There Was an Old Woman (1943)
The Murderer Is a Fox (1945)
The Case Book of Ellery Queen (1945) short stories
Ten Days' Wonder (1948)
Cat of Many Tails (1949)
Double, Double (1950)
The Origin of Evil (1951)
The King Is Dead (1952)
Calendar of Crime (1952) short stories
The Scarlet Letters (1953)
QBI—Queen's Bureau of Investigation (1955) short stories
Inspector Queen's Own Case (1956)
The Finishing Stroke (1958)
The Player on the Other Side (1963) with Theodore Sturgeon
And on the Eighth Day (1964) with Avram Davidson
The Fourth Side of the Triangle (1965) with Avram Davidson
A Study in Terror (1966) film novelization
Face to Face (1967)
The House of Brass (1968) with Avram Davidson
The Last Woman in His Life (1970)
A Fine and Private Place (1971)
The Lamp of God (1951)
Queens Full (1966) short stories
QED—Queen's Experiments in Detection (1968) short stories
The Best of Ellery Queen (1985) includes one previously uncollected story
The Tragedy of Errors (1999) includes one unpublished synopsis by Dannay

Ghost-written Ellery Queen, Jr., Works

Samuel Duff McCoy, Frank Belknap Long or James Clark Carlisle, Jr.
The Black Dog Mystery (1941)
The Golden Eagle Mystery (1942)
The Green Turtle Mystery (1944)
The Red Chipmunk Mystery (1946)
The Brown Fox Mystery (1948)
The White Elephant Mystery (1950)
The Yellow Cat Mystery (1952)
The Blue Herring Mystery (1954)
The Mystery of the Merry Magician (1954)
The Mystery of the Vanished Victim (1954)
The Purple Bird Mystery (1966)

Ellery Queen Pastiches

Norma Schier, *The Anagram Detectives* (1979) includes "The Adventure of the Solitary Bride"
Julian Symons, *The Great Detectives: Seven Criminal Investigations* (1981)

Pastiches in Leroy King Juvenile Series

James Holding, *The Norwegian Apple Mystery* (1960); *The African Fish Mystery* (1961); *The Italian Tile Mystery* (1961); *The Hong Kong Jewel Mystery* (1963); *The Zanzibar Shirt Mystery* (1963); *The Tahitian Powder Box Mystery* (1964); *The Japanese Card Mystery* (1965); *The New Zealand Bird Mystery* (1967); *The Philippine Key Mystery* (1968); *The Borneo Snapshot Mystery* (1972)

CRAIG RICE

John J. Malone

Craig Rice (1908–1975) was the first mystery writer to grace *Time* magazine's cover, Jan. 28, 1946. Her series character John J. Malone is an attorney who favors a screwball drink, and sometimes is involved with a screwball pair, press agent Jake Justis and his socialite wife Helen. To the dismay of Homicide Captain Daniel Von Flanagan, they manage to solve a number of murder cases.

Born Georgiana Ann Craig, the author worked in radio and public relations in Chicago, finally finding a publisher for her fiction with *Eight Faces at Three* in 1939. She ghostwrote crime novels for Gypsy Rose Lee and George Sanders. She collaborated with Stuart Palmer and Ed McBain. She wrote screenplays for Falcon and other film series.

Stuart Palmer completed People Vs. Withers and Malone, a book that featured his Hildegarde Withers character as well as Rice's Malone. Larry M. Harris (b. 1933) contributed one book after Rice's death.

Original John J. Malone Works

Eight Faces at Three (1939) aka *Death at Three*
The Corpse Steps Out (1940)
The Wrong Murder (1940)
The Right Murder (1941)
Trial by Fury (1941)
The Big Midget Murders (1942)
Having a Wonderful Crime (1943)
Lucky Stiff (1945)

The Fourth Postman (1948)
My Kingdom for a Hearse (1957)
Knocked for a Loop (1957) aka *The Double Frame*
The Name is Malone (1958)
People Vs. Withers and Malone (1963) with Stuart Palmer
But the Doctor Died (1967)

Pastiche

Larry M. Harris, *The Pickled Poodles* (1960)

VIRGINIA RICH

Two cooks in the kitchen

Virginia Rich (1914–85) wrote three culinary mysteries featuring Eugenia Potter, a widow and exceptional cook. The first was *The Cooking School Murders*. 'Genia returns to her childhood Iowa hometown and organizes an adult education class, to be taught by a famous chef. After the first class, one of the students turns up dead. "Rich has captured well the emotions of a sixties-ish woman returning home for the first time in many years," wrote Susan Dunlap in *1001 Midnights* (1986). "...In addition to her grasp of cooking, Rich has a good feel for the idiosyncrasies of small-town living; and the pace of the narrative is like the pace of a small-town summer evening before it settles into full night."

After Rich's death, Nancy Pickard was commissioned to complete *The 27-Ingredient Chili Con Carne Murders*, "based on a story and notes left by Virginia Rich at the time of her death," according to Jean Swanson and Dean James in *By A Woman's Hand*. Pickard had her own successful mystery series with Jenny Cain, director of a philanthropic foundation in Port Frederick, Massachusetts. The first in the revived series was *Bum Steer* (1990).

"It was hell. It was really hard," Pickard said of finishing the Rich novel. Her comments appeared in *Rediscovering Nancy Drew* edited by Carolyn Stewart Dyer and Nancy Tillman Romalov. "But ever since I got it finished, it's been just a real kick. I've had the best time and the response has been such fun. But it was real tough to get into somebody else's voice, particularly since it was third person — my novels are first person. And the protagonist was a much older woman. Ten years had intervened since I first read the novels and what I liked in mysteries had changed, to some extent, and my own mysteries had changed a great deal, so I had to do a fair amount of hard work to get into the mood to do that book." Pickard said she began with about 60 typewritten pages of scenes and an outline. "But it turned out that book didn't work. I actually wrote two books, because I had to go through what she had started to find out that it wasn't going to work. And I think that she would have come to the same conclusion...."

A strong response from readers prompted Pickard to do more pastiches.

Original Eugenia Potter Mysteries

The Cooking School Murders (1982)   *The Nantucket Diet Murders* (1985)
The Baked-Bean Supper Murders (1983)

Posthumous Collaboration

Nancy Pickard, *The 27-Ingredient Chili Con Carne Murders* (1993)

Pastiches

Nancy Pickard, *The Blue Corn Murders* (1999); *The Secret Ingredient Murders* (2002)

ELLIOTT ROOSEVELT

Eleanor Roosevelt on the case

Elliott Roosevelt (1910–1990), the son of Franklin D. and Eleanor Roosevelt, flew 300 combat missions with the U.S. Army Air Force during World War II. He went on to own a Texas radio station, lived on a horse ranch in Portugal and served as Miami Beach mayor. He collaborated with James Brough on a memoir of his parents. A series of mystery stories featuring his mother bore his sole byline, although, according to mystery authority Jon L. Breen, they were ghosted by William Harrington, who in the first book is given the credit "my mentor in the craft of mystery writing." Harrington also wrote novelizations of the *Columbo* television series.

The publisher brought out more books after Roosevelt's death, making them posthumous ghostly collaborations. By *Murder at the President's Door*, Harrington's work was widely known.

Original Eleanor Roosevelt Mysteries

Murder and the First Lady (1984)
The Hyde Park Murder (1985)
Murder at Hobcaw Barony (1986)
The White House Pantry Murder (1987)

Murder at the Palace (1987)
Murder in the Rose Garden (1989)
Murder in the Oval Office (1989)
Murder in the Blue Room (1990)

Eleanor Roosevelt Posthumous Collaborations

William Harrington, *A First-Class Murder* (1991); *Murder in the Red Room* (1992); *Murder in the West Wing* (1993); *A Royal Murder* (1994); *Murder in the Executive Mansion* (1995); *Murder in the Chateau* (1996); *Murder at Midnight* (1997); *Murder in the Map Room* (1998); *Murder in Georgetown* (1999); *Murder in the Lincoln Bedroom* (2000); *Murder at the President's Door* (2001)

REBECCA ROTHENBERG

Garden mysteries

Rebecca Rothenberg (1948–1998) built a trio of Claire Sharples Botanical Mysteries around a gardening theme. She was an epidemiologist and amateur botanist, as well as writer and musician.

Following her death from a brain tumor, Rothenberg's friend Taffy Cannon, author of the Nan Robinson mysteries, completed the manuscript for *The Tumbleweed Murders*. Cannon in an introduction explained she had gotten to know Rothenberg and "learned that she was witty, wise, accomplished, self-deprecating, and possessed of an enviable gift for language. She had been a songwriter in Nashville and an epidemiologist in Los Angeles. What's more, she had seized the vast and arguably unlovable San Joaquin Valley for her Claire Sharples series and had invested the region with charm and appeal."

Original Claire Sharples Mysteries

The Bulrush Murders (1992)   The Shy Tulip Murders (1996)
The Dandelion Murders (1994)

Posthumous Collaboration with Taffy Cannon

The Tumbleweed Murders (2001)

LAWRENCE SANDERS

McNally

American mystery writer Lawrence Sanders (1920–1998) was discharged from the Marine Corps in 1946. He became a writer with *Mechanics Illustrated* and *Science and Mechanics*. His first novel, *The Anderson Tapes*, won an Edgar Award when it came out in 1970. His character Archy McNally is a private detective based in Palm Beach who works for the rich and weird.

After Sanders' death, Putnam's contracted mystery writer Vincent Lardo to pick up the series. "That authorship was not immediately revealed," according to Internet columnist Stephen Leary. "In 2000, a fan of the books of Lawrence Sanders filed a class-action lawsuit claiming Sanders' estate and the publisher misled fans into believing Sanders was still alive (he died in 1998) by publishing *McNally's Dilemma* under his name. A settlement was reached and consumers received $13 if they bought the hardcover copy of the book. In that novel, the ghostwriter's name (Vincent Lardo) was listed in small type on the copyright page."

Original McNally Works

McNally's Secret (1992)   McNally's Trial (1995)
McNally's Luck (1992)   McNally's Puzzle (1996)
McNally's Risk (1993)   McNally's Gamble (1997)
McNally's Caper (1994)

McNally Pastiches

Vincent Lardo, *McNally's Dilemma* (1999); *McNally's Folly* (2000); *McNally's Chance* (2001); *McNally's Alibi* (2002); *McNally's Dare* (2003); *McNally's Bluff* (2004)

JOHN A. SAXON

Sam Welpton

John A. Saxon (1886–1847) wrote stories under his own name and as Rex Norman. He sold stories to pulp magazines such as *Spicy Mystery Stories*. He wrote one book about Sam Welpton of Lane & Welpton, insurance investigators.

Robert Leslie Bellem wrote a second Welpton novel after his friend's death.

Original Welpton Work
Liability Limited (1947) aka *This Was No Accident*

Pastiche
Robert Leslie Bellem writing as John A. Saxon, *Half-Past Mortem* (1947)

DOROTHY L. SAYERS

Lord Peter Wimsey

Dorothy L. Sayers (1893–1957) was born at Oxford, where her father was chaplain of Christ Church. She attended Somerville College, Oxford, to study modern languages. She wrote mystery stories featuring Lord Peter Death Bredon Wimsey, who has an independent income, plays cricket and noses into crime puzzles. The stories explore interesting social themes at the same time as they reveal murderers. Sayers once explained she gave Wimsey a large independent source of income as a cheap relief for herself when she felt low on funds. Later books in the series explored the relationship between Wimsey and Harriet Vane.

Jill Paton Walsh (b. 1937), an English novelist and children's book author, continued the series, the first a completion of a Sayers manuscript, the second based on the "Wimsey Papers," published "letters" written by Wimsey family members (meaning Sayers herself) to *The Spectator* during World War II.

"With *Thrones, Dominations*, I was working in the dark with a plot that had been worked out," Walsh told Leonard Picker of *Publishers Weekly*. "In *A Presumption of Death*, all I had to use were propaganda letters, and so I had a completely free hand with the plot. The characters then became the difficulty, because this time they needed to be moved into a situation that was so different from when we last saw them in her hands."

Original Works
Whose Body? (1923)
Clouds of Witness (1926)
Unnatural Death (1927) aka *The Dawson Pedigree*

The Unpleasantness at the Bellona Club (1928)
Lord Peter Views the Body (1928)
Strong Poison (1930)

The Documents in the Case (1930) short
stories, with Robert Eustace
The Five Red Herrings (1931) aka
Suspicious Characters
Have His Carcase (1932)
Murder Must Advertise (1933)
Hangman's Holiday (1933) short stories
The Nine Tailors (1934)
Gaudy Night (1935)

Busman's Honeymoon (1937) adapted
from the play by Sayers and Muriel
St. Clare Byrne
In the Teeth of the Evidence (1939)
Striding Folly (1972)
*Abominable History of the Man with
Copper Fingers* (1982) short stories
*Lord Peter: The Complete Lord Peter
Wimsey Stories* (1986)

Pastiches

Norma Schier, *The Anagram Detectives* (1979)
Jill Paton Walsh, *Thrones, Dominations* (1998); *A Presumption of Death* (2002)

Fictional Biography

C.W. Scott-Giles, *The Wimsey Family* (1977)

Cookbook

Elizabeth Ryan, *Lord Peter Wimsey Cookbook* (1981)

GEORGES SIMENON

Inspector Maigret

Belgian-born writer Georges Simenon (1903–1989) came to the United States in
1945 from Quebec and lived in several locations before settling on Shadow Rock
Farm in Lakeville, Connecticut. A fast writer, he produced twenty-eight Jules
Maigret short stories as well as seventy-five other novels beginning in 1931.

　　A Parisian police inspector, Maigret toils long hours, smokes a pipe inces-
santly and enjoys many a home-cooked meal served by Madame Maigret.

　　Italian writers Carlo Fruttero and Franco Lucentini include Maigret with
other series detectives in their 1983 novel.

Original Maigret Works

The Strange Case of Peter the Lett (1931)
aka *The Case of Peter the Lett* aka
Maigret and the Enigmatic Lett
The Crime at Lock 14 (1931) aka *Maigret
Meets a Milord* aka *Lock 14*
The Death of Monsieur Gallet (1931) aka
Maigret Stonewalled
The Crime of Inspector Maigret (1931)
Maigret and the Hundred Gibbets

A Battle of Nerves (1931) aka *Maigret's
War of Nerves* aka *A Man's Head*
A Face for a Clue (1931) aka *Maigret and
the Concarneau Murders* aka *Maigret
and the Yellow Dog* aka *The Yellow Dog*
The Crossroad Murders (1931) aka *Maigret at the Crossroads*
A Crime in Holland (1931) aka *Maigret
in Holland*

The Sailor's Rendezvous (1931)

At the "Gai Moulin" (1931) aka Maigret at the "Gai Moulin"

Guinguette by the Seine (1931) aka Maigret and the Tavern by the Seine aka The Bar on the Seine

The Shadow in the Courtyard (1932) aka Maigret Mystified

Maigret and the Countess (1932) aka The Saint-Fiacre Affair aka Maigret Goes Home aka Maigret on Home Ground

The Flemish Shop (1932) aka Maigret and the Flemish Shop

Death of a Harbor Master (1932) aka Maigret and the Death of a Harbor Master

The Madman of Bergerac (1932)

Liberty Bar (1932) aka Maigret on the Riviera

The Lock at Charenton (1933)

Maigret Returns (1934)

Maigret and the Hotel Majestic (1942)

Maigret in Exile (1942)

Maigret and the Spinster (1942)

To Any Lengths (1944) aka Maigret and the Fortuneteller

Maigret and the Toy Village (1944)

Maigret's Rival (1944) aka Inspector Cadaver

Maigret in Retirement (1947)

Maigret in New York (1947) aka Inspector Maigret in New York's Underworld aka Maigret in New York's Underworld

A Summer Holiday (1948) aka No Vacation for Maigret aka Maigret on Holiday

Maigret's Dead Man (1948) aka Maigret's Special Murder

Maigret's First Case (1949)

My Friend Maigret (1949) aka The Methods of Maigret

Maigret at the Coroner's (1949)

Maigret and the Old Lady (1950)

Madame Maigret's Own Case (1950) aka Madame Maigret's Friend aka The Friend of Madame Maigret

Maigret's Memoirs (1951)

Maigret and the Strangled Stripper (1951) aka Maigret in Montmartre aka Inspector Maigret and the Strangled Stripper

Maigret Takes a Room (1951) aka Maigret Rents a Room

Inspector Maigret and the Burglar's Wife (1951) aka Maigret and the Burglar's Wife

Inspector Maigret and the Killers (1952) aka Maigret and the Gangsters

Maigret's Revolver (1952)

Maigret and the Man on the Boulevard (1953) aka Maigret and the Man on the Bench

Maigret Afraid (1953)

Maigret's Mistake (1953)

Maigret Goes to School (1954)

Inspector Maigret and the Dead Girl (1954) aka Maigret and the Young Girl

Maigret and the Minister (1955) aka Maigret and the Calame Report

Maigret and the Headless Corpse (1955)

Maigret Sets a Trap (1955)

Maigret's Failure (1956)

Maigret's Little Joke (1957) aka None of Maigret's Business

Maigret and the Millionaires (1958)

Maigret Has Scruples (1958)

Maigret and the Reluctant Witnesses (1959)

Maigret Has Doubts (1959)

Maigret in Court (1960)

Maigret in Society (1960)

Maigret and the Lazy Burglar (1961)

Maigret and the Black Sheep (1962)

Maigret and the Saturday Caller (1962)

Maigret and the Dosser, Maigret and the Bum (1963)

Maigret Loses His Temper (1963)

Maigret and the Ghost (1964) aka Maigret and the Apparition

Maigret on the Defensive (1964)

The Patience of Maigret (1965) aka Maigret Bides His Time

Maigret and the Nahour Case (1967)

Maigret's Pickpocket (1967)
Maigret Takes the Waters (1968) aka
  Maigret in Vichy
Maigret Hesitates (1968)
Maigret's Boyhood Friend (1968)
Maigret and the Killer (1969)

Maigret and the Wine Merchant (1970)
Maigret and the Madwoman (1970)
Maigret and the Loner (1971)
Maigret and the Flea (1971) aka *Maigret
  and the Informer*
Maigret and Monsieur Charles (1972)

Pastiches

Carlo Fruttero and Franco Lucentini, *The D Case: Or, The Truth About the Mystery of Edwin Drood* (1993)

Julian Symons, *Great Detectives: Seven Original Investigations* (1981) includes "About Maigret and the Stolen Papers"

CHARLES MERRILL SMITH
The Reverend Randollph

Charles Merrill Smith (1919–1986), a United Methodist minister, wrote a half dozen mystery novels featuring a liberal clergyman, the Reverend C.P. Randollph.

Smith left an unfinished manuscript at his death and his son, Terrance Love Smith, completed it. Terrance Smith himself died in an automobile accident, however, before he would write further entries in the series.

Original Works

Reverend Randollph and the Wages of Sin (1974)
Reverend Randollph and the Avenging Angel (1977)
Reverend Randollph and the Fall from Grace Inc. (1978)

Reverend Randollph and the Holy Terror (1982)
Reverend Randollph and the Unholy Bible (1984)

Posthumous Collaboration with Terrance Love Smith

Reverend Randollph and the Splendid Samaritan (1987)

MICKEY SPILLANE
Mike Hammer

Mickey Spillane (1918–2006), born in Brooklyn, New York, the son of an Irish-American bartender and a Scottish mother, started writing while in high school. He served in the Army Air Corps during World War II. From writing text stories for comic book publishers he moved up to books with *I, the Jury* (1948), the first case for hard-boiled Mike Hammer, private eye. The book sold more than six million copies, its sex and violence finding a ready post-war audience. Many critics were outraged. He wrote more Hammer novels, and several books featuring a secret agent, Tiger Mann. The Hammer books were made into radio, films and a TV series in 1984 to 1987. Spillane himself played the dick in *The Girl Hunters* (1963).

After Spillane died, fellow crime writer and longtime admirer Max Allan Collins completed the manuscript for the unfinished Spillane story *Dead Street*. "Spillane broke down the barriers, where sex and violence were concerned, and this pissed people off. Also, he was perceived as right-wing. The vigilante approach Hammer used turned the stomachs of many liberals," Collins said in a *January Magazine* interview. Collins has contracted to complete other Hammer manuscripts.

Original Mike Hammer Works

I, The Jury (1947)
My Gun in Quick (1950)
Vengeance Is Mine! (1950)
One Lonely Night (1951)
The Big Kill (1951)
Kiss Me, Deadly (1952)
The Girl Hunters (1962)

The Snake (1964)
The Twisted Thing (1966)
The Body Lovers (1967)
Survival ... Zero! (1970)
The Killing Man (1989)
Black Alley (1997)

Posthumous Mike Hammer Collaboration

Max Allan Collins, *The Goliath Bone* (2008)

Posthumous Collaboration

Max Allan Collins, *Dead Street* (2008)

RICHARD STARK

Parker

Donald Edwin Westlake (1931–2008) was a prolific fiction writer known particularly for the Dortnumder humorous crime caper stories issued under his own name and the hard-boiled Parker crime thrillers written under the Richard Stark byline. He also wrote as Edwin West, Tucker Coe, and Samuel Holt. He wrote on a manual typewriter.

Australian mystery writer Garry Disher's Wyatt series and Max Allan Collins' Nolan books both owe a strong debt to the Parker model. But Dan Simmons, in the first of his trio of Joe Kurtz books, indicates his character is the illegitimate son of Parker, and the book is thus, technically, a pastiche.

Original Parker Novels

The Hunter (1962) retitled *Point Blank* (1967), retitled *Payback*
The Man With the Getaway Face (1963) retitled *Steel Hit* (Great Britain)
The Outfit (1963)
The Mourner (1963)
The Score (1963) retitled *Killtown* (Great Britain, 1973)
The Jugger (1965)
The Seventh (1966) retitled *The Split* (1968)
The Handle (1966) retitled *Run Lethal* (Great Britain, 1973)
The Rare Coin Score (1967)
The Green Eagle Score (1967)
The Black Ice Score (1968)

The Sour Lemon Score (1969)
Slayground (1971)
Deadly Edge (1971)
Plunder Squad (1972)
Butcher's Moon (1974)
Child Heist (1974) a fake Parker novel included in the Dortmunder novel *Jimmy the Kid*
Comeback (1997)
Backflash (1998)
Flashfire (2000)
Firebreak (2001)
Breakout (2002)
Nobody Runs Forever (2004)
Ask the Parrot (2006)
Dirty Money (2008)

Pastiches featuring Joe Kurtz

Dan Simmons, *Hardcase* (2002); *Hard Freeze* (2003); *Hard as Nails* (2004)

REX STOUT

Wolfe and Goodwin

Rex Stout (1886–1975) sent his manuscripts to his editors as first-drafts from his typewriter. The Indiana native, educated in Kansas, was a whiz in math as a youth, and after service in the U.S. Navy (he was warrant officer on President Theodore Roosevelt's yacht) he co-invented a school banking system that was implemented nationally. He wrote several novels before the Nero Wolfe mysteries became popular. He was named Mystery Writers of America Grand Master in 1959. Wolfe, a hefty stay-at-home, prefers to solve mysteries from his home at West 35th Street, sending his associate Archie Goodwin to obtain clues, grill suspects and deal with the police. The series, popular on radio and in movies, featured Timothy Hutton and Maury Chaykin in the early 2000s.

Robert Goldsborough (b. 1937), a fan of Nero Wolfe novels since his teens, crafted a handful of pastiches, with permission of the Stout estate. He wrote the first one especially for his mother, another Stout fan. Goldsborough was a longtime reporter and editor with the Chicago *Tribune* and *Advertising Age*. Mystery writer Loren D. Estleman set a series of short stories in *Ellery Queen Mystery Magazine* beginning in 2008 squarely in the Wolfe-Goodwin universe. Yet to be collected in a book, they feature crime-solving Claudius Lyon, a Wolfe wannabe, and his right hand, Arnie Woodbine. Two of Lawrence Block's four Chip Harrison novels—*Make Out with Murder* (1974) and *The Topless Tulip Caper* (1975)—find the young man working for Leo Haig in a relationship that resembles the Wolfe/ Goodwin one. Randall Garrett's Lord Darcy fantasy novels are Stout-like; the main character investigates a puzzle with the help of Lord Bontriomphe (French for "good win"). John Lescroart's *Son of Holmes* (1986) and *Rasputin's Revenge: The Further Startling Adventures of Auguste Lupa — Son of Holmes* (1987) give a lot of clues to being about Wolfe.

Original Nero Wolfe Mysteries

Fer-de-Lance (1934)
The League of Frightened Men (1935)
The Rubber Band (1936)
The Red Box (1937)
Too Many Cooks (1938)
Some Buried Caesar (1939)
Over My Dead Body (1940)
Where There's a Will (1940)
Black Orchids (1942)
Not Quite Dead Enough (1944)
The Silent Speaker (1946)
Too Many Women (1947)
And Be A Villain (1948)
The Second Confession (1949)
Trouble in Triplicate (1949)
In the Best Families (1950)
Three Doors to Death (1950)
Curtains for Three (1951)
Murder by the Book (1951)
Prisoner's Base (1952)
Triple Jeopardy (1952)
The Golden Spiders (1953)
The Black Mountain (1954)
Three Men Out (1954)
Invitation to Murder (1954)

Before Midnight (1955)
Might As Well Be Dead (1956)
Three Witnesses (1956)
If Death Ever Slept (1957)
Three for the Chair (1957)
And Four to Go (1958)
Murder Is No Joke (1958)
Champagne for One (1958)
Plot It Yourself (1960)
Three at Wolfe's Door (1960)
Too Many Clients (1960)
The Final Deduction (1961)
Homicide Trinity (1961)
Gambit (1962)
The Mother Hunt (1963)
A Right to Die (1964)
The Doorbell Rang (1965)
Trio for Blunt Instruments (1965)
Death of a Doxy (1965)
The Father Hunt (1968)
Death of a Dude (1969)
Please Pass the Guilt (1973)
Corsage (1977)
Death Times Three (1985)

Pastiches

Carlo Fruttero and Franco Lucentini, *The D Case: Or, The Truth About the Mystery of Edwin Drood* (1993)
Robert Goldsborough, *Murder in E Minor* (1986); *Death on Deadline* (1987); *The Bloodied Ivy* (1988); *The Last Coincidence* (1989); *Fade to Black* (1990); *Silver Spire* (1992); *The Missing Chapter* (1994)
Norma Schier, *The Anagram Detectives* (1979)
Julian Symons, *The Great Detectives: Seven Criminal Investigations* (1981)

Fictional Biographies

William S. Baring-Gould, *Nero Wolfe of West Thirty-Fifth Street* (1969)
Ken Darby, *The Brownstone House of Nero Wolfe* (1983)

Cookbook

Editors of Viking Press, *The Nero Wolfe Cookbook* (1973)

MURRAY THOMAS

Inspector Wilkins

Thomas Murray Ragg (1897–?) was a British writer who used the byline Murray Thomas for his Inspector Ragg police series.

Years later, another British writer, James Anderson (b. 1936), added to the sequence.

Original Inspector Wilkins Works

Buzzards Pick the Bones (1932)   *Inspector Wilkins Sees Red* (1934)
Inspector Wilkins Reads the Proofs (1935)

Pastiches

James Anderson, *The Affair of the Bloodstained Egg Cozy* (1975); *The Affair of the Muti-lated Mink Coat* (1981)

ARTHUR W. UPFIELD

Bony Bonaparte

Arthur W. Upfield (1890–1964) wrote mysteries featuring the half–Aboriginal, half white Queensland, Australia, Detective Inspector Napoleon "Bony" Bonaparte. Born in Hampshire, England, Upfield joined the First Australian Imperial Force during World War I and served in Egypt and France. He moved to Australia with his family and began his career as a writer.

Upfield at his death left an unfinished manuscript and notes. J.L. Price and Dorothy Strange completed the text.

Original Napoleon Bonaparte Works

Barrakee Mystery (1928) aka *Lure of the Bush*   *Winds of Evil* (1937)
Sands of Windee (1931)   *Bone Is Pointed* (1938)
Wings Above the Diamantina (1936) aka   *Mystery of Swordship Reef* (1939)
   Winged Mystery aka *Wings Above the*   *Bushranger of the Skies* (1940) aka *No*
   Claypan   *Footprint in the Bush*
Mister Jelly's Business (1937) aka *Murder*   *Death of Swagman* (1945)
   Down Under   *Devil's Steps* (1946)

Author Bites the Dust (1948)
Mountains Have a Secret (1948)
Widows of Broome (1950)
Bachelors of Broken Hill (1950)
New Shoe (1952) aka *Clue of the New Shoe*
Venom House (1953)
Murder Must Wait (1953)
Death of a Lake (1954)
Cake in the Hatbox (1954) aka *Sinister Stones*
Battling Prophet (1956)
Man of Two Tribes (1956)
Bony Buys a Woman (1957) aka *Bushman Who Came Back*

Bony and the Mouse (1959) aka *Journey to the Hangman*
Bony and the Black Virgin (1959)
Bony and the Kelly Gang (1960) aka *Valley of Smugglers*
Bony and the White Savage (1961) aka *White Savage*
Will of the Tribe (1962)
Madman's Bend (1963) aka *Body at Madman's Bend*
Breakaway House (1987)
The Great Melbourne Cup Mystery (1996)

Posthumous Collaboration

J.L. Price and Dorothy Strange, *The Lake Frome Monster* (1966)

S.S. VAN DINE

Philo Vance

Virginia native Willard Huntington Wright (1888–1939), using the penname S.S. Van Dine, created the erudite amateur criminologist Philo Vance. In the first book, *The Benson Murder Case* (1926), the Manhattan sleuth helps his friend, District Attorney Markham, break a murderer's alibi. By *The Gracie Allen Murder Case* in 1938, even Wright was falling into near farce. Raymond Chandler noted in an essay in *The Simple Art of Murder*, "Philo Vance needs a kick in the pance."

Humorist and outdoors writer Corey Ford (1902–1969) couldn't resist writing his own variation on Philo Vance. Vance inspired numerous unlisted parodies, including "The Pinke Murder Case" by N.O.T. Von Dime in *The Mixture As Before* (1930).

Original Philo Vance Works

The Benson Murder Case (1926)
The Canary Murder Case (1927)
The Greene Murder Case (1928)
The Bishop Murder Case (1929)
The Scarab Murder Case (1930)
The Kennel Murder Case (1933)

The Dragon Murder Case (1934)
The Casino Murder Case (1934)
The Garden Murder Case (1935)
The Kidnap Murder Case (1936)
The Gracie Allen Murder Case (1938)
The Winter Murder Case (1939)

Pastiches

Jon L. Breen, *Hair of the Sleuthhound* (1982)
Corey Ford writing as John Riddell, *The John Riddell Murder Case* (1930)

CORNELL WOOLRICH

Darkly Criminal

Cornell Woolrich (1903–1968) produced crime and detective stories for the pulps under his own name and as George Hopley and William Irish. His 1942 short story "It Had to Be Murder" evolved into Alfred Hitchcock's 1954 motion picture *Rear Window*.

Although he was briefly married, Woolrich was a homosexual, and eventually an alcoholic, and lived reclusively for thirty-five years in the same residential hotel in Harlem as his mother. His earliest writing showed the influence of F. Scott Fitzgerald. His later writings evinced the suspenseful, darkly paranoiac and obsessive prose that earned him the label "father of noir" and "Poe of the 20th century."

Veteran mystery writer Lawrence Block (b. 1938) completed an unfinished Woolrich manuscript.

Posthumous Collaboration

Lawrence Block, *Into the Night* (1987)

Espionage

The passing of the original writers at the height of their series characters' popularity — Edward S. Aarons or Ian Fleming, are good examples — practically obliged publishers to find new writers to keep up the momentum. Of these, James Bond outlived the heyday of paperback espionage fiction in the 1960s. Robert Ludlum reinvented the genre in the 1980s.

EDWARD S. AARONS

Cajun

Edwards S. Aarons (1916–1975), a Philadelphia native, majored in literature and history at Columbia University. He was a Coast Guard chief petty officer during World War II. He wrote under his own name and as Paul Ayres and Edward S. Ronns. His hero Sam Durell (code name Cajun), who emerged in the same Cold War era as James Bond, is a durable agent for the CIA's K section.

Will B. Aarons (1914–2002), the author's brother, purportedly continued the series, though literary historians have verified that Lawrence Hall actually wrote the books.

Original Series

Assignment to Disaster (1955)
Assignment—Suicide (1956)
Assignment—Treason (1956)
Assignment—Budapest (1957)
Assignment—Stella Marni (1957)
Assignment—Angelina (1958)
Assignment—Madeleine (1958)
Assignment—Carlotta Cortez (1958)
Assignment—Helene (1959)
Assignment—Lili Lamaris (1959)

Assignment—Mara Tirana (1959)
Assignment—Zoraya (1961)
Assignment—Ankara (1961)
Assignment—Lowlands (1961)
Assignment—Burma Girl (1961)
Assignment—Karachi (1962)
Assignment—Sorento Siren (1963)
Assignment—Manchurian Doll (1963)
Assignment—Sulu Sea (1964)
Assignment—The Girl in the Gondola (1964)

Assignment—The Cairo Dancers (1965)
Assignment—Palermo (1956)
Assignment—Cong Hai Kill (1956)
Assignment—School for Spies (1966)
Assignment—Black Viking (1967)
Assignment—Moon Girl (1968)
Assignment—Nuclear Nude (1968)
Assignment—Peking (1969)
Assignment—Star Stealers (1970)
Assignment—White Rajah (1970)
Assignment—Tokyo (1971)

Assignment—Bangkok (1972)
Assignment—Golden Girl (1972)
Assignment—Maltese Maiden (1972)
Assignment—Ceylon (1973)
Assignment—Silver Scorpion (1973)
Assignment—Amazon Queen (1974)
Assignment—Sumatra (1974)
Assignment—Black Gold (1975)
Assignment—Quayle Question (1975)
Assignment—Afghan Dragon (1976)
Assignment—Unicorn (1976)

Pastiches

Lawrence Hall writing as Will B. Aarons, *Assignment Sheba* (1976); *Assignment Tiger Devil* (1977); *Assignment 13th Princess* (1977); *Assignment Mermaid* (1979); *Assignment Tyrant's Bride* (1980); *Assignment Death Ship* (1983)

DESMOND BAGLEY

In the shadows

Simon Bagley (1923–1983) was born in England's Lake District and grew up in his parents' theatrical boarding house. During World War II, he was employed in the aviation industry. He lived in Uganda and South Africa, and worked in gold and asbestos mines before becoming a freelance broadcast writer.

His first novel, *The Golden Keel*, came out in 1962. His thrillers, published under the penname Desmond Bagley, featured exotic locations. Max Stafford, a security consultant, and the spy Slade appeared in two books each. The Bagleys later lived in Italy and England and the Channel Islands. The author's wife, Joan Margaret Brown, completed his last two novels after his death.

Posthumous Collaborations

Joan Margaret Brown, *Night of Error* (1984); *Juggernaut* (1985)

JOHN BUCHAN

Richard Hannay

Thriller writer John Buchan (1875–1940) served as a governor general of Canada. Born in Perth, Scotland, he juggled a rich life of political service and literature. He set his Prester John adventure books in South Africa. His *The Thirty-Nine Steps,* which takes place in Europe prior to World War I, is about shadowy operative Richard Hannay. Alfred Hitchcock filmed the story with great success.

Jack Smithers brought three established adventure characters together for his pastiche.

Original Richard Hannay Works

The Thirty-Nine Steps (1915)
Greenmantle (1916)
Mr. Standfast (1919)
The Three Hostages (1924)

The Courts of the Morning (1929)
The Island of Sheep (1936)
Sick Heart River (1940)

Pastiche

Dick Johns. Adapted by Patrick Barlow from an original concept by Simon Corble and Nobby Dimon. *The 39 Steps*. Broadway farce. (2009)

Jack Smithers, *Combined Forces: Being the Latter-Day Adventures of Maj. Gen. Sir Richard Hannay, Captain Hugh (Bulldog) Drummond, and Berry & Co.* (1983)

ERSKINE CHILDERS

Sands

Two sailing adventurers stumble on a devious German plan for the invasion of England, in *The Riddle of the Sands* by Erskine Childers.

Born in London to Protestant Irish parents, Childers (1870–1922) studied at Haileybury College and Trinity College, Cambridge. He clerked at the House of Commons for a time. He was an avid yachtsman. He served in the artillery during the Second Boer War and was wounded. During his recovery, he wrote *The Riddle of the Sands*, an early novel of espionage and intrigue that is still in print. He wrote two more books but became embroiled in Irish Free State political matters and was tried for possessing a pistol and executed. His son, Erskine Hamilton Childers, went on to become president of Ireland.

Sam Llewellyn was born on Tresco, Isles of Scilly, and lives in Herefordshire, England, with his wife, Canadian author Karen Wallace.

Original Work

The Riddle of the Sands (1903)

Pastiche

Sam Llewellyn, *The Shadows in the Sands* (1998)

IAN FLEMING

007

James Bond. More than a half century since the British secret agent 007 appeared in Ian Fleming's *Casino Royale*, the hero remains a popular culture phenomenon. Blockbuster motion pictures appear regularly. Graphic novels capture the spirit of the original writing while new authors bring out contemporary adventures featuring the suave spymaster.

One might consider Ian Fleming a relic of the Cold War. But critic Christopher Hitchens suggests otherwise in the introduction to a reprint of *From Russia With Love*: "By some latent intuition, Fleming was able to peer beyond the Cold War limitations of mere spy fiction and to anticipate the emerging milieu of the Colombian cartels, Osama bin-Laden and indeed the Russian mafia — as well as the nightmarish idea that some such fanatical freelance megalomaniac would eventually collar some weapons-grade plutonium."

Fleming (1908–1964), the son of a Conservative Member of Parliament, read the adventure novels of Sapper, John Buchan, Sax Rohmer and Robert Louis Stevenson as a boy. He played sports at Eton, attended Royal Military College at Sandhurst and completed his education in Switzerland, Munich and Geneva. He joined the Reuters news agency in 1929 and was assigned to the Moscow bureau. In 1939, he took a post as personal assistant to the British director of Naval Intelligence, Admiral John Godfrey. Ranked a lieutenant commander, he traveled around the world. He established an intelligence unit that saw action during the invasion of Germany. Fleming had a beach house retreat called Goldeneye in Jamaica, and each winter he began to write novels there.

Fleming's books are marked by a flamboyant, cultured hero who drives a 1933 4.5 liter Bentley (and later an Aston Martin), drinks his dry martinis shaken, not stirred, smokes blended Morland cigarettes and carries a concealed .25 Beretta. A mark of Fleming's prose that differentiated him from Sapper and other early adventure writers was his attention to detail and his crafting of a refined character.

President John F. Kennedy revealed his pleasure in reading the spy tales. Motion picture versions of *Dr. No*, *Goldfinger* and *From Russia, With Love* featured the Scots actor Sean Connery as Bond and brought even greater popularity to the books.

"He had not set out to be a writer. He did not, in fact, write his first book, *Casino Royale*, until he was forty-three. But he had always loved writing and he had always loved books," niece Kate Fleming said on the Ian Fleming Centre Web site.

Original James Bond Works

Casino Royale (1954) aka *You Asked for It* (1955)
Live and Let Die (1954)

Moonraker (1955) retitled *Too Hot to Handle* (1957)
Diamonds Are Forever (1956)

From Russia, With Love (1957)

Doctor No (1958)

Goldfinger (1959)

For Your Eyes Only: Five Secret Exploits of James Bond (1960) in Great Britain as *For Your Eyes Only: Five Secret Occasions in the Life of James Bond* (1960) reissued as *Quantum of Solace* (2008)

Thunderball (1961)

Spy Who Loved Me (1962)

On Her Majesty's Secret Service (1963)

Bonded Fleming (1965) includes *Thunderball, For Your Eyes Only* and *The Spy Who Loved Me*

Man with the Golden Gun (1965)

You Only Live Twice (1964)

More Gilt-Edged Bonds (1965) includes *Live and Let Die, Moonraker,* and *Diamonds Are Forever*

Octopussy (1965) in Great Britain as *Octopussy and The Living Daylights* (1966)

Man with the Golden Gun (1965)

Berlin Escape: The Last Great Adventures of James Bond (1985)

Quantum of Solace: The Complete James Bond Stories (2008)

Pastiches

Kingsley Amis writing as Robert Markham, *Colonel Sun* (1968)

Raymond Benson, *Zero Minus Ten* (1997); *Tomorrow Never Dies* (1997) movie novelization; *Facts of Death* (1998); *High Time to Kill* (1999); *World Is Not Enough* (1999) movie novelization; *Doubleshot* (2000); *Never Dream of Dying* (2001); *Man with the Red Tattoo* (2002); *Die Another Day* (2003) movie novelization

Sebastian Faulks, *Devil May Care* (2008)

Charles Higson, *SilverFin* (2005) Young Bond Series; *Blood Fever* (2006) Young Bond Series; *Double or Die* (2007) Young Bond Series

Henry Gammidge and John McClusky, *James Bond: Goldfinger* (2004) graphic novel; *James Bond: Dr. No* (2005) graphic novel

John Gardner, *License Renewed* (1981); *For Special Services* (1982); *Ice Breaker* (1983); *Role of Honour* (1984); *Nobody Lives Forever* (1986); *No Deals, Mr. Bond* (1987); *Scorpion* (1988); *Win, Lose or Die* (1989); *Brokenclaw* (1991); *Death Is Forever* (1992); *Never Send Flowers* (1993); *Seafire* (1994); *License to Kill* (1995) movie novelization; *Goldeneye* (1995) movie novelization; *Cold* (1996) aka *Cold Fall*

Anthony Hern, Henry Gammidge, and John McClusky, *James Bond: Casino Royale* (2005) graphic novel

Jim Lawrence, *James Bond: Octopussy* (2004) graphic novel

Jim Lawrence and Yaroslav Horak, *James Bond: The Man with the Golden Gun* (2004) graphic novel; *James Bond: Spy Who Loved Me* (2005) graphic novel; *James Bond: Spy Who Loved Me* (2005) graphic novel; *James Bond: Golden Ghost* (2006) graphic novel; *James Bond: Death Wing* (2007) graphic novel; *James Bond: Phoenix Project* (2007) graphic novel; *James Bond: Trouble Spot* (2007) graphic novel

Jim Lawrence, Yaroslav Horak and Kingsley Amis, *James Bond: Colonel Sun* (2005)

Jim Lawrence, Yaroslav Horak and Alan J. Porter, *James Bond: Shark Bait* (2008) graphic novel

Doug Moench, *James Bond 007: Serpent's Tooth* (1995) graphic novel

R.L. Stine, *James Bond in Win, Place, or Die* (1985)

Dr. Kate Westbrook, *Moneypenny Diaries: Guardian Angel* (2005)

Christopher Wood, *James Bond, the Spy Who Loved Me* (1977) movie novelization; *James Bond and Moonraker* (1979) movie novelization

Fictional Biography

John Pearson, *James Bond: The Authorized Biography* (1973)
John Cork and Collin Stutz, *James Bond Encyclopedia* (2007)

ROBERT LUDLUM

Jason Bourne

Robert Ludlum (1927–2001) was born in New York City, grew up in New Jersey and went to school in Connecticut. At age sixteen, he landed a part in a Broadway show. He saw action in the South Pacific from 1945 to 1947. He graduated from Wesleyan University in 1951. From 1952 to 1959, Ludlum and his wife, Mary Ruducha, acted in summer stock and on and off Broadway. He was in some 200 television drama episodes including *Studio One, Robert Montgomery Presents* and *Kraft Television Theater.* Ludlum's first novel, *The Scarlatti Inheritance,* about a group of European financiers who after World War I put up the cash for Adolf Hitler's charge into the Third Reich, climbed onto the bestseller list, as did each of the nearly dozen books which followed. "Life is extremely complicated," Ludlum said in an interview for *Bookreporter.* "I try as best I can to enter the realm of nuances of human behavior and alternatives of that behavior."

Ludlum's hallmark is the arena of mega-power. His twisting, turning tales delve into governmental secrets, huge conspiracies and vile corruption. From such a dark morass rises the Ludlum hero, an idealist, a democrat, an individualist, tolerant yet strong and loyal. "Ludlum chooses somewhat ordinary men as his heroes to fight against these evils [cabals and enemy governments]. They are often in their 40s, of upper-middle class backgrounds, and with strong ideas of what is morally right," explained Karen Hinckley in *St. James Guide to Crime & Mystery Writers.*

"It is somehow fitting that a novelist who specialized in complex conspiracy theories and international espionage should have left behind a conundrum to baffle even Bourne himself. In the years since his death, 12 new works bearing his name have hit the bookshelves and beach-towels of the world. None was penned by Ludlum himself—and at least three have not been credited to any other writer. These include *The Bancroft Strategy,* published last year, which sold 102,000 copies in hardback alone," said a writer in *The Independent* in 2007.

Ludlum's editor, Keith Kahla, is believed to have completed or written some books; his agent, Henry Morrison, claims to have finished a manuscript. Some posthumous sequel writers have been identified. Eric Von Lustbader is continuing the Jason Bourne books. James Cobb has written Covert One books. Ludlum is said to have put together the concept for a series to feature an elite, top-secret team of troubleshooters headed by Col. Jonathan Smith, whose mission was to fight crime and corruption at the highest levels. The novels have been written by others including Gayle Lynds, who observed on Mystery Ink, "As a writer of fiction, Robert Ludlum opened many doors for all of us not only politically but literarily. He brought passion, an informed sense of history, and a deep concern for the future to all his works. He was also unafraid to create strong female characters."

Original Bourne Works

The Bourne Identity (1980)   *The Bourne Ultimatum* (1990)
The Bourne Supremacy (1986)

Jason Bourne Pastiches

Eric Van Lustbader, *Robert Ludlum's The Bourne Legacy* (2004); *Robert Ludlum's The Bourne Betrayal* (2007); *Robert Ludlum's The Bourne Sanction* (2008)

Posthumous Collaborations

Keith Kahla, *The Sigma Protocol* (2001); *The Janson Directive* (2002); *The Tristan Betrayal* (2003)

Posthumous Covert One Collaborations

Gayle Lynds, *The Hades Factor* (2000); *The Paris Option* (2002)
Jonathan Smith, *The Cassandra Compact* (2001)

Covert One Pastiches

James Cobb, *The Arctic Event* (2007)
Patrick Larkin, *The Lazarus Vendetta* (2004); *The Moscow Vector* (2005)
Gayle Lynds, *The Altman Code* (2003)

Other Pastiches

Anonymous, *The Ambler Warning* (2005); *The Bancroft Strategy* (2007)

EUGÈNE VIDOCQ

Eugene Vidocq

Eugène Vidocq (1775–1857) was a circus performer and soldier and professional thief sentenced to prison for his crimes. He was an informer during the Napoleonic wars. He wrote an autobiography.

British writer Dick Donovan (1842–1924) and American writer Vincent McConnor (1907–?) fictionalized Vidocq's exploits.

Original Work

Memoirs of Vidocq (1828) aka *Memoirs of Vidocq, Principal Agent of the French Police Until 1827; and Now Proprietor of the Paper Manufactory at St Mande;* *Written by Himself* aka *Memoirs of Vidocq, French Police Agent* aka *Vidocq, the Police Spy*

Pastiches

Dick Donovan, *Eugène Vidocq, Soldier, Thief, Spy, Detective: A Romance Founded on Facts* (1895)

Vincent McConnor, *I Am Vidocq* (1965)

Fantasy and Horror

The Robert E. Howard estate let things get a bit out of hand in the 1970s and 1980s with dozens of pastiche fantasy tales of Conan the Barbarian and of late has reined back and concentrated on reprinting the original stories in new editions. V.C. Andrews' publisher successfully nurtured her gothic horror style well beyond the original author's eight books. And no one was in control of Bram Stoker's archetypal Dracula franchise, though many writers have shaped their own variations with other literary vampires and skipped by Dracula altogether.

V. C. ANDREWS

Flowers in the Attic

Virginia Cleo Andrews (1923–1986), whose peculiar gothic horror stories sold millions of copies worldwide, grew up in a working-class environment and was educated in Portsmouth, Virginia, where she was born. As a child she read avidly the writings of Jules Verne, Edgar Allan Poe, Edgar Rice Burroughs and the Brontë sisters. In her teen years, Andrews developed orthopedic problems and eventually was confined to a wheelchair. She worked as a fashion illustrator and commercial artist. She began to write, and sold *Flowers in the Attic*. In it, the four Dollanganger children, offspring of an incestuous union, are locked in the attic of an old mansion so their grandfather will not learn of their existence and disinherit their mother. Physically abused by their grandmother, they turn to each other for comfort and love.

After Andrews died of cancer, her family and publisher continued to bring out books under Andrews' name, at first claiming they were her work. It was soon acknowledged horror writer Andrew Neiderman (b. 1940) was continuing the series.

Original Works

Flowers in the Attic (1979) Dollanganger Series

Petals on the Wind (1980) Dollanganger Series

If There Be Thorns (1981) Dollanganger
    Series
My Sweet Audrina (1982)
Seeds of Yesterday (1984) Dollanganger
    Series

Heaven (1985) Casteel Family Series
Dark Angel (1986) Casteel Family Series
Garden of Shadows (1987) Dollanganger
    Series

Pastiches by Andrew Neiderman

Fallen Hearts (1990) Casteel Family Series
The Gates of Paradise (1990) Casteel Family Series
Web of Dreams (1990) Casteel Family Series
Dawn (1990) Cutler Family Series
Secrets of the Morning (1991) Cutler Family Series
Twilight's Child (1992) Cutler Family Series
Midnight Whispers (1992) Cutler Family Series
Darkest Hour (1993) Cutler Family Series
Ruby (1994) Landry Family Series
Pearl in the Mist (1994) Landry Family Series
All That Glitters (1995) Landry Family Series
Hidden Jewel (1995) Landry Family Series
Tarnished Gold (1996) Landry Family Series
Melody (1996) Logan Series
Heart Song (1997) Logan Series
Unfinished Symphony (1997) Logan Series
Music in the Night (1998) Logan Series
Olivia (1999) Logan Series
Butterfly (1998) Orphans Series
Crystal (1998) Orphans Series
Brooke (1998) Orphans Series
Raven (1998) Orphans Series
Runaways (1998) Orphans Series
Misty (1999) Wildflower Series
Star (1999) Wildflower Series
Jade (1999) Wildflower Series
Cat (1999) Wildflower Series
Into the Garden (1999) Wildflower Series
Rain (2000) Hudson Series
Lightning Strikes (2000) Hudson Series
Eye of the Storm (2000) Hudson Series
The End of the Rainbow (2001) Hudson Series
Gathering Clouds (2001) Hudson Series
Cinnamon (2001) Shooting Stars Series
Ice (2001) Shooting Stars Series
Rose (2001) Shooting Stars Series
Honey (2001) Shooting Stars Series
Falling Stars (2001) Shooting Stars Series
Cage of Love (2001) short stories
The Little Psychic (2001) short stories

Willow (2002) DeBeers Series
Wicked Forest (2002) DeBeers Series
Twisted Roots (2002) DeBeers Series
Into the Woods (2003) DeBeers Series
Hidden Leaves (2003) DeBeers Series, includes *Dark Seed*
Broken Wings (2003) Broken Wing Series
Midnight Flight (2003) Broken Wing Series
Celeste (2004) Gemini Series
Black Cat (2004) Gemini Series
Child of Darkness (2005) Gemini Series
April Shadows (2005) Shadows Series
Girl in the Shadows (2006) Shadows Series
Broken Flower (2006) Early Spring Series
Scattered Leaves (2007) Early Spring Series
Secrets in the Attic (2007) Secrets Series
Secrets in the Shadows (2008) Secrets Series
Delia's Crossing (2008) Delia Series
Delia's Heart (2008) Delia Series
Delia's Gift (2009) Delia Series

ROBERT LYNN ASPRIN

No Myth-takes

Robert Lynn Asprin (1946–2008) wrote comic fantasy takes in his Myth and Phule's Company series. Born in St. Johns, Michigan, he attended University of Michigan then joined the U.S. Army. He was married twice and had two children. He belonged to the Society for Creative Anachronism. His first novel, *The Cold Cash War*, came out in 1977. With his then-wife Lynn Abbey Asprin he edited the Thieves' World shared universe series. His first pun-filled MythAdventure of Skeeve and Aahz appeared in 1978. Asprin took a writing hiatus, in part due to financial issues with the IRS, and when he again began writing, it was in collaboration with other authors including Jody Lynn Nye. The listing includes only their collaborations; the last one, as the book came out after Asprin's death, technically a posthumous collaboration. Nye said on her Web site, "I will continue to write the books that Bob and I planned. We had big plans, some of which I can't talk about yet, but I hope you will enjoy the results. I have loved the series and the characters since I first read the books, almost thirty years ago, and I respect them."

Myth Adventures with Jody Lynn Nye

Myth-Told Tales (2003)
Myth-Alliances (2003)
Myth-Taken Identity (2004)

Class Dis-Mythed (2005)
Myth-Gotten Gains (2006)
Myth-Chief (2008)

Posthumous Collaboration

Jody Lynn Nye, *Myth-Fortunes* (2008)

Pastiches

Announced; no title or publication information

ALGERNON BLACKWOOD
Weirdness

Algernon Blackwood (1869–1951) was a journalist who wrote fiction of the supernatural. Born in London, Blackwood was a farmer in Canada, proprietor of a hotel, manager of a factory, a "psychical researcher" and finally a newsman in New York City. Again living in England, he began to write his distinct fiction. His story "The Willow" was highly praised by horror master H.P. Lovecraft, and inspired a sequel of sorts by Irish author Caitlin R. Kiernan (b. 1964).

Original work

The Listener and Other Stories (1907) includes "The Willow"

Pastiche

Caitlin R. Kiernan, *Threshold* (2001)

MARION ZIMMER BRADLEY
Avalon

Marion Zimmer Bradley (1930–1999) brought a strong feminist attitude to her fantasy novels. A native of Albany, New York, she sold her first story in 1952. She and Robert Alden Bradley were married from 1949 to 1964. She later married Walter H. Breen, until they divorced in 1990. The author graduated from Hardin-Simmons University in Texas. She created the Darkover setting (a planet colonized by people from Earth) for many of her books but *The Mists of Avalon* was her best-known. It told the Camelot story from the perspective of Morgan Le Fay and Gwenhwyfar. She edited a *Sword and Sorceress* annual for many years. "She believed that a fantasy writer must be well-versed in all fields of humanity, so she studied psychology, parapsychology, mythology, religions, to bring authenticity to her writing," commented a writer on the AllSands website.

California writer Diana L. Paxson (b. 1943) assisted Marion Zimmer Bradley, her sister-in-law, with *Mists* and wrote sequels after Bradley's death. Paxson has written her own Chronicles of Westria fantasy books. Bradley also collaborated with Deborah J. Ross on the Clingfire trilogy, and Ross continued books in the Darkover sequence after Bradley's passing.

Original Darkover Works

The Planet Savers (1958)
The Sword of Aldones (1962)
The Bloody Sun (1964) rewritten and expanded edition (1979)
Star of Danger (1965)
The Winds of Darkover (1970)
The World Wreckers (1971)
Darkover Landfall (1972)
The Spell Sword (1974) with Paul Edwin Zimmer uncredited
The Heritage of Hastur (1975)
The Shattered Chain (1976)
The Forbidden Tower (1977)
Stormqueen! (1978)
Two to Conquer (1980)
Sharra's Exile (1981)
Hawkmistress! (1982)

Thendara House (1983)
City of Sorcery (1984)
The Heirs of Hammerfell (1989)
Rediscovery (1993) with Mercedes Lackey
Exile's Song (1996) with Adrienne Martine-Barnes
The Shadow Matrix (1997) with Adrienne Martine-Barnes
Traitor's Sun (1999) with Adrienne Martine-Barnes
The Fall of Neskaya (2001) with Deborah J. Ross, Clingfire Trilogy
Zandru's Forge (2003) with Deborah J. Ross, Clingfire Trilogy
A Flame in Hali (2004) with Deborah J. Ross, Clingfire Trilogy

Posthumous Darkover Collaborations

Deborah J. Ross, *The Alton Gift* (2007); *The Children of Kings* (announced)

Original Mists of Avalon Works

The Mists of Avalon (1979) with Diana L. Paxson, uncredited
The Forest House (1993) with Diana L. Paxson, uncredited, retitled *The Forests of Avalon*

Lady of Avalon (1997) with Diana L. Paxson, uncredited

Posthumous Sequels

Diana L. Paxson, *Ancestors of Avalon* (2004); *Ravens of Avalon* (2007); *Sword of Avalon* (2009)

AVRAM DAVIDSON

Fantasy

Avram Davidson (1923–1993), a Hugo and World Fantasy Award winner, was a Navy medic during World War II. His first writing was as a Talmudic scholar in the 1950s. He belonged to the Swordsmen and Sorcerers' Guild of America. His books included Doctor Eszterhazy, Limekiller and Virgil Magnus series entries and the novel *Rork!* (1965). Besides nineteen novels he wrote more than 200 short stories and essays. He lived in Mexico, Belize, Washington and California.

His one-time collaborator, his former wife, Grania Davis, collected his stories for publication and completed his last work.

Posthumous Collaborations

Grania Davis, *The Boss in the Wall: A Treatise on the House Devil* (1998)
Michael Swanwick, *Moon Dogs* (2000) includes "Mickelrede or the Slayer and the Staff" and "Vergil Magus: King Without Country"

DAVID GEMMELL
Historical fantasy

David Gemmell (1948–2006) had a knack for writing heroic fantasy novels.

Born in West London, he became a journalist and newspaper editor. His first novel, *The Siege of Dros Delnoch*, was written in a white heat of creativity when he was diagnosed (erroneously) as having cancer. It came out in 1984 with the title *Legend*. Gemmell continued to write battle-intense prose in his eleven-novel Drenai and four-book Rigante series. He had started the final volume of his historical Troy trilogy when he died of heart disease. His wife and researcher, Stella Gemmell, familiar with the book's plot and relying on Gemmell's notes and outline, finished the manuscript. The books are about characters familiar from history, but with different personalities and no compulsion to follow their true historical course.

To replicate her husband's style, Stella Gemmell told *Times* reporter Jane Wheatley, she "'Read and reread the battle scenes, deconstructed them, then built my own. David used to act out fights in his study with various swords and helmets he'd collected.' She smiles, 'I didn't do that.'"

Original Troy works

Troy: Lord of the Silver Bow (2005)   *Troy: Shield of Thunder* (2006)

Posthumous collaboration

Stella Gemmell, *Troy: Fall of Kings* (2007)

ROBERT E. HOWARD
Conan and the Barbarians

Seventeen of Robert E. Howard's fantastic Conan tales of a heroic barbarian warrior battling fierce Picts and ghoulish demons appeared in *Weird Tales* magazine beginning with "The Phoenix on the Sword" in the December 1932 issue.

"There is no literary work, to me, half as zestful as rewriting history in the guise of fiction," wrote Howard in "On Reading—And Writing," reprinted in *The Last Celt: A Bio-bibliography of Robert Ervin Howard* edited by Glenn Lord (1976).

The son of a doctor, Texas-born Howard (1906–1936) took up exercise and body building as a frail teen. A reading diet of poetry and mythology helped develop his active imagination. He began writing at age seventeen and soon found a steady market with the pulp fiction magazines in the 1920s and '30s. He turned out horror, boxing, Western and detective tales as well as swords-and-sorcery. When his mother was near death in 1936, he took his own life.

"In a genre now labeled Heroic Fantasy, Howard truly came into his own, welding together various elements into a form which would not achieve its maximum popularity until thirty years after his death," said James Cawthorn and Michael Moorcock in *Fantasy: The 100 Best Books*. "And towering over all of the heroes created for this genre is Conan the Cimmerian, greatest warrior of the Hyborian Age."

Howard's muscular writing might not have survived had not Gnome Press collected his Conan stories in the 1950s. Oscar J. Friend, acting as agent for the Howard heirs in 1954, following issue of four Gnome editions of Conan stories, suggested that an author be found to carry on the character. Friend offered $1,250 for all rights to the literary property, but then-owner Dr. P.M. Kuykendall, declined, saying in a letter (quoted in part in Don Herron's *The Dark Barbarian*), "I do realize that there is a possibility that over the years his characterizations will exhaust themselves, nevertheless we think it would be better for the estate to gamble on this, rather than take the amount offered."

It took time, but the gamble proved a sound one. Fragments and other Howard stories were expanded or adapted by fantasy writer L. Sprague de Camp. Sprague de Camp continued with new stories when a paperback house, Lancer, brought out paperback editions in the mid–1960s.

Lord, literary agent for the Howard estate, in a 1978 letter suggested how Conan finally found a paperback audience: "I assume that the sudden surge of interest in fantasy at about the time the Lancer paperbacks came out certainly helped; no doubt the popularity of J.R.R. Tolkien's *Lord of the Rings* helped a great deal. And the Frank Frazetta covers on the Conan paperbacks probably helped. And I like to think that readers were captivated by the Howard stories; he was quite popular in *Weird Tales* during his lifetime…. The cheap paperback editions certainly brought his works before the public, whereas the limited editions of the hardbacks were known only to a few."

Motion pictures in 1982 and '84 featuring Arnold Schwarzenegger continued the Conan publishing momentum. An animated television series entered syndication in 1992.

Marvel Comics in 1970 began issuing a comic book version of the sword-swinging hero. "Everyone has his own idea of what Conan should be," said comics scripter Roy Thomas in *Conan Saga* No. 73 (April 1993), "only Robert E.

Howard's prose version is the authentic McConan — not de Camp, not Marvel, not Schwarzenegger."

The Howard book pastiches came in four waves. Sprague de Camp and also Carter dominated the early revival. After Lancer went bankrupt, rights were tied up for several years. Zebra took the opportunity to reprint Howard's lesser works and also sequels by new hands. Of these characters, Black Vulmea is a pirate; Bran Mak Morn is the king of the Picts of Caledonia; Cormac Mac Art is a sword-swinging Irish warrior; and Kull sits on the barbarian throne of Valusia.

Red Sonja was originally called Red Sonya in a single Howard short story appearing in *The Magic Carpet Magazine* for January 1934. She was made into a comic book companion to Conan, and later a heroine of her own comics by writer Thomas and in six Ace paperback books by David C. Smith and Richard L. Tierney. She appeared in a motion picture in 1985 starring Brigitte Nielsen and Schwarzenegger.

When Conan rights again became available, Berkley re-issued the old books while Bantam obtained rights to publish new Conan stories, looking to veteran fantasy and science fiction scribes such as Poul Anderson for stories. When Tor took on the franchise in 1982, it found new, up-and-coming fantasy writers who, after a Conan or three, often moved on to their own novels or series.

"Howard's style is not hard for a reasonably competent prosaist to imitate; since it is so clean, straightforward and unobtrusive," wrote L. Sprague de Camp (1907–2000) in an essay, "Editing Conan," which was reprinted in *The Blade of Conan*. "If one writes the best and clearest action narrative one can, it comes out pretty close to Howard, and it is easy to sprinkle in the little clichés and epithets to which he was addicted." Sprague de Camp is an editor and freelance writer of non-fiction as well as fiction works.

Lin Carter (1930–1988), born in Florida, wrote several science fiction and fantasy series including those featuring Callisto and Zarkon, Lord of the Unknown.

Bjorn Nyberg was a Swedish fan of Howard's writing who submitted a complete manuscript to Gnome Press. After editing by Sprague de Camp, it was published.

Karl Edward Wagner (b. 1945) holds a degree in psychiatry but has been a full-time writer since 1975.

David C. Smith (b. 1952) worked in advertising and taught English before teaming with Forest Service veteran, editor and writer Richard L. Tierney (b. 1936 in Iowa).

Poul William Anderson (b. 1926) writes both science fiction with a firm scientific basis and fantasy derived from Nordic mythology.

Andrew Jefferson Offutt (b. 1934) worked as a salesman and agency manager before becoming a full-time writer.

Robert Jordan (1948–2007) has written the extended Wheel of Time fantasy novels as well as seven entries in the Conan series.

Roland Green (b. 1944) has also written the Wandor heroic fantasy series. "I had read only two Conans when I started writing, and at that time Conan was an example of the kind of hero I didn't want," he said in an interview in *The Bar-*

barian Scroll No. 15. "However, by the time I actually started writing *Conan the Valiant*, I had read pretty much all the Conan canon, and had a clearer and more favorable impression of the character."

"Conan and I go back a long way," said Leonard Carpenter, author of nine Conan pastiches, in an interview in *The Hyborian Report*. "I first encountered him in eighth grade, back in about 1960, in some of the old Gnome Press editions in our local library. He helped me survive adolescence. Conan captivated me because he was an uncompromising, forceful character, not stereotyped or prettified like the milk-drinking cowboys we had in my boyhood, and not coldly paranoid like the later 'adult Western' heroes."

In his lifetime, Howard suffered heavy editing at times. "Jack Byrne did some rewriting of the boxing stories he published at Fiction House," according to bibliographer Leon Nielsen, "cutting 10,000 words from *Iron Men*, while the editors at *Argosy All-Story* made cuts to *Crowd Horror*. After Howard's death in 1936, Otis Adelbert Kline rewrote some of his Western stories to get them published." Otto Binder, he suggested, used Howard's notes to finish *Almuric* for *Weird Tales* in 1939.

This listing omits comic books and graphic novels. In some cases, the first publication was of versions completed by others. The Howard listing is of original works either complete or incomplete. Howard works listed are only the ones with characters carried on by other writers; he also wrote cowboy, boxing, horror and other stories.

Original Book Publication of Black Vulmea Works
Black Vulmea's Vengeance (1976)

Black Vulmea Pastiche
David C. Smith, *The Witch of the Indies* (1977)

Original Book Publication of Bran Mak Morn Works
Bran Mak Morn (1996) seven stories and   edited by David Weber
  one fragment about Bran Mak Morn,

Uniform Edition of Howard's Original Bran Mak Morn Tales and Fragments
Bran Mak Morn: The Last King (2005)

Bran Mak Morn Pastiches
David C. Smith and Richard Tierney, *For the Witch of the Mists* (1978)
Karl Edward Wagner, *Legion from the Shadows* (1976)

Original Book Publication of Conan Works
Skull-Face and Others (1946) contains   *Conan the Conqueror* (1950) aka *The Hour*
  five Conan stories   *of the Dragon* (1977) Conan novel

King Conan (1953) five stories about Conan

The Coming of Conan (1953) four stories about Conan, one edited by L. Sprague de Camp

Conan the Barbarian (1954) five stories about Conan

The Sword of Conan (1954) four stories about Conan

Uniform Editions of Howard's Original Tales and Fragments

The Coming of Conan (2003) edited by Patrice Louinet
The Bloody Crown of Conan (2004) edited by Patrice Louinet
The Savage Tales of Solomon Kane (2004)
The Conquering Sword of Conan (2005) edited by Patrice Louinet

Pastiches about Conan the Barbarian (and Some Posthumous Collaborations)

Poul Anderson, *Conan the Rebel* (1980)

Leonard Carpenter, *Conan the Renegade* (1986); *Conan the Raider* (1986); *Conan the Warlord* (1988); *Conan the Hero* (1989); *Conan the Great* (1990); *Conan the Outcast* (1991); *Conan the Savage* (1992); *Conan of the Red Brotherhood* (1993); *Conan, Scourge of the Bloody Coast* (1994); *Conan the Gladiator* (1995); *Conan, Lord of the Black River* (1996)

Roland Green, *Conan the Valiant* (1988); *Conan the Guardian* (1991); *Conan the Relentless* (1992); *Conan and the Gods of the Mountain* (1993); *Conan at the Demon's Gate* (1994)

John C. Hocking, *Conan and the Emerald Lotus* (1995)

Robert Jordan, *Conan the Invincible* (1982); *Conan the Defender* (1982); *Conan the Triumphant* (1983); *Conan the Unconquered* (1983); *Conan the Magnificent* (1984); *Conan the Destroyer* (movie adaptation; original story by Roy Thomas and Gerry Conway, screenplay by Stanley Mann, 1984); *Conan the Victorious* (1984)

Roger E. Moore, *Conan and the Prophecy* (1984); *Conan the Outlaw* (1985)

Sean A. Moore, *Conan the Hunter* (1994); *Conan and the Shaman's Curse* (1996)

Andrew J. Offutt, *Conan and the Sorcerer* (1978); *Conan: The Sword of Skelos* (1979); *Conan the Mercenary* (1981)

Steve Perry, *Conan the Fearless* (1986); *Conan the Defiant* (1987); *Conan the Indomitable* (1989); *Conan the Free Lance* (1990); *Conan the Formidable* (1990)

John Maddox Roberts, *Conan the Valorous* (1985); *Conan the Champion* (1987); *Conan the Marauder* (1988); *Conan the Bold* (1989); *Conan the Rogue* (1991); *Conan and the Treasure of Python* (1993); *Conan and the Manhunters* (1994); *Conan and the Amazon* (1995)

L. Sprague de Camp, *Tales of Conan* (1955) four posthumous Howard collaborations with L. Sprague de Camp; *Conan the Adventurer* 1966) four stories, one Howard story completed by L. Sprague de Camp; *Conan the Usurper* (1967) four Howard stories, one edited and one completed by L. Sprague de Camp; *Conan and the Spider God* (1980)

L. Sprague de Camp and Lin Carter, *Conan* (1967) seven stories, one completed by Sprague de Camp, one completed by Carter, two pastiches by Sprague de Camp and Carter; *Conan the Wanderer* (1968) four stories, one completed by Sprague de Camp, one by Sprague de Camp and Lin Carter; *Conan the Freebooter* (1968) five stories, two completed by Sprague de Camp; *Conan of the Isles* (1969); *Conan of Cimmeria* (1969) eight stories, one completed by Sprague de Camp, one completed

by Sprague de Camp and Carter, three pastiches by Sprague de Camp and Carter;
Conan the Buccaneer (1971); *Conan of Aquilonia* (1977) four stories; *Conan the Liberator* (1979); *Conan the Barbarian* (movie adaptation; original script by John Milius and Oliver Stone, 1982)

L. Sprague de Camp, Lin Carter and Bjorn Nyberg, *Conan the Swordsman* (1978) seven stories, five by Sprague de Camp and Carter, two by Sprague de Camp and Nyberg

L. Sprague de Camp and Bjorn Nyberg, *Conan the Avenger* (1968)

Harry Turtledove, *Conan of Venarium* (2003)

Karl Edward Wagner, *Conan: The Road of Kings* (1979)

James M. Ward, *Conan the Undaunted* (1984)

Original Book Publication of Cormac Mac Art Works

Tigers of the Sea (1974) four Cormac Mac Art stories, two edited and completed by Richard L. Tierney

Cormac Mac Art (1995) includes two stories completed by editor David Drake

Cormac Mac Art Pastiches

Andrew J. Offutt, *Sword of the Gael* (1975); *The Undying Wizard* (1976); *The Sign of the Moonbow* (1977); *The Mists of Doom* (1977)

Andrew Offutt and Keith Taylor, *When Death Birds Fly* (1980); *The Tower of Death* (1982)

Original Book Publication of Kull Works

Kull (1995) edited by David Drake

Uniform Editions of Howard's Original Kull Tales and Fragments

Kull: Exile of Atlantis (2008)

Pastiches About Kull

Lin Carter, *King Kull* (1967) thirteen King Kull stories, one edited by Carter, three edited and completed by Carter

Sean A. Moore, *Kull the Conqueror* (based on a screenplay by Charles Edward Pogue, 1997)

Original Book Publication of Red Sonja Works

"The Shadow of the Vulture" Red Sonya story included in *The Sowers of the Thunder* (1973)

Red Sonja Pastiches

David C. Smith and Richard L. Tierney, *Red Sonja: The Ring of Ikribu* (1981); *Red Sonja: Demon Night* (1982); *Red Sonja: When Hell Laughs* (1982); *Red Sonja: Endithor's Daughter* (1982); *Red Sonja: Against the Prince of Hell* (1983); *Red Sonja: Star of Doom* (1983)

Skull Face Pastiches

Richard A. Lupoff, *Return of Skull Face* (1977)

Original Book Publication of Solomon Kane Works

Solomon Kane (1968)

The Moon of Skulls (1968) Solomon
  Kane stories

The Hand of Kane (1968) Solomon
  Kane stories

Posthumous Collaborations

Ramsey Campbell, *Solomon Kane* (1995) original stories and fragments and three stories newly completed

Michael Moorcock, Frank Belknap Long, A.E. van Vogt, H. Warner Munn, Manly Wade Wellman and Brian Lumley, *Ghor Kin-Slayer* (1997) fragment completed

Pastiches Based on Howard's Hyborian Age Mythos

Loren L. Coleman, *Legends of Kern 1: Blood of Wolves* (2005); *Legends of Kern 2: Cimmerian Rage* (2005); *Legends of Kern 3: Songs of Victory* (2005)

Richard A. Knaak, *A Soldier's Quest 1: The God in the Moon* (2006); *A Soldier's Quest 2: The Eye of Charon* (2006); *A Soldier's Quest 3: The Silent Enemy* (2006)

Jeff Mariotte, *Marauders 1: Ghost of the Wall* (2006); *Marauders 2: Winds of the Wild Sea* (2006); *Marauders 3: Dawn of the Ice Bear* (2006)

J. Steven York, *Anok, Heretic of Stygia 1: Scion of the Serpent* (2005); *Anok, Heretic of Stygia 2: Heretic of Set* (2005); *Anok, Heretic of Stygia 3: Venom of Luxur* (2005)

ROBERT JORDAN

Wheel of Time

Most of his readers knew fantasy writer James Oliver Rigney, Jr. (1948–2007), as Robert Jordan. His first book, the launch of a family saga, *The Fallon Blood*, came out under yet another name, Reagan O'Neal. He wrote Westerns as Jackson O'Reilly. While an editor with Tor, he wrote several Conan pastiches as Robert Jordan. He continued the fantasy vein, and the name, for his popular Wheel of Time series.

A South Carolina native, he served two tours in Vietnam as an Army helicopter gunner. He graduated from The Citadel with a degree in physics and worked for the U.S. Navy as a nuclear engineer.

At his death, the last volume in Jordan's saga, *A Memory of Light*, was incomplete. Brandon Sanderson finished it in three volumes.

Original Wheel of Time Works

The Eye of the World (1990)

The Great Hunt (1990)

The Dragon Reborn (1991)

The Shadow Rising (1992)

The Fires of Heaven (1993)

Lord of Chaos (1994)

A Crown of Swords (1996)

The Path of Daggers (1998)

Winter's Heart (2000)

Crossroads of Twilight (2003)

New Spring: The Novel (2004)

Knife of Dreams (2005)

Posthumous Collaboration

Brandon Sanderson, *The Gathering Storm* (announced 2009)

ROBERT KORNWISE

Sorcery

Robert Kornwise was a high school student. He died in an auto accident at age 16, because of a drunk driver. Friends sent his incomplete manuscript to Kornwise's favorite writer, Piers Anthony (b. 1934), creator of the Xanth series, and asked if he would complete it. He did.

Posthumous Collaboration with Piers Anthony

Through the Ice (1992)

RICHARD LAYMON

Scary

Windy City native Richard Laymon (1947–2001) grew up in California. He attended Willamette University in Oregon and Loyola University in Los Angeles. He wrote short stories and novels with themes of horror and fantasy under his own name and as Carl Laymon and Richard Kelly. Several works came out after his death from a heart attack.

Posthumous Restoration

The Woods are Dark (2008) restored and complete edition of his 1981 novel

Posthumous Pastiche/Tribute

Edited by Kelly Laymon, Steve Gerlach and Richard Chizmar, *In Laymon's Terms* (2009)

FRITZ LEIBER

Fafhrd and the Gray Mouser

Fritz Leiber (1910–1992), a prolific and influential writer of fantasy, horror and science tales, crafted a number of stories about sword-and-sorcery heroes Fafhrd (a seven-foot barbarian from the north) and Gray Mouser (an apprentice-wizard-turned-thief) who find adventure in the world of Nehwon. Leiber's first story, and first story about the pair, "Two Sought Adventure," appeared in *Unknown* in 1939, and was collected in *Swords Against Death* as "The Jewels in the Forest." Leiber's friend Harry Otto Fischer (1910–1986) — Leiber based the characters on himself (Mouser) and Fischer (Fafhrd) — wrote part of the 1964 novella "The Lords of Quarmall," which first appeared in *Fantastic* in 1964 and was collected in *Swords in the Mist* (1968). Most of the stories appeared first in periodicals or anthologies edited by others. "Ill Met in Lankhmar, collected in *Swords and Deviltry*, won the author Nebula and Hugo awards in 1970.

Award-winning fantasy author Robin Wayne Bailey extended the series for one book. He has also written Frost, Brothers of the Dragon and DragonKin stories.

Original works

Two Sought Adventure (1957)
Swords in the Mist (1968) stories
Swords Against Wizardry (1968) stories
Swords of Lankhmar (1968)
Swords and Deviltry (1970) stories

Swords Against Death (1970) stories
Swords and Ice Magic (1977) stories
The Knight and Knave of Swords (1988) stories

Pastiche

Robin Wayne Bailey, *Swords Against the Shadowland* (1998)

H.P. LOVECRAFT

Macabre

Howard Phillips Lovecraft (1890–1937), the reclusive, effete master of gothic horror, fantasy and science fiction of a distinctly weird variety, seldom ventured far from Providence, Rhode Island. His work appeared in *Argosy, Weird Tales* and other pulp magazines. Lovecraft wrote a cosmic horror; other writers expanded on this Cthulhu Mythos, as Lovecraft's publisher August Derleth (1909–1971) of Arkham House called it. Lovecraft corresponded with other writers such as Clark Ashton Smith, Robert E. Howard and Robert Bloch. His influence is felt yet today on modern writers of horror tales.

This book does not list writers who toiled in the Cthulhu shared universe.

Derleth worked diligently to keep Lovecraft's work before the public. After Lovecraft died, Derleth expanded fragments and notes into new stories, several of which appeared in *Weird Tales* and later in books. The collaborations are not without controversy; some challenge that many are simply Derleth stories with Lovecraft's name attached.

Selected Original Work

The Shadow Over Innsmouth (1936)

Posthumous Collaborations

August Derleth, *The Lurker at the Threshold* (1945); *The Survivor* (1954); *Wentworth's Day* (1957); *The Gable Window* (1957); *The Shadow Out of Space* (1957); *The Ancestor* (1957); *The Lamp of Alhazred* (1957); *The Peabody Heritage* (1957); *The Shuttered Room* (1959); *The Dark Brotherhood* (1966); *The Horror from the Middle Span* (1967); *Innsmouth Clay* (1971); *The Watchers Out of Time* (1974)

T.S. Joshi, *The Dunwich Horror and Others* (1984) short stories, revised; *At the Mountains of Madness and Other Novels* (1986) revised; *Dragons and Other Tales* (1987) revised

The Shadows Over Innsmouth Pastiche

Kim Newman, *Famous Monsters* (1995) includes "The Big Fish"

MICHAEL MCDOWELL
Candles aflame

Michael McDowell (1950–1999), who wrote the Blackwater series about the Caskeys (they could reshape themselves as reptiles), as well as stories that inspired the motion pictures *The Nightmare Before Christmas* and *Beetlejuice*, died before he could complete his last manuscript.

Born in Alabama, he received degrees from Harvard and Brandeis. His first paperback original novels *The Amulet* (1979) and *Cold Moon Over Babylon* (1980) were in the gothic horror tradition. He later wrote mysteries in collaboration with Dennis Schuetz.

Maine writer Tabitha King (b. 1949) finished the story at the request of McDowell's family. It is something of a Southern gothic novel about a seven-year-old named Calley who is entangled in the supernatural.

Posthumous Collaboration with Tabitha King

Candles Burning (2006)

A. MERRITT
Fantasy

Abraham Merritt (1884–1943) was born in New Jersey but grew up in Philadelphia. He studied law but became a newspaper reporter and editor. He was assistant editor at *American Weekly* from 1912 to 1937, when he stepped up to editor. He was twice married and lived on Long Island. *The Ship of Ishtar* is among his best-known fantasy novels.

Merritt's friend and occasional collaborator, the illustrator Hannes Bok (1914–1964), completed a Merritt fragment and added to it for *The Fox Woman and the Blue Pagoda*. (The fragment was published by itself in *The Fox Woman and Other Stories* [1949].) Bok also used unpublished Merritt material to shape *The Black Wheel*.

Posthumous Collaborations

Hannes Bok, *The Fox Woman and the Blue Pagoda* (1946); *The Black Wheel* (1948)

ANDRE NORTON

Quag Keep

Andre Norton (1812–2005) wrote fantasy, science fiction and historical novels. Born in Cleveland, Ohio, she was the first female recipient of the Gandalf Grand Master Award from the World Science Fiction Society in 1977.

Collaborations with writers Lyn McConchie and Jean Rabe began before the author's death, and continued beyond.

Posthumous Collaborations

Lyn McConchie, *Beast Master's Quest* (2006)
Sasha Miller, *The Knight of the Red Beard* (2008)
Jean Rabe, *Return to Quag Keep* (2006); *Dragon Mage* (2008)

MERVYN PEAKE

Gothic fantasy

Mervyn Peake (1911–1968), an illustrator as well as poet and novelist, was born in Jiangzi, China, but lived for many years in England. His *Rhymes Without Reason* (1944) was a collection of nonsense poems. He later wrote *Mr. Pye*, a comic novel. But his main literary work was the story of Titus Groan. Peake planned *Titus Alone* as the concluding book in his Gormenghast trilogy. He fell ill with Parkinson's Disease before finishing it and his wife, Maeve Gilmore, turned the manuscript and notes over to the publisher. The publisher misunderstood the notes and issued the manuscript in a form not satisfactory to all.

Langdon Jones re-edited *Titus Alone* for another publisher. The start of another manuscript, *Titus Awakes*, remains incomplete and unpublished, though Gilmore worked on it before her death. A few pages were printed in a 1995 edition that collected all three Gormenghast works.

Original Gormenghast Works

Titus Groan (1946)
Gormenghast (1950)
Sometime, Never: Three Tales of Imagi-

nation (1956) includes "Boy in Dark-ness"
Titus Alone (1959)

Posthumous Restoration

Langdon Jones, *Titus Alone* (1970)

JOHN WILLIAM POLIDORI

Original vampire

Bram Stoker's wasn't the first literary vampire. John William Polidori (1795–1821) set up the vampire sub-genre of horror/fantasy fiction with his story, "The Vampyre," a tale of Lord Ruthven that appeared in *New Monthly Magazine* in April 1819. It was at first attributed to Lord Byron but has appeared in several book editions in the years since bylined by Polidori.

Polidori, the son of an Italian scholar and his English wife, attended Ample-forth College and the University of Edinburgh, where he received a medical degree. He became personal physician to Lord Byron, made friends in literary circles. He began to write, though with minimal success. He apparently committed suicide.

Cyprien Berard wrote an unauthorized sequel, which was for some reason widely attributed to Charles Nodier. Nodier, however, wrote *Le Vampyre*, a play based on the same character and situation.

Original Work

"The Vampyre" (1819)

Pastiche

Cyprien Berard, *Lord Ruthwen ou les Vampires* (1820)

M.P. SHIEL

Fantastic

Matthew Phipps Shiel (1865–1947) was a British writer of fantasy and the super-natural. Born in the West Indies, he first wrote short stories, then a novel, *The Rajah's Sapphire* (1896). Publishing under the name M.P. Shiel, he wrote a number of serials under contract. Among his best-known books are *The Purple Cloud* (1901) and *The Yellow Danger* (1898).

Terrance Ian Fytton Armstrong (1912–1970), better known as John Gawsworth, found three unfinished Shiels stories and had Oswell Blakeston complete them for the 1936 anthology *Masterpieces of Thrills*. Gawsworth apparently completed other stories himself. Shiels was still alive but disinterested in the project. Oswell Blakeston (1907–1985) was an artist and writer. Other collections with collaborations appeared after Shiel's death.

Posthumous Collaborations

Masterpieces of Thrills (1936) edited by John Gawsworth, includes "Dr. Todoro," "The Mystery of the Red Road" and "The Hanging of Ernest Clark," with Oswell Blakeston and John Gawsworth

Thrills (1936) edited by John Gawsworth, includes "A Case for Deducation" with Fytton Armstrong (a John Gawsworth penname)

Crimes, Creeps and Thrills (1936) edited by John Gawsworth, includes "The Falls Scandal," with Fytton Armstrong

Works of M.P. Shiel Updated, Vol. 2 (1980) includes "The Missing Merchants" with John Gawsworth

Prince Zaleski and Cummings King Monk (1977) includes "The Return of Prince Zaleski," heavily revised by Gawsworth

Prince Zaleski (2002) includes "The Return of Prince Zaleski," heavily revised by Gawsworth

L. SPRAGUE DE CAMP AND FLETCHER PRATT

Harold Shea

L. Sprague de Camp (1907–2000) and Fletcher Pratt (1897–1956) collaborated on fantasy stories about psychologist Harold Shea and the magical parallel world he lived in for *Unknown* magazine, *Beyond Fantasy* and *Fantasy Magazine*. They collected the stories in *The Incomplete Enchanter* and *The Castle of Iron*. Those two books were merged with *Wall of Serpents* for *The Complete Compleat Enchanter* (1988).

After Pratt died, Sprague de Camp, in something of a half-pastiche, recruited a new partner, Christopher Stasheff (b. 1944), for more stories.

Original Harold Shea Works

The Incomplete Enchanter (1941)   *Wall of Serpents* (1960)
The Castale of Iron (1950)

Half-Pastiches

L. Sprague de Camp with Christopher Stasheff, *The Enchanter Reborn* (1992); *The Exotic Enchanter* (1995)

Harry Turtledove, editor, *The Enchanter Completed: A Tribute Anthology for L. Sprague de Camp* (2005) includes "Return to Xanadu" by Lawrence Watt-Evans

BRAM STOKER
The Count

Bram Stoker (1847–1912), a theater critic, wrote the Gothic horror masterpiece *Dracula* in 1897. The book, about Dr. Van Helsing's pursuit of the legendary Transylvanian vampire, inspired a mini-industry of B-movies, as well as pastiches. Born near Dublin, Stoker was not a healthy child. He attended Trinity College, graduated with honors and went into Civil Service work. He managed the Lyceum Theatre in London for a decade. He wrote reviews for the *Dublin Evening Mail*. He married actress Florence Balcombe. Among his lesser known novels is one about Egyptian mummies, *The Jewel of Seven Stars* (1903).

Such a rich character inspired myriad impersonations. Dracula novels are listed. Other vampire variations are not. The Stoker family authorized great-grand-nephew Dacre Stoker to write a sequel. *Dracula: The Undead* came out in 2009.

Original Works

Dracula (1897)   *Dracula's Guest* (1914)

Pastiches

Marta Acosta, *The Bride of Casa Dracula* (2008); *Happy Hour at Casa Dracula* (2008)
Brian Wilson Aldis, *Dracula Unbound* (1991)
Victor Gyozo Ambrus, *Dracula* (1980); *Dracula Bedtime Storybook* (1981); *Son of Dracula* (1986)
C. Dean Anderson, *I Am Dracula* (1998)
Roderick Anscombe, *The Secret Life of Laszlo, Count Dracula* (1994)
Etiene Aubin, *Dracula and the Virgin of the Undead* (1974)
Michael Augustyn, *Vlad Dracula: The Dragon Prince* (2004)
Ronald Chetwynd-Hayes, *Dracula's Children* (1987); *House of Dracula* (1987)
Asa Drake, *Crimson Kisses* (1981)
Carl Dreadstone, *Dracula's Daughter* (1977) movie novelization
Loren D. Estleman, *Sherlock Homes Versus Dracula* (1978) aka *The Adventures of the Sanguinary Count*
Nancy Garden, *Prisoner of Vampires* (1984)
Larry Mike Garmon, *Dracula: Return of Evil* (2001)
Angus Hall, *Scars of Dracula* (1971) movie novelization
Jeanne Kalogridis, *Covenant with the Vampire* (1994); *Children of the Vampire* (1995)
Kideyuki Kikuchi, *Vampire Hunter D* (2005); *Raiser of Gales* (2005) Vampire Hunter D series; *Demon Deathchase* (2006) Vampire Hunter D series; *Vale of the Dead Town* (2006) Vampire Hunter D series; *The Stuff of Dreams* (2006) Vampire Hunter D series; *Pilgrimage of the Sacred and the Profane* (2006) Vampire Hunter D series;

Mysterious Journey to the North Sea, Part 1 (2007) Vampire Hunter D series; *Mysterious Journey to the North Sea, Part 2* (2007) Vampire Hunter D series; *The Rose Princess* (2007) Vampire Hunter D series; *Dark Nocturne* (2008) Vampire Hunter D series; *Pale Fallen Angel, Part 1* (2008) Vampire Hunter D series; *Pale Fallen Angel, Part 2* (2008) Vampire Hunter D series; *Pale Fallen Angel, Part 3* (2009) Vampire Hunter D series

Gail Kimberly, *Dracula Began* (1976)

Marie Kiraly, *Mina* (1994)

Elizabeth Kostova, *The Historian* (2005)

Allen Conrad Kupler, *The Journal of Professor Abraham Van Helsing* (2004)

Michael Lawrence and Chris Mould, *Young Dracula* (2002)

Richard Laymon, Ed Gorman, Max Allan Collins, Rex Miller and Nancy Collins, *Dracula: Prince of Darkness* (1992)

Robert Lory, *Dracula Returns* (1973); *Hand of Dracula* (1973); *Dracula's Brother* (1973); *Dracula's Gold* (1973); *Drums of Dracula* (1974); *Witching of Dracula* (1974); *Dracula's Lost World* (1974); *Dracula's Disciple* (1975); *Challenge to Dracula* (1975)

Tim Lucas, *The Book of Renfield: A Gospel of Dracula* (2005)

Carole Marsh, *The Mystery at Dracula's Castle: Transylvania, Romania* (2008)

Douglas Myles, *Prince Dracula: Son of the Devil* (1988)

Kim Newman, *Anno Dracula* (1993); *Blood Red Baron* (1996)

Dean Owen, *Brides of Dracula* (1969) movie novelization

Michel Parry, *Countess Dracula* (1971) movie novelization

James Reese, *The Dracula Dossier: A Novel of Suspense* (2008)

Anne Rice, *The Ultimate Dracula* (1992)

John Ruddy, *Bargain* (1990)

Raymond Rudorff, *The Dracula Archives* (1971)

Fred Saberhagen, *The Dracula Tapes* (1975); *Holmes-Dracula File* (1978); *Old Friends of the Family* (1979); *Thorn* (1980); *Dominion* (1982); *A Matter of Taste* (1992); *Question of Time* (1992); *A Sharpness on the Neck* (1998); *A Coldness in the Blood* (2003)

Javier Garcia Sanchez, *Ella, Dracula/she, Dracula* (2006)

Stephen Seitz, *Sherlock Holmes and the Plague of Dracula* (2007)

John Shirley, *Dracula in Love* (1990)

Robin Spriggs, *The Dracula Poems: A Poetic Encounter with the Lord of Vampires* (1992)

Dacre Stoker and Ian Holt, *Dracula: The Undead* (2009)

Jack Hamilton Teed, *Blood of Dracula* (1977)

Peter Tremayne, *Dracula Unborn* (1977); *Revenge of Dracula* (1978); *Dracula, My Love* (1980)

Martin Waddell, *Little Dracula's First Bite* (1986); *Little Dracula's Christmas* (1986); *Little Dracula at the Seaside* (1987); *Little Dracula Goes to School* (1987)

Jan Wahl, *Dracula's Cat* (1981); *Dracula's Cat and Frankenstein's Dog* (1990)

Fred Warrington, *Dracula the Undead* (1997)

Paul Witcover, *Dracula: Asylum* (2006)

Jeanne Youngson, *Further Perils of Dracula* (1979)

J.R.R. TOLKIEN
Middle-earth

John Ronald Reuel Tolkien (1892–1973) was born in Bloemfontein, South Africa, the son of a bank manager. At age three, his mother brought Tolkien and his brother back to England for health reasons. Tolkien began to study the classics at Exeter College in Oxford, but switched to English and literature. He wrote poetry. He continued an interest in language, and in making up his own, supposedly spoken by elves.

Tolkien served as a signal officer during the First World War. The loss of two close friends inspired him to start writing *The Silmarillion*, an epic work. After the war, he taught. At age thirty-three he became one of Oxford's youngest professors. He wrote *The Hobbit*, and, after a fashion, the Rings trilogy.

"All historians of children's literature ... agree in placing that book among the very highest achievements of children's authors during the 20th cent.," according to Humphrey Carpenter and Mari Prichard in *The Oxford Companion to Children's Literature*. "Tolkien himself came to believe that no author could write especially 'for' children — the first edition of *The Hobbit* contains a number of patronizing 'asides' to the child-audience, but many of these were removed later, when its author's views on the subject changed."

Tolkien had held up publication of the Lord of the Rings opus in order to include *Silmarillion*. He never finished it. *The Fellowship of the Ring* and *The Two Towers* eventually saw print in 1954, *The Return of the King* the next year. By 1965, international copyright on the books lapsed. An American paperback publisher, Ace, brought the trilogy out in softcover, but without paying royalties. Tolkien revised the work slightly for a new, "authorized" edition from his own publisher. The notoriety of the royalties dispute brought wide attention to the books, which were very popular with college students. Ace later paid royalties to Tolkien and withdrew its edition. By the end of 1968, about three million copies of the Lord of the Rings had sold worldwide.

Christopher Tolkien (b. 1924), who edited his father's History of Middle-earth series, with the assistance of Canadian fantasy fiction writer Guy Gavriel Kay (b. 1954) completed *The Silmarillion* and it was published in 1977.

Original Middle-earth Works

The Hobbit; or, There and Back Again (1937)
The Fellowship of the Ring (1954)
The Two Towers (1954)

The Return of the King (1955)
Bilbo's Last Song (1990) verse extracted from *The Hobbit*

Posthumous Collaborations

Christopher Tolkien and Guy Gabriel Kay, *The Silmarillion* (1977)
Christopher Tolkien, *The Children of Hurin* (1997)

MANLY WADE WELLMAN
John the Balladeer

Manly Wade Wellman (1903–1986) was a native of Kamundongo (Angola), Portuguese West Africa, where his father was a British physician. Wellman graduated from Wichita (Kansas) Municipal University and Columbia, lived for many years in North Carolina and absorbed many of its folk legends. He was married to Frances Obrist, who wrote for *Weird Tales* under the name Frances Garfield. He was a journalist for newspapers in Wichita. He served in the military during World War II. He wrote mysteries, historical novels, juveniles and non-fiction works.

His first short story, "The Lion Roared," for *Thrilling Tales* in 1927, was based on some of the magic stories he heard while growing up in Africa. He set many of his fantasy and horror stories in the Appalachian mountains. He ghost-wrote scripts for Will Eisner's The Spirit comics. His best known series featured an occult detective, Judge Pursuivant, an adventurer, John Thunstone, and a roaming forest minstrel, Silver John. John first appeared in a short story in *Fantasy and Science Fiction* in December 1951.

Arkham House revised the earliest stories to give them a semblance of novel-like continuity. Karl Edward Wagner collected all of the John the Balladeer stories and reprinted them just as they had originally run in periodicals or anthologies.

Original John the Balladeer Works

Who Fears the Devil? (1963) short stories   *The Lost and the Lurking* (1981)
The Old Gods Waken (1979)   *The Hanging Stones* (1982)
After Dark (1980)   *The Voice of the Mountain* (1984)

Posthumous Restoration

Karl Edward Wagner, editor, *John the Balladeer* (1988); *Owl Hoots in the Daytime and Other Omens: Selected Manly Wade Wellman Stories*, Vol. 5 (2003)

CHERRY WILDER
Rulers of Hylor

Cherry Barbara Lockett Grimm (1930–2002) was born in Auckland, New Zealand. She began to write science fiction and fantasy in 1974 and sold more than fifty short stories and novels under the name Cherry Wilder.

After Wilder's death, science fiction writer Katya Reimann (b. 1965), author of the Tielmaran Chronicles, completed Cherry's fourth Rulers of Hylor book.

Original Rulers of Hylon Works
A Princess of the Chameln (1984)
Yoath the Wolf (1984)
The Summer's King (1986)

Posthumous Collaboration
Kayta Reimann, *The Wanderer* (2004)

AUSTIN TAPPAN WRIGHT

Utopia

Austin Tappan Wright (1883–1931), born in Hanover, New Hampshire, and educated at Harvard, was a legal scholar at the University of California at Berkeley Law School. In his lifetime he wrote a single short story, for *Atlantic Monthly*. After his death, his widow, Margaret, found a mass of papers and notes for a Utopian fantasy, *Islandia*. She typed the manuscript and later her daughter Sylvia, with the assistance of Mark Saxton (1914–1988), brought the book into print. The book, condensed from Wright's draft, relates the adventures of John Lang in an imaginary world near Antarctica.

Saxton, longtime editor with Farrar & Rinehart, wrote one sequel and two prequels.

Original Work
Islandia (1942)

Pastiches
Mark Saxton, *The Islar, Islandia Today: a Narrative of Lang III* (1969); *The Two Kingdoms: A Novel of Islandia* (1979); *Havoc in Islandia* (1982)

Humor

Fondness for characters well done inspired Tom Holt to write more Mapp and Lucia stories, and Stuart Donald to take Para Handy on board his puffer again. Motives pure and just. Julius Lester and Toni Morrison had a different agenda in revisiting Joel Chandler Harris's Br'er Rabbit and cohorts — are the originals racist mockery or are they dialect-precise tellings? Thorne Smith's ghosts and P.G. Wodehouse's upper society twits are impossibly original, thus the few attempts at pastiche.

E. F. BENSON

Mapp and Lucia

Emeline Lucas, known as Lucia, dominates the social order of Riseholme, in Southern England. Her husband, Peppino, writes poetry. Elizabeth Mapp rules over her own community, Tilling. Both ladies appeared in stories by E.F. Benson, and they eventually met in the book *Mapp and Lucia* (1931), in which the two were rescued at sea by an Italian fishing boat.

The author, Edward Frederick Benson (1867–1940), was born in Berkshire, England, where his father was Wellington College headmaster. Benson loved music, excelled at sports, became an archaeologist and began to write fiction. Although he also wrote other novels, ghost stories and memoirs, the Make Way for Lucia books were his most enduring, and inspired a BBC-TV mini-series.

Comic novelist Tom Holt carried the characters forward into the World War II era with his pastiches. Guy Fraser-Sampson filled in a gap between *Miss Mapp* and *Mapp and Lucia*.

Original Map and Lucia Works

Queen Lucia (1920)
Miss Mapp (1922)
Lucia in London (1927)
Mapp and Lucia (1931)

Lucia's Progress (1935) aka *The Worshipful Lucia*
Trouble for Lucia (1939)

178

Pastiches

Guy Fraser-Sampson, *Major Benjy* (2008)
Tom Holt, *Lucia in Wartime* (1986); *Lucia Triumphant* (1988)

HUGH FOULIS
Para Handy

Para Handy is the nickname of Peter Macfarlane, primary figure in a long run of short stories written by Neil Munro for the *Glasgow Evening News* under the pen-name Hugh Foulis. The stories are about the skipper of the *Vital Spark*, a puffer (steamboat) that delivered goods along the River Clyde and coast of Scotland in the early 20th century. The stories of the captain, the engineer Dan Macphail, the mate Dougie and the deckhands The Tar or Sunny Jim, inspired three television adaptations.

Munro (1864–1930) was born in Inverary, Argyll, Scotland, of the Campbell clan. He worked for several newspapers over the years, and wrote serious books under his real name. The humorous Para Handy stories, with thick dialect, however, proved to be his most popular.

Stuart Donald, born in Renfrewshire, manager of Cowal Highland Gathering in Dunoon and a freelance writer, composed sequel stories. "I grew up with the Para Handy tales, and know them — literally — almost off by heart. I therefore approached the whole task with both affection and respect for their creator," Donald said in the introduction to *Para Handy Sails Again*. Donald died before he could compile a planned third volume of short stories. He also wrote *Para Handy's Scotland: In the Wake of the Vital Spark* (1994), a nonfiction tribute.

Original Works

The Vital Spark (1906)
In Highland Harbours with Para Handy (1911)
Hurricane Jack of the Vital Spark (1923)
Para Handy Tales (1955)
Para Handy: First Complete Edition (1992)

Pastiches

Stuart Donald, *Para Handy Sails Again* (1995); *Para Handy: All at Sea* (1996)

GEORGE GROSSMITH
Nobody

Diary of a Nobody, a comedic account of Charles Pooter's self-absorbed social life, was written by George Grossmith (1847–1912) and first appeared *Punch* in 1888 and 1889. Grossmith was a singer and actor (primarily in Gilbert and Sullivan operettas) as well as writer. He also did a solo act with song and piano.

Keith Waterhouse (b. 1929) took Pooter's wife Carrie's side in his sequel.

Original Work
Diary of a Nobody (1892)

Pastiche
Keith Waterhouse, *Mrs. Pooter's Diary* (1983)

JOEL CHANDLER HARRIS
Brer Rabbit

Georgia native Joel Chandler Harris (1848–1908) worked as a journalist, and wrote numerous Uncle Remus tales strong on dialect and African storytelling. Brer Rabbit is the trickster, able to outwit Brer Fox at every turn. Harris certainly tapped the African tradition for his stories. He also apparently borrowed from Algonquian tales, and from Brer Rabbit stories Robert Roosevelt (1829–1906), uncle to Theodore Roosevelt, wrote for *Harper's Weekly*.

Harris was white. His stories after a fashion became an embarrassment, decried for appropriating black tradition, snubbed for perceived racism — until Julius Lester (b. 1939), a professor at the University of Massachusetts at Amherst, and Toni Morrison (b. 1931), a well-known novelist, decided to revisit them. Lester told interviewer Janice Del Negro for *Booklist*, "When I retell folk tales, I really feel that I have an obligation to be true to both the culture out of which the stories came and the culture as it is now. Doing the Uncle Remus tales was a daunting prospect. There are white people who have great love for the Uncle Remus tales as Joel Chandler Harris wrote them and feel they should not be touched, and there are black people who are antagonistic to the stories because of slavery. The frightening thing about doing the stories was that sense of responsibility to the culture, both past and present, as well as future." Morrison, well known for her novel *Beloved*, spun *Tar Baby* into an exploration of tensions between blacks and whites and the need to create mythologies.

Original Works

Uncle Remus: His Songs and his Sayings (1880)

Nights with Uncle Remus (1883)

Daddy Jake, the Runaway, and Short Stories Told After Dark by Uncle Remus (1889)

Uncle Remus and His Friends (1892)

Told by Uncle Remus (1905)

Uncle Remus and Brer Rabbit (1907)

Uncle Remus and the Little Boy (1910)

Uncle Remus Returns (1918)

Witch Wolf (1921)

Pastiches

Julius Lester, *Tales of Uncle Remus: The Adventures of Brer Rabbit* (1987); *More Tales of Uncle Remus: The Further Adventures of Brer Rabbit, His Friends, Further Tales of Uncle Remus: The Misadventures of Brer Rabbit, Brer Fox, Brer Wolf, the Doodang, and Other Creatures* (1990); *The Last Tales of Uncle Remus* (1994)
Toni Morrison, *Tar Baby* (1981)

THORNE SMITH
Ghosts

James Thorne Smith, Jr. (1892–1934), known simply as Thorne Smith to readers of his popular novels, wrote breezy humorous tales that brimmed with sensuality, social drinking and the supernatural. A native of Annapolis, Maryland, he attended Dartmouth College and worked in the advertising field before he became a writer. The hero Cosmo Topper, in *Topper* and its sequel, is a banker who encounters a pair of playful apparitions, Marion and George Kirby.

Norman H. Matson (1893–1965) completed Smith's last novel, *The Passionate Witch*, the story of shy millionaire T. Wallace Wooly, Jr., and his witch wife, Jennifer, which appears to have been one of the inspirations for the television series *Bewitched*. Matson wrote a sequel; the book, with its bare heroine on the cover, leaves little doubt as to the ribald contents.

Posthumous Collaboration

Norman H. Matson, *The Passionate Witch* (1941) aka *I Married a Witch*

Pastiche

Norman H. Matson, *Bats in the Belfry* (1942) sequel to *The Passionate Witch*

P.G. WODEHOUSE
Jeeves

Pelham Grenville Wodehouse's upper class British twit Bertie Wooster and the resourceful man-servant Jeeves first appeared in the story "Extricating Young Gussie" in the 18 September 1915 issue of *The Saturday Evening Post*. Wodehouse (1881–1975) was born and educated in England, but later lived in America. He began writing a humorous newspaper column in 1903. He was interned by Germany during World War II. In his career he turned out nearly 100 books, several in series such as Psmith, Ukridge and the Drones Club. There were thirty-five Jeeves stories in total (including two which were rewrites of earlier, non–Jeeves stories) and eleven novels.

"The duo is as momentous in literary history as the other great tandems — Don Quixote and Sancho Panza, Sherlock Holmes and Dr. Watson. Of the two, Wooster is by far the more interesting. He is a character. Jeeves, to the end of his days, remains a type — the *deus ex machina* who saves the day when all seems lost, the great artificer who ties up the loose ends and who rescues Bertie from the consequences of his repeated follies," explains Alexander Cockburn in an introduction to the 1975 Vintage edition of *The Code of the Woosters*.

Jeeves and Wooster appeared in two plays, a long-play recording, a BBC radio dramatization, two motion pictures and two British television productions, the most recent beginning in 1990 with Stephen Fry as Jeeves and Hugh Laurie as Wooster.

C. Northcote Parkinson wrote a fictionalized biography of Jeeves while Geoffrey Jaggard performed much the same function for Bertie with a reader's companion, *Wooster's World: A Companion to the Wooster-Jeeves Cycle of P.G. Wodehouse, LL.D.* (1967) and Daniel H. Garrison with *Who's Who in Wodehouse* (1987). The last two are considered non-fiction reference works, for purposes of this survey. P.H. Cannon's Jeeves stories are at the same time retellings of H.P. Lovecraft horror stories. Jonathan Ames' novel is at least a partial pastiche as the main character, Alan Blair, has in his employ a manservant named Jeeves. Stage adaptations include the musical *By Jeeves* by Alan Ackbourn and Andrew Lloyd Webber in 1996. Hugh Laurie and Stephen Fry brought the Wodehouse characters alive in a Granada Television series in the 1990s.

Original Bertie Wooster and Jeeves Works

The Man with Two Left Feet (1919) short stories

My Man Jeeves (1919)

The Inimitable Jeeves (1923) aka *Jeeves* (1923) short stories

Carry On, Jeeves (1925) short stories

Very Good, Jeeves (1930) short stories

Thank You, Jeeves (1934)

Brinkley Manor (1934) aka *Right Ho, Jeeves* (1934)

The Code of the Woosters (1938)

Joy in the Morning (1946) aka *Jeeves in the Morning* (1983)

The Mating Season (1949)

Ring for Jeeves (1953) aka *The Return of Jeeves* (1954)

Jeeves and the Feudal Spirit (1954) aka *Bertie Wooster Sees It Through* (1955)

How Right You Are, Jeeves (1960) aka *Jeeves in the Offing* (1960)

Stiff Upper Lip, Jeeves (1963)

Much Obliged, Jeeves (1971) aka *Jeeves & the Tie That Binds* (1971)

Aunts Aren't Gentlemen (1974) aka *The Cat-Nappers* (1974)

Pastiches

Jonathan Ames, *Wake Up, Sir!* (2004)

P.H. Cannon, *Scream for Jeeves* (1994)

Fictional Biographies

Daniel H. Garrison, *Who's Who in Wodehouse* (1987)

C. Northcote Parkinson, *Jeeves: A Gentleman's Personal Gentleman* (1979)

Juveniles (19th Century)

Whatever rules of pastiching hold for adult fiction carry over to juveniles. Horatio Alger was a brand, for instance, so of course his name was perpetuated for as long as possible by his various publishers. Anna Sewell could never get away with only one book, one as good as *Black Beauty*, thus there have been new sequels.

WILLIAM ADAMS

Charlton School

The Rev. William Adams (1814–1848), author of *The Shadow of the Cross* and other books, left a manuscript of schoolboy fiction at his death.

The Rev. Henry Cadwallader Adams (1817–1899) edited his brother's manuscript about Charles Warbeck, Henry Mertoun and others for publication in 1851 and contributed a sequel. In a preface to *The Cherry-Stones*, H.C. remarked that after his brother's death, "many friends, who remembered the delight with which the Story had been listened to, were desirous that it should be given to the world, and it was placed in my hands with that intention. I found it could not be published in its then state. It was little more than a rough draft, with marginal notes, and some portions not written at all ... I have ... ventured to rewrite the Book, retaining as far as possible the original MSS., and supplying a continuation and conclusion in keeping with it. That the Story must, under such circumstance, lose much of the beauty and interest, which it would have possessed if it had been completed by the mind by which it was originally conceived, is sufficiently obvious; but I trust enough remains to justify the Publication, and to render the Work interesting as well as valuable to its youthful Readers, for whose perusal it is principally designed."

Posthumous Collaboration

H.C. Adams, *The Cherry-Stones: A Tale* (1851) aka *Charlton School: A Tale for Youth*

Pastiche
H.C. Adams, *First of June* (1856) aka *Schoolboy Rivalry*

HORATIO ALGER, JR.

Out for Business

Massachusetts native Horatio Alger, Jr. (1834–1899), gave up a career as a Unitarian minister to write adventure stories for boys. A graduate of Harvard Divinity School, Alger was ever optimistic that one can persevere against life's travails and achieve wealth and fame. His young dime novel heroes Ragged Dick and Tattered Tom (actually a girl) did just that, in tale after tale of Alger's 135-book output (an estimated 20 million copies made their way into print).

The next generation of boys' books authors saw Edward Stratemeyer (1862–1930) at the forefront. Stratemeyer, who would eventually so overflow with ideas he engaged a stable of authors to craft his Tom Swift, Nancy Drew, Hardy Boys and other adventures, learned from the master. Stratemeyer, at Alger's request, completed a book Alger was unable to finish. After Alger's death, and pleased with the results of the collaboration, Stratemeyer acquired the copyrights and purportedly completed another ten Alger manuscripts or outlines for the Rise of Life series. Chances are he plotted most of them himself.

Marilyn S. Greenwald in *The Secret of the Hardy Boys* (2004) said Stratemeyer "admired Alger, and appreciated how much the author had taught him." Stratemeyer went on to success with the Rover Boys, issued under the penname Arthur M. Winfield. He established a syndicate and farmed out the writing of boys' and girls' books to others, who worked anonymously on his characters and outlines.

Several authors have parodied the Alger style, or rendered modern novels in an Alger vein — Mark Twain, Theodore Dreiser, F. Scott Fitzgerald, Lawrence Sanders and Nathaniel West (*A Cool Million*, 1934) among them — though none has succeeded in a straight-faced replication of the author who in his day gave Twain a run for the money.

Posthumous Collaborations

Edward Stratemeyer writing as Horatio Alger
Out for Business: or, Robert Frost's Strange Career (1900)
Falling in with Fortune; or, The Experiences of a Young Secretary (1900)
Young Captain Jack; or, The Son of a Soldier (1901)
Nelson the Newsboy; or, Afloat in New York (1901)
Jerry, the Backwoods Boy; or, The Parkhurst Treasure (1904)
Lost at Sea; or, Robert Roscoe's Strange Cruise (1904)
From Farm to Fortune; or, Nat Nason's Strange Experience (1905)
The Young Book Agent; or, Frank Hardy's Road to Success (1905)

Joe, the Hotel Boy; or, Winning Out by Pluck (1906)
Randy of the River; or, The Adventures of a Young Deck Hand (1906)
Ben Logan's Triumph; or, The Boys of Boxwood Academy (1908)

HELEN BANNERMAN
Sambo in India

Helen Bannerman (1862–1946) was born in Edinburgh, Scotland, but spent most of her life in the British commonwealth country India. Her husband was in the Indian Medical Service. The character in her first book, though not racist in its original depiction, is widely considered as such and has experienced considerable censorship and controversy; yet, it never went out of print. Fred Marcellino changed the names of the characters for a recent republication. Julius Lester rewrote the story. Day Bannerman wrote of *Little White Squibba* based on notes left by her mother — with a little white girl as heroine. (Bannerman herself had previously written a similarly titled *Little Black Quibba* in 1902.)

Original Works
The Story of Little Black Sambo (1899)

Posthumous Sambo Collaboration
Julius Lester, *Sam and the Tigers: A New Telling of "Little Black Sambo"* (1996)
Fred Marcellino, *The Story of Little Babaji* (1996)

Posthumous Collaboration
Day Bannerman, *Little White Squibba* (1965)

LEWIS CARROLL
Alice

'Twas brillig, Lewis Carroll's stroll into the imagination. Charles Lutwidge Dodgson (1832–1898) was an English mathematician, photographer and writer. His tales of Alice and his witty poems, such as "Jabberwocky," caught the public's imagination and are considered classics. The character Alice is believed to be based on Alice Liddell, the daughter of the dean of Christ Church and a family friend.

Alice inspired numerous parodies, as well as sequels by other hands, including some, oddly enough, in cyberpunk or futuristic or mathematical veins.

Original Works

Alice's Adventures in Wonderland (1865)   *Through the Looking Glass and What Alice Found There* (1871)

Pastiches

Peter Abrahams, *Down the Rabbit Hole* (2005)
Gilbert Adair, *Alice Through the Needle's Eye* (1984)
Nadine Amadio, *New Adventures of Alice in Rainforest Land* (1988)
Frank Beddor, *The Looking Glass Wars* (2004); *Seeing Redd* (2007)
Charles Edward Carryl, *Davy and the Goblin; or, What Followed Reading 'Alice's Adventures in Wonderland'* (1884)
Brad Craddock, *Alice's Misadventures Underground* (2006)
Robert Gilmore, *Alice in Quantumland* (1995)
Jonathan Lethem, *As She Climbed Across the Table* (1997)
Jeff Noon, *Automated Alice* (1996)
Eugene Orlando, *A Journey with Alice to Wonderland* (2004)
Ernest La Prade, *Alice in Orchestralia* (1925) aka *Alice in Orchestra Land* aka *Alice in Music Land*; *Marching Notes* (1929)
Anna Matlock Richards, *New Alice in the Old Wonderland* (1895)
Patrick Senecal, *Aliss* (2000)
Yales Wilson, *More Alice* (1959)

OLIVER OPTIC

Blue and Gray

William Taylor Adams (1822–1897) was best known to his young nineteenth-century readers as Oliver Optic. The Boston native taught public school before he took up the pen to write periodical and hardcover fiction. He was so successful that he turned in chalk and pointer in 1865 and picked up pen to write some 1,000 short stories and 115 novels. While Adams' heroes were as self-determined as Alger's, Adams' were more adventurous and militaristic. He often set his heroes at sea — literally, in Boat Club, Army and Navy and other series.

Just as he had with Horatio Alger, Jr., New Jersey native Edward Stratemeyer (1862–1930) picked up the reins following Adams' death and completed the last of Optic's Blue and Gray — On Land series, under contract to the publisher.

Posthumous Collaboration

Edward Stratemeyer writing as Oliver Optic, *An Undivided Union* (1899)

ANNA SEWELL

Black Beauty

If you're only ever going to write one book, *Black Beauty's* not a bad choice. Anna Sewell (1820–1878) was a bank manager's daughter who grew up in Yarmouth, Norfolk, England. Her mother Mary Wright Sewell wrote children's books. Anna learned compassion in the Quaker household, and when she was injured at age fourteen and became increasingly disabled, she developed a keen interest in horses. She became a skilled carriage driver, though refused to use the whip. Her message is loud and strong in *Black Beauty*: treat animals kindly. Sewell wrote the novel in her later years, when she was confined to her home. She died a year after it came out. Four motion pictures and one television series have been based on the work.

An interesting trio of prolific British sisters in the 1970s and early 1980s wrote sequels about other horses but in the *Black Beauty* universe. They were Josephine Pullein-Thompson (b. 1924), Christine Pullein-Thompson (1925–2005) and Diana Pullein-Thompson (b. 1925).

Original work

Black Beauty: The Autobiography of a Horse (1877)

Pastiches

Phyllis Briggs, *Son of Black Beauty* (1950)

Christine Pullein-Thompson, *Black Velvet* (1975); *Black Blossom* (1978); *Black Pioneer* (1982)

Diana Pullein-Thompson, *Black Princess* (1978); *Black Romany* (1978); *Black Piper* (1982)

Josephine Pullein-Thomson, *Black Ebony* (1975); *Black Nightshade* (1978); *Black Raven* (1982)

JOHANNA SPYRI

Heidi

Heidi the Swiss miss appeared in an 1880 novel written by Johanna Spyri (1827–1901). Born Johanna Louise Heusser in Hirzel, Switzerland, the author married Bernhard Spyri, a lawyer. She wrote fictional accounts of country life, and stories for children. The adventures of Heidi, the orphan girl who came to live with her grandfather in the Alps, became a popular motion picture with Shirley Temple in the title role. Spyri followed her first Heidi tale with a second, and the two were combined in one volume for subsequent publication. Spyri's English translator, Charles Tritten, wrote two sequels after her death. Other titles have been reported.

Original Work

Heidi (1880) includes *Heidi's Apprenticeship* and *Years of Wandering*

Pastiches

Anonymous, *Defend Yourself, Heidi; Heidi and the Little Orphan Boy; Heidi's Niece; Heidi the Detective; Heidi Goes to Camp; Heidi and the Bear; Heidi and the Injured Bird; Heidi and the Phantom of the Alps; Heidi and the Honey Thief; Heidi and Her Friend Arrive from the Sky*
Charles Tritten, *Heidi Grows Up* (1938); *Heidi's Children* (1939)

Juveniles (20th Century)

Enid Blyton wrote for children, and children welcomed more books in her Famous Five or Secret Seven series after her death. L. Frank Baum wrote for children, but it was adults who went crazy collecting his early books and nurturing new sequels. Lassie is an interesting literary creation in that almost none of the later books about the collie share either characters or setting. Most derive from a rather non-derivative American television series. Similarly, Walt Disney's version of Winnie the Pooh and other denizens of Six-Acre Woods has dominated bookshelves, with only recently an attempt to revive the original A.A. Milne aura. J.K Rowling's enormously popular Harry Potter fantasies have had to stave off a handful of illegal Chinese clones. No one has ventured to translate the bogus stories into English.

ROBERT ARTHUR, JR.

Three Investigators

Jupiter Jones, Pete Crenshaw and Bob Andrews were youthful private detectives in southern California, featured in a series of books purported by their publisher to have been conceived and introduced by Alfred Hitchcock.

Robert Arthur, Jr. (1909–1969), actually conceived and wrote the first nine and number 11 in the Alfred Hitchcock and the Three Investigators series, and left notes for others. He was born on Corregidor Island, the Philippines, where his father was stationed with the U.S. Army. He attended William and Mary College and the University of Michigan, from which he graduated in 1930 with a B.A. in journalism. He wrote for the pulp fiction magazines during the Depression. He was associate editor of *Photo-Story* and edited *Pocket Detective Magazine*. Arthur and a friend from a broadcast writing class, David Kogan, wrote scripts for *The Mysterious Traveler* radio series. In Hollywood, Arthur wrote scripts for *The Twilight Zone* and was a story editor for *Alfred Hitchcock Presents*. He edited several Hitchcock anthologies and was a natural choice to launch the Three Investigators series. Walter Retan was the original editor of the series.

After Arthur's death, Edgar Award–winning writer Dennis Lynds (1924–2005) (author of the Dan Fortune mystery series under the name Michael Collins), Edgar Award–winning Kin Platt (1911–2003) and Mary V. Carey wrote new books. Books bear the credit "based on characters created by Robert Arthur." The name of the series was changed to The 3 Investigators — Crimebusters in 1989. New authors included Megan Stine and H. William Stine, G.H. Stone (really Gayle Lynds, later a popular thriller writer under her own name) and William MacCay. Some early books were rewritten after Hitchcock's death, and he was replaced with a new host, Hector Sebastian. Legal issues between Random House and the Arthur heirs apparently ended the series in the United States, though it continued in Germany.

Original Three Investigators Works

The Secret of Terror Castle (1964)
The Mystery of the Stuttering Parrot (1964)
The Mystery of the Whispering Mummy (1965)
The Mystery of the Green Ghost (1965)
The Mystery of the Vanishing Treasure (1966)

The Secret of Skeleton Island (1966)
The Mystery of the Fiery Eye (1967)
The Mystery of the Silver Spider (1967)
The Mystery of the Screaming Clock (1968)
The Mystery of the Talking Skull (1969)

Three Investigators Pastiches

William Arden (Dennis Lynds), *The Mystery of the Moaning Cave* (1968); *The Mystery of the Laughing Shadow* (1969); *The Secret of the Crooked Cat* (1970); *The Mystery of the Shrinking House* (1972); *The Secret of Phantom Lake* (1973); *The Mystery of the Dead Man's Riddle* (1974); *The Mystery of the Dancing Devil* (1976); *The Mystery of the Headless Horse* (1977); *The Mystery of the Deadly Double* (1978); *The Secret of Shark Reef* (1979); *The Mystery of the Purple Pirate* (1982); *The Mystery of the Smashing Glass* (1984); *The Mystery of the Wrecker's Rock* (1986); *Hot Wheels* (1989)

Marc Brandel (Marcus Beresford), *The Mystery of the Two-Toed Pigeon* (1984); *The Mystery of the Rogues' Reunion* (1985); *An Ear for Danger* (1989)

M.V. Carey (Mary Virginia Carey), *The Mystery of the Flaming Footprints* (1971); *The Mystery of the Singing Serpent* (1972); *The Mystery of Monster Mountain* (1973); *The Secret of the Haunted Mirror* (1974); *The Mystery of the Invisible Dog* (1975); *The Mystery of Death Trap Mine* (1976); *The Mystery of the Magic Circle* (1978); *The Mystery of the Sinister Scarecrow* (1979); *The Mystery of the Scar-Faced Beggar* (1981); *The Mystery of the Blazing Cliffs* (1981); *The Mystery of the Wandering Cave Man* (1982); *The Mystery of the Missing Mermaid* (1983); *The Mystery of the Trail of Terror* (1984); *The Mystery of the Creep-Show Crooks* (1985); *The Mystery of the Cranky Collector* (1987); *Case of the Savage Statue* (1987)

Rose Estes, *Case of the Dancing Dinosaur* (1985)

William MacCay, *Funny Business* (1989); *Shoot the Works* (1990)

Megan Stine and H. William Stine, *Case of the Weeping Coffin* (1985); *Case of the House of Horrors* (1985); *Murder to Go* (1989); *Thriller Diller* (1989); *Long Shot* (1990)

G.H. Stone (Gayle Lynds), *Rough Stuff* (1989); *Reel Trouble* (1989); *Fatal Error* (1990)
Nick West (Kin Platt), *The Mystery of the Coughing Dragon* (1970); *The Mystery of the Nervous Lion* (1971)

WILBERT AWDRY
Thomas the Tank Engine

The Rev. Wilbert Vere Awdry (1911–1997), in case you couldn't guess, was a railroad enthusiast. Born in Romsey, Hampshire, England, and educated at St. Peter's Hall and Wycliffe Hall in Oxford, he was ordained an Anglican priest in 1936. He served in curacies at several locations in Great Britain. He married Margaret Wale and they had a son, Charles, who was greatly amused by stories his father invented about an imaginary Sodor island and the animated engines and vehicles that dwelled there.

Awdry put his stories to paper, and *The Three Railroad Engines* appeared in 1945. It was based on the Talyllyn Railway in Mid-Wales. "To add to the story telling, the Rev. Awdry drew simple pictures of steam locomotives on the paper along with the stories. A head on view being the easiest to draw, he drew a row of locomotives standing in an engine shed with a human face and expression on each locomotive's smokebox door," according to Ian Gunn. C. Reginald Dalby illustrated the first published books. Thomas, for those in the know, was a 0-6-OT Class E2 shuttling engine dating from the Victorian era.

Awdry wrote twenty-five more books before he retired and turned the series over to Christopher Awdry (b. 1940). Christopher Awdry wrote his first book when his own son Richard was three. Christopher was born in Wiltshire and grew up in South Birmingham. He wrote articles about railway preservation for the periodical *Steam Railway*.

Both men produced other children's books, but when Thomas the Tank Engine appeared on television, it gained huge popularity. Egmont Books ended the book series after Christopher Awdry's fourteen titles, then revived it again for *Thomas and Victoria* in 2007. There were several books produced under Christopher Awdry's hand featuring the Sodor trains, but not part of the official series.

Original Railway Series Works

WILBERT V. AWDRY
The Three Railway Engines (1945)
Thomas the Tank Engine (1946)
James the Red Engine (1948)
Tank Engine Thomas Again (1949)
Troublesome Engines (1950)
Henry the Green Engine (1951)
Toby the Tram Engine (1952)

Gordon the Big Engine (1953)
Edward the Blue Engine (1954)
Four Little Engines (1955)
Percy the Small Engine (1956)
The Eight Famous Engines (1957)
Duck and Diesel Engine (1958)
The Little Old Engine (1959)
The Twin Engines (1960)

Branch Line Engines (1961)
Gallant Old Engine (1962)
Stepney the Bluebell Engine (1963)
Mountain Engines (1964)
Very Old Engines (1965)
Main Line Engines (1966)
Small Railway Engines (1967)
Enterprising Engines (1968)

Oliver the Western Engine (1969)
Duke and the Lost Engine (1970)
Tramway Engines (1972)

WILBERT V. AWDRY WITH GEORGE
    AWDRY

The Island of Sodor: Its People, History and Railways (1987)

Railway Series Pastiches

Christopher Awdry, *Really Useful Engines* (1983); *James and the Diesel Engines* (1984); *Great Little Engines* (1985); *More About Thomas the Tank Engine* (1986); *Gordon the High Speed Engine* (1987); *Toby, Trucks and Trouble* (1988); *Thomas and the Twins* (1989); *Jock the New Engine* (1990); *Thomas and the Great Railway Show* (1991); *Thomas Comes Home* (1992); *Henry and the Express* (1993); *Wilbert the Forest Engine* (1994); *Thomas and the Fat Controller's Engines* (1995); *New Little Engine* (1996); *Thomas and Victoria* (2007)

Related Thomas the Tank Engine Pastiches

Christopher Awdry, *Thomas and the Missing Christmas Tree* (1986); *Thomas and the Evil Diesel* (1987); *Thomas and the Hurricane* (1992); *Bad Days for Thomas and His Friends* (2001); *More Bad Days for Thomas and His Friends* (2001); *Sodor; Reading Between the Lines* (2005)

Selected Thomas-Related Pastiches for Younger Readers

James and the Balloons, Percy and the Kite, Thomas and the Birthday Party, Henry and the Ghost Train, Thomas and the Dinosaurs, Thomas and the Pony Show, Thomas Goes to School, Henry Goes to the Hospital, The Snowy Special, Alfie, Annie and Clarabel, 'Arry and Bert, Arthur, Bertie, Bill and Ben, Billy, Boco, Bulgy, Bulstrode, Caroline, Cranky, Daisy, Dennis, Disel, Donald and Douglas, Duck, Duncan, Edward, Elizabeth, Emily, Fat Controller, Fergus, Freddie, George, Gordon, Harold, Harvey, Hector, Henry, Jack, James, Jeremy, Mavis, Mighty Mac, Molly, Murdoch, Neville, Oliver, Percy, Peter Sam, Rheneas, Rocky, Rosie, Rusty, Salty, Sir Handel, Skarloey, Spencer, Stepney, Terence, Thomas, Toby, Trevor and Whiff

ENID BAGNOLD

National Velvet

Enid Bagnold (1889–1981), born in Rochester, Kent, England, wrote the popular play *The Chalk Garden* (1956) and the horse story *National Velvet* (1935). Enid had begun to write as a girl living in Jamaica, where her father was assigned with the Royal Engineers. She was educated in England and on the continent. As a debutante, she lived a carefree life in London, writing occasional pieces for periodicals. She was a nurse and ambulance driver during World War I. She married Sir Roderick Jones, owner of Reuter's New Agency, in 1920.

National Velvet, illustrated by Bagnold's daughter Laurienne Jones, is about Velvet Brown, whose huge dream is to own and train a horse of her own. She wins a raffle, and a horse named Piebald, which she readies for the Grand National race. She disguises herself as a male in order to ride the horse. Elizabeth Taylor played the lead in a 1944 film version of the story. There was a *National Velvet* television series that ran from 1960 to 1962. A 1978 film, *International Velvet*, is about an American, Sarah Brown, orphaned and sent to live with her aunt, Velvet Brown. Together they relive the dream. Bryan Forbes directed the film, wrote the script and wrote the book.

Original work
National Velvet (1935)

Pastiche
Bryan Forbes, *International Velvet* (1992) based on the motion picture

J. M. BARRIE
Tinkerbelle

James Matthew Barrie's *Peter Pan*, the story of a boy who wouldn't grow up, has had a long life on stage and screen. Barrie (1860–1937) was a Scotsman who wrote novels and stage plays. Peter was first a character in Barrie's *The Little White Bird* (1902). After a 1904 production of *Peter Pan, or, The Boy Who Wouldn't Grow Up* became popular, the publisher Hodder and Stoughton reworked and issued the Peter Pan section as a separate book. Barrie's own book version of Pan didn't appear until 1911.

Several writers have produced both unauthorized and authorized sequels. (The characters are in public domain.)

Original Works
Peter Pan in Kensington Gardens (1906)   *When Wendy Grew Up* (1957)
Peter Pan (1911) aka *Peter Pan and Wendy*

Pastiches
Gilbert Adair, *Peter Pan and the Only Children* (1987)
Dave Barry and Ridley Pearson, *Peter and the Starcatchers* (2004) Starcatchers series; *Peter and the Shadow Thieves* (2006) Starcatchers series; *Peter and the Secret of Rundoon* (2007) Starcatchers series; *Peter and the Sword of Mercy* (2009) Starcatchers series; *Escape from the Carnivale* (2006) Neverland Adventures; *Cave of the Dark Wind* (2006) Neverland Adventures; *Blood Tide* (2008) Neverland Adventures

Terry Brooks, *Hook* (1991) screenplay novelization
Toby Forward, *Neverland* (1989)
Laurie Fox, *The Lost Girls* (2004)
Vincent Harris Jefferds, *Peter Pan and the Troll* (1985)
James V. Hart, *Captain Hook: The Adventures of a Notorious Youth* (2005)
Justine Korman, *Peter Pan Saves the Day* (1988)
R. Scott Leatherwood, *Neverland: The Early Adventures of Peter Pan* (2001)
Geraldine McCaughrean, *Peter Pan in Scarlet* (2006)
J.E. Somma, *After the Rain: A New Adventure for Peter Pan* (1999)
Karen Wallace, *Wendy* (2003)

L. FRANK BAUM
Off to See the Wizard

A cyclone sweeps off Dorothy Gale, the plucky girl from Kansas, and her frisky dog Toto to the fantastic land of Oz. Desperate to find her way home, Dorothy follows the Yellow Brick Road to the Emerald City. She befriends unlikely sidekicks: a Tin Woodman who wants a heart, a Cowardly Lion who wants courage and a Scarecrow who wants intelligence. Tussling with wicked witches and flying monkeys, she seeks out the Wizard of Oz in hopes that he will help her. The story is widely known, if not from the original children's books, then from the 1939 motion picture which is aired over network television annually.

New York–born writer Lyman Frank Baum turned children's book publishing on its ear with *The Wonderful Wizard of Oz*.

"L. Frank Baum's book is a classic of its kind because it makes a vivid appeal to the reader's imagination," said Allen Eyles in *The World of Oz* (1985). "Dorothy is an average, bright, but unremarkable girl who could be any young reader. There is a fantastic array of characters, each different from the last. And there is a variety of settings."

Baum (1856–1919) was tutored at home because of poor health and then briefly attended Peekskill Military Academy and Syracuse Classical School. He managed an opera house, worked in the family oil business, raised poultry and co-produced Baum's Castorine, an axle grease. He also ran a variety store, edited a newspaper and traveled as a crockery salesman. He wrote a book about breeding chickens, another about decorating windows in dry goods stores.

Then, having written text to accompany W.W. Denslow's illustrations for the best-selling *Father Goose: His Book* (1899), Baum the next year penned *The Wizard of Oz*. It appeared in 1900 with Denslow illustrations (the remainder of his Oz books sparkled with drawings by John R. Neill, who also wrote three of the books in the early 1940s).

In an introduction in the first Oz tale, Baum described it as something different, "for the time has come for a series of newer 'wonder tales' in which the stereotyped genie, dwarf and fairy are eliminated, together with all the horrible and blood-curdling incidents devised by their authors to point a fearsome moral to each tale." Baum populated his stories with witches good and bad, and with magic elements not that far removed from the old fairy tales, but added a degree of familiarity which caught the fancy of young readers. And he didn't preach.

With the success of *Oz*, Baum became a writer full-time. He eventually moved to California, to an estate he called "Ozcot." In a baker's dozen sequels he expanded upon characters such as Glinda, Ozma and Billina. He turned out other children's book series under his own name and pseudonyms, including Snuggle Tales, Boy Fortune Hunter Series as "Floyd Akers," Twinkle Tales as "Laura Bancroft" and Aunt Jane's Nieces as "Edith Van Dyne." He wrote several musicals based on his Oz stories.

Motion pictures were made based on *The Wizard of Oz*, several in Baum's lifetime and two based on his scripts. The first, from Selig in 1910, starred Bebe Daniels as Dorothy. But the best known was the 1939 version directed by Victor Fleming. "This well-loved film survives as Hollywood's best retelling of a fairy story, mainly because of the delightful score by Harold Arlen and E.Y. Harburg, and because Judy Garland, who, though actually too old for Dorothy, success-fully portrayed the essential innocence and wonder which make such stories live," opined Leslie Halliwell in *The Filmgoer's Companion* (1975).

Other hands continued the books after Baum's death. The publisher Reilly & Lee, according to Eyles, was "particularly impressed by the work of Ruth Plumly Thompson, whose first book of fantasy for children, *The Perhappsy Chaps*, appeared in 1918 from another Chicago publisher. She came from Philadelphia (like Denslow and Neill) and at the time was in her late twenties. Each week a chil-dren's page appeared under her name in one of the Philadelphia papers."

Thompson (1891–1976), a newspaper and free-lance writer, created addi-tional characters in her role as the second "Royal Historian of Oz." Her writing was marked by a fondness for puns and for the introduction of people from exotic, real lands such as China and Turkey. Critics suggest that Thompson more than continued the series, she transformed it into her own fantastic universe.

When Thompson gave up the series, Neill (d. 1943), as mentioned, wrote three entries, offering even more incredible characters such as the oily-eyed Heel-ers and the wooden whale Davy Jones.

Frank J. Baum, L. Frank's oldest son, wrote one book and also co-authored with Russell P. MacFall *To Please a Child*, the 1961 biography of his father.

Jack Snow, a lifelong Oz enthusiast and author of the non-fiction *Who's Who in Oz* (1954), wrote two Oz books.

Rachel C. Payes (b. 1922 in Maryland) began her professional writing career with an Oz pastiche and wrote several other young adult novels under the "Rachel Cosgrove" penname. Texan Susan Saunders (b. 1945) contributed an Oz story to the canon, while Eloise Jarvis McGraw (b. 1915 in Texas), an art and writing teacher, wrote two with her daughter Lauren Lynn (McGraw) Wagner. Martin Gard-ner expanded the offerings with Visitors from Oz, who confessed to *Bookpage* in

November 1998, "Like Baum, I cannot decide whether this book is solely for young-sters, or also for older readers who are still young at heart."

Gregory Maguire (b. 1954 in Albany, New York) had no doubts of his adult audience when he took the Oz characters far beyond Baum in a proposed trio of books beginning with *Wicked*, based in part on a Broadway musical.

Not really intended as part of the Oz canon, but borrowing characters and themes, are Keith Laumer's *The Other Side of Time* (1965) and Ray Bradbury's "The Exiles," a short story from 1951. Philip José Farmer included the Tin Wood-man, Scarecrow and Glinda as well as Dorothy and Baum in his novel *A Barn-stormer in Oz* (1982) while in Geoff Ryman's *Was...* (1992) Dorothy and Toto meet not only Baum but Judy Garland for good measure!

Oz fans make a distinction between the canonical, or "Famous Forty," Oz books written by Baum, Thompson, Neil, Snow, Cosgrove and the McGraws and later works. This listing omits fan, very-small-press and parodic works.

See also Edith Van Dyne.

Original Baum Wizard of Oz Works

The Wonderful Wizard of Oz (1900) aka
  The New Wizard of Oz (1903)
*The Marvelous Land of Oz, Being an
  Account of the Further Adventures of
  the Scarecrow and Tin Woodman*
  (1904) aka *The Land of Oz* (1904)
Ozma of Oz (1907)
Dorothy and the Wizard of Oz (1908)
The Road to Oz (1909)
The Emerald City of Oz (1910)
The Patchwork Girl of Oz (1913)
Tik-Tok of Oz (1914)

The Scarecrow of Oz (1915)
Tinkitink in Oz (1916)
The Lost Princess of Oz (1917)
The Tin Woodsman of Oz (1918)
The Magic of Oz (1919)
Glinda of Oz (1920)
The Visitors from Oz (1960)
*All Things Oz: The Wonder, Wit and
  Wisdom of The Wizard of Oz* (2003)
  includes Baum short stories not
  previously collected

Pastiches

Frank Joslyn Baum, *The Laughing Dragon of Oz* (1935)
Roger S. Baum, *Dorothy of Oz* (1989); *The Rewolf of Oz* (1990); *The SillyOZbuls of Oz* (1991); *The SillyOZbul of Oz and Toto* (1992); *The SillyOZbul of Oz and the Magic Merry-Go-Round* (1992); *Lion of Oz and the Badge of Courage* (1992); *The Green Star of Oz* (2000); *Toto in Candy Land* (2000); *The Oz Odyssey* (2006)
Polly Berends, *Ozma and the Wayward Wand* (1985)
Rachel R. Cosgrove, *The Hidden Valley of Oz* (1951); *The Wicked Witch of Oz* (1993)
Edward Einhorn, *Paradox in Oz* (2000); *The Living House of Oz* (2005)
Philip José Farmer, *A Barnstormer in Oz* (1982)
Martin Gardner, *Visitors from Oz: The Wild Adventures of Dorothy, the Scarecrow and the Tin Woodman* (1998)
Dorothy Haas, *Dorothy and the Seven-Leaf Clover* (1985); *Dorothy and Old King Crow* (1986)
James Howe, *Mr. Tinker in Oz* (1985)
Stephen King, *Wizard and Glass* (1997)

Gregory Maguire, *The Life and Times of the Wicked Witch of the West* (1995) Wicked Years series; *Son of a Witch* (2005) Wicked Years series; *A Lion Among Men* (2008) Wicked Years series

Dick Martin, *The Ozmapolitan of Oz* (1986)

Eloise Jarvis McGraw, *The Rundelstone of Oz* (2001)

Eloise Jarvis McGraw and Lauren Lynn McGraw, *The Forbidden Fountain of Oz* (1980)

Eloise Jarvis McGraw and Lauren Lynn Wagner, *Merry Go Round in Oz* (1963)

John R. Neill, *The Wonder City of Oz* (1940); *The Scalawagons of Oz* (1941); *Lucky Bucky in Oz* (1942); *The Runaway in Oz* (1995)

Eugene Orlando, *A Journey with Dorothy to Oz* (electronic, ca 2004)

Darren Reid, *The Sword of Oz* (2007)

Geof Ryman, *Was* (1992)

Susan Saunders, *Dorothy and the Magic Belt* (1985)

Eric Shanower, *The Enchanted Apples of Oz* (1986) graphic novel; *The Secret Island of Oz* (1987) graphic novel; *The Ice King of Oz* (1988) graphic novel; *The Forgotten Forest of Oz* (1989) graphic novel; *The Blue Witch of Oz* (1992) graphic novel

Sherwood Smith, *The Emerald Wand of Oz* (2005); *Trouble Under Oz* (2006)

Jack Snow, *The Magic Mimics in Oz* (1946); *The Shaggy Man of Oz* (1949)

Gilbert M. Sprague, *The Patchwork Bride of Oz* (1997)

L. Sprague de Camp, *Sir Harold and the Gnome King* (1991)

Ruth Plumly Thompson, *The Royal Book of Oz* (1921) issued as by Baum; *Kabumpo in Oz* (1922) carrying the credit "Founded on and continuing the famous Oz stories by L. Frank Baum"; *The Cowardly Lion of Oz* (1923) carrying the credit "Founded on and continuing the famous Oz stories by L. Frank Baum"; *Grampa in Oz* (1924); *The Lost King of Oz* (1925); *The Hungry Tiger of Oz* (1925); *The Gnome King of Oz* (1927); *The Giant Horse of Oz* (1928); *Jack Pumpkinhead of Oz* (1929); *The Yellow Knight of Oz* (1930); *Pirates in Oz* (1931); *The Purple Prince of Oz* (1932); *Ojo in Oz* (1933); *Speedy in Oz* (1934); *The Wishing Horse of Oz* (1935); *Captain Salt in Oz* (1936); *Handy Mandy in Oz* (1937); *The Silver Princess in Oz* (1938); *Ozoplaning with the Wizard of Oz* (1939); *Yankee in Oz* (1972); *The Enchanted Island of Oz* (1976)

Joan D. Vinge, *Return to Oz* (1985)

Alexander Volkov, *The Wizard of the Emerald City* (1939/1959)

Gina Wickwar, *The Hidden Prince of Oz* (2000); *Toto of Oz* (2007)

LUDWIG BEMELMANS

Madeline

Award-winning children's book author and illustrator Ludwig Bemelmans (1898–1962) created the character of Madeline for six books. Born in Austria, the author later lived in the United States, where he worked in the hotel and restaurant trade. His first children's book was *Hans* (1934). The Madeline books feature a schoolgirl and her nanny-nun, Miss Clavel. The second book about the characters won the Caldecott Medal in 1954.

Bemelmans left an unfinished manuscript, "Madeline's Christmas in Texas," that his son, John Bemelmans Marciano (b. 1970), discovered and completed, and gave a new title.

Original Madeline Works

Madeline (1939)
Madeline and the Bad Hat (1945)
Madeline's Rescue (1953)

Madeline and the Gypsies (1959)
Madeline in London (1961)
Madeline's Christmas (1985)

Posthumous Collaboration

John Bemelmans Marciano, *Madeline in America, and Other Holiday Tales* (1999)

Pastiche

John Bemelmans Marciano, *Madeline Says Merci: The Always-Be-Polite Book* (2001)

JOHN BELLAIRS

Frosty

John Anthony Bellairs (1938–1991) wrote the fantasy novel *Face in the Frost*. A graduate of the University of Notre Dame and the University of Chicago, Bellairs was an English professor at colleges in New England and the Midwest. J.R.R. Tolkien's *The Lord of the Rings* inspired his *The Face in the Frost*. In another genre, his Johnny Dixon, Lewis Barnavelt and Anthony Monday books are gothic mysteries for young adult readers.

At his death at age 53, Bellairs left two unfinished manuscripts and two synopses. His estate engaged Brad Strickland (b. 1947) to completed the works. Strickland was born in Georgia. His first novel, *To Stand Beneath the Sun*, came out in 1985.

Original Lewis Barnavelt Works

The House with a Clock in Its Walls (1973)
The Figure in the Shadows (1975)

The Doom of the Haunted Opera (1998)

Posthumous Lewis Barnavelt Collaborations

Brad Strickland, *The Ghost in the Mirror* (1994); *The Vengeance of the Witch-finder* (1993); *The Specter from the Magicians Museum* (1998); *The Beast Under the Wizard's Bridge* (2002); *The Tower at the End of the World* (2001); *The Whistle, the Grave, and the Ghost* (2003); *The House Where Nobody Lived* (2006)

Original Johnny Dixon Works

The Curse of the Blue Figurine (1983)

The Mummy, the Will, and the Crypt (1983)

The Spell of the Sorcerer's Skull (1984)
The Revenge of the Wizard's Ghost (1985)
The Trolley to Yesterday (1989)

The Chessmen of Doom (1989)
The Secret of the Underground Room (1990)
The Drum, the Doll and the Zombie (1994)

Posthumous Johnny Dixon Collaboration

Brad Strickland, *The Letter, the Witch, and the Ring* (1976)

Johnny Dixon Pastiches

Brad Strickland, *The Hand of the Necromancer* (1996) Johnny Dixon series; *The Bell, the Book, and the Spellbinder* (1997) Johnny Dixon series; *The Wrath of the Grinning Ghost* (1999) Johnny Dixon series; *The Sign of the Sinister Sorcerer* (2008) Johnny Dixon series

ENID BLYTON

Famous Five and Secret Seven

Enid Blyton (1897–1968) wrote scads of British children's and boarding school stories and novels in several series. The Famous Five (tomboy Georgina, known as "George," and Timmy appeared in six books on their own, then began a new series when joined by Julian, Dick and Anne) and Secret Seven (a club made up of siblings Peter and Janet and friends Jack, Colin, George, Pam and Barbara and their dog Scamper) were about children who work independently of adults to solve various puzzles. Two series are set at girls' schools: St. Clare's, featuring twins Pat and Isabel O'Sullivan, and Whiteleafe, whose students include Naughtiest Girl Elizabeth Allen.

Blyton sold an estimated 400 million copies of her books. Born in London, the daughter of a cutlery salesman, she attended St. Christopher's School, where she was head girl. She trained as a teacher at Ipswich High School and became a teacher until her writing took hold. She was married to Major Hugh Alexander Pollock, an editor with George Newnes, and, after a divorce, to Kenneth Fraser Darrell Waters.

French readers, in particular, enjoyed the series, and were eager for the many pastiches.

Original Famous Five Works

Five on a Treasure Island (1942)
Five Go Adventuring Again (1943)
Five Run Away Together (1944) aka *Five Run Away to Danger*
Five Go to Smuggler's Too (1945)
Five Go Off in a Caravan (1946)
Five on Kirrin Island Again (1947)

Five Go Off to Camp (1948) aka *Five on the Track of a Spook Train*
Five Get Into Trouble (1949) aka *Five Caught in a Treacherous Plot*
Five Fall Into Adventure (1950)
Five on a Hike Together (1951)
Five Have a Wonderful Time (1952)

Five Go Down to the Sea (1953)
Five Go to Mystery Moor (1954)
Five Have Plenty of Fun (1955)
Five on a Secret Trail (1956)
Five Go to Billycock Hill (1957)
Five Get Into a Fix (1958)

Five on Finniston Farm (1960)
Five Go to Demon's Rocks (1961)
Five Have a Mystery to Solve (1962)
Five Are Together Again (1963)
Short Stories about the Famous Five (1995)

Famous Five Pastiches

Claude Voilier, *Les Cinq sont les plus forts* (1971) aka *The Famous Five and the Mystery of the Emeralds; Les Cinq au bal des espions* (1971) aka *The Famous Five in Fancy Dress; Le Marquis appelle les Cinq* (1972) aka *The Famous Five and the Stately Homes Gang; Les Cinq au Cap des tempêtes* (1972) aka *The Famous Five and the Missing Cheetah; Les Cinq à la télévision* (1973) aka *The Famous Five Go on Television; Les Cinq et les pirates du ciel* (1973) aka *The Famous Five and the Hijackers; Les Cinq contre le Masque noir* (1974) aka *The Famous Five Versus the Black Mask; Les Cinq et le galion d'or* (1974) aka *The Famous Five and the Golden Galleon; Les Cinq font de la brocante* (1975) aka *The Famous Five and the Inca God; Les Cinq se mettent en quatre* (1975) aka *The Famous Five and the Pink Pearls; Les Cinq dans la cité secrète* (1976) aka *The Famous Five and the Secret of the Caves; La Fortune sourit aux Cinq* (1976) aka *The Famous Five and the Cavalier's Treasure; Les Cinq et le rayon Z* (1977) aka *The Famous Five and the Z-Rays; Les Cinq vendent la peau de l'ours* (1977) aka *The Famous Five and the Blue Bear Mystery; Les Cinq aux rendez-vous du diable* (1978) aka *The Famous Five in Deadly Danger; Du neuf pour les Cinq* (1978) aka *The Famous Five and the Strange Legacy; Les Cinq et le diamant bleu* [The Famous Five and the Blue Diamond] (1979) aka *Les Cinq et le rubis d'Akbar* [The Famous Five and the Ruby of Akbar] (1980); *Les Cinq et le trésor de Roquepine* (1979) aka *The Famous Five and the Knights' Treasure; Les Cinq en croisière* [The Famous Five on a Cruise] (1980); *Les Cinq jouent serre* (1980) aka *The Famous Five and the Strange Scientist; Les Cinq contre les fantômes* [The Famous Five Against the Ghosts] (1981); *Les Cinq en Amazonie* [The Famous Five in the Amazon] (1983)

Original Naughtiest Girl Works

The Naughtiest Girl in the School (1940)
The Naughtiest Girl Again (1942)
The Naughtiest Girl Is a Monitor (1945)

Enid Blyton's Omnibus! (1952) includes "Here's the Naughtiest Girl!"
Here's the Naughtiest Girl! (1997)

Naughtiest Girl Pastiches

Anne Digby, *The Naughtiest Girl Keeps a Secret* (1999); *The Naughtiest Girl Helps a Friend* (1999); *The Naughtiest Girl Saves the Day* (1999); *Well Done, the Naughtiest Girl!* (1999); *The Naughtiest Girl Wants to Win* (2000); *The Naughtiest Girl Marches On* (2000)

Original Secret Seven Works

The Secret Seven (1949) aka *The Secret Seven and the Mystery of the Empty House*

Secret Seven Adventure (1950) aka *The Secret Seven and the Circus Adventure*

Well Done, Secret Seven (1951) aka *The Secret Seven and the Tree House Adventure*

Secret Seven on the Trail (1952) aka *The Secret Seven and the Railroad Mystery*

Go Ahead Secret Seven (1953) aka *The Secret Seven Get Their Man*

Good Work, Secret Seven (1954) aka *The Secret Seven and the Case of the Stolen Car*

Secret Seven Win Through (1955) aka *The Secret Seven and the Hidden Cave Adventure*

Three Cheers Secret Seven (1956) aka *The Secret Seven and the Grim Secret*

Secret Seven Mystery (1957) aka *The Secret Seven and the Missing Girl Mystery*

Puzzle for the Secret Seven (1958) aka *The Secret Seven and the Case of the Music Lover*

Secret Seven Fireworks (1959) aka *The Secret Seven and the Bonfire Adventure*

Good Old Secret Seven (1960) aka *The Secret Seven and the Old Fort Adventure*

Shock for the Secret Seven (1961) aka *The Secret Seven and the Case of the Dog Lover*

Look Out Secret Seven (1962) aka *The Secret Seven and the Case of Missing Medals*

Fun for the Secret Seven (1963) aka *The Secret Seven and the Case of the Old Horse*

The Secret Seven Short Story Collection (1997)

Secret Seven Pastiches

Evelyne Lallemand, *Les Sept à la chasse au lion* (1976) aka *The Seven and the Lion Hunt; Les Sept sont dans de Beaux Draps* (1978) aka *The Seven Go Haunting; Les Sept et le Magicien* (1977) aka *The Seven and the Magician; Les Sept et las Déesse d'or* (1977) aka *The Seven Strike Gold; Les Sept et les bulldozers* (1978) aka *The Seven to the Rescue; Les Sept font du Cinéma* (1977) aka *The Seven on Screen; Les Sept et les Soucoupes volantes* (1979) aka *The Seven and the UFOs; Les Sept ne croient pas au Père Noël* (1981) aka *The Seven and Father Christmas; Les Sept à 200 à l'heure* (1982) aka *The Seven and the Racing Driver*

Original St. Clare's Works

The Twins at St. Clare's (1941)

The O'Sullivan Twins (1942) aka *The O'Sullivan Twins Again*

Summer Term at St. Clare's (1943)

Second Form at St. Clare's (1944)

Claudine at St. Clare's (1944)

Fifth Formers at St. Clare's (1945)

St. Clare's Pastiches

Pamela Cox, *Third Form at St. Clare's* (2000); *Sixth Form at St. Clare's* (2000)

Margaret Wise Brown

Moon

Caldecott Medal winner Margaret Wise Brown (1910–1952) is the author of children's classics *Goodnight Moon* and *The Runaway Bunny* (1942) and a hundred other books, most with animals as the main characters. Born in New York City, she attended Hollins College and Columbia University. She studied at Writers Laboratory of the Bureau of Educational Experiments. She became a children's book editor and then a writer. She died of complications from surgery for a burst appendix.

Brown's sister Roberta became executor for her estate and organized unpublished manuscripts, some of which she submitted to publishers. Other manuscripts she tucked away to await rediscovery in 1987. "Amazingly, this unpublished manuscript lay incomplete and forgotten in a cedar trunk in a Vermont barn," according to the publisher Thomas Nelson. "When it was discovered, the onionskin paper had yellowed and the paperclips that held the pages together had rusted. Children's book publisher Laura Minchew, a longtime fan of Brown, took on the challenge to complete the work." The text is based on the New England Sampler prayer "God Bless the Moon and God Bless Me."

Posthumous Collaboration

Laura Minschew, *The Moon Shines Down* (2008)

FRANCES HODGSON BURNETT

The Secret Garden

Frances Hodgson Burnett (1849–1924) wrote a now-classic story of Mary Lennox, a not-terribly-healthy daughter of British parents who is cared for by a nanny, Ayah, while growing up in India. Orphaned, she is sent to Yorkshire, in the care of her father's brother-in-law, Archibald Craven, who mourns his wife's death. The housekeeper Mrs. Medlock is stern with the child, who soon discovers and explores a secret garden — the key to her uncle's story. Burnett, reared in poverty in England, later lived in Tennessee, where she had to support her siblings with her writing.

English mystery/suspense writer Susan Moody added to the story.

Original Work

The Secret Garden (1909)

Pastiche

Susan Moody, *Misselthwaite: The Sequel to the Secret Garden* (1995) aka *Return to the Secret Garden* (1998)

Julie Campbell
Trixie Belden

The world of boys' and girls' fiction in the late nineteenth and early twentieth centuries found a variety of circumstances: authors held creative rights to their characters; authors themselves engaged ghost-writers when they no longer wanted to continue a series; syndicates and publishers created or purchased rights and hired authors to write books.

Now look at Julie Campbell (1908–1999). Born in Flushing, New York, she married Charles Tatham, Jr., in 1933. She was proprietor of her own literary agency and was the author of four book series. She wrote Ginny Gordon books from 1948–1956. She wrote Trixie Belden books from 1948 to 1958. She filled in for Helen Wells and wrote a half dozen books each in the Cherry Ames and Vicki Barr series, using her married name Julie Tatham. Wells eventually returned to write more of her earlier series.

Trixie Belden of Crabapple Farm near Sleepyside-on-the-Hudson, New York, is a curious teen who with her friend Honey Wheeler and others solve such puzzles as the disappearing sheep on Uncle Andrew's farm and where has Diana Lynch's Uncle Monty been all these years?

Campbell owned rights to the Belden series, and negotiated a royalty on the second half-dozen books in the run. But she had to give up rights to Western Publishing, which farmed out the work under the name "Kathryn Kenney" to Nicolete Meredith Stack, Gladys Baker Bond, Polly Curren Fedosiuk, Carl Henry Rathjen, Laura French and others.

Original Trixie Belden Works

Trixie Belden and the Secret of the Mansion (1948)

Trixie Belden and the Red Trailer Mystery (1950)

Trixie Belden and the Gatehouse Mystery (1951)

Trixie Belden and the Mysterious Visitor (1954)

Trixie Belden and the Mystery Off Glen Road (1956)

Trixie Belden and the Mystery in Arizona (1958)

Pastiches

The Mysterious Code (1961)
The Black Jacket Mystery (1961)
The Happy Valley Mystery (1962)
The Marshland Mystery (1962)
The Mystery at Bob-White Cave (1963)
The Mystery of the Blinking Eye (1963)
The Mystery on Cobbett's Island (1964)
The Mystery of the Emeralds (1965)
The Mystery on the Mississippi (1965)
The Mystery of the Missing Heiress (1970)

The Mystery of the Uninvited Guest (1977)
The Mystery of the Phantom Grasshopper (1977)
The Secret of the Unseen Treasure (1977)
The Mystery of Old Telegraph Road (1978)
The Mystery of the Castaway Children (1978)
The Mystery at Mead's Mountain (1978)
The Mystery of the Queen's Necklace (1979)
The Mystery at Saratoga (1979)

The Sasquatch Mystery (1979)

The Mystery of the Headless Horseman (1979)

The Mystery of the Ghostly Galleon (1979)

The Hudson River Mystery (1979)

The Mystery of the Velvet Gown (1980)

The Mystery of the Midnight Marauder (1980)

The Mystery at Maypenny's (1980)

The Mystery of the Whispering Witch (1980)

The Mystery of the Vanishing Victim (1980)

The Mystery of the Missing Millionaire (1980)

The Mystery of the Memorial Day Fire (1984)

The Mystery of the Antique Doll (1984)

The Pet Show Mystery (1985)

The Indian Burial Ground Mystery (1985)

The Mystery of the Galloping Ghost (1986)

MATT CHRISTOPHER

Batter-up

His death in 1997 from complications from surgery for a brain tumor didn't slow the pace of Matt Christopher books, fiction and nonfiction, for middle readers.

The author was born in 1917 in Bath, Pennsylvania, one of nine children. Christopher found baseball a fascinating sport as a youth, and played on his high school team. He wrote poetry and short stories and at age eighteen submitted a story to a Writer's Digest competition. Though he didn't win, he kept writing, and eventually sold a story. Married and working at a factory, he finished the manuscript for *The Lucky Baseball Bat*. Little Brown accepted it for publication in 1954. He continued to write sports stories and mysteries for juvenile readers while working a regular job until he became a fulltime writer in 1963.

After his death, his publisher kept his name alive with ghostwritten books. Only fiction is listed here. *Behind the Desk with Matt Christopher* (2004) is Dale Christopher's biography of his father.

Original Return of the Home Run Kid Work

Return of the Home Run Kid (1992)

Home Run Kid Pastiche

Comeback of the Home Run Kid (2006)

Pastiches

The Catcher's Mask (1998)

Center Court Sting (1998)

Mountain Bike Mania (1998)

Prime-Time Pitcher (1998)

Roller Hockey Radicals (1998)

Soccer Scoop (1998)

The Dog Called the Pitch (1998)

The Captain Contest (1999)

Operation Babysitter (1999)

Long-Arm Quarterback (1999)

Snowboard Showdown (1999)

Spike It! (1999)

Soccer Duel (2000)

Tennis Ace (2000)

Hat Trick (2000)
Secret Weapon (2000)
Skateboard Renegade (2000)
Cool as Ice (2001)
Football Nightmare (2001)
The Captain Contest (2001)
Dive Right In (2002)
All Keyed Up (2003)
Nothin' but Net (2003)
You Lucky Dog (2003)
Master of Disaster (2003)
Slam Dunk (2004)
Stealing Home (2004)
Snowboard Champ (2004)
Roller Hockey Rumble (2004)
Catch That Pass! (2005)
Challenge at Second Base (2005)

Lacrosse Face-off (2006)
Catching Waves (2006)
Soccer Hero (2007)
All Star Fever (2008)
Double Play at Short (2008)
Fairway Phenom (2008)
Rock On (2008)
Wild Ride (2008)
Baseball Turnaround (2008)
Body Check (2008)
Baseball Flyhawk (2008)
Soccer Duel (2008)
Football Double Threat (2008)
Lacrosse Firestorm (2008)
Shadow Over the Back Court (2008)
Karate Kick (2009)

JAMES OLIVER CURWOOD

Kazan

Michigan-born James Oliver Curwood (1879–1927) wrote novels of Alaska and the Canadian Northwest. He wrote Mountie novels including *Steele of the Royal Mounted* (1911) and gold seeker tales. And he wrote dog books.

Movie adaptations of *Kazan* prompted Whitman Publishing to commission two pastiches in the 1940s. Henry E. Vallely (ca1881–1950) wrote one of them. The other appeared under Curwood's name.

Original Dog Works
Kazan: Wolf Dog of the North (1914) aka
   Kazan: Father of Baree

Baree, Son of Kazan (1917) aka Baree:
   The Story of a Wolf-Dog

Pastiches
Kazan, King of the Pack (1940)
Henry E. Vallely, Kazan in Revenge of the North (1937)

JEAN DE BRUNHOFF

Babar

Paris-born Jean de Brunhoff (1899–1937) created the children's book hero Babar the Elephant for his wife, Cecile de Brunhoff, to read to their sons including

Laurent. De Brunhoff studied at L'École Alsacienne. He served in the French Army during World War I. An established artist, he wrote seven Babar books for publication. The firm Hachette acquired publication rights after de Brunhoff's death to tuberculosis.

Laurent de Brunhoff (b. 1925) took over writing the series. He is an illustrator as well as writer and now lives in the United States.

Original Babar Stories

Histoire de Babar, le petit éléphant (1931) aka The Story of Babar, the Little Elephant (1933)

Le Voyage de Babar (1932) aka The Travels of Babar (1934)

Le Roi Babar (1933) aka Babar the King (1935)

Les Vacances de Zephir (1934) aka Zephir's Holidays (1937) aka Babar and Zephir (1942) aka Babar's Friend Zephir (1937)

ABC de Babar (19334) aka ABC of Babar (1936)

Babar en famille (1938) aka Babar and His Children (1938)

Babar and Father Christmas (1940) aka Babar et le père Noël (1941)

Babar Pastiches

Laurent de Brunhoff, Babar et ce coquin d'Arthur (1947) aka Babar's Cousin: That Rascal Arthur (1948); Pique-Nique chez Babar (1949) aka Babar's Picnic (1949); Babar dans l'île aux oiseaux (1951) aka Babar's Visit to Bird Island (1952); La Fête de Celesteville (1954) aka Babar's Fair (1954); Babar et le Professeur Grifaton (1956) aka Babar and the Professor (1957); Le Château de Babar (1961) aka Babar's Castle (1962); Babar's French Lessons (1963); Babar's Spanish Lessons (1965) Spanish text by Roberto Eyzaguirre; Babar Comes to America (1965); Babar fait du ski (1966) aka Babar Goes Skiing (1969); Babar jardinier (1966) aka Babar the Gardener (1969); Babar en promenade (1966) aka Babar Goes on a Picnic (1969); Babar à la mer (1966) aka Babar at the Seashore (1969); Babar Loses His Crown (1967); Babar's Games (1968); Babar fait du sport (1969) aka Babar the Athlete (1971); Babar campeur (1969) aka Babar the Camper (1971); Babar et le docteur (1969) aka Babar and the Doctor (1971); Babar artiste peintre (1969) aka Babar the Painter (1971); Babar aux sports d'hiver (1969); Babar's Moon Trip (1969); Babar's Birthday Surprise (1970); Babar patissier (1970) aka Babar Bakes a Cake (1974); Babar musicien (1970), translation published as Babar's Concert (also see below) (1974); Babar aviateur (1970) aka Babar to the Rescue (1974); Babar et l'arbre de Noël (1970) aka Babar's Christmas Tree (1974); Babar Visits Another Planet (1972) aka Babar sur la planète molle (1972); Meet Babar and His Family (1973); Babar and the Wully-Wully (1975) aka Babar et le Wouly-Wouly (1975); Babar Saves the Day (1976); Babar's Mystery (1978); Babar Learns to Cook (1978); Babar the Magician (1980); Babar and the Ghost (1981); Babar's ABC (1983); Babar's Book of Color (1984); Babar's Counting Book (1986); Babar's Little Girl (1987); Babar's Little Circus Star (1988); Babar's Busy Year: A Book about Seasons (1989); Babar's Colors and Shapes (1989); Babar's Number Fun (1989); Babar's Paint Box Book (1989); Babar's Busy Week (1990); Isabelle's New Friend (1990) aka Babar's Little Girl Makes a Friend (2002); Hello, Babar! (1991); Babar's Battle (1992) aka La Victoire de Babar (1992); Babar: The Show Must Go On (1992); Babar's Bath Book (1992); Babar's Car (1992); Babar's Peekaboo Fair (1993); The Rescue of Babar (1993) aka Babar's Rescue (2004);

Babar's French and English Word Book (1994); *Babar and the Succotash Bird* (2000); *Babar's Yoga for Elephants* (2002); *Babar's Little Girl Makes a Friend* (2002); *Babar and the Christmas House* (2003); *Babar's Museum of Art* (2003); *Babar Goes to School* (2003); *Babar and the Gift for Mother* (2004); *Babar Loses His Crown* (2004); *Babar and the Runaway Egg* (2004); *Babar's World Tour* (2005); *Babar's Gallery* (2006)

DR. SEUSS
Diffendoofer

Theodor Geisel (1904–1991) was a cartoonist and writer who developed one of the most distinctive and influential styles of prose and illustration in children's books in the twentieth century. The Springfield, Massachusetts, native published more than 60 books, including *The Cat in the Hat* (1957) and *Green Eggs and Ham* (1960).

Geisel mentioned to his Random House editor in 1988 that he had an idea about a teacher. After his death, Geisel's widow Audrey collected sketches Geisel had left in his office and approached the publisher about a new book. "Children's poet Jack Prelutsky helped complete the verses, and artist Lane Smith was drafted to finish Geisel's drawings. Random House eventually published *Hooray for Diffendoofer Day!* in 1998," according to Dorothy Pomerantz in *Forbes*.

Posthumous Collaboration
Jack Prelutsky, *Hooray for Diffendoofer Day!* (1998)

Original Grinch Work
How the Grinch Stole Christmas (1957)

Pastiche
Louise Gikow, *Dr. Seuss' How the Grinch Stole Christmas!* (2000) based on motion picture screenplay by Jeffrey Price and Peter S. Seaman

WALTER FARLEY
Black Stallion

Walter Farley (1915–1989) began to write his first Black Stallion book while still in high school, and completed it as a student at Columbia University. It tells the story of young Alec Ramsey and a bold horse stranded on a desert island after the ship they were on sank. Rescued, they work with an old trainer, Henry Daily, so the Black can race.

Farley used royalties to travel to Mexico, Hawaii, South America and Europe. He served in the Army during World War II, and worked on the staff of *Yank* while with the Fourth Armored Division. He continued to write about horses the rest of his life. Most of his books were about Black Stallion or Island Stallion. The Black Stallion has four times appeared in motion pictures, beginning in 1979.

The author's son has continued the series.

Original Works

The Black Stallion (1941)
The Black Stallion Returns (1945)
Son of the Black Stallion (1947)
The Island Stallion (1948)
The Black Stallion and Satan (1949)
The Black Stallion's Blood Bay Colt (1951)
Island Stallion's Fury (1951)
Black Stallion's Filly (1952)
Black Stallion Revolts (1953)
Black Stallion's Sulky Colt (1954)
The Island Stallion Races (1955)
Black Stallion's Courage (1956)

The Black Stallion Mystery (1957)
The Horse Tamer (1958)
The Black Stallion and Flame (1960)
Man O' War (1962)
The Black Stallion Challenged! (1964)
The Black Stallion's Ghost (1969)
The Black Stallion and the Girl (1971)
The Black Stallion Legend (1983)
The Young Black Stallion: A Wild and Untamable Spirit! (1989) written with Steven Farley

Pastiches

Steven Farley, *The Black Stallion's Steeplechaser* (1997); *Young Black Stallion—The Promise* (1998); *Young Black Stallion—A Horse Called Raven* (1998); *Young Black Stallion—The Homecoming* (1998); *Young Black Stallion—Wild Spirit* (1999); *Young Black Stallion—The Yearling* (1999); *Young Black Stallion—Hard Lessons* (1999); *Black Stallion's Shadow* (2000)

RACHEL FIELD

Hitty

Rachel Field (1894–1942), great niece of Cyrus Field, who laid the Atlantic cable, Stephen J. Field, an associate justice of the Supreme Court, Matthew Field, a civil engineer, and David Dudley Field, Jr., a New York lawyer of note, grew up in western Massachusetts. She enjoyed drawing and writing verse as a girl, and had a taste of success with a one-act play she penned while at Harvard-Radcliffe. She wrote movie scenarios for several years, and found a niche writing books for children.

Field's *Hitty*, the story of a wooden doll, has not gone out of print since it appeared in 1929, with illustrations by Dorothy P. Lathrop. Field went on to write for older readers, including the popular novel *All This, and Heaven, Too* (1938), but *Hitty* remained her enduring hit, and each year draws hundreds of fans to the Stockbridge, Massachusetts, Library, where the original doll is on display.

Fans writer Rosemary Wells and artist Susan Jeffers shortened and reshaped Field's original story for a 1999 book, which was for many readers an invitation to read the original. There followed in 2001 new chapter book adventures, *Hitty's Travels*, at the hands of Ellen Weiss and illustrator Betina Ogden.

Original Work

Hitty: Her First Hundred Years (1929)

Pastiches

Rosemary Wells, *Rachel Field's Hitty: Her First Hundred Years* (1999)
Ellen Weiss, *Civil War Days* (2001); *Gold Rush Days* (2001); *Voting Rights Days* (2002);
  Ellis Island Days (2002)

LOUISE FITZHUGH

Harriet spies some more

Louise Fitzhugh's middle-reader stories of Harriet M. Welsch depict an eleven-year-old living in New York City. Harriet observes everyone around her and writes about what they do — to the extent she relies more on her notebook than her own wits. She's an outsider, much as the author was. Anita Silvey in *100 Best Books for Children* (2004) said Harriet was a flawed but real character. Harriet saw things people didn't want seen, said more than she should have. She had snits. She saw a psychiatrist. "She's a young woman with a really great sense of herself. She even says, 'I love myself,'" Silvey said.

Fitzhugh (1928–1974), a native of Memphis, Tennessee, had a fractured life. Her parents divorced. She attended several schools and universities. She was married briefly. *Harriet the Spy* (1964) was her best-known book, with its atypical heroine and unexpectedly realistic characters. It was made into a motion picture in 1996. Beth Ellen and Sport, characters from the book, appeared in their own adventures. Fitzhugh illustrated many of her own books. She died of a brain aneurysm.

Helen Ericson continued the adventures under contract to publisher Random House, with nurse Ole Golly returning from Montreal to care for Harriet when her parents take a vacation in Paris. Maya Gold also wrote a sequel.

Original Stories

Harriet the Spy (1964)   *Sport* (1979)
The Long Secret (1965)

Pastiches

Helen Ericson, *Harriet Spies Again* (2003)
Maya Gold, *Harriet the Spy, Double Agent* (2007)

DON FREEMAN
Corduroy the bear

Artist Don Freeman (1908–1978) created the children's literature favorite *Corduroy*, though he was equally comfortable working in the fine arts, depicting inner city scenes in the style of the Ash Can School.

Born in San Diego, California, he grew up in Missouri he studied under John Sloan and Harry Wickey at Art Students League in New York City. He found Honore Daumier to be a particularly inviting artistic influence. He struggled through the Depression but found work for theaters in the city. During World War II, his art appeared in various military publications. He worked as a painter, printmaker and cartoonist and began to illustrate children's books. He wrote some books with his wife, Lydia Freeman. His first Corduroy children's book came out in 1968. Other writers have continued the series about the toy bear who is companion to a girl named Lisa.

Original Corduroy Works

Corduroy (1968)   *A Pocket for Corduroy* (1978)

Corduroy Pastiches

B.G. Hennessey, *Corduroy's Christmas* (1992); *Corduroy at the Zoo* (2001); *Corduroy Goes to School* (2002); *Corduroy Goes to the Fire Station* (2003); *Happy Easter, Corduroy* (2004); *Corduroy's Snowy Day* (2005); *Corduroy Goes to the Library* (2005); *Corduroy Lost and Found* (2006); *Corduroy Goes to the Beach* (2006)
Alisa Inches, *Corduroy Makes a Cake* (2001); *Corduroy's Hike* (2003); *Corduroy's Garden* (2004); *Corduroy Writes a Letter* (2004)
Emilie Kong (illustrator), *Halloween Is Here, Corduroy* (2007)
Leonard M. Marcus, *Corduroy & Company* (2001)
Lisa McCue (illustrator), *Corduroy's Day* (1985); *Corduroy's Party* (1985); *Corduroy Goes to the Doctor* (1987); *Corduroy's Busy Street* (1987); *Corduroy's Christmas Surprise* (1992); *Corduroy's Best Halloween Ever* (2001); *Corduroy's Thanksgiving* (2006)

KENNETH GRAHAME
Wind in the Willows

Kenneth Grahame (1859–1932) brought amphibians and rodents to life in the classic children's book *The Wind in the Willows*. Born in Edinburgh, Scotland,

Kenneth's mother died of scarlet fever when he was only five. He overcame the disease, with longlasting effect. During the last of his childhood, under the care of his maternal grandmother, he resorted to a world of imagination. Unable to continue his education, he worked as a clerk, eventually joining the staff of the Bank of England. He wrote for periodicals and his first collection of stories, *The Golden Age*, came out in 1893. Other tales were of orphans who lived difficult lives. His writing eventually became profitable.

Grahame married Elspeth Thomson in 1899. He told stories to their nearly blind son, Alistair. These stories became letters and eventually ended up in print in *The Wind in the Willows*, the fast-paced human-like adventures of Rat and Mole and Toad and Badger in the Berkshire countryside. (Mapledurham House apparently inspired Toad Hall.) The book, illustrated by E.H. Shepard and today considered a classic, was so successful that Grahame quit the bank and went into gentle retirement.

A.A. Milne adapted part of *Willows* as a stage play, *Toad of Toad Hall*, in 1929. Other dramatic versions included Allan Bennett's in 1991. The stories also prompted screen and television versions. (Disneyland has a *Mr. Toad's Wild Ride* ride in California.) Jan Needle's version of the story is somewhat satirical. The Brian Trueman and Nicholas Jones books are based on a television series. Sequels by Duncton Chronicles author William Horwood (b. 1944) include *The Willows in Winter*, which was made into an animated film in 1997.

"Implicit in the writing of sequels is an admission of unoriginality," reviewer Christopher Lehman-Haupt wrote in *The New York Times*. "And Mr. Horwood, an English writer of children's books for all ages, concedes this gracefully enough when he writes in an afterword of 'the universality of the four great characters Grahame first created in those stories told to his young son': the loyal Mole, the resourceful Water Rat, the stern but wise Badger and most of all the capricious Mr. Toad."

Selected Original Works

The Wind in the Willows (1908)
The First Whisper of "The Wind in the Willows" (1944) edited by Elspeth Grahame, includes "Bertie's Escapade," from a manuscript in the Bodleian Library, Oxford

Pastiches

Nicholas Jones and Brian Trueman, *Grand Annual Show* (1984); *Mole's Cousin* (1984); *Weasel's Trap* (1984); *Alfred and the Caravan* (1984); *Buried Treasure* (1985); *Burglary at Toad Hall* (1985); *Harvest* (1985); *Labyrinth* (1985); *Winter Sports* (1986); *Rescue* (1986); *Bankruptcy* (1986); *Toad, Photographer* (1986)
John Gilmore, *If Only Toads Could Fly* (1993)
William Horwood, *The Willows in the Winter* (1993); *Toad Triumphant* (1995); *The Willows and Beyond* (1996); *Willows in Winter Series: Mole Gets Lost* (1997); *Willows in Winter Series: Flying into Danger* (1997); *Willows in Winter Series: Toad in Trouble* (1997); *The Willows at Christmas* (1998)

Jan Needle, *Wild Wood* (1981)
Dixon Scott, *A Fresh Wind in the Willows* (1984)

Hardie Gramatky
Tugboat

Hardie Gramatky (1907–1979) was an artist, illustrator and writer of children's books, including the popular story of an East River tugboat (based on one of the Moran towcraft he saw from his studio window), *Little Toot* (1939).

A native of Dallas, Texas, he attended Stanford University and the Chouinard Art Institute. He painted watercolors and he worked for a half dozen years as a senior animator for Walt Disney Studios. (*Little Toot* was included in a *Melody Time* Disney short in 1948.) He produced training films for the U.S. Air Force during World War II. He later lived in Connecticut and concentrated on illustrations for leading periodicals including *American* and *Reader's Digest.*

Gramatky wrote four sequels to *Little Toot* and had most of a fifth completed at the time of his death. The family waited until the fiftieth anniversary of *Little Toot* to complete the book and bring it to publication. "Sometimes I wondered why it took me so long to continue with this book, the story my father planned before his death," Linda Gramatky Smith told Shirley Horner of *The New York Times.* "Other times I know precisely what kept me away — the feeling that I could never come up to the high standards of his work. After all, he was a master, a proven success, and he could work with that assurance. Or so it seemed to me."

Smith said on the Little Toot Web site: "When my father died in 1979, one of the last things he did creatively was to ask me if I knew dictation so that I could 'take down the final version of the Loch Ness book' that he had been lying there thinking about. So Mom and I knew how important that book was to Dad." Gramatky's manuscript sketches were more than sufficient to persuade a Putnam reader to go ahead with the project. Gramatky's widow Dorothea, herself an illustrator, added a few more scenes. The story was animated for Shelley Duvall's *Bedtime Stories* program on Showtime. There have also been derivative publications of Gramatky's original for young children.

Original Little Toot Works

Little Toot (1939)
Little Toot on the Thames (1964)
Little Toot on the Grand Canal (1968)

Little Toot on the Mississippi (1973)
Little Toot Through the Golden Gate (1975)

Posthumous collaboration

Linda Gramatky Smith and Dorothea Cooke Gramatky, *Little Toot and the Loch Ness Monster* (1989)

Pastiche

Linda Gramatky Smith, *Little Toot and the Lighthouse* (1999)

JOHNNY GRUELLE

Raggedy Ann and Andy

Johnny Gruelle (1880–1938) illustrated as well as wrote a series of children's books about Raggedy Ann and Raggedy Andy. He registered and marketed Raggedy Ann dolls (Patent 47789, 1915). He manufactured them near his home in Connecticut.

Gruelle was born in Arcola, Illinois, the son of a portraitist and landscape painter. He became a political cartoonist and illustrator. His first book came out in 1914. Family tradition has it Gruelle's daughter Marcella, found an old rag doll in a trunk in her grandmother's attic. It had no face, so Gruelle made one, and told Marcella stories about Raggedy Ann to entertain. Marcella suffered an infection due to smallpox vaccine and died at age thirteen. The first Raggedy Ann book came out in 1918. There's a Raggedy Ann and Andy Museum in Arcola.

Other writers have continued the series.

Original Works

Raggedy Ann Stories (1918)
Raggedy Andy Stories (1920)
Raggedy Ann and Andy and the Camel with the Wrinkled Knees (1924)
Raggedy Andy's Number Book (1924)
Raggedy Ann's Wishing Pebble (1925)
Raggedy Ann's Alphabet Book (1925)
Beloved Belindy (1926)
The Paper Dragon: A Raggedy Ann Adventure (1926)
Wooden Willie (1927)
Raggedy Ann's Fairy Stories (1928)
Raggedy Ann's Magical Wishes (1928)
Marcella: A Raggedy Ann Story (1929)
Raggedy Ann in the Deep Deep Woods (1930)
Raggedy Ann's Sunny Songs (1930)
Raggedy Ann in Cookie Land (1931)
Raggedy Ann's Lucky Pennies (1932)
Raggedy Ann in the Golden Meadow (1935)
Raggedy Ann and the Left-Handed Safety Pin (1935)

Raggedy Ann's Joyful Songs (1937)
Raggedy Ann in the Magic Book (1939)
Raggedy Ann and the Laughing Brook (1940)
Raggedy Ann and the Golden Butterfly (1940)
Raggedy Ann and the Hoppy Toad (1940)
Raggedy Ann Helps Grandpa Hoppergrass (1940)
Raggedy Ann Goes Sailing (1941)
Raggedy Ann and Andy and the Nice Fat Policeman (1942)
Raggedy Ann and Betsy Bonnet String (1943)
Raggedy Ann and Andy (1944)
Raggedy Ann in the Snow White Castle (1946)
Raggedy Ann's Adventures (1947)
Raggedy Ann and the Slippery Slide (1947)
Ragged Ann's Mystery (1947)
Raggedy Ann and Marcella's First Day at School (1952)

Raggedy Ann's Merriest Christmas (1952)   *Raggedy Ann's Secret* (1959)
Raggedy Andy's Surprise (1953)   *Raggedy Ann and the Golden Ring* (1961)
Raggedy Ann's Tea Party (1954)   *Raggedy Ann and the Hobby Horse* (1961)

Pastiches

Anonymous, *Raggedy Ann and the Happy Meadow* (1961); *Raggedy Ann and the Wonderful Witch* (1961); *Raggedy Ann and the Tagalong Present* (1971); *Raggedy Andy's Treasure Hunt* (1973); *Raggedy Ann's Cooking School* (1974); *Raggedy Ann and Andy and the Kindly Rag Man* (1975); *Raggedy Ann and Andy and Witchie Kissaby* (1977); *More Raggedy Ann and Andy Stories* (1977)

Mary Virginia Carey, *Raggedy Ann and the Sad and Glad Days* (1972)

Kathleen N. Daly, *Raggedy Ann and Andy* (1977) movie novelization

Danielle Doll, *Meet Raggedy Ann* (2008)

Janet Fulton, *Raggedy Ann* (1969)

Patricia Hall, *Raggedy Ann & Andy: Day at the Fair* (2000); *Raggedy Ann & Andy: Going to Grandma's* (2001); *Raggedy Ann & Andy: Easter Treats* (2001); *Raggedy Ann & Andy: Old Friends, New Friends* (2002); *Raggedy Ann & Andy: Hooray for Reading!* (2002)

Barbara Shook Hazen, *Raggedy Ann and Fido* (1969); *Raggedy Ann and the Cookie Snatcher* (1972); *Raggedy Ann and Andy and the Rainy Day Circus* (1973)

Alison Inches, *Marcella's New Doll* (2000)

Jean Lewis, *Raggedy Ann and Andy Meet Raggedy Cat* (1988)

Jan Palmer, *How Raggedy Ann Got Her Candy Heart* (2001); *Raggedy Ann's Wishing Pebble* (2002)

Doris Thorner Salzberg, *Raggedy Granny Stories* (1977)

Elizabeth Silbaugh, *Raggedy Ann's Tea Party Book* (1999)

Nora Smaridge, *Raggedy Ann—A Thank You, Please, and I Love You Book* (1976)

Jan Sukus, *Raggedy Ann and Raggedy Andy Book* (1973)

Patricia Thackray, *Raggedy Ann at the Carnival* (1977)

Dean Whalley, *Raggedy Ann and the Daffy Taffy Pull* (1972)

HERGÉ

Tintin

Belgian writer Georges Remi (1907–1983), under the penname Hergé, researched, wrote and illustrated the adventures of youthful journalist Tintin and his fox terrier Milou (Snowy) and Captain Haddock and other characters in twenty-three graphic novels.

Born in Brussels, Remi studied for a time at Saint-Boniface, a Catholic secondary school. His early drawings appeared in the school's Boy Scout publication in the 1920s. Remi was a professional artist by 1928, and created Tintin in 1929. Many Tintin stories keyed off on world events. *The Blue Lotus*, for example, took its impetus from an incident that triggered the Chinese-Japanese War in 1934.

"Tintin's slightly priggish character fitted the times," suggested a writer in *The Economist* in 2008. "His simple ethical code — seek the truth, protect the weak and stand up to bullies — appealed to a continent waking up from the shame of war." Health reasons eventually forced the artist to work with collaborators. A twenty-fourth Tintin tale was published in incomplete form, as he asked that no other artist work on it.

Tintin characters appeared in an unauthorized graphic novel, *Breaking Free*, by the pseudonymous Jack Daniels, issued in England without copyright. *Tintin in Thailand*, distributed in French and English, is in black and white, includes profanity and departs significantly from the original. The Remi estate pursued and enforced its rights to have the work withdrawn. Yves Rodier, a French-Canadian comic strip artist, wrote unauthorized comic book pastiches of Tintin and completed a version of *Tintin and Alph-art*. The estate never sanctioned it. Readers in Spain, for whom *The Blue Lotus* is a favorite, were offended when Antonio Altarriba in *The Pink Lotus* depicted an older Tintin and included suggestive scenes, and several bookshops withdrew the book from circulation. Frederick Tuten's novel reimagines the hero in a more serious vein.

Original Tintin Series
(original publication dates, but English titles)

Tintin in the Land of the Soviets (1929–1930)
Tintin in the Congo (1930–1931)
Tintin in America (1931–1932)
Cigars of the Pharaoh (1932–1934)
The Blue Lotus (1934–1935)
The Broken Ear (1935–1937)
The Black Island (1937–1938)
King Ottokar's Sceptre (1938–1939)
The Crab with the Golden Claws (1940–1941)
The Shooting Star (1941–1942)
The Secret of the Unicorn (1942–1943)
Red Rackham's Treasure (1943–1944)

The Seven Crystal Balls (1943–1948)
Prisoners of the Sun (1946–1949)
Land of Black Gold (1948–1950)
Destination Moon (1950–1953)
Explorers on the Moon (1950–1954)
The Calculus Affair (1954–1956)
The Red Sea Sharks (1958)
Tintin in Tibet (1960)
The Castafiore Emerald (1963)
Flight 714 (1968)
Tintin and the Picaros (1976)
Tintin and Alph-Art (1986) expanded (2004)

Pastiches

Michel Regnier as Greg, *Tintin and the Lake of Sharks* (1972) based on the film *Tintin et le lac aux requins*
Antonio Altarriba, *The Pink Lotus* (2008)
Jack Daniels, *Breaking Free* (1989)
Yves Rodier, *Tintin and Alph-Art* (1986) completes Hergé story
Frederick Tuten, *Tintin in the New World* (1996)
Bud E. Weyser, *Tintin in Thailand* (1999)

Anthony R.M. Hodges

Rainbow

Anthony Hodges, of England, half-wrote a book. His granddaughter Naomi A. Moore, of New Zealand, with her own literary aspirations, found Hodges' manuscript after his death, and finished it. The family published the 100-page children's fantasy, *Chasing the Rainbow*, set in Sussex, England, and gave copies to family members. It was too good to contain, and the book is now available through a website, along with two new books by Naomi. It's not your typical posthumous collaboration.

Posthumous Collaboration
Naomi Moore, *Chasing the Rainbow* (2008)

Caroline Emilia Jacobs

Blue Bonnet

Caroline Emilia Jacobs was a penname of Emilia Elliot (1872–1909). Apparently she died not long after her manuscript for *A Texas Blue Bonnet* found a publisher.

Edyth Ellerbeck Read completed the next three entries in the girls' book series, perhaps based on outlines. Lela Horn Richards wrote the last three books. Several of the books are still in print.

Original Work
A Texas Blue Bonnet (1910)

Posthumous Collaborations
Edyth Ellerbeck Read, *Blue Bonnet's Ranch Party* (1912); *Blue Bonnet in Boston* (1914); *Blue Bonnet Keeps House* (1916)

Pastiches
Lela Horn Richards, *Blue Bonnet: Debutante* (1917); *Blue Bonnet of the Seven Stars* (1919); *Blue Bonnet's Family* (1929)

Ezra Jack Keats

Children of all cultures

A hallmark of children's books crafted by Ezra Jack Keats (1916–1983) were multicultural characters and themes. Born Jacob Ezra Katz, to Polish immigrant parents in Brooklyn, New York, he made his first income from his art at age eight, when he painted a sign for a merchant. With nurturing (though impoverished) parents, an award from Scholastic Publishing and scholarships to art school, Keats painted WPA murals during the Depression. He illustrated *Captain Marvel* comic books. After military service in World War II (he painted camouflage patterns on aircraft), he broke into the field of magazine illustration, working for *Reader's Digest, Colliers* and *Playboy*, among others. Discrimination against his Jewish religion prompted his sympathy for those who suffered ethnic injustice. He broke new ground in depicting urban settings in his books.

The first children's book he illustrated was *Jubilant for Sure* (1954) by Elisabeth Hubbazrd Lansing. The first children's book he wrote, *My Dog Is Lost*, came out in 1960. *The Snowy Day* in 1963 earned Keats the Caldecott Award. The boy Peter, featured in the book, appeared in six more books. At his death from a heart attack, Keats had written and illustrated twenty-four books and illustrated in his distinct gouache and collage style a total of more than eighty-five.

Recent pastiches are based on characters, including Peter, Archie, Amy, Willie the dog and the neighborhood created by Keats.

Original Peter Works

The Snowy Day (1963)   *A Letter to Amy* (1968)
Whistle for Willie (1964)   *Goggles!* (1969)
Peter's Chair (1967)   *The Pet Show* (1972)

Peter Pastiches

Anastasia Suen, *Willie's Birthday* (2001); *Hamster Chase* (2002); *The Loose Tooth* (2003); *The Clubhouse* (2003)

Original Roberto Works

Dreams (1974)   *Louie* (1975)

Roberto Pastiches

Janice N. Harrington, *Roberto Walks Home* (2008)

ERIC KNIGHT

Lassie, find Timmy

Eric Knight (1897–1942) was born in Yorkshire, England. His father, a diamond merchant, deserted the family in South Africa and Eric's mother remarried and located to the United States. Eric graduated from Cambridge School of Latin in Massachusetts and studied art at New York National Academy of Design. He became a feature writer for the Syndicate Bureau and reviewed movies for the Philadelphia *Public Ledger*.

He and his wife, Jere, lived on a farm in Pennsylvania and later settled in Hollywood, where a Collie puppy named Toots became a favorite. Knight visited England during the Great Depression, and conceived a story set in Yorkshire that became *Lassie Come Home*. *The Saturday Evening Post* published it Dec. 17, 1938, and two years later it came out as a book. MGM made a film of the story in 1942, by which time Knight had died in action during World War II.

Lassie became a television fixture through several series over the years. It is this Americanized Lassie featuring Jeff Miller or Timmy Martin, Corey Stuart or others that inspired the bulk of the book sequels.

Original work

Lassie Come Home (1940)

Pastiches

Anonymous, *Challenge to Lassie* (1949) based on MGM film that took its story from *Greyfriars Bobby* by Eleanor Atkinson; *The Painted Hills: A Story of Lassie the Famous Film Dog* (1930) based on MGM film that took its story from *Shep of the Painted Hills* by Alexander Hull; *Lassie and the Kittens* (1956); *Lassie's Brave Adventure* (1958); *Lassie Wins the Prize* (1958); *M-G-M's Lassie: Rescue in the Storm* (1951)

Sheila Black, *Lassie: Best Friends Are Forever* (1994) aka *Lassie* (1994) based on a screenplay by Matthew Jacobs, Gary Ross and Elizabeth Anderson

Marion Borden, *Hooray for Lassie* (1964)

Marion Bray, *Under the Big Top* (1995); *Treasure at Eagle Mountain* (1995); *Lassie to the Rescue* (1995); *Hayloft Hideout* (1995); *Danger at Echo Cliffs* (1996)

Stuart Corey and Lassie, *Forest Ranger Handbook* (1967)

L.G. Edmonds, *Lassie: The Wild Mountain Trail* (1966)

George S. Elrick, *Lassie: Adventure in Alaska* (1967); *Lassie and the Shabby Sheik* (1968); *Lassie: Old One-Eye* (1975)

Jean Fiedler, *Lassie: The Sandbar Rescue* (1964); *Lassie and the Deer Mystery* (1966)

Steve Frazee, *Lassie: The Mystery of Bristlecone Pine* (1967); *Lassie: The Secret of the Smelter's Cave* (1968); *Lassie: Lost in the Snow* (1969); *Lassie: Trouble at Panter's Lake* (1972)

Kennon Graham, *Lassie and the Big Clean-Up Day* (1972); *Lassie and the Secret Friend* (1972)

Earl Hammer and Don Spies, *Lassie: A Christmas Story* (1997)

Monica Hill, *Lassie Shows the Way* (1957)

Cecily Ruth Hogan, *Lassie and Her Friends* (1975)

Nancy E. Krulik, *Lassie: The Puppy Problem* (1989); *Lassie: Digging Up Danger* (1989); *Lassie: The Big Blowup* (1990); *Lassie: Water Watchdog* (1990); *Lassie: The Skateboard Dare* (1990); *Lassie: Dangerous Party* (1990); *Lassie: A Boy's Best Friend & Buried Treasure* (1990); *Lassie: Party Nightmare & Water Watchdog* (1990); *Lassie: Skateboard Stunt & Danger Zone* (1990)

Leon Lazarus, *Lassie and the Lost Explorer* (1958)

Jean Lewis, *Lassie: The Busy Morning* (1973)

Florence Michelson, *Lassie and the Cub Scout* (1966); *Lassie and the Fire Fighters* (1968)

Diane Muldrow, *Lassie: The Great Escape* (1998)

Irwin Shapiro, *Lassie Finds a Way: A New Story of the Famous Dog* (1957)

Dorothy J. Snow, *Lassie and the Mystery at Blackberry Bog* (1956); *Lassie and the Secret of the Summer* (1958)

Doris Schroeder, *Lassie: The Forbidden Valley* (1959)

Stephanie St. Pierre, *Lassie's Forest Adventure* (1994); *Lassie and the Little Lost Sheep* (1994)

Charles S. Strong, *Lassie: Treasure Hunter* (1960)

Theresa, *Lassie Finds a Friend* (1960)

Charles Spain Verral, *Lassie and the Daring Rescue* (1956); *Lassie and Her Day in the Sun* (1957)

Robert Weverka, *The Magic of Lassie* (1978) based on a screenplay by Jean Holoway, Robert B. Sherman and Richard M. Sherman

Rae Lambert
Furlings

Rae Lambert of Wales, a television writer, created *The Furlings*, the story of cute animals including Abigail the mouse, Edgar the mole and Russell the hedgehog. The derivative animated motion picture *Once Upon a Forest* in 1993 inspired a companion book by Elizabeth Isele.

Original Work
A Furling's Story (1989)

Pastiche
Elizabeth Isele, *Once Upon a Forest* (1993)

Hugh Lofting
Doctor Dolittle

Hugh Lofting (1886–1947), a native of Maidenhead, England, as a child kept a variety of small animals in his own private zoo in his mother's cupboard. He studied civil engineering at university and traveled widely. He had great success writing children's books including the Doctor Dolittle series, which grew out of stories he wrote to his children while serving in the military during World War I. Chubby, affable Doctor Dolittle can converse with animals. Lofting received the Newbery Medal in 1923.

After Lofting's death, his sister-in-law, Olga Fricker, assembled both published and incomplete stories for two more collections.

Original Doctor Dolittle Works

The Story of Doctor Dolittle: Being the History of His Peculiar Life at Home and Astonishing Adventures in Foreign Parts Never Before Printed (1920) retitled *Doctor Dolittle*
The Voyages of Doctor Dolittle (1922) retitled *Doctor Dolittle and the Pirates*
Doctor Dolittle's Post Office (1923)

Doctor Dolittle's Circus (1924)
Doctor Dolittle's Zoo (1925)
Doctor Dolittle's Caravan (1926)
Doctor Dolittle's Garden (1927)
Doctor Dolittle in the Moon (1928)
Doctor Dolittle's Return (1933)
Doctor Dolittle and the Secret Lake (1948)

Posthumous Collaborations

Olga Fricker, *Doctor Dolittle and the Green Canary* (1950); *Doctor Dolittle's Puddleby Adventure* (1952)

Doctor Dolittle Pastiches or Condensations

Anonymous, *Dr. Dolittle's Animals* (1998) based on motion picture; *Doctor Dolittle to the Rescue* (1999); *Doctor Dolittle in Trouble* (2000); *Doctor Dolittle Saves the Day* (2000); *Doctor Dolittle and the Lighthouse* (2000); *Doctor Dolittle's First Adventure* (2000); *Doctor Dolittle Takes Charge* (2000); *Doctor Dolittle's Ambulance* (2000)
Hugh Jason, *Doctor Dolittle and His Friends: Special Motion Picture Edition* (1967)
N.J. Kleinbaum, *Doctor Dolittle meets the Pushmi-Pullyu* (1999); *Doctor Dolittle and Tommy Stubbins* (1999)
Al Perkins, *Hugh Lofting's Doctor Dolittle and the Pirates* (1968)

BETTY MACDONALD

Mrs. Piggle-Wiggle

The imaginative Betty MacDonald (1908–1958) wrote children's books about Mrs. Piggle-Wiggle, the vibrant woman who lives in an upside-down house and is forever curing the neighborhood children of ailments and bad habits.

Perhaps better known to adult readers was the author's *The Egg and I* (1945), her novel of fictionalized experiences on a rural chicken farm. The novel was turned into a motion picture and introduced the rustic characters of Ma and Pa Kettle, who went on to have their own successful series of movies.

The author was born Anne Elizabeth Campbell Bard in Boulder, Colorado. She graduated from Roosevelt High School in Butte, Montana. She married Robert Heskett in 1927 and the couple lived on a farm on the Olympic Peninsula. In her second marriage, to Donald C. MacDonald, she moved to California began to write books.

Daughter Anne MacDonald Canham used some of her mother's material and created new stories of her own to continue the children's series.

Original Works

Mrs. Piggle-Wiggle (1947)

Mrs. Piggle-Wiggle's Magic (1949)

Mrs. Piggle-Wiggle's Farm (1954)

Hello, Mrs. Piggle-Wiggle (1957)

Pastiches

Anne MacDonald Canham, *Happy Birthday, Mrs. Piggle-Wiggle* (2007)

ELLEN MACGREGOR

Miss Pickerell

Comically eccentric Miss Pickerell had adventures on earth, in the sea, on the moon and on Mars. She was perhaps the earliest science fiction character meant for younger readers.

Author Ellen MacGregor (1906–1954) was born in Baltimore, Maryland, and lived with her family in Wisconsin and Washington. She majored in science at the University of Washington and did her postgraduate studies at the University of California. She became a librarian in Hawaii and Florida. She wrote a short story for *Liberty* in 1950, and eventually expanded it into her first book *Miss Pickerell Goes to Mars* (1951).

McGraw-Hill engaged Dora Pantell (b. 1915) to continue the series following MacGregor's death. Pantell at first worked from MacGregor's notes, then created her own plots. It's not clear where the break came, but several of the later books deal with issues MacGregor wouldn't have encountered such as computers and the energy crisis.

Original Works

Miss Pickerell Goes to Mars (1951)

Miss Pickerell Goes Undersea (1953)

Miss Pickerell and the Geiger Counter (1953)

Miss Pickerell Goes to the Arctic (1954)

Posthumous Collaborations

Dora Pantell, *Miss Pickerell on the Moon* (1965); *Miss Pickerell Goes on a Dig* (1966); *Miss Pickerell Harvests the Sea* (1968)

Pastiches

Dora Pantell, *Miss Pickerell and the Weather Satellite* (1971); *Miss Pickerell Meets Mr. H.U.M.* (1974); *Miss Pickerell Takes the Bull by the Horns* (1976); *Miss Pickerell and the Supertanker* (1977); *Miss Pickerell to the Earthquake Rescue* 1977); *Miss Pickerell and the Blue Whales* (1978); *Miss Pickerell Tackles the Energy Crisis* (1980); *Miss Pickerell on the Trail* (1981); *Miss Pickerell and the Blue Whale* (1982); *Miss Pickerell and the War of the Computers* (1984); *Miss Pickerell and the Lost World* (1985)

A.A. MILNE
Pooh

Alan Alexander Milne (1882–1956), a native of Hampstead, London, England, grew up at a boarding school where his father was headmaster. He served in the British Army during World War I. His best-known stories are about Christopher Robin, Winnie-the-Pooh, Tigger, Eye-ore, Owl and the others.

Milne's book of thirty-five verses for children, *Now We Are Six*, inspired Christopher Matthew to reshape them for older readers. The Pooh books, in the hands of Walt Disney, generated scads of animated films and book spin-offs. The Milne interests cleared the way for what was described as "the first authorized sequel" in 2009: novelist and playwright David Benedictus's *Return to the Hundred Acre Wood*.

Original Pooh Works

Winnie the Pooh (1926)   *The House at Pooh Corner* (1928)
Now We Are Six (1927)

Pooh Pastiches

Anonymous, *Adventures of Winnie the Pooh: I See the Sun* (1995); *The Big Fat Bee* (1994); *Christopher Robin Goes to School* (2005); *Falling Leaves* (2005); *My Very First Encyclopedia with Winnie the Pooh and Friends: Nature* (2003); *My Very First Encyclopedia with Winnie the Pooh and Friends: Animals* (2003); *Pooh Opposites* (2005); *Pooh's Grand Adventure: The Search for Christopher Robin* (1997); *Walt Disney's Winnie the Pooh Goes to School* (2001); *Walt Disney's Winnie the Pooh: Feelings* (1999); *Where Are You Roo?* (2003); *Winnie the Pooh and Some Bees* (1990); *Winnie the Pooh and the Honey Tree* (1999); *Winnie the Pooh: I'm Really Sorry* (2000); *Winnie the Pooh's ABC* (2001); *Winnie the Pooh's Busy Book* (2001); *Winnie the Pooh's Giant Lift the Flap Book* (1999); *Winnie the Pooh's Thinking Spot Series No. 1: How Do You Hop So High?* (2005); *Winnie the Pooh's Thinking Spot Series No. 2: What Is that Rumbly in my Tummy?* (2005); *Winnie the Pooh's Thinking Spot Series No. 3: Why Don't Things Fall Up?* (2005); *Winnie the Pooh's Thinking Spot Series No. 4: Why Does It Have to Rain?* (2005); *Winnie the Pooh's Thinking Spot Series No. 5: Does it Float?* (2005); *Winnie the Pooh's Thinking Spot Series No. 6: Is My Shirt Getting Smaller?* (2005); *Winnie the Pooh's Thinking Spot Series No. 7: What Good are Bugs?* (2005); *Winnie the Pooh's Thinking Spot Series No. 8: Why Is the Day All Gray?* (2005); *Winnie the Pooh's Thinking Spot Series No. 9: How Does Your Garden Grow?* (2005); *Winnie the Pooh's Thinking Spot Series No. 10: Where Did the Rain Puddle Go?* (2005); *Winnie the Pooh's Thinking Spot Series No. 11: Who's Hiding?* (2005); *Winnie the Pooh's Thinking Spot Series No. 12: Who Said Whoo?* (2005); *Winnie the Pooh's Thinking Spot Series No. 13: How Did You Make That Web?* (2005); *Winnie the Pooh's Thinking Spot Series No. 14: Where Does the Sun Go at Night?* (2005); *Winnie the Pooh's Thinking Spot Series No. 15: Why Aren't You Asleep?* (2005)
Sarah Albee, *Piglet and the Stormy Day* (2005)

David Benedictus, *Return to the Hundred Acre Wood* (2009)

Ann Braybrooks, *Pooh's Best Friend* (1998)

Betty Birney, *I Am Winnie the Pooh* (2004)

Stephanie Calmenson, *Winnie the Pooh and Tigger Too* (1994)

Janet Campbell, *Walt Disney's Winnie the Pooh and the Honey Tree* (1993)

Don Ferguson, *Walt Disney's Winnie the Pooh's A to ZZzz* (1992)

Isabel Gaines, *Pooh's Honey Tree* (1998); *Bounce, Tigger, Bounce* (1998); *Pooh and the Storm That Sparkled* (1999); *The Giving Bear* (1999)

Andrew Grey, *All About Kanga and Roo* (2007)

Mary Russell Hicks, *Winnie the Pooh and the Honey Tree* (2000)

Benjamin Hoff, *The Tao of Pooh* (1983)

Ellen Milnes, *Winnie the Pooh: Sweet Dreams* (2002)

Nancy Parent, *Walt Disney's Winnie the Pooh: Everyone Is Special* (2000); *Walt Disney's Winnie the Pooh: Home Sweet Home* (2000)

Teddy Slater, *Walt Disney's Winnie the Pooh and the Blustery Day* (1993); *Winnie the Pooh and a Day for Eeyore* (1994)

Shirley Stepp-Awea, *Pooh & Friends Spell It Out* (2004)

Bruce Talkington, *Winnie the Pooh and the Perfect Christmas Tree* (1994); *Winnie the Pooh's Halloween* (1995)

Kathleen W. Zoehfeld, *Pooh's Mailbox* (1998); *Pooh Plays Doctor* (1999); *Pooh's First Day of School* (1999); *Winnie the Pooh's Big Book of First Words* (2000); *Pooh's Jingle Bells* (2000)

Cookbooks

Virginia Ellison, *The Pooh Cook Book* (1969)

Dawn Martin, *Winnie-the-Pooh's Cookie Book* (1996)

Six Pastiche

Christopher Matthew, *Now We Are Sixty (and a Bit)* (1999)

LUCY MAUD MONTGOMERY

Anne Shirley

Lucy Maud Montgomery's impetuous, red-headed orphan, Anne Shirley, was not the boy expected by the Prince Edward Island couple Marilla Cuthbert and her brother Matthew Cuthbert who adopted her. Nevertheless, the fictional heroine worked her way into their hearts and into the hearts of several generations of young adult and adult readers. Canadian author Montgomery (1874–1942), whose mother died when she was two years old, was raised by her strict, Presbyterian maternal grandparents. Her isolation, she wrote in a journal, "drove me in on myself and early forced me to construct for myself a world of fancy and imagination very different indeed from the world in which I lived." Obliged to care for step-siblings, she eventually became a schoolteacher. She worked for a newspaper in Nova Scotia. She began writing fiction. *Anne of Green Gables* was published in 1908. Anne and the writer's other heroines such as Emily were children who never quite grew up. They continued to display a rebellious streak — key to their appeal. There have been several film and television adaptations, the most popular of the latter featuring Megan Follows.

"L.M. Montgomery has given us characters that live with us all our lives and inform our understanding of what it means to be engaged with life," Elizabeth R. Epperly, founder of the L.M. Montgomery Institute, told *Canadian Geographic* in April 2008.

The Anne of Avonlea books by a variety of writers provided young readers with new adventures. Budge Wilson, a Canadian writer of children's fiction, wrote a prequel in 2008, at the request of the estate, to mark the centennial of Anne's first appearance. "I am still vaguely troubled by the idea that L.M. Montgomery would perhaps not want this done," she said in a Reuters interview in 2008. Anne grew up in an orphanage. "You saw what a lively, cheerful, articulate person she was, but she should have been a basket case after what she'd been through. I realized that this was a huge puzzle — and a puzzle that I might like to try to solve."

Original Anne Shirley and Related Works

Anne of Green Gables (1908)
Anne of Avonlea (1909)
Chronicles of Avonlea, in Which Anne Shirley of Green Gables and Avonlea Plays Some Part (1912)
Anne of the Island (1915)
Anne's House of Dreams (1917)
Rainbow Valley (1919)

Further Chronicles of Avonlea: Which Have to Do with Many Personalities and Events in and About Avonlea (1920)
Rilla of Ingleside (1921)
Anne of Windy Poplars (1936) aka *Anne of Windy Willows* (1936)
Anne of Ingleside (1939)

Pastiches in *Road to Avonlea* Series

Dennis Adair and Janet Rosenstock, *The Journey Begins* (1991)
Heather Conkie, *The Materializing of Duncan McTavish* (1991); *Malcolm and the Baby* (1992); *Sara's Homecoming* (1993); *Old Quarrels, Old Love* (1993); *Dreamer of Dreams* (1993); *The Ties That Bind* (1994); *Friends and Relations* (1995)
Amy J. Cooper, *Aunt Abigail's Beau* (1992)
Gail Hamilton, *The Story Girl Earns Her Name* (1991; *Felicity's Challenge* (1992); *Nothing Endures but Change* (1993); *Aunt Hetty's Ordeal* (1993); *Family Rivalry* (1993); *May the Best Man Win* (1993); *A Dark and Stormy Night* (1994); *Vows of Silence* (1995)
Marlene Matthew, *But When She Was Bad...* (1994); *Double Trouble* (1994)
Fiona McHugh, *Song of the Night* (1991); *Quarantine at Alexander Abraham's* (1992); *Of Corsets and Secrets and True, True Love* (1993)
Janet Rosenstock, *Misfits and Miracles* (1994); *Felix and Blackie* (1994)

Anne of Green Gables Pastiches

Eugene Orlando, *A Journey with Anne of Green Gables* (2005)
Budge Wilson, *Before Green Gables* (2008)

Cookbook

Kate McDonald, *The Anne of Green Gables Cookbook* (2006)

JACK O'BRIEN
Silver Chief

John Sherman O'Brien (1898–1938), who wrote young adult adventure books and historical biographies under the name Jack O'Brien, featured RCMP Sgt. Jim Thorpe and his part–Siberian, part-wolf Silver Chief in a series of book.

O'Brien was chief surveyor on Byrd's Antarctic expedition, in charge of dogs. It's little wonder the extreme north figures in some of the plots. (O'Brien's nonfiction *By Dog Sled for Byrd: 1600 Miles Across Antarctic Ice* came out in 1931.)

In later entries, perhaps by a hired writer, the hero's nephew Peter Thorne and a Silver Chief offspring take front stage. After O'Brien's death, Pennsylvania native Albert G. Miller (b. 1905) wrote a last book in the series.

Original Works

Silver Chief, Dog of the North (1933)   *Royal Red* (1951)
Silver Chief to the Rescue (1937)   *Silver Chief's Revenge* (1954)
The Return of Silver Chief (1943)

Pastiche

Albert G. Miller, *Silver Chief's Big Game Trail* (1961)

ROBERT C. O'BRIEN
Rats

Robert C. O'Brien's *Mrs. Frisby and the Rats of N.I.M.H.* won the Newbery Medal in 1972. It is about a field mouse who recruits escaped laboratory rats to help protect her home from a farmer's plow.

The author was born Robert Leslie Conly (1918–1973) but used Robert C. O'Brien for many of his works. He studied at Juilliard and earned a bachelor of arts degree in English from the University of Rochester. He wrote three other children's books besides *Mrs. Frisby*.

Jane Leslie Conly (b. 1948) continued her father's premise in two more novels. She won a Newbery Honor for her separate novel *Crazy Lady*.

Selected Original Work

Mrs. Frisby and the Rats of N.I.M.H. (1971) aka *The Secret of N.I.M.H.* (1972)

Pastiches

Jane Leslie Conly, *Racso and the Rats of N.I.M.H.* (1986); *R-T, Margaret, and the Rats of N.I.M.H.* (1990)

SCOTT O'DELL
Chief Joseph

California-born Scott O'Dell (1898–1989) worked as a cameraman and technical director in Hollywood before becoming a full-time writer in 1934. His credits include two dozen juvenile books, among them *Island of the Blue Dolphins* (1960) and *Streams to the River, River to the Sea: A Novel of Sacagawea* (1986). O'Dell won four Newbery Medals for his books.

"O'Dell is, in a very real way, a different person each time he tells a story. This gives each of his books an individual quality that is uniquely suited for its natural and cultural setting," observed James E. Higgins in *Twentieth-Century Children's Writers* (1989).

After the author's death, *Thunder Rolling in the Mountains* was completed by his wife, Elizabeth Hall, a longtime research collaborator as well as librarian, writer and editor of fiction and non-fiction. She was born in 1929 in California. The joint book, told through the eyes of Sound of Running Feet, a Nez Perce girl, is about Chief Joseph and the tragic defeat of the tribe and its retreat to Canada.

"Their story of courage and determination in the face of cruelty, betrayal and bureaucratic ignorance" moved O'Dell deeply, according to Hall in a foreword. "So deeply that he continued to work on the manuscript in the hospital until two days before he died."

Posthumous collaboration

Elizabeth Hall, *Thunder Rolling in the Mountains* (1992)

PEGGY PARISH
Amelia Bedelia

Peggy Parish (1927–1988), a South Carolinian by birth, created the super-literal children's book housemaid heroine Amelia Bedelia. When she makes a sponge cake, she puts in real sponges.

Parish earned a bachelor of arts degree in English from the University of South Carolina. She became a teacher of dancing, and later, living in Oklahoma, third grade. She wrote two other children's books before her breakthrough with

Amelia Bedelia. Her nephew, Herman Parish, continued the books after Parish died of an aneurysm. His background is in advertising.

Original Books

Amelia Bedelia (1963)

Thank You, Amelia Bedelia (1964)

Amelia Bedelia and the Surprise Shower (1966)

Come Back, Amelia Bedelia (1971)

Play Ball, Amelia Bedelia (1972)

Good Work, Amelia Bedelia (1976)

Teach Us, Amelia Bedelia (1977)

Amelia Bedelia Helps Out (1979)

Amelia Bedelia and the Baby (1981)

Amelia Bedelia Goes Camping (1985)

Merry Christmas, Amelia Bedelia (1986)

Amelia Bedelia's Family Album (1988)

Pastiches

Herman Parish, Good Driving, Amelia Bedelia (1996); Bravo, Amelia Bedelia! (1997); Amelia Bedelia 4 Mayor (1999); Calling Doctor Amelia Bedelia (2002); Amelia Bedelia and the Christmas List (2003); Amelia Bedelia, Bookworm (2003); Happy Haunting, Amelia Bedelia (2004); Amelia Bedelia Goes Back to School (2004); Be My Valentine, Amelia Bedelia (2004); Amelia Bedelia, Rocket Scientist? (2005); Amelia Bedelia's Masterpiece (2007); Amelia Bedelia Under Construction (2007); Amelia Bedelia and the Cat (2008)

ELEANOR H. PORTER

Pollyanna

Pollyanna Whittier and her siblings Junior, Judy, Ruth and Jimmy appeared in Eleanor H. Porter's 1913 bestseller Pollyanna. An orphan living with her Aunt Polly in Vermont, Pollyanna is effervescently optimistic even in her poor circumstances.

Born in New Hampshire, Porter had trained as a singer but, while living in Massachusetts, began to write books for children, including three Miss Billy titles. She also wrote adult titles such as Sister Sue (1921). Porter (1868–1920) wrote one Pollyana sequel. A near-dozen more Glad Books appeared, after her death, by other hands.

Original Works

Pollyanna (1913)

Pollyanna Grows Up (1915)

Pastiches

Elizabeth Borton, Pollyanna in Hollywood (1931); Pollyanna's Castle in Mexico (1934); Pollyanna's Door to Happiness (1936); Pollyanna's Golden Horseshoe (1939); Pollyanna and the Secret Mission (1951)

Margaret Piper Chalmers, Pollyanna's Protégés (1944)

Virginia May Moffitt, Pollyanna at Six Star Ranch (1948); Pollyanna of Magic Valley (1949)

Colleen L. Reece, *Pollyanna Come Home* (1995); *Pollyanna Plays the Game* (1995)
Harriet Lummis Smith, *Pollyanna of the Orange Blossoms* (1924); *Pollyanna's Jewels*
  (1925); *Pollyanna's Debt of Honor* (1927); *Pollyanna's Western Adventure* (1929)

BEATRIX POTTER
Peter Rabbit

Helen Beatrix Potter (1866–1943) was an English author and illustrator. Of her
twenty-three best-selling children's books, *The Tale of Peter Rabbit* was the first
and most popular. Potter's parents were well-to-do and protective.

Potter's education was at the hands of a governess. She was isolated as a
child, but managed to make some headway in the field of fungi study. She clan-
destinely became engaged to her publisher, Norman Warne, but he died before
they married. She later married William Heelis. With her publishing success she
became financially independent of her parents and purchased and lived on a farm
in the Lake District. It is now owned by The National Trust.

Her publisher Frederick Warne & Co. in later years authorized retellings of
the stories of Peter and his sisters Flopsy, Mopsy and Cottontail.

Original Work
The Tale of Peter Rabbit (1902)

Pastiches
Anonymous, *It's Halloween, Peter Rabbit* (2003); *Merry Christmas, Peter Rabbit* (2003);
  Peter Rabbit's Easter (2003); *Peter Rabbit's Five Fluffy Bunnies* (2005)
Ladybird editions, *Mr. Jeremy Fisher Dives for Treasure* (1986); *A Birthday Party for
  Mrs. Tiggy-Winkle* (1986); *Mrs. Tiggy-Winkle's Windy Day* (1986); *The Tale of Peter
  Rabbit* (1987 and 1992); *Peter Rabbit's Big Adventure* (1989)
Sarah Toast, *The Tale of Peter Rabbit* (1995)

H. A. AND MARGARET REY
Curious George

Hans A. Rey (1898–1977) introduced the children's book character Curious George
and his keeper, the Man in the Yellow Hat, in *Cecily G. and the Nine Monkeys*.
The chimpanzee was such an inviting character, he was soon given his own series,
illustrated by the author's wife, Margaret Rey (1906–1996). Both were Jews. Margaret was born in Germany but fled the Nazis to live in Brazil. She met Hans and
they married in 1935. They worked from Paris, which they had to flee as World

War II broke out. They ended up in New York City, and later Cambridge, Massachusetts.

"The books displayed a social consciousness: In the 1942 British edition, Curious George was renamed Zozo. The publisher objected to the monkey's name because George VI sat on the throne and, in London slang, 'curious' meant 'gay,'" John R. Miller wrote in the *Wall Street Journal* in 2006.

The books inspired a series of more than 100 cartoons written by Margaret Rey and Alan J. Shalleck and (1929–2006) and directed by Shalleck. Color animation cells were used to illustrate book editions of several of the cartoons. After both Reys had died, other writers continued the series.

Original Works written by H.A. and Margaret Rey

Cecily G. and the Nine Monkeys (1939)
Curious George (1941)
Curious George Takes a Job (1947)
Curious George Rides a Bike (1952)
Curious George Gets a Medal (1957)
Curious George Flies a Kite (1958)
Curious George Learns the Alphabet (1963)
Curious George Goes to the Hospital (1966)

Works written by Margaret Rey and Alan J. Shalleck

Curious George Goes to the Aquarium (1984)
Curious George Visits the Zoo (1985)
Curious George and the Pizza (1985)
Curious George Plays Baseball (1986)
Curious George Walks the Pets (1986)
Curious George at the Airport (1987)
Curious George and the Dump Truck (1988)
Curious George Goes Fishing (1988)
Curious George at the Fire Station (1988)
Curious George at the Ballet (1988)
Curious George Goes Sledding (1988)
Curious George at the Beach (1988)
Curious George at the Laundromat (1988)
Curious George Goes to a Restaurant (1988)
Curious George Goes to the Circus (1988)
Curious George Visits a Police Station (1988)
Curious George at the Railroad Station (1988)
Curious George Goes Hiking (1988)
Curious George Visits an Amusement Park (1988)
Curious George Goes to the Dentist (1989)
Curious George Goes to an Ice Cream Shop (1989)
Curious George Goes to School (1989)
Curious George and the Dinosaur (1989)
Curious George Goes to a Toy Store (1989)
Curious George Goes Camping (1990)
Curious George Goes to an Air Show (1991)
Curious George Bakes a Cake (1993)

Pastiches

Curious George Goes to a Chocolate Factory (1998)
Curious George and the Puppies (1998)
Curious George Makes Pancakes (1998)
Curious George Feeds the Animals (1998)
Curious George Goes to a Movie (1998)
Curious George and the Hot Air Balloon (1998)
Curious George in the Snow (1998)
Curious George's Dream (1998)
Curious George Goes to the Beach (1999)
Curious George and the Dump Truck (1999)
Curious George Goes Camping (1999)
Curious George at the Parade (1999)
Curious George Goes to a Costume Party (2001)
Curious George in the Big City (2001)

Curious George Takes a Train (2002)
Curious George Visits a Toy Store (2002)
Curious George and the Birthday Surprise (2003)
Curious George Visits the Library (2003)
Curious George and the Firefighters (2004)
Curious George's First Day of School (2005)

Curious George's Dinosaur Discovery (2006)
Curious George at the Baseball Game (2006)
Merry Christmas, Curious George (2006)
Curious George at the Aquarium (2007)

DOROTHY RICHARDS

Tasseltip

Dorothy Richards' Tasseltip cute rabbit stories for the British Ladybird 474 imprint were illustrated by Ernest A. Aris and are prized by collectors. Sarah Cotton rewrote the books in the 1970s for the publisher's 497 series. The new books featured the same Aris illustrations.

Original Tasseltip Works

The Flickerdick (1947)
Mr. Mole's House Warming (1947)
A Little Silk Apron (1947)

Clatter! Clatter!! Bang!!! (1948)
The Flower Show (1950)
The First Day of Spring (1950)

Tasseltip Pastiches

Sarah Cotton, *Tasseltip Buys a Present* (1975); *Tasseltip Takes a Ride* (1975); *Tasseltip Has a Lucky Day* (1975); *Tasseltip Saves the Day* (1975); *Tasseltip and the Boozle* (1975); *Tasseltip Plays Truant* (1975)

FRANK RICHARDS

Greyfriars School

Amazingly prolific English author Charles H. St. John Hamilton (1876–1961) produced a string of school boy stories for *The Magnet*, a weekly, beginning in 1908. They were about Billy Bunter and his mates at Greyfriars School and they appeared under the name Frank Richards. And that was only a small portion of the author's enormous output. Titles after 1968 are reproductions of issues of *The Magnet*. Richards created a comparable female character, Bessie Bunter, under the pen-name Hilda Richards, for *The School Friend*. Other authors reportedly added to her repertoire as well.

Critic and novelist David Hughes (1931–2005) wrote one recent Billy Bunter pastiche.

Original Billy Bunter Works

Billy Bunter of Greyfriar's School (1947)
Billy Bunter's Barring-out (1948)
Billy Bunter's Banknote (1948)
Billy Bunter in Brazil (1949)
Billy Bunter's Christmas Party (1949)
Billy Bunter Among the Cannibals (1950)
Billy Bunter's Benefit (1950)
Billy Bunter Butts In (1951)
Billy Bunter's Postal Order (1951)
Billy Bunter and the Blue Mauritus (1952)
Billy Bunter's Beanfeast (1952)
Billy Bunter's Brainwave (1953)
Billy Bunter's First Case (1953)
Billy Bunter the Bold (1954)
Bunter Does His Best (1954) aka *Billy Bunter Does His Best*
Backing Up Billy Bunter (1955)
Billy Bunter's Double (1955)
Banishing of Billy Bunter (1956)
Lord Billy Bunter (1956)
Billy Bunter Afloat (1957)
Billy Bunter's Bolt (1957)
Billy Bunter the Hiker (1958)
Billy Bunter's Bargain (1958)
Bunter Comes for Christmas (1959) aka *Billy Bunter Comes for Christmas*
Bunter Out of Bounds (1959)
Bunter Keeps It Dark (1960)
Bunter the Bad Lad (1960)
Billy Bunter at Butlin's (1961)
Billy Bunter's Treasure-hunt (1961)
Bunter the Ventriloquist (1961)
Billy Bunter's Bodyguard (1962)
Bunter the Caravaner (1962)
Just Like Bunter (1961)
Big Chief Bunter (1963)
Bunter the Stowaway (1964)
Thanks to Bunter (1964)
Bunter and the Phantom of the Towers (1965)
Bunter the Racketeer (1965)
Bunter the Sportsman (1965)
Bunter the Tough Guy of Greyfriars (1965)
Bunter's Holiday Cruise (1965)
Bunter's Last Fling (1965)
Billy Bunter and the Man from South America (1967)
Billy Bunter and the School Rebellion (1967)
Billy Bunter and the Secret Enemy (1967)
Billy Bunter's Big Top (1967)
Billy Bunter and the Bank Robber (1968)
Billy Bunter, Sportsman (1968)
Billy Bunter and the Crooked Captain (1968)
Billy Bunter's Convict (1968)
Billy Bunter in the Land of the Pyramids (1969)
Billy Bunter of Bunter Court (1969)
Rebellion of Harry Wharton (1969)
Billy Bunter and the Courtfield Cracksman (1970)
Billy Bunter and the Terror of the Form (1970)
Mystery of Wharton Lodge (1971)
Bunter and the Greyfriars Mutiny (1972)
My Lord Bunter (1972)
Bunter on the Nile (1972)
Schemer of the Remove (1972)
Six Boys in a Boat (1972)
Alonzo the Great (1973)
Billy Bunter's Christmas (1973)
Black Sheep of Greyfriars (1973)
Calling Mister Quelch (1973)
Greyfriars Hikers (1973)
Harry Wharton's Enemy (1973)
Tyrant of Greyfriars (1973)
Bargain for Bunter (1974)
Billy Bunter in China (1974)
Billy Bunter's Circus (1974)
Joker of Greyfriars (1974)
Kidnapped Schoolboys (1974)
Mystery of the Moat House (1974)
Shadow over Harry Wharton (1974)
Billy Bunter's Coronation Party (1975)
Billy Bunter's Hat Trick (1975)
Billy Bunter's Lucky Day (1975)
Bob Cherry's Big Bargain (1975)
Bunter Tells the Truth (1975)
Bunter's Seaside Caper (1975)
Burglar of Greyfriars (1975)

Ghost of Polpelly (1975)
Greyfriars Cowboys (1975)
Sit-in Strike at Greyfriars (1975)
Sleuth of Greyfriars (1975)
Billy Bunter's Hair Raid (1976)
Dictator of Greyfriars (1976)
Dunmen of Greyfriars (1976)
Popper Island Rebels (1976)
Schoolboy Smuggler (1976)
Bounder's Rebellion (1977)
Bunter the Lion Tamer (1977)
Bunter's Funny Turn (1977)
Mystery Man of Greyfriars (1977)
Vernon Smith's Rival (1977)

Big Bang at Greyfriars (1978)
Bunter's Orders (1978)
Schoolboy Tourists (1978)
Bully of Greyfriars (1979)
Greyfriars' Second Eleven (1979)
Rogue of the Remove (1979)
Shylock of Greyfriars (1979)
Greyfriars Mysteries (1981)
Odd Fellows of Greyfriars (1981)
Persecution of Billy Bunter (1981)
Billy Bunter Expelled (1982)
Billy Bunter's Wembley Party (1983)
Billy Bunter: Film Star (1986)
Society for Reforming Billy Bunter (1986)

Billy Bunter Pastiche

David Hughes, *But for Bunter* (1985) aka *The Joke of the Century*

Original Bessie Bunter Works

Bessie Bunter of Cliff House (1949)
Bessie Bunter Joins the Circus (1967)

Bessie Bunter and the Gold Robbers (1967)

Bessie Bunter Pastiches

Issued as by Hilda Richards, *Bessie Bunter and the School Informer* (1968); *Bessie Bunter and the Missing Fortune* (1992)

J.K. ROWLING

Harry Potter-san

Harry Potter is a writer's fantasy — the bestselling series of the millennium, conceived when the author had little means and little expectation of success. Joanne Kathleen Rowling was born in Bristol, England, in 1966. Her favorite school subject was English. She earned a degree in French at Executer University. She worked for Amnesty International as a researcher and secretary. Divorced, she began to write in 1990. She envisioned a seven-book series set around Hogwarts School of Witchcraft and Wizardry, the story of orphan Harry Potter and his friends Ron Weisley and Hermione Granger and foes Lord Voldemort and others. The books (400+ million copies sold) and derivative film series achieved enormous popularity.

Rowling and her publisher Scholastic have been vigilant in protecting the franchise. In 2008, they sought injunction against writer Steve Vander Ark, who wrote an encyclopedia of the Hogworts universe. Rowling said she planned her own guide. Ark severely revised his manuscript to comply with the court's decision, and *The Lexicon: An Unauthorized Guide to Harry Potter Fiction and Related Materials* went back into production.

Rowling did endorse fan Melissa Anelli's *Harry, a History: The True Story of a Boy Wizard, His Fans, and Life Inside the Harry Potter Phenomenon* the same year, though. Scholastic and Rowling went to international court to prevent publication of a Russian children's book, *The Magic Double Bass* by Dmitry Yemets, claiming its story of girl wizard Tanya Grotter was too close to *Harry Potter and the Philosopher's Stone*. Parodies such as Michael Gerber's *Barry Trotter and the Unauthorized Parody* (2002) were to be expected. But Rowling and Scholastic had to battle a charge by a Pennsylvania woman, Nancy Stouffer, that Rowling had stolen her *Rah and the Muggles* featuring Larry Potter, allegedly written in the 1980s.

Fans could barely wait for each new installment. In fact, in some countries, they didn't. *Harry Potter and the Leopard Walk Up to Dragon* "by English person J.K. Rowling," was published in China in 2002, for example, the fifth violation of international copyright law. Chinese authorities said they had little recourse against "The tale in which Harry turns into a hairy dwarf after a 'sour-sweet rain,'" *USA Today* reported in 2002.

Original Books

Harry Potter and the Philosopher's Stone (1997) aka *Harry Potter and the Sorcerer's Stone* (1998)

Harry Potter and the Chamber of Secrets (1998)

Harry Potter and the Prisoner of Azkaban (1999)

Harry Potter and the Goblet of Fire (2000)

Harry Potter and the Order of the Phoenix (2003)

Harry Potter and the Half-Blood Prince (2005)

Harry Potter and the Deathly Hallows (2007)

Illegal Chinese Pastiches

Anonymous, *Harry Potter and the Leopard Walk Up to Dragon* (2002); *Harry Potter and the Chinese Porcelain Doll; Harry Potter and the Waterproof Pearl; Harry Potter and the Half-Blooded Relative Prince; Harry Potter and the Filler of Big* (aka *Harry Potter and the Big Funnel); Harry Potter and Platform Nine and Three-Quarters; Harry Potter and the Chinese Overseas Students at the Hogwarts School of Witchcraft and Wizardry; Harry Potter and the Showdown; Harry Potter and the Big Dipper; Harry Potter and Beaker and Burn; Cho Chang and the Monastery Murders; Harry Potter and the Chinese Empire; Harry Potter and the Hiking Dragon*

H.L. SAYLER

Airship Boys

The Airship Boys Ned Napier and Alan Hope explore inaccessible lands and discover lost races in the series written by H.L. Sayler in the earliest days of aviation.

Author Harry Lincoln Sayler (1863–1913) also wrote books in the Boys Big Game Series under the pseudonym Elliot Whitney and Aeroplane Boys books as Ashton Lamar.

Publisher Reilly & Britton engaged DeLysle F. Cass to write an eighth volume about the rescue of the Boys' reporter friend Robert Russell.

Original Works

The Airship Boys; or, The Quest of the Aztec Treasure (1909)

The Airship Boys Adrift; or, Saved by Aeroplane (1909)

The Airship Boys Due North; or, By Balloon to the Pole (1910)

The Airship Boys in the Barren Lands; or, The Secret of the White Eskimos (1910)

The Airship Boys in Finance; or, The Flight of the Flying Cow (1911)

The Airship Boys'; Ocean Flyer; or, New York to London in Twelve Hours (1911)

The Airship Boys as Detectives; or, On Secret Service in Cloudland (1913)

Pastiche

De Lysle Ferree Cass writing as H.L. Sayler, *The Airship Boys in the Great War; or, The Rescue of Bob Russell* (1915)

RICHARD SCARRY

Busytown

Boston-born Richard McClure Scarry (1919–1994) studied at the Museum of Fine Arts School. He was an art director, editor and writer for U.S. military publications during World War II. He married Patricia Murphy in 1948, as he began a career as a free-lance artist. His first illustrated book was *Two Little Miners* in 1949 for Golden Books. His *Best World Book Ever* (1963) found a huge audience, as did *Busy, Busy World* two years later. Each was illustrated with, well, busy drawings of animal characters in workaday activities. (Later editions have made the text more politically correct.) Scarry moved his studio from Connecticut to Switzerland in 1968. Canada-produced *The Busy World of Richard Scarry* was televised in Nickelodeon from 1995 to 2000.

Richard McClure Scarry, Jr. (b. 1953), known as Huck Scarry, wrote and illustrated new books in his father's style.

Selected Original Busytown Works

Best World Book Ever (1963)

Busy, Busy World (1965)

What Do People Do All Day? (1968)

Pastiches

Huck Scarry, *Richard Scarry's A Day at the Airport* (2001); *Richard Scarry's A Day at the Fire Station* (2003); *Richard Scarry's Father Cat's Christmas Tree* (2003); *Richard Scarry's A Day at the Police Station* (2004)

DODIE SMITH

Dogs everywhere

Dorothy Gladys Smith, nicknamed Dodie, was a successful dramatist. Born in Whitefield, England, Smith sought to become an actress, but instead became toy buyer for a London retailer and, under the name C.L. Anthony, wrote the play *Autumn Crocus* (1931). She married Alec Beesley and they lived in London and later the United States, where she wrote her first novel, *I Capture the Castle* (1948). She sold rights to Walt Disney for her *The Hundred and One Dalmatians* (1956), and several pastiches about Cruella de Vil's dognapping plottings derived from that relationship.

Original Dog Works

101 Dalmations (1948)   *The Starlight Barking* (1967)

Pastiches

Anonymous, *Speak Up, Patch* (1993)
R.H. Disney, *Disney's 1021 Dalmatians* (2000)
Alice Downes, *102 Dalmatians* (2000)
Sue Kassirer, *Wizzer's Christmas* (1997)
Judy Katschke, *Disney's 102 Dalmatians: Where's Oddball?* (2000); *102 Dalmatians First Reader* (1002)

MARGARET SUTTON

Judy Bolton, girl detective

Margaret Sutton (1903–2001) created the Judy Bolton young adult crime solver series in 1932 and produced thirty-eight books for Grosset & Dunlap through 1967. The first book was based on the real breaching of a dam in Austin, Potter County, Pennsylvania, in 1911. She also wrote books in Palace Wagon Family, Jemima, Daughter of Daniel Boone and Gail Gardner nurse series.

The author was born Rachel Beebe in Odin, Pennsylvania. She was a secretary and worked in a print shop. She was twice married, to William Sutton then to Everett Hunting.

Linda Joy Singleton completed Sutton's unfinished manuscript and privately published *The Talking Snowman* in 1997. Sutton reviewed the pages before publication, but it technically is a pastiche because Sutton did not commission Singleton's effort.

Original Judy Bolton Works

The Vanishing Shadow (1932)	*The Clue of the Stone Lantern* (1950)
The Haunted Attic (1932)	*The Secret of Fog Island* (1951)
The Invisible Chimes (1932)	*The Black Cat's Clue* (1952)
Seven Strange Clues (1932)	*The Forbidden Chest* (1953)
The Ghost Parade (1933)	*The Haunted Road* (1954)
The Yellow Phantom (1933)	*The Clue in the Ruined Castle* (1955)
The Mystic Ball (1934)	*The Trail of the Green Doll* (1956)
The Voice in the Suitcase (1935)	*The Haunted Fountain* (1957)
The Mysterious Half Cat (1936)	*The Clue of the Broken Wing* (1958)
The Riddle of the Double Ring (1937)	*The Phantom Friend* (1959)
The Unfinished House (1938)	*The Discovery at the Dragon's Mouth* (1960)
The Midnight Visitor (1939)	
The Name on the Bracelet (1940)	*The Whispered Watchword* (1961)
The Clue in the Patchwork Quilt (1941)	*The Secret Quest* (1962)
The Mark on the Mirror (1942)	*The Puzzle in the Pond* (1963)
The Secret of the Barred Window (1943)	*The Hidden Clue* (1964)
The Rainbow Riddle (1946)	*The Pledge of the Twin Knights* (1965)
The Living Portrait (1947)	*The Search for the Glowing Hand* (1966)
The Secret of the Musical Tree (1948)	*The Secret at the Sand Castle* (1967)
The Warning on the Window (1949)	

Collaborative Judy Bolton Pastiche

Linda Joy Singleton and Margaret Sutton, *The Talking Snowman* (1997)

ALBERT PAYSON TERHUNE

Laddie

Albert Payson Terhune's love of animals came through in his prose. Terhune (1872–1942) graduated from Columbia University and worked as an *Evening World* reporter from 1894 to 1914. His father was the Rev. Edward Payson Terhune. His mother was Mary Virginia Terhune, a novelist under the name Marion Harland. He spent much of his life at Sunnybank Park in Wayne, New Jersey, which is now maintained by a nonprofit organization and is open to visitors. Terhune wrote for periodicals, but his books involving various dogs (including Lad the collie) of Sunnybank were his most popular works. Lad fans gather annually at Sunnybank to celebrate Lad's birthday — and contribute toward a fund for breed health research.

Margo Lundell wrote pastiche Lad books for beginning readers.

Original Works

Lad, a Dog (1918)
Further Adventures of Lad (1922) retitled
  Dog Stories Every Child Should Know
  (1941)

Lad of Sunnybank (1929)

Lad Pastiches

Margo Lundell, *Lad, a Dog: Lad to the Rescue* (1997); *Lad, a Dog: Lad Is Lost* (1998);
  Lad, a Dog: The Bad Puppy (1998)

BARBARA EUPHAN TODD

The scarecrow

Barbara Euphan Todd (1890–1976) wrote books for young readers, her best-known being *Worzel Gummidge; or, The Scarecrow of Scatterbrook*, about a straw creature that came to life at Ten Acre Field. He made friends with young John and Sue Peters. Todd was born in Doncaster, Yorkshire, and attended girls' school in Surrey. She found early success as a writer of children's stories. In 1932, she married Commander John Graham Bower of the Royal Navy, and they often wrote together.

   After her death, the walking scarecrow character appeared on radio and television (he was especially popular in New Zealand) and inspired new sequels.

Original Worzel Gummidge Work

*Worzel Gummidge; or, The Scarecrow of
  Scatterbrook* (1936)
Worzel Gummidge Again (1937)
More About Worzel Gummidge (1938)
Worzel Gummidge and Saucy Nancy
  (1947)
Worzel Gummidge Takes a Holiday (1949)

Earthy Mangold and Worzel Gummidge
  (1954)
Worzel Gummidge Railway Scarecrows
  (1955)
Worzel Gummidge at the Circus (1956)
Worzel Gummidge Treasure Ship (1958)
Detective Worzel Gummidge (1963)

Worzel Gummidge Pastiches

Keith Waterhouse and Willis Hall, *The Television Adventures of Worzel Gummidge*
  (1979); *More Television Adventures of Worzel Gummidge* (1980); *Worzel Gummidge
  at the Farm* (1980); *Worzel Gummidge Goes to the Seaside* (1980); *Trials of Worzel
  Gummidge* (1980); *New Television Adventures of Worzel Gummidge and Aunt Sally*
  (1981); *Worzel Gummidge's Birthday* (1981); *Worzel Gummidge: A Musical* (1984);
  Worzel Gummidge Down Under (1987)

EDITH VAN DYNE
Bluebird Books

L. Frank Baum wrote three children's book series under the name Edith Van Dyne. They featured Aunt Jane's Nieces, Flying Girls and Mary Louise (the Bluebird Books). His son, Harry Neal Baum, apparently helped with *Mary Louise Solves a Mystery*.

After Baum's death in 1919, Emma Speed Sampson wrote five more entries for Baum's publisher, Reilly & Britton. As Baum himself had become more interested in the girl detective Josie O'Gorman, in these books Sampson began to incorporate that character more deeply in the stories. The last two books were originally published under Sampson's byline.

Original Works

Mary Louise (1915)   *Mary Louise and the Liberty Girls* (1918)
Mary Louise in the Country (1916)   *Mary Louise Adopts a Soldier* (1919)
Mary Louise Solves a Mystery (1917)

Pastiches

Emma Speed Sampson, *Mary Louise at Dorfield* (1920); *Mary Louise Stands the Test* (1921); *Mary Louise and Josie O'Gorman* (1922); *Josie O'Gorman* (1923); *Josie O'Gorman and the Meddlesome Major* (1924)

CHARLES SPAIN VERRAL
Brains Benton

Ontario-born Charles Spain Verral (1904–1990) was a frequent contributor to fiction magazines and also worked as an illustrator and editor. He succeeded Major Malcolm Wheeler-Nicholson as writer of the Bill Barnes stories for *Bill Barnes Air Adventures* and *Air Trails* pulp magazines under the house name George L. Eaton, writing 41 stories in all. He wrote for other magazines and also for radio, comic books and, in the 1950s, wrote juvenile books including adaptations of popular television programs.

The Case of the Missing Message is a young adult mystery series set in the small town of Crestwood. Technical whiz Barclay "Brains" Benton and his narrator sidekick Jimmy Carson, known secretly as "X" and "Operative 3" of the Benton and Carson International Detective Agency, very much in the Sherlock Holmes and Dr. Watson mold, help a boy, Skeets Fenton, regain rightful control of the Fenton Circus. Only a secret message left by the boy's late father can establish his claim.

The publisher wanted sequels, but "I was so tied up with contracted work that I couldn't see how I could turn out a succession of mysteries," Verral wrote in a letter to *The Mystery & Adventure Series Review* No. 18 (Spring 1987). So other writers were brought in. Verrall edited the next two entries, assuring a continuity of characterization. Some suggest Verral had contractual obligations and didn't want too many books under his name, and so simply ghost-wrote his own books. Whoever wrote it, the final book in the series is more densely plotted and longer than the other entries.

Original Brains Benton mystery

The Case of the Missing Message (1959)

Pastiches

"George Wyatt," *The Case of the Counterfeit Coin* (1960) edited by Verral; *The Case of the Stolen Dummy* (1961) edited by Verral; *The Case of the Roving Rolls* (1961) edited by Carrie Greenberg; *The Case of the Waltzing Mouse* (1961) edited by Carrie Greenberg; *The Case of the Painted Dragon* (1961) edited by Carrie Greenberg

GERTRUDE CHANDLER WARNER

Boxcar Children

A grammar school teacher for thirty-two years, Connecticut-born Gertrude Chandler Warner (1890–1979) came from a musical family. Ill health as a teen forced her to leave high school, though she completed requirements with a tutor, and during World War I became a first-grade teacher. Another bout of illness was fortuitous: while laid-up, she penned a children's book. She conceived *The Boxcar Children* in 1924, she said, because she couldn't find the kind of fun-to-read stories she wanted for her students.

"Miss Warner drew on her own experiences to write each mystery," according to an afterword in recent series entries. "As a child she spent hours watching trains go by on the tracks opposite her family home. She often dreamed about what it would be like to set up housekeeping in a caboose or freight car — the situation the Alden children find themselves in." The book was published in 1942.

Orphaned Henry, Jessie, Violet and Benny Alden after the first book found security with their well-to-do grandfather, James Alden. Subsequent entries ventured to various settings and frequently introduced eccentric characters. Most stories contained an element of mystery. And the youngest, Benny, never tired of eating.

The continuing popularity of the series prompted the publisher Albert Whitman & Co. to continue it without byline but credited as "created by Gertrude Chandler Warner." The publisher also added a second mystery series.

Original Boxcar Children Series

The Boxcar Children (1942)
Surprise Island (1949)
The Yellow House Mystery (1953)
Mystery Ranch (1958)
Mike's Mystery (1960)
Blue Bay Mystery (1961)
The Woodshed Mystery (1962)
The Lighthouse Mystery (1963)
Mountain Top Mystery (1964)
Schoolhouse Mystery (1965)

Caboose Mystery (1966)
Houseboat Mystery (1967)
Snowbound Mystery (1968)
Tree House Mystery (1969)
Bicycle Mystery (1970)
Mystery in the Sand (1971)
Mystery Behind the Wall (1973)
Bus Station Mystery (1974)
Benny Uncovers a Mystery (1976) edited
    by Caroline Rubin

Pastiches

The Haunted Cabin Mystery (1991)
The Deserted Library Mystery (1991)
The Animal Shelter Mystery (1991)
The Old Motel Mystery (1992)
The Mystery of the Hidden Painting (1992)
The Amusement Park Mystery (1992)
The Mystery of the Mixed Up Zoo (1992)
The Camp-Out Mystery (1992)
The Mystery Cruise (1992)
The Disappearing Friend Mystery (1992)
The Mystery of the Singing Ghost (1992)
The Pizza Mystery (1993)
The Mystery Horse (1993)
The Mystery at the Dog Show (1993)
The Castle Mystery (1993)
The Mystery of the Lost Village (1993)
The Mystery on the Ice (1993)
The Mystery of the Lost Village (1993)
The Mystery of the Purple Pool (1994)
The Ghost Ship Mystery (1994)
The Mystery in Washington D.C. (1994)
The Mystery of the Hidden Beach (1994)
The Mystery of the Missing Cat (1994)
The Mystery at Snowflake Inn (1994)
The Mystery on Stage (1994)
The Dinosaur Mystery (1995)
The Mystery of the Stolen Music (1995)
The Mystery at the Ballpark (1995)
The Chocolate Sundae Mystery (1995)
The Mystery of the Hot Air Balloon (1995)
The Mystery Bookstore (1995)
The Pilgrim Village Mystery (1995)
The Mystery of the Stolen Boxcar (1995)
Mystery in the Cave (1996)

The Mystery on the Train (1996)
The Mystery of the Lost Mine (1996)
The Guide Dog Mystery (1996)
The Hurricane Mystery (1996)
The Mystery of the Secret Message (1996)
The Firehouse Mystery (1997)
The Mystery in San Francisco (1997)
The Mystery at the Alamo (1997)
The Outer Space Mystery (1997)
The Soccer Mystery (1997)
The Growling Bear Mystery (1997)
The Mystery of the Lake Monster (1998)
The Mystery at Peacock Hall (1998)
The Black Pearl Mystery (1998)
The Cereal Box Mystery (1998)
The Panther Mystery (1998)
The Stolen Sword Mystery (1998)
The Basketball Mystery (1999)
The Movie Star Mystery (1999)
The Mystery of the Pirate's Map (1999)
The Ghost Town Mystery (1999)
The Mystery in the Mall (1999)
The Gymnastics Mystery (1999)
The Poison Frog Mystery (2000)
The Mystery of the Empty Safe (2000)
The Great Bicycle Race Mystery (2000)
The Mystery of the Wild Ponies (2000)
The Mystery of the Computer Game (2000)
The Mystery at the Crooked House (2000)
The Hockey Mystery (2001)
The Mystery of the Midnight Dog (2001)
The Summer Camp Mystery (2001)
The Copycat Mystery (2001)
The Haunted Clock Tower Mystery (2001)

The Disappearing Staircase Mystery (2001)
The Mystery on Blizzard Mountain (2002)
The Mystery of the Spider's Clue (2002)
The Mystery of the Mummy's Curse (2002)
The Mystery of the Star Ruby (2002)
The Stuffed Bear Mystery (2002)
The Mystery at Skeleton Point (2002)
The Tattletale Mystery (2003)
The Comic Book Mystery (2003)
The Ice Cream Mystery (2003)
The Midnight Mystery (2003)
The Mystery of the Fortune Cookie (2003)
The Radio Mystery (2003)
The Mystery of the Runaway Ghost (2004)
The Finders Keepers Mystery (2004)
The Mystery of the Haunted Boxcar (2004)
The Clue in the Corn Maze (2004)

The Ghost of the Chattering Bones (2005)
The Sword of the Silver Knight (2005)
The Game Store Mystery (2005)
The Mystery of the Orphan Train (2005)
The Vanishing Passenger (2006)
The Giant Yo-Yo Mystery (2006)
The Creature in Ogopogo Lake (2006)
The Rock 'n' Roll Mystery (2006)
The Secret of the Mask (2007)
The Seattle Puzzle (2007)
The Ghost in the First Row (2007)
The Box That Watch Found (2007)
A Horse Named Dragon (2008)
The Great Detective Race (2008)
The Ghost at the Drive-In Movie (2008)
The Mystery of the Traveling Tomatoes (2008)

Pastiches in the Boxcar Children Special Mysteries Series

The Mystery on the Ice (1993)
The Mystery in Washington, D.C. (1994)
The Mystery at Snowflake Inn (1994)
The Mystery at the Ballpark (1995)
The Pilgrim Village Mystery (1995)
The Mystery at the Fair (1996)
The Pet Shop Mystery (1996)
The Niagara Falls Mystery (1997)
The Mystery in the Old Attic (1997)
The Windy City Mystery (1998)

The Mystery of the Queen's Jewels (1998)
The Mystery of the Black Raven (1999)
The Home Run Mystery (2000)
The Honeybee Mystery (2000)
The Mystery of the Screech Owl (2001)
The Mystery of the Tiger's Eye (2001)
The Candy Factory Mystery (2002)
The Mystery of the Alligator Swamp (2002)
The Great Shark Mystery (2003)
The Black Widow Spider Mystery (2003)

Cookbook

Diane Blain, *The Boxcar Children Cookbook* (1991)

KATE DOUGLAS WIGGIN

Rebecca of Sunnybrook Farm

Kate Douglas Wiggin (1856–1923) wrote the popular tale of headstrong Rebecca Rowena Randall, who eventually wins the heart of her stern Aunt Matilda in *Rebecca of Sunnybrook Farm*.

Philadelphian Kate Douglas Smith (she later married Samuel B. Wiggin) was a kindergarten teacher in California and a prolific author of essays and articles for education publications. Proceeds from her fiction supported her efforts with the San Francisco Silver Street Kindergarten. After her husband's death, the author married George C. Riggs. She had no children of her own.

Eric E. Wiggin (b. 1939), a clergyman and writer and a distant cousin of the author's first husband, wrote original stories and reshaped and expanded his mother's original stories into three books. He also wrote Hannah's Island Christian novels.

Original Works

Rebecca of Sunnybrook Farm (1903)   New Chronicles of Rebecca (1906)

Pastiches

Eric E. Wiggin, *Rebecca of Sunnybrook Farm: The Child* (1989); *Rebecca of Sunnybrook Farm: The Girl* (1990); *Rebecca of Sunnybrook Farm: The Woman* (1991); *Rebecca Returns to Sunnybrook* (1994); *Rebecca of the Brick House* (1994)

LAURA INGALLS WILDER

Little House

Laura Ingalls Wilder (1867–1957) grew up in the Midwest in the late 1800s and she captured the pioneer time and the people marvelously in a series of books for younger readers. Born in the Big Woods section of Wisconsin, the author's parents Charles and Caroline Ingalls raised a family of five children. They homesteaded in Indian Territory in Kansas, and lived in Minnesota and Iowa before homesteading again in Dakota Territory. Laura became a teacher. She married Almanzo Wilder and they raised a family. They too moved frequently, and ended up at Rocky Ridge Farm in Missouri.

Laura wrote of her experiences and her daughter Rose Wilder (1886–1968), a skilled writer, shaped her drafts and may have rewritten portions of them for publication. Following her mother's death, Rose inherited the literary estate for her lifetime, after which it went to the Mansfield, Missouri Library. After Rose Wilder Lane died, her adopted grandson Roger Lea MacBride (1929–1995) assumed control of the book copyrights. Following his death, the Mansfield Library sought to regain control of the rights. The result was a settlement with the MacBride heirs. The books had generated a considerable franchise with Michael Landon's *Little House on the Prairie* television show, which ran from 1974 to 1983.

Cynthia Rylant wrote a pastiche purportedly about the two years Wilder neglected to cover in her books, based on unpublished memoirs. MacBride wrote some books about his mother. Recent series for young readers tell stories of Charlotte Tucker, Laura's grandmother, and Caroline Quiner, Laura's mother.

Original Little House Books by Laura Ingalls Wilder as prepared by Rose Wilder

Little House in the Big Woods (1932)   Farmer Boy (1933)

Little House on the Prairie (1935)
On the Banks of Plum Creek (1937)
By the Shores of Silver Lake (1939)
Long Winter (1940)

Little Town on the Prairie (1941)
These Happy Golden Years (1943)
The First Four Years (1971)
West from Home (1974)

Pastiches

Elizabeth Levy, *Father Murphy's First Miracle* (1983)

Roger Lea MacBride, *Little House on Rocky Ridge* (1993) Little House: The Rose Years series; *Little Farm in the Ozarks* (1994) Little House: The Rose Years series; *In the Land of the Big Red Apple* (1995) Little House: The Rose Years series; *On the Other Side of the Hill* (1995) Little House: The Rose Years series; *Little Town in the Ozarks* (1996) Little House: The Rose Years series; *New Dawn on Rocky Ridge* (1997) Little House: The Rose Years series; *On the Banks of the Bayou* (1998) Little House: The Rose Years series; *Bachelor Girl* (1999) Little House: The Rose Years series

Cynthia Rylant, *Old Town in the Green Groves; Laura Ingalls Wilder's Lost Little House Years* (2004)

Larry Weinberg, *Father Murphy's Promise* (1982)

Melissa Wiley, *Little House by Boston Bay* (1999) Little House: The Charlotte Years series; *On Tide Mill Lane* (2001) Little House: The Charlotte Years series; *The Road from Roxbury* (2002) Little House: The Charlotte Years series; *Across the Pudding-stone Dam* (2004) Little House; The Charlotte Years series

Marie D. Wilkes, *The Little House in Brookfield* (1996) Little House: The Caroline Years series; *Little Town at the Crossroads* (1997) Little House: The Caroline Years series; *Little Clearing in the Woods* (1998) Little House: The Caroline Years series; *On Top of Concord Hill* (2000) Little House: The Caroline Years series

Celia Wilkins, *Across the Rolling River* (2001) Little House: The Caroline Years series; *Little City by the Lake* (2003) Little House: The Caroline Years series

Poets

Poetry's short form means it is most often pastiched (or, more likely, parodied) in brief bursts. It's a poet's feeling, or unusual construction or settings that comes in for replication, rather than characters or situations. Thus the Robert Frost or Emily Dickinson latter-generation collections are as much tributes to the old poets as full-blown meanders into their styles. *Unauthorized Versions: Poems and Their Parodies*, edited by Kenneth Baker (Faber & Faber, 1990) is a gem, pairing original verses with takeoffs/tributes/sneers.

SAMUEL TAYLOR COLERIDGE
Christabel

Samuel Taylor Coleridge (1772–1834), an English Lake District poet, with good friend William Wordsworth, initiated the Romantic Movement. "The Rime of the Ancient Mariner" is perhaps his best known work, along with "Kubla Khan." "Christabel" is in two parts, the first written in 1797, the second three years later. A planned third section never appeared. Called by some a lesbian vampire poem, it describes Christabel's encounter in the woods with someone who is fleeing from abductors, Geraldine.

Martin Farquhar Tupper (1810–1889), an English attorney, writer and poet, made his mark with *Proverbial Philosophy*, which is, as it sounds, a compilation of moralistic essays.

Original Work

"Christabel" (1797–1800)

Pastiche

Martin Farquhar Tupper, *Geraldine: A Sequel to Coleridge's Christabel, with Other Poems* (1846)

EMILY DICKINSON
Gentle verse

Amherst, Massachusetts, recluse Emily Elizabeth Dickinson (1830–1886) saw publication of only a handful of her poems in the *Springfield Republican* in her lifetime. Her punctuation was made uniform, her unusual rhyme patterns altered and some of her words edited. After her death, her sister Lavinia Dickinson (1833–1899) discovered her 1,800 or so poems.

After a family squabble about the poems, Thomas Wentworth Higginson and Mabel Loomis Todd (brother William Dickinson's mistress) heavily edited the poems for the publication of a collection in 1890. A niece, Martha Dickinson Bianchi, published more verses 1914–1929. It was not until *The Poems of Emily Dickinson* came out in 1955 that readers saw the restored originals.

Posthumous Collaboration

Thomas Wentworth Higginson and Mabel Loomis Todd, *Poems* (1890); *Poems: Second Series* (1891); *Poems: Third Series* (1896)

Martha Dickinson Bianchi, *The Single Hound* (1914); *The Complete Poems of Emily Dickinson* (1925); *Further Poems of Emily Dickinson* (1929)

Posthumous Restoration

The Poems of Emily Dickinson (1955)

Pastiches, Tributes and Parodies

Sheila Coghill and Thom Tammaro, editors, *Visiting Emily; Poems Inspired by the Life and Work of Emily Dickinson* (2000)

WILLIAM HENRY DRUMMOND
Franglais

William Henry Drummond (1854–1907), "the poet of the habitant," was born in Ireland and lived in Canada. A clergyman, he wrote poetry in a fractured French-English spoken by Quebecers. "They should be heard, as most Canadians are privileged to hear them, repeated round a camp-fire by someone competent in French-Canadian English patois, or recited at cigar-time after dinner ... [when] it suffices that a poem should be humorous and human," according to *The Cambridge History of English and American Literature*.

Alexander MacGregor Rose (1846–1898) was born in Scotland. He became an ordained minister but pursued a career as a journalist in California. He eventually went to work for the *Montreal Gazette*. While no one has directly accused

Rose of writing Drummond pastiches, he used the same colloquial French-Canadian lingo as Drummond. Rose's works appeared originally in newspapers, and were later collected in books.

Original Works

The Habitant and Other French-
    Canadian Poems (1898)
Johnnie Courteau and Other Poems
    (1901)

Phil-o'Rum's Canoe and Madeleine
    Vercheres (1903)
The Voyager and Other Poems (1905)
The Great Fight (1909)

Pastiches

A. MacGregor Rose, *Sir Wilfrid's Progress Through England and France in the Jubilee Year* (1897); *Hoch der Kaiser; Myself and Gott* (1900); *Poems of A. MacGregor Rose* (no date)

ROBERT FROST

Country verse

Pulitzer Prize–winning Robert Frost (1874–1963) wrote of the rural life of New England, and of human nature. Born in San Francisco, where both parents were teachers and his father soon became editor of the *Daily Evening Post*, Frost had difficulties in school and was home-educated. Following his father's death, the family moved to Massachusetts, and then to New Hampshire. He published his first verse in 1890 in the *Lawrence High School Bulletin*. He attended classes at both Dartmouth College and Harvard College. He and his family with wife Elinor White lived on small farms while he taught at various schools. His poetry increasingly finds its way into print. *A Boy's Will* came out in England in 1913 and *North of Boston* appeared the next year. His life became one of gentleman farming, poeticizing and public speaking. He recited "The Gift Outright" at President John F. Kennedy's inauguration in 1961.

Two editors compiled tributes and a few takeoffs.

Original Works

North of Boston (1914)
Mountain Interval (1916)
Selected Poems (1923)
New Hampshire (1923)
Several Short Poems (1924)
A Further Range (1926) aka New Poems
    (1936)
Selected Poems (1928)
West-Running Brook (1929)

The Lovely Shall Be Choosers (1929)
Collected Poems of Robert Frost (1930)
The Lone Striker (1933)
Selected Poems: Third Edition (1934)
Three Poems (1935)
The Gold Hesperidee (1935)
From Snow to Snow (1936)
A Further Range (1936)
Collected Poems of Robert Frost (1939)

A Witness Tree (1942)
Come In, and Other Poems (1943)
Steeple Bush (1947)
Complete Poems of Robert Frost (1949)
Hard Not to Be King (1951)
Aforesaid (1954)

A Remembrance Collection of New Poems (1959)
You Come Too (1959)
In the Clearing (1962)
The Poetry of Robert Frost (1969)

Pastiches, Tributes and Parodies

Sheila Coghill and Thom Tammaro, editors, *Visiting Frost; Poems Inspired by the Life and Work of Robert Frost* (2005)

JOYCE KILMER
Trees

Alfred Joyce Kilmer (1886–1918), born in New Brunswick, New Jersey, was a journalist, poet and critic. His oft-recited "Trees" (1914) inspired several parodies and tributes. Kilmer, a sergeant with the U.S. 165th Infantry, was killed in the Second Battle of the Marne. There's a Joyce Kilmer Memorial Forest (with remnants of old-growth trees) in North Carolina.
   Ogden Nash (1902–1971) wrote a takeoff, "Song of the Open Road."

Original Work

Trees, Trees and Other Poems (1914)

Pastiche

Ogden Nash, *I Wouldn't Have Missed It, Selected Poems of Ogden Nash* (1975) includes "Song of the Open Road"
Walter Irving Clarke, "To the Editor," *New York Times*, Aug. 24, 1918 (uncollected)

ARCHIBALD LAMPMAN
Poet of the North

Archibald Lampman (1861–1899) was born in Morpeth, Ontario, and attended Trinity College. He left a career as a teacher to become a postal clerk in Ottawa. He self-published his first book, *Among the Millet* (1888), but his second, *Lyrics of Earth* (1895), found a Boston publisher. He was one of the Confederation Poets with Charles G.D. Roberts, Susanna Moodie, Catherine Parr Trail, Duncan Campbell Scott and William Wilfred Campbell. His frequent topic was Canada's countryside and hardworking inhabitants. He, Scott and Campbell wrote a weekly column for the Toronto *Globe* from 1892 to 1893. An annual Canadian literary prize is named for him.

Scott (1862–1947) and Lampman shared "a love of poetry and the Canadian wilderness. During the 1890s the two made a number of canoe trips together in the area north of Ottawa," according to the Famous Poems and Poets Web site. "When Lampman died in 1899, Scott devoted himself to keeping his friend's literary reputation alive, and, from 1900 to 1947, edited a number of editions of Lampman's poetry. Although Scott has been criticized for taking editorial liberties with the manuscripts, he was responsible for bringing Lampman's works to the attention of 20th-century readers."

Scott compiled four editions of Lampman verse that came out after the poet's death. Scott and Edward Killoran Brown (1905–1951) turned Lampman's incomplete manuscript into *At the Long Sault*, a lyric depiction of a 1660 skirmish between Iroquois and French at Montreal.

Posthumous Collaborations

Duncan Campbell Scott and Edward Killoran Brown, *At the Long Sault* (1943)

Posthumous Restoration

Lyrics of Earth (1978)

CLEMENT CLARKE MOORE

Jolly Elf

Clement Clarke Moore (1779–1863), who taught divinity at Columbia College (now University), is most associated with the verse "A Visit from St. Nicholas," published anonymously in the *Troy (New York) Sentinel* in 1823. The poem became a classic and codified the Santa Claus mythos.

A case has been argued that Henry Livingston, Jr. (1748–1828), an upper New York state land baron and occasional poet, was the actual author of the verse.

Many hands have written takeoffs on "'Twas the Night Before Christmas, and all through the house...." Some are collected in an anthology. A string of children's books make regional and occupational twists on the theme.

Original Work

An American Anthology, 1787–1900, edited by Edmund Clarence Stedman (1844) includes "A Visit from St. Nicholas"

Pastiches

Sarah Kirwan Blazek, *An Irish Night Before Christmas* (1995)

Kimbra L. Cutlip, *Sailor's Night Before Christmas* (1999); *Firefighter's Night Before Christmas* (2002)

David Davis, *Librarian's Night Before Christmas* (2007); *Nurse's Night Before Christmas* (2003); *Redneck Night Before Christmas* (1997)

Christine Ford, *The Soldiers' Night Before Christmas* (2006)

Ed Gardner, editor, *The Annotated Night Before Christmas; a collection of Sequels, Parodies, and Imitations of Clement Moore's Immortal Ballad About Santa Claus* (1991)

Leon A. Harris, *Night Before Christmas, in Texas That Is* (1977)

Stephen L. Layne, *The Teachers' Night Before Christmas* (2001); *The Principal's Night Before Christmas* (2004); *Preacher's Night Before Christmas* (2006)

Amanda McWilliams, *Ozark Night Before Christmas* (2004)

Jenny Jackson Moss, *Cajun Night After Christmas* (2000)

Geraty and James Rice, *Gullah Night Before Christmas* (1998)

James Rice, *Texas Night Before Christmas* (1986); *Trucker's Night Before Christmas* (1999)

Trosclair, *Cajun Night Before Christmas* (1992)

Thomas Noel Turner, *Hillbilly Night Afore Christmas* (1983); *Country Music Night Before Christmas* (2003)

Chet Williamson, *Pennsylvania Dutch Night Before Christmas* (2000)

BANJO PATERSON

Snowy River

Australian poet Andrew Barton "Banjo" Paterson (1864–1941) wrote ballads about the bush, about ranch life and outback tragedy. Among his verses are "Waltzing Matilda," widely known in its musical version, and "The Man from Snowy River." The latter was first published in *The Bulletin* in 1890 and is about the capture of a racehorse that has escaped into the wild.

"The Man from Snowy River" was made into a film (1982) and sequel (1988) and a television series (1990s). Elyne Mitchell (1913–2002), author of the Silver Brumby children's books, wrote a novelization based on the screenplay.

Original Work
The Man from Snowy River (1890)

Pastiche
Elyne Mitchell, *The Man from Snowy River* (1982)

SYLVIA PLATH

Ariel

The publication of *Ariel* by Sylvia Plath (1932–1963) brought her great fame. The American novelist, poet and short story writer also composed a partially autobiographical novel, *The Bell Jar*, published as by Victoria Lucas. When it first appeared, *Ariel* was not in the form she had left it at her death. Her husband and literary executor, Ted Hughes, had edited it.

A 2004 edition places the poems in Plath's intended order, and affords facsimile reproductions of several manuscript pages. Her daughter, Frieda Hughes, provided a foreword.

Original Work

Ariel (1965)

Posthumous Restoration

Ariel: The Restored Edition (2004)

ERNEST LAWRENCE THAYER
No joy in Mudville

"Casey at the Bat" appeared June 3, 1888, under the pseudonym "Phin," in William Randolph Hearst's *San Francisco Examiner*. Massachusetts-born Ernest Lawrence Thayer (1863–1940), the son of a textile mill owner and a Harvard graduate, didn't acknowledge his authorship for many years, as "Casey" steadily grew into an enduring baseball lyric, and by which time others claimed it as theirs.

Thayer "is a prize specimen of the 'one-poem poet,'" according to Martin Gardner in *The Annotated Casey at the Bat*. "He wrote nothing else of merit. No one imagines that Casey is 'great' in the sense that the poetry of Shakespeare or Dante is great; a comic ballad obviously must be judged by different standards.... By some miracle of creativity, in harmony with those curious laws of humor and popular taste that no one seems to think worth investigating, he managed to produce the nation's best known piece of comic verse."

Beginning in 1888, comic actor DeWolf Hopper recited "Casey" from the stage, to wild applause. "*Casey's* fame was spurred on by the American craze for baseball that began during the Civil War period, when the sport was played by a few amateurs. By 1900 professionals had come to dominate the diamonds, and John J. McGraw, A.G. Spaulding, and Connie Mack were national figures," according to James Gilreath in an introduction to the Library of Congress edition of a 1909 Hopper recording of the poem.

Hopper appeared in a Casey film in 1916 and a 1927 re-make featured Wallace Beery. Walt Disney made animated cartoon versions in *Make Mine Music* in 1946 and *Casey Bats Again* in 1953. *The Mighty Casey* was an opera version that premiered in 1953 with music by William Schuman and a libretto by Jeremy Gury.

Pasticheurs frequently sought revenge for Casey's dreadfully embarrassing strikeout, as, for example, in "The Coming Back of Casey" by Charles E. Jestings. Several poets offered distaff variations such as "Casey's Sister at the Bat" by James O'Dea and "Casey's Daughter at the Bat" by Al Graham. All are included in the Gardner compilation.

Frank Deford, a senior writer for *Sports Illustrated*, tacked a new ending on the traditional tale while Burgess Fitzpatrick redeemed the family name through a grandson.

Original work

"Casey at the Bat" (1900)

Pastiches

Frank Deford, *Casey on the Loose* (1989)
Ellen M. Dolan, *Casey at the Bat* (1987) prose retelling
Burgess Fitzpatrick, *Casey's Redemption* (1958)
Martin Gardner, editor, *The Annotated Casey at the Bat: A Collection of Ballads about the Mighty Casey* with an introduction and notes (1967, 1984) contains pastiche poems by Ray Bradbury, Les Desmond, Don Fairbairn, Al Graham, Charles E. Jestings, Harry E. Jones, William F. Kirk, J.A. Lindon, the editors of *Mad*, Neil McConlogue, Clarence P. McDonald, James O'Dea, Nitram Rendrag, Grantland Rice, William F. Robertson, Herman J. Schiek, "Sparkus," and several unknown versifiers with an appendix of other parodies and sequels

HENRY DAVID THOREAU

Walden in verse

Henry David Thoreau (1817–1862) borrowed an ax, hewed timbers and shaped notches and tenons when he built his remote dwelling in Concord, Massachusetts, in spring 1845. "At length, in the beginning of May, with the help of some of my acquaintances, rather to improve so good an occasion for neighborliness than from any necessity, I set up the frame of my house," he wrote in *Walden*. "No man was ever more honored in the character of his raisers than I. They are destined, I trust, to assist at the raising of loftier structures one day."

Thoreau is one of America's most influential non-fiction writers, for *Walden*, for his essay "On Civil Disobedience" and for his outrageously independent and embracing character as someone who loved nature and freedom. Several editors have reshaped Thoreau's voluminous journals for new books. And Bradley P. Dean manhandled the Concordian's unfinished final book into shape in a posthumous collaboration. But Thoreau's rare flights of poetry also inspired pastiche.

Maine-born Robert Maurice Chute (1926), a Native American, has taught biology at Bates, Middlebury, and San Fernando Valley State Colleges and Lincoln University. He channeled Thoreau for a collection of new verse. A reviewer,

Terry Plunkett, in *Kennebec Journal* said of *Woodshed on the Moon*: "Sometimes Chute speaks in H.D.'s voice, sometimes in his own. Sometimes he recreates for himself events Thoreau describes. Sometime it is unclear which of the two is speaking, describer or Doppelganger. The effect is wonderful." Another reviewer, Marion K. Stocking, in *Beloit Poetry Journal*, said, "Chute brings to Thoreau many appropriate virtues, not least the scientist's skill in accurate, unsentimental observation to perceive what Hopkins called the inscape — not just the leaf and twig, but the intrinsic form. Another of Chute's works is *Heat Wave in Concord* (1996).

Original Poetic Works

Poems of Nature edited by H.S. Salt and Frank B. Sanborn (1895)
Collected Poems of Henry Thoreau edited by Carl Bode (1943) enlarged edition (1964)

Pastiche Poetry

Robert Chute, *Woodshed on the Moon* (1991)

WALT WHITMAN

Leaves of Grass

Walt Whitman (1819–1892) was a poet, journalist and essay writer. Born on Long Island, he was a teacher, government clerk and nurse during the Civil War. His *Leaves of Grass* (1855) broke creative ground and brought its author wide renown. "It is truly American poetry without any European inspiration. Between 1855 and 1892 it went through six editions and nine successive printings during his lifetime. In each edition Whitman made alterations or deletions, but the book grew apace with the nation," according to the Walt Whitman Birthplace Association website. Nevertheless, Whitman's life was one of constant job hopping, mostly from newspaper to newspaper. He also was a housing speculator and contractor.

The range of Whitman's influence shows in a salutatory collection issued in 2003.

Original Works

Leaves of Grass (1855)

Tributes, Pastiches and Parodies

Sheila Coghill and Thom Tammaro, editors, *Visiting Walt; Poems Inspired by the Life and Work of Walt Whitman* (2003)

WILLIAM WORDSWORTH
Daffodils

William Wordsworth (1770–1850), along with his friend Samuel Taylor Coleridge, initiated the English Romantic Movement. Born in the Lake District to a literary family (his sister Dorothy was a poet), Wordsworth came into print in 1787 with the publication of a sonnet. Thanks to an inheritance, he enjoyed a comfortable literary life. "I Wandered Lonely as a Cloud" is an oft-read verse.

Wordsworth wrote "Peter Bell" in 1796 but withheld it from publication for many years. He was busy working with Coleridge on *Lyrical Ballads*. The character Peter Bell sees the errors of his ways and renounces his immoral life, and becomes England's poet laureate.

Poet and essayist John Hamilton Reynolds (1794–1852) penned a takeoff, after being at Wordsworth's publisher and having seen the proofs of the original. Reynolds' lines appeared in print before Wordsworth's original. "There is a legend that Wordsworth received a copy of the parody from the postman thinking it was his own, which was then in press," according to a *New York Times* story in 1901. Percy Bysshe Shelley (1792–1822), another of the Romantic poets, grabbed Peter Bell for his own twist right after it came out, though his lines did not come into print until after his death. Shelley made the main character a Methodist whose life was preordained. His title indicated it was the third variation on the theme.

Original Work
"Peter Bell" (1819)

Pastiches
John Hamilton Reynolds, *Peter Bell: A Lyrical Ballad* (1819)
Percy Bysshe Shelley, *Peter Bell the Third* (1839)

Pulps

Pulp fiction magazines — so-called because of the inexpensive newsprint on which they were printed — democratized American fiction in the 1910s through 1940s and nurtured many writers who went on to successful careers writing mysteries, science fiction, Westerns and other novels for book publication. Some publishers found success with magazines built around a single character, such as the crimefighters Black Bat or The Spider, or the cowboy Jim Hatfield, Texas Ranger, or the space-hopping Lensmen (see Science Fiction). These characters were often created by magazine editors, who farmed out writing to one or more scribes for hire. The characters enter our definition of pastiche when, years and publishers later, they have been resurrected for an entirely new generation.

LARS ANDERSON
The Domino Lady

Socialite Ellen Patrick, the daughter of deceased District Attorney Owen Patrick, disguises herself in a domino mask and strapless white dress to seek vengeance on thugs and criminals in semi-spicy stories by Lars Anderson. The marginally risqué stories appeared in *Saucy Romantic Adventures* (five stories in 1936) and *Mystery Adventure Magazine* (one story in 1936). Anderson is something of a cipher. He wrote for a brief period in the mid- to late 1930s then disappeared.

Decades later, several writers came up with new adventures in an anthology edited by Lori Gentile. James Steranko, best known as a graphic artist and designer, wrote a new tale for a reprint collection of the original stories.

Original Works
Compliments of the Domino Lady (2004)

Pastiches

Nancy Holder, Chuck Dixon, C.J. Henderson, Martin Powell, Ron Fortier, James
   Chambers, Bobby Nash and Gail McCabee, *The Domino Lady: Sex as a Weapon*
   (2009) short stories
James Steranko, *Domino Lady: The Complete Collection* (2004) includes "Aroused"

BERTHA M. CLAY

Dime novelist

Bertha M. Clay was "a writer of mushy love stories for the English lower classes,"
in the view of dime novel historian Albert Johannsen. "Mrs. Brame was a voluminous writer, contributing mostly to various London periodicals. Few of her
stories appeared in book form during her lifetime, but after her death they were
published in many editions, both in England and in America. She was the real
simon-pure 'Bertha M. Clay' and 'Dora Thorne.'"

   The American publisher Street & Smith published a flexible schedule of
dime novels, the *Bertha Clay Library* from 1900 to 1917, then until 1932 the *New
Bertha M. Clay Library*. These were reprints of stories originally issued in Great
Britain. "Of all the women's dime novelists, the stories published under the name
Bertha M. Clay had the longest running popularity. For after the author's death
in 1884, the name was in continual use by Street & Smith and others until the
early 1930s," according to American Women's Dime Novel Project. The stories
in this series were primarily reprints of stories that appeared in earlier series such
as the *New York Weekly*.

   Bertha M. Clay (1836–1884) was really Charlotte M. Brame, born Charlotte
Mary Law in Leicestershire, England. She was a governess when she married jew-
eler Philip Brame (sometimes spelled Braeme). She was a British writer who, in
order to sell to American periodicals, took a new name. She scrambled her initials
and in 1876 became Bertha M. Clay. She is credited with having written some
800 titles, perhaps the best known being *Dora Thorne*. For a time it was believed
English writer Thomas W. Hanshew, creator of Cleek, was behind the Bertha M.
Clay penname.

   "When she died in 1886, the name was continued as a 'house name' for
Street & Smith. At various points, up to twelve different writers published under
the name Bertha M. Clay," according to American Women's Dime Novel Project. "After her death it became a stock name with Street and Smith, and under
it appeared stories by Frederick V. Dey, John R. Coryell, and others. Some of
Mrs. Brame's novels were published, in both England and America, as 'By the
author of "Dora Thorne,"' or even as by 'Dora Thorne.' Sixty-eight novels are
listed by [bibliographer] Allibone, but it is not certain that all of them were written by her," said Johannsen.

MAXWELL GRANT
The Shadow knows

Was playboy Lamont Cranston really The Shadow? Or aviator Kent Allard? Walter B. Gibson (1897–1985) had a lot of fun with diversions and illusions as he wrote the adventures of this pulp hero. Street & Smith introduced a shadowy character on a radio show it was affiliated with. The character went over, so the publisher sought to capitalize on its popularity with a magazine. Gibson, veteran journalist and amateur magician, was a good choice to write the stories. The magazine at first came out quarterly, but was so popular, it soon appeared twice a month. Grant wrote at a frantic pace, 285 adventures in all. Theodore Tinsley and Bruce Elliot filled out the forty stories Gibson didn't write during the years 1931 to 1949. All were masked by the penname Maxwell Grant. (Gibson also used the alias for his Norgil the Magician stories.)

Gibson was born in Germantown, Pennsylvania, and attended school in Philadelphia. As a youth he haunted magic shops. He attended Colgate University and became a reporter with the *Philadelphia North American*, and later the *Evening Ledger*. He wrote features for the Ledger Syndicate. As time went by, he wrote books about magic tricks, psychics, crime and puzzles. He ghostwrote books for Houdini and Thurston. In 1931 he contracted to write The Shadow, little anticipating he would in 1932 alone produce twenty-four 60,000-word stories on his Corona manual typewriter. And that wasn't the whole of his output!

The Shadow had a small group of operatives, including Harry Vincent, The Shadow's right-hand man; Shrevvie the cab driver; Burbank, in charge of communications; Clyde Burke, a newspaper reporter; and Cliff Marsland, a reformed mobsman. Margot Lane appeared in later stories, when the character was introduced on the radio show and listeners expected to find her in the pulps as well.

A paperback publisher briefly resurrected the character in the 1960s, when secret agents were the rage. Listed are only those magazine stories that have been reprinted in books. The stories are arranged in the order of original pulp publication.

Reprinted Original Works in Magazine Order,
by Walter B. Gibson writing as Maxwell Grant (Unless Noted)

The Living Shadow (April 1, 1931) (1931)
The Eyes of the Shadow (July 1, 1931) (1931)
The Shadow Laughs (October 1, 1931) (1931)
The Red Menace (Nov. 1, 1931) (1975)
Gangdom's Doom (Dec. 1, 1931) (1970)
The Death Tower (Jan. 1, 1932) (1969)
The Silent Seven (Feb. 1, 1932) (1975)
The Black Master (March 1, 1932) (1874)

Mobsmen on the Spot (April 1, 1932) (1974)
Hands in the Dark (May 1, 1932) (1975)
Double Z (June 1, 1932) (1975)
The Crime Cult (July 1, 1932) (1975)
Hidden Death (Sept. 1, 1932) (1970)
Green Eyes (Oct. 1, 1932) (1977)
The Ghost Makers (Oct. 15, 1932) (1970)
The Romanoff Jewels (Dec. 1, 1932) (1975)
Kings of Crime (Dec. 15, 1932) (1976)

Shadowed Millions (Jan. 1, 1933) (1976)
The Creeping Death (Jan. 15, 1933) (1977)
The Shadow's Shadow (Feb. 1, 1933)
    (1977)
Six Men of Evil (Feb. 15, 1933) (2007)
Fingers of Death (March 1, 1933) (1977)
Murder Trail (March 15, 1933) (1977)
The Silent Death (April 1, 1933) (1978)
The Shadow's Justice (April 15, 1933)
    (2007)
The Death Giver (May 15, 1933) (1978)
The Red Blot (June 1, 1933) (2006)
The Grove of Doom (Sept. 1, 1933) (1969)
Road of Crime (Oct. 1, 1933) (2007)
Mox (Nov. 15, 1933) (1975)
The Wealth Seeker (Jan. 15, 1934) (1978)
The Black Falcon (Feb. 1, 1934) (2006)
Gray Fist (Feb. 15, 1934) (1977)
The Cobra (April 1, 1934) (2007)
Charg, Monster (July 1, 1934) (1977)
The Chinese Disks (Nov. 1, 1934) (2006)
The Unseen Killer (Dec. 1, 1934) (2008)
The Blue Sphinx (Jan. 15, 1935) (2008)
The Plot Master (Feb. 1, 1935) (2008)
Crooks Go Straight (March 1, 1935)
    (2007)
Lingo (April 1, 1935) (2007)
Gray Ghost (May 1, 1936) (2009)
The Fate Joss (July 1, 1935) (2008)
The London Crimes (Sept. 15, 1935)
    (2007)
Zemba (Dec. 1, 1935) (1977)
Castle of Doom (Jan. 15, 1936) (2007)
The Voodoo Master (March 1, 1936)
    (2006)
The Third Shadow (March 15, 1936)
    (2007)
The Salamanders (April 1, 1936) (2006)
The City of Doom (May 15, 1936) (2007)
The Crime Oracle (June 1, 1936) (1975)
The Broken Napoleons (July 15, 1936)
    (2007)
The Golden Masks (Sept. 1, 1936) (2008)
Jibaro Death (Sept. 15, 1936) (2008)
City of Crime (Oct. 1, 1936) (2008)
Partners of Peril (Nov. 1, 1936) (2007)
Vengeance Is Mine (Jan. 1, 1937) (2009)

Quetzal (Feb. 15, 1937) (2008)
Washington Crime (April 1, 1937) (2008)
Crime, Insured (July 1, 1937) (2006)
The Shadow Unmasks (Aug. 1, 1937)
    (2008)
Teeth of the Dragon (Nov. 15, 1937) (1975)
The Murder Master (Feb. 15, 1938) (2006)
The Golden Pagoda (March 1, 1938)
    (2008)
Serpents of Siva (April 15, 1938) (2007)
Voodoo Trail (June 1, 1938) (2008)
The Golden Vulture (July 15, 1938) (2006)
Death Jewels (Aug. 1, 1938) (2008)
Shadow Over Alcatraz (Dec. 1, 1938)
    (2008)
Battle of Greed (April 15, 1939) (2009)
Death's Harlequin (May 1, 1939) (2008)
    Theodore Tinsley
Smugglers of Death (June 1, 1939) (2008)
The Golden Master (Sept. 15, 1939)
    (1984)
The Masked Lady (Oct. 15, 1939) (2008)
Shiwan Khan Returns (Dec. 1, 1939)
    (1984)
The Hooded Circle (Jan. 15, 1939) (2008)
The Fifth Face (Aug. 15, 1940) (2007)
The Blackmail King (Nov. 1, 1941)
    (2008)
The Devil Monsters (Feb. 1, 1943) (2007)
House of Ghosts (Sept 1, 1943) (1981)
Murder by Moonlight (Dec. 1, 1943)
    (1966)
The Freak Show Murders (May 1, 1944)
    (1978)
Voodoo Death (June 1, 1944) (1966)
The Mask of Mephisto (July 1, 1945)
    (1975)
Murder by Magic (Aug. 1, 1945) (1975)
A Quarter of Eight (Oct. 1, 1945) (1978)
The White Skulls (Nov. 1945) (2009)
The Mother Goose Murders (March 1,
    1946) (1979)
Crime Over Casco (April 1, 1946) (1979)
Malmordo (July 1, 1946) (2006)
Jade Dragon (Sept. 1, 1948) (1981)
The Magigals Mystery (Winter 1949)
    (2007)

Shadow Pastiches

Walter Gibson, *Return of the Shadow* (1963); *The Duende History of the Shadow* (1980)
   includes "Blackmail Bay"; *The Shadow Scrapbook* (1979) includes "The Riddle of
   the Rangoon Ruby"
James Luceno, *The Shadow* (1994) movie novelization
Dennis Lynds, *The Shadow Strikes* (1964); *Shadow Beware* (1965); *Cry Shadow!* (1965);
   The Shadow's Revenge (1965); *Mark of the Shadow* (1966); *Shadow — Go Mad!* (1966);
   The Night of the Shadow (1966); *The Shadow Destination: Moon* (1967)

KENNETH ROBESON

The Man of Bronze & The Avenger

Missouri-born Lester Dent (1904–1959), a member of the Explorers Club, wrote
all but twenty of the 181 pulp magazine adventures of Clark "Doc" Savage, Jr.,
for Street & Smith in the 1930s and '40s. Doc was a trained surgeon, scientist,
researcher and inventor. Operating from an office in a New York City skyscraper,
he fights all manner of evil-doers. He often operated on the brains of captured
villains, to remove their criminous tendencies. His greatest foe was John Sun-
light, who appeared in two stories. Assisting the hero are chemist Monk Mayfair, lawyer Ham Brooks, engineers Renny Renwick and Long Tom Roberts and
geologist Johnny Littlejohn. Savage's cousin Patricia Savage has no lack of talent
but is generally overshadowed in this man's world.

   Bantam reprinted all of the Doc Savage novels in paperbacks (not in their
original order), resurrected a neglected Dent manuscript, commissioned a new
novel from Philip José Farmer and engaged Will Murray to complete Lester Dent
outlines for another seven. Recent two-to-a-book reprints of Doc Savage adventures have in some cases restored original Dent material edited out for the magazines.

   The Avenger was Richard Benson, an adventurer who goes into a rage when
the killers of his wife and daughter elude capture. Benson has the unusual ability of being able to reshape his face and change his appearance. He and his small
crew of assistants including Cole Wilson and Nellie Gray appeared in stories written by Paul Ernst (1899–1985) under the Street & Smith house name Kenneth
Robeson for a magazine of the same title. After the periodical ceased, five short
stories by Emile Tepperman as Kenneth Robeson appeared in *Clues Detective* and
one in *The Shadow* magazines. (These stories were reprinted in the late 1970s in
the fan journal *Pulp*, issues 8 to 13.)

   When 1970s paperback reissue proved popular, Warner Books contracted
for a dozen more by science fiction writer and comic books and pulps historian
Ron Goulart. Decades later, several writers contributed stories to a new anthology. The stories are arranged in the order of original pulp publication.

Original Avenger Works

Justice Inc. (October 1939) (1972)
The Yellow Hoard (October 1939) (1972)
The Sky Walker (November 1939) (1972)
The Devil's Horns (December 1939)
   (1972)
The Frosted Death (January 1940) (1972)
The Blood Ring (March 1940) (1972)
Stockholders in Death (April 1940) (1972)
The Glass Mountain (February 1940)
   (1973)
Tuned for Murder (May 1940) (1973)
The Smiling Dogs (June 1940) (1973)
River of Ice (July 1940) (1973)
The Flame Breathers (September 1940)
   (1973)

Murder on Wheels (November 1940)
   (1973)
Three Gold Crowns (January 1941) (1973)
House of Death (March 1941) (1973)
The Hate Master (May 1941) (1973)
Nevlo (July 1941) (1973)
Death in Slow Motion (September 1941)
   (1973)
Pictures of Death (November 1941) (1973)
The Green Killer (January 1942) (1974)
The Happy Killers (March 1942) (1974)
The Black Death (May 1942) (1974)
The Wilder Curse (July 1942) (1974)
Midnight Murder (September 1942)
   (1974)

Avenger Pastiches

Ron Goulart, *The Man from Atlantis* (1974); *Red Moon* (1974); *The Purple Zombie* (1974); *Dr. Time* (1974); *The Nightwitch Devil* (1974); *Black Chariots* (1974); *The Cartoon Crimes* (1974); *The Death Machine* (1974); *The Blood Countess* (1975); *The Glass Man* (1975); *The Iron Skull* (1975); *Demon Island* (1975)

Will Murray, Joe Gentile, Richard Dean Starr, Tom DeFalco, Ron Goulart, Robert Greenberger, Clay Griffith, Susan Griffith, C.J. Henderson, Howard Hopkins, Robert Jeschonek, Paul Kupperberg, Chris Mills, Gary Phillips, Martin Powell, Andy Bennett, Dave Aikins and Max McCoy, *The Avenger Chronicles* (2008)

Original Doc Savage Works in order of magazine date, by Lester Dent except as noted, all under Kenneth Robeson byline

The Man of Bronze (March 1933) (1964)
The Land of Terror (April 1933) (1965)
Quest of the Spider (May 1933) (1972)
The Polar Treasure (June 1933) (1965)
Pirate of the Pacific (July 1933) (1967)
The Red Skull (August 1933) (1967)
The Lost Oasis (September 1933) (1965)
The Sargasso Ogre (October 1933) (1967)
The Czar of Fear (November 1933) (1968)
The Phantom City (December 1933)
   (1966)
Brand of the Werewolf (January 1934)
   (1965)
The Man Who Shook the Earth (February
   1934) (1969)
Meteor Menace (March 1934) (1964)

The Monsters (April 1934) (1965)
The Mystery on the Snow (May 1934)
   (1972)
The King Maker (June 1934) (1975)
The Thousand-Headed Man (July 1934)
   (1964)
The Squeaking Goblin (August 1934)
   (1969)
Fear Cay (September 1934) (1966)
Death in Silver (October 1934) (1968)
The Sea Magician (November 1934)
   (1970)
The Annihilist (December 1934) (1968)
The Mystic Mullah (January 1935) (1965)
Red Snow (February 1935) (1969)
Land of Always-Night (March 1935) (1966)

The Spook Legion (April 1935) (1967)
The Secret in the Sky (May 1935) (1967)
The Roar Devil (June 1935) (1977)
The Quest of Qui (July 1935) (1966)
Spook Hole (August 1935) (1972)
The Majii (September 1935) (1971)
Dust of Death (October 1935) (1969)
Murder Melody (November 1935) (1967) by Norman Daniels
The Fantastic Island (December 1935) (1966)
Murder Mirage (January 1936) (1969) by Norman Daniels
Mystery Under the Sea (February 1936) (1968)
The Metal Master (March 1936) (1973)
The Men Who Smiled No More (April 1936) (1970) by Norman Daniels
The Seven Agate Devils (May 1936) (1973)
Haunted Ocean (June 1936) (1970) by Norman Daniels
The Black Spot (July 1936) (1974) by Norman Daniels
The Midas Man (August 1936) (1970)
Cold Death (September 1936) (1968) by Norman Daniels
The South Pole Terror (October 1936) (1974)
Resurrection Day (November 1936) (1969)
The Vanisher (December 1936) (1970)
Land of Long Juju (January 1937) (1970) by Norman Daniels
The Derrick Devil (February 1937) (1973)
The Mental Wizard (March 1937) (1970)
The Terror in the Navy (April 1937) (1969)
Mad Eyes (May 1937) (1969)
The Land of Fear (June 1937) (1973)
He Could Stop the World (July 1937) (1970) by Norman Daniels
Ost (August 1937) aka *The Magic Island* (1977)
The Feathered Octopus (September 1937) (1970)
Repel (October 1937) aka *Deadly Dwarf* (1968)
The Sea Angel (November 1937) (1970)
The Golden Peril (December 1937) (1970)

The Living Fire Menace (January 1938) (1971)
The Mountain Monster (February 1938) (1976)
Devil on the Moon (March 1938) (1970)
The Pirate's Ghost (April 1938) (1971)
The Motion Menace (May 1938) (1971)
The Submarine Mystery (June 1938) (1971)
The Giggling Ghosts (July 1938) (1971)
The Munitions Master (August 1938) (1971)
The Red Terrors (September 1938) (1976)
Fortress of Solitude (October 1938) (1968)
The Green Death (November 1938) (1971)
The Devil Genghis (December 1938) (1974)
Mad Mesa (January 1939) (1972)
The Yellow Cloud (February 1939) (1971)
The Freckled Shark (March 1939) (1972)
World's Fair Goblin (April 1939) (1969)
The Gold Ogre (May 1939) (1969)
The Flaming Falcons (June 1939) (1968)
Merchants of Disaster (July 1939) (1969)
The Crimson Serpent (August 1939) (1974)
Poison Island (September 1939) (1971)
The Stone Man (October 1939) (1976)
Hex (November 1939) (1969)
The Dagger in the Sky (December 1939) (1969)
The Other World (January 1940) (1968)
The Angry Ghost (February 1940) (1977)
The Spotted Men (March 1940) (1977)
The Evil Gnome (April 1940) (1976)
The Boss of Terror (May 1940) (1976)
The Awful Egg (June 1940) (1978)
The Flying Goblin (July 1940) (1977)
Tunnel Terror (August 1940) (1979)
The Purple Dragon (September 1940) (1978)
Devils of the Deep (October 1940) (1984)
The Awful Dynasty (November 1940) (1988)
The Men Vanished (December 1940) (1988)
The Devil's Playground (January 1941) (1968) by Alan Hathaway
Bequest of Evil (February 1941) (1990)

The All-White Elf (March 1941) (1986)

The Golden Man (April 1941) (1984)

The Pink Lady (May 1941) (1984)

The Headless Men (June 1941) (1984) by Alan Hathaway

The Green Eagle (July 1941) (1968)

Mystery Island (August 1941) (1987)

Birds of Death (October 1941) (1989)

The Invisible-Box Murders (November 1941) (1989)

Peril in the North (December 1941) (1984)

The Rustling Death (January 1942) (1987) by Alan Hathaway

Men of Fear (February 1942) (1987)

The Too-Wise Owl (March 1942) (1989)

The Magic Forest (April 1942) (1988)

Pirate Isle (May 1942) (1983)

The Speaking Stone (June 1942) (1983)

The Man Who Fell Up (July 1942) (1982)

The Three Wild Men (August 1942) (1984)

The Laugh of Death (October 1942) (1984)

They Died Twice (November 1942) (1981)

The Devil's Black Rock (December 1942) (1989)

The Time Terror (January 1943) (1981)

Waves of Death (February 1943) (1989)

The Black, Black Witch (March 1943) (1981)

The King of Terror (April 1943) (1984)

The Talking Devil (May 1943) (1982)

The Running Skeletons (June 1943) (1986)

Mystery on Happy Bones (July 1943) (1979)

The Mental Monster (August 1943) (1989)

Hell Below (September 1943) (1980)

The Goblins (October 1943) (1985)

The Secret of the Su (November 1943) (1985)

The Spook of Grandpa Eben (December 1943) (1987)

According to Plan of a One-Eyed Mystic (January 1944) aka *One-Eyed Mystic* (1982)

Death Had Yellow Eyes (February 1944) (1982)

The Derelict of Skull Shoal (March 1944) (1990)

The Whisker of Hercules (April 1944) (1981)

The Three Devils (May 1944) (1987)

The Pharaoh's Ghost (June 1944) (1981)

The Man Who Was Scared (July 1944) (1981)

The Shape of Terror (August 1944) (1982)

Weird Valley (September 1944) (1989)

Jiu San (October 1944) (1981)

Satan Black (November 1944) (1980)

The Lost Giant (December 1944) (1980)

Violent Night (January 1945) aka *The Hate Genius* (1979)

Strange Fish (February 1945) (1987)

The Ten-Ton Snake (March 1945) (1982)

Cargo Unknown (April 1945) (1980)

Rock Sinister (May 1945) (1987)

The Terrible Stork (June 1945) (1988)

King Joe Cay (July 1945) (1987)

The Wee Ones (August 1945) (1989)

Terror Takes 7 (September 1945) (1989)

The Thing That Pursued (October 1945) (1987)

Trouble on Parade (November 1945) (1989)

The Screaming Man (December 1945) (1981)

Measures for a Coffin (January 1946) (1987)

Se-Pa-Poo (February 1946) (1990)

Terror and the Lonely Widow (March 1946) (1989)

Five Fathoms Dead (April 1946) (1988)

Death Is a Round Black Spot (May 1946) (1990)

Colors for Murder (June 1946) (1990)

Fire and Ice (July 1946) (1988)

Three Times a Corpse (August 1946) (1990)

The Exploding Lake (September 1946) (1990)

Death in Little Houses (October 1946) (1990)

The Devil Is Jones (November 1946) (1990)

The Disappearing Lady (December 1946) (1988) by William Bogart

Target for Death (January 1947) (1990)
by William Bogart
The Death Lady (February 1947) (1990)
by William Bogart
Danger Lie East (March-April 1947)
(1988)
No Light to Die By (May-June 1947)
(1988)
The Monkey Suit (July-August 1947)
(1988)
Let's Kill Ames (September-October
1947) (1988)
Once Over Lightly (November-December 1947) (1988)

I Died Yesterday (January-February 1948)
(1988)
The Pure Evil (March-April 1948) (1987)
Terror Wears No Shoes (May-June 1948)
(1990)
The Angry Canary (July-August 1948)
(1986)
The Swooning Lady (September-
October 1948) (1986)
The Green Master (Winter 1949) (1990)
Return from Cormoral (Spring 1949)
(1990)
Up From Earth's Center (Summer 1949)
(1990)

Doc Savage Posthumous Collaborations

Will Murray, issued as by Lester Dent, *Python Isle* (1991); *White Eyes* (1992); *The Frightened Fish* (1992); *The Jade Ogre* (1992); *Flight into Fear* (1993); *The Whistling Wraith* (1993); *The Forgotten Realm* (1993)

Doc Savage Posthumous Restorations

The Squeaking Goblin (2007)
The Evil Gnome (2007)
Dust of Death (2007)

The Stone Man (2007)
The Polar Treasure (2007)
Mystery Under the Sea (2008)

Doc Savage Pastiches

Lester Dent, *The Red Spider* (1979)
Philip José Farmer, *Escape from Loki* (1991)

Fictional Biography

Philip José Farmer, *Doc Savage: An Apocalyptic Life* (1973)

GRANT STOCKBRIDGE

The Spider

The Spider, a popular pulp fiction hero in his day, owed his delineation to initial writer R.T. Maitland Scott (1882–1966), who composed the first two stories for Popular Publications. Scott went on to other projects and Norvell Page, Emile C. Tepperman, Wayne Rogers, Prentice Winchell and Donald C. Cormack continued the series, all writing under the house name Grant Stockbridge. *The Spider* ran for 118 magazine issues from 1933 to 1943.

The Spider was Richard Wentworth, a millionaire avenger who stamped a spider imprint on the forehead of each criminal he grappled with. The police had little use for The Spider, though police commissioner Stanley Kirkpatrick was a close friend to Wentworth. The Spider often took on criminals with a blazing .45 in each hand.

Scott, who created the template for The Spider, was born in Woodstock, Ontario, and attended Royal Military College. He also wrote stories about Secret Service Smith for *Adventure* magazine.

Popular purchased a manuscript entitled "Slaughter, Inc." but never published it. The novel was rediscovered in 1978 and published in paperback the next year, with The Spider's name changed to Blue Steel for copyright reasons. The author was credited as Spider Page. Several writers came up with new versions of The Spider decades after his last pulp appearance. The list includes only those pulp tales that have been reissued in books. The stories are arranged in the order of original pulp publication.

Reprinted original works in order of periodical appearance

The Spider Strikes (October 1933) (1969) as by R.T.M. Scott

The Wheel of Death (November 1933) (1969) as by R.T.M. Scott

Wings of the Black Death (December 1933) (1969) hereafter as by Grant Stockbridge (Norvell Page except where noted)

City of Flaming Shadows (January 1934) (1970)

Empire of Doom (February 1934) (2007)

The Citadel of Hell (March 1934) (2007)

Serpent of Destruction (April 1934) (2007)

The Mad Horde (May 1934)

Satan's Death Blast (June 1934) (1984)

Corpse Cargo (July 1934) (1985) (2008)

Prince of Red Looters (August 1934) aka *The Prince of Evil* (1985)

Reign of the Silver Terror (September 1934) (2007)

Builders of the Black Empire (October 1934) (1980)

Death's Crimson Juggernaut (November 1934) (2007)

The Red Death Rain (December 1934) (1993)

The City Destroyer (January 1935) (1975)

The Pain Emperor (February 1935) (1992)

The Flame Master (March 1935) (2007)

Slaves of the Crime Master (April 1935) (2007)

Reign of the Death Fiddler (May 1935) (2007)

Hordes of the Red Butcher (June 1935) (1975)

Dragon Lord of the Underworld (July 1935) (2007)

Master of the Death-Madness (August 1935) (2007)

King of the Red Killers (September 1935) (1993)

Overlord of the Damned (October 1935) (1980)

Death Reign of the Vampire King (November 1935) (1975)

Emperor of the Yellow Death (December 1935) (2007)

The Mayor of Hell (January 1936) (2007)

Slaves of the Murder Syndicate (February 1936) (2007)

Green Globes of Death (March 1936) (1993)

The Cholera King (April 1936) (2007)

Slaves of the Dragon (May 1936) (2007)

Legions of Madness (June 1936) (2007)

Laboratory of the Damned (July 1936) (2007)

Satan's Sightless Legions (August 1936) (2007)

The Coming of the Terror (September 1936) (2007)

The Devil's Death Dwarfs (October 1936) (2007)

City of Dreadful Night (November 1936) (2007) Emile Tepperman

Reign of the Snake Men (December 1936) (2007)

Dictator of the Damned (January 1937) (1991) Emile Tepperman

The Milltown Massacres (February 1937) (1991) Emile Tepperman

Scourge of the Yellow Fangs (April 1937) (2009)

Master of the Flaming Horde (November 1937) (1995)

Legions of the Accursed Light (January 1938) (1993)

The Spider and the Faceless One (November 1939) (2008)

Satan's Murder Machines (December 1939) (1993)

The Spider and The Pain Master (January 1940) (1991) Emile Tepperman

Slaves of the Laughing Death (March 1940) (1993)

Judgment of the Damned (June 1940) (1993)

The Council of Evil (October 1940) (2008)

Death and the Spider (April 1941) (2009)

The Devil's Paymaster (May 1941) (1993)

Death and The Spider (January 1942) (1975)

Slaves of the Ring (April 1942) (2008)

Secret City of Crime (February 1943) (1991)

Pastiches

Norvell Page writing as Spider Page, *Slaughter, Incorporated* (1979)

John Jakes, Mort Castle, Bill Crider, Shannon Denton, Chuck Dixon, Steve Englehart, Ron Fortier, Joe Gentile, Rich Harvey, John Halfers, C.J. Henderson, Howard Hopkins, Anthony Kuhoric, Elizabeth Massie, Christopher Mills and Tom Floyd, *The Spider Chronicles* (2007)

Romances

Only five writers are included in this section, but oh, what writers! Jane Austen is one of the most adored of her generation. A virtual flood of sequels to her several novels has emerged in recent decades, for readers who can't get enough after the real thing.

JANE AUSTEN
Comedies of manners

Jane Austen (1775–1817) lived a relatively simple life as the daughter of a rector in Hampshire, England. One of a large family, she attended boarding school with her sister Cassandra, but otherwise was home educated. She read widely in her father's library, among other books, the novels of Fielding and Richardson. She wrote humorous parodies during her youth, mostly to amuse her family. By the late 1790s, she had begun work on several of her comedies of middle class manners. The family in 1800 relocated to Bath, where Jane met a young man who fell in love with her. There were other romantic interludes, but she never married. The family eventually returned to Hampshire, by which time Austen had completed her novel *Sense and Sensibility*. It was published in 1811. Its success prompted her to finish other works, though she died in 1817 before she completed what became *Sanditon*.

Her popularity has only grown. Many credit her familiar, well-drawn characters as spurring her appeal. Austen enthusiasm re-emerged in the 1870s and blossomed in the 1970s. "Jane Austen joined the debate over the moral value of novels not by theorizing, but by showing that what a novel imitates is far less important than its technical 'forms of expression.' Gaiety, persistence and painstaking work with the technical challenges of her story were everything to her," in the opinion of biographer Park Honan in *Jane Austen Her Life* (1987).

Austen novels inspired voluminous pastiches.

Mansfield Park is about Fanny Price, who is adopted by a rich and frivolous family. Jane Gillespie worked two characters from *Mansfield Park* into her extension, *Ladysmead*, in which a small-town clergyman hopes to find advantageous marriages for his seven daughters. English-born Joan Aiken's *Mansfield Revisited* tells the story of Susan Price, Fanny's younger sister.

Emma is about a restless small town woman who, after the marriage of her companion, attends her widowed father and tries to arrange the affairs of her friends. Gillespie's *Aunt Celia* takes characters from *Emma*— such as Mr. Weston, the squire of Randalls, and his daughter Celia, into new plot directions. Aiken's *Jane Fairfax* is sub-titled "Jane Austen's Emma, through another's eyes."

Pride and Prejudice is about the Bennets of Hertfordshire, who have five daughters but only a male cousin to pass along their real property. Gillespie's *Teverton Hall* follows the fortunes of two young people who are offspring of one of the marriages contracted in the Austen book. British novelist Emma Tennant's sequel relates Elizabeth Bennet's fortunes after her marriage to Fitzwilliam Darcy. Seth Grahame-Smith, Ben H. Winters and Steve Hockensmith added outrageous new scenes to Austen's originial prose to produce the popular *Pride and Prejudice and Zombies* (2009), *Sense and Sensibility and Sea Monsters* (2009) and *Dawn of the Dreadfuls* (2010), respectively.

Sense and Sensibility tells of sisters Elinor and Marianne and their unfortunate love affairs. *Brightsea* by Gillespie resurrects the conceited sisters, Misses Nancy and Lucy Steele: the latter is now married, the former, apparently doomed to spinsterhood. Lucy accepts a chaperone's position at the summer resort Brightsea — and finds her fortunes changing.

Original Brothers Work

Fragment of a Novel Written by Jane Austen January–March 1817 (also known as *The Brothers,* or *Sanditon,* 1925)

Posthumous collaboration on incomplete manuscript *The Brothers,* or *Sanditon*

"Another Lady" (Marie Dobbs as Anne Telscombe), *Sanditon* (1975)
"Julia Barrett" (Julia Braun Kessler), *Charlotte* (2000)
Alice Cobbett, *Somehow Lengthened: A Development of Sanditon* (1932)
D.J. Eden, *Sanditon* (2002)
Anna Austen Leroy, *Sanditon: A Continuation* (1983)
Juliette Shapiro, *A Completion of Sanditon* (2004)

Selected *Emma* Work

Emma (1816)

Emma Pastiches

Joan Aiken, *Jane Fairfax: The Secret Story of the Second Heroine of Jane Austen's Emma* (1990)

Rachel Billington, *Perfect Happiness* (1996)

Diane Birchall, *Mrs. Elton in America* (2004, trilogy of short works, *In Defense of Mrs. Elton, Mrs. Elton in America* and *The Courtship of Mrs. Elton*)

Joan Ellen Delman, *Lover's Perjuries; or, the Clandestine Courtship of Jane Fairfield and Frank Churchill: A Retelling of Jane Austen's Emma* (2007)

Brenda Finn, *Anna Weston: A Sequel to Emma by Jane Austen* (2000)

Jane Gillespie, *Aunt Celia* (1990); *Truth and Rumor* (1995)

Amanda Grange, *Mr. Knightly's Diary* (2007)

Charlotte Grey, *The Journal of Jane Fairfax* (1983)

Joan Leigh-Austen, *A Visit to Highbury: Another View of Emma* (1995); *Later Days at Highbury* (1996)

Katharine Moore, *Donwell Abbey* (2007)

Debra White Smith, *Amanda* (2006)

Naomi Royde Smith, *Jane Fairfax* (1940)

Emma Tennant, *Emma in Love: Jane Austen's Emma Continued* (1997)

Original Lady Susan Work

Lady Susan and *The Watsons* (1882)

Lady Susan Pastiche

Phyllis Ann Karr, *Lady Susan* (1980)

Original *Mansfield Park* Work

Mansfield Park (1814)

Mansfield Park Pastiches

Joan Aiken, *Mansfield Revisited* (1984); *The Youngest Miss Ward* (1999); *The Admiral's Lady* (1995)

Paula Atchia, *Mansfield Letters: A Sequel to Mansfield Park* (1996)

Carrie Bebris, *The Matters at Mansfield; or, The Crawford Affair* (2008)

Mrs. Francis Brown (Edith Charlotte Brown), *Susan Price; or, Resolution* (1930)

Jane Gillespie, *Ladysmead* (1982); *The Reluctant Baronet* (1998)

Victor Gordon, *Mrs. Rushworth* (1989)

Amanda Grange, *Edmund Bertram's Diary* (2007)

Victor Gordon, *Mrs. Rushworthy* (1990)

Willis Hall, *Mansfield Park: A Play* (1994)

Jane Menzies, *Gambles and Gambols—A Visit to Old Friends* (1983)

Dorothy Allen and Ann Owen, *Mansfield Park: An Alternative Ending* (1989)

Debra White Smith, *Central Park* (2005)

Judith Terry, *Miss Abigail's Part: or, Version and Diversion* (1986)

Northanger Abbey Pastiches

Jane Gillespie, *Uninvited Guests: A Sequel to Jane Austen's Northanger Abbey* (1994)

Debra White Smith, *Northpointe Chalet* (2005)

Orginal *Persuasion* Work

Northanger Abbey and *Persuasion* (1817)

Persuasion Pastiches

Grania Beckford, *Virtues and Vices* (1981)

Jane Gillespie, *Sir Willy* (1992)

Amanda Grange, *Captain Wentworth's Diary* (2007)

Laurie Horowitz, *The Family Fortune* (2006)

Susan Kaye, *None But You* (2006) Captain Frederick Wentworth, Book 1; *For You Alone* (2007) Captain Frederick Wentworth, Book 2

June Menzies, *His Cunning or Hers: A Postscript to Persuasion* (1993)

Melissa Nathan, *Persuading Annie* (2004)

Karen V. Siplin, *Such a Girl* (2004)

Debra White Smith, *Possibilities* (2006)

Original *Pride and Prejudice* Work

Pride and Prejudice (1813)

Pride and Prejudice Pastiches

Pamela Aidan, *An Assembly Such as This: A Novel of Fitzwilliam Darcy, Gentleman* (2005); *Duty and Desire* (2006); *These Three Remain: A Novel of Fitzwilliam Darcy, Gentleman* (2006)

Joan Aiken, *Lady Catherine's Necklace* (2000)

Sara Angelini, *The Trials of the Honorable F. Darcy* (2007)

Elizabeth Aston, *Mr. Darcy's Daughter* (2004); *The Exploits & Adventures of Miss Alethea Darcy* (2005); *The True Darcy Spirit* (2006); *The Second Mrs. Darcy* (2007); *The Darcy Connection* (2008)

Jane Aylmer, *Mr. Darcy's Story* (1996)

Ted Bader and Marilyn Bader, *Desire & Duty: A Sequel to Jane Austen's Pride and Prejudice* (1997); *Virtue and Vanity* (2000)

"Julia Barrett" (Julia Braun Kessler and Gabrielle Donnelly), *Presumption: An Entertainment* (1993)

E. Barrington, *Ladies* (1927)

Carrie Bebris, *Pride and Prescience* (2004); *North by Northanger; or, The Shades of Pemberley, a Mr. & Mrs. Darcy Mystery* (2007)

Linda Berdoll, *Mr. Darcy Takes a Wife: Pride and Prejudice Continues* (2003); *Darcy & Elisabeth: Nights and Days at Pemberley* (2005)

Diana Birchall, *Mrs. Darcy's Dilemma: A Sequel to Jane Austen's Pride and Prejudice* (2003)

Dorothy Alice Bonavia-Hunt, *Pemberley Shades: A lightly Gothic tale of Mr. and Mrs. Darcy* (1949)

Sylvia G. Brinton, *Old Friends and New Fancies: An Imaginary Sequel to the Novels of Jane Austen* (1913)

Judith Brocklehurst, *A Letter from Lady Catherine* (2007)

Skylar Hamilton Burris, *Conviction: A Sequel to Pride and Prejudice* (2006)

Rebecca Ann Collins, *Mr. Darcy's Daughter* (2007); *The Ladies of Longbourn* (2007); *Pemberley Chronicles* (2008); *The Women of Pemberley* (2008); *Netherfield Park Revisited* (2008); *The Women of Pemberley* (2000)

Jane Dawkins, *Letters from Pemberley* (1999); *More Letters from Pemberley* (2008)

Joan Ellen Delman, *Miss de Bourgh's Adventure* (2005)

Anne Fafoutakis, *Mrs. Fitzwilliam Darcy* (2002)

Marjorie Fasman, *The Diary of Henry Fitzwilliam Darcy* (1998)

Kate Fenton, *Vanity and Vexation: A Novel of Pride and Prejudice* (2004); *Lions and Liquorice* (1995)

Phyllis Furley, *The Darcys: Scenes from a Married Life* (2004)

Jane Gillespie, *Teverton Hall* (1984); *Deborah* (1995)

Seth Grahame-Smith, *Pride and Prejudice and Zombies* (2009)

Amanda Grange, *Mr. Darcy's Diary* (2007); *Mr. Darcy, Vampyre* (2009)

Helen Halstead, *Mr. Darcy Presents His Bride* (2007)

Anne Hampson, *Pemberley Place* (1998)

Regina Jeffers, *Darcy's Passion: Fitzwilliam Darcy's Story* (2007); *Darcy's Hunger* (2009)

Sharon Lathan, *Two Shall Become One; Mr. & Mrs. Fitzwilliam Darcy* (2007)

Kara Louise, *Pemberley's Promise* (2007); *Drive and Determination* (2007); *Assumed Engagement* (2007)

Colleen McCullough, *The Independence of Mary Bennett* (2008)

Isobel Scott Moffat, *The Mistress of Pemberley* (2008)

Frances Morgan, *Darcy and Elizabeth* (2003)

Melissa Nathan, *Pride, Prejudice and Jasmin Field* (2001)

Elizabeth Newark, *Consequence; or, Whatever Became of Charlotte Lucas* (1997); *The Darcys Give a Ball: A Gentle Joke, Jane Austen Style* (2008)

Jane Odiwe, *Lydia Bennet's Story* (2007)

Warrene Piper, *Son of John Wintringham* (1930); *The Sun in His Own House* (1931)

Alexandra Potter, *Me and Mr. Darcy* (2007)

Abigail Reynolds, *By Force of Instinct: A Pemberley Variation* (2007); *From Lambton to Longbourn: A Pride & Prejudice Variation* (2007); *The Last Man in the World: A Pride & Prejudice Variation* (2007); *Impulse & Initiative: A Pride & Prejudice Variation* (2007); *Without Reserve: A Pride & Prejudice Variation* (2007); *Pemberley by the Sea: A Pride & Prejudice Variation* (2008)

Anne and Arthur Russell, *The Wedding at Pemberley: A Footnote to Pride and Prejudice* (1949)

Juliette Shapiro, *Excessively Diverted: The Sequel to Jane Austen's Pride & Prejudice* (2002); *Fitzwilliam Darcy's Memoirs* (2004); *Mr. Darcy's Decision* (2008)

Mary Lydon Simpsen, *Pemberley Remembered* (2007)

Debra White Smith, *First Impressions* (2004)

Mary Street, *The Confession of Fitzwilliam Darcy* (2008)

Emma Tennant, *Pemberly; Or, Pride and Prejudice Continued* (1993); *An Unequal Marriage; or, Pride and Prejudice Twenty Years Later* (1994); *Pemberley Revisited* (2005)

Cedric Wallis, *The Heiress of Rosings* (1956)

Emma Campbell Webster, *Being Elizabeth Bennett* (2007)

T.H. White, *Darkness at Pemberley* (1932)

Genevieve Rose Wimer, *Honour and Humility* (2002)

Original *Sense and Sensibility* Work

Sense and Sensibility (1811)

Sense and Sensibility Pastiches

Joan Aiken, *Eliza's Daughter: A Sequel to Sense and Sensibility* (1994)
"Julia Barrett" (Julia Braun Kessler), *The Third Sister: A Sequel to Sense & Sensibility* (1996)
Lily Adams Beck, *The Ladies! A Shining Constellation of Wit and Beauty* (1922)
Mrs. Francis Brown (Edith Charlotte Brown), *Margaret Dashwood: or, Interference* (1929)
Jane Gillespie, *Brightsea* (1986)
Debra White Smith, *Reason and Romance* (2004)
Emma Tennant, *Elinor and Marianne* (1996)
Ben H. Winters, *Sense and Sensibility and Sea Monsters* (2009)

Posthumous Collaborations on Incomplete Manuscript *The Watsons*

Joan Aiken, *Emma Watson: Jane Austen's Unfinished Novel Completed (The Watsons)* (1996)
Edith Charlotte Brown and Francis Brown, *The Watsons: Completed in Accordance with Her Intentions* (1928)
John Coates, *The Watsons: Jane Austen's Fragment Continued and Completed* (1958)
Catherine Anne Hubback, *The Younger Sister* (1850)
L. Oulton, *The Watsons* (1923)
Merryn Williams, *The Watsons* (2005)

CHARLOTTE BRONTË

Jane Eyre

Charlotte Brontë (1816–1855) was one of a literary family, daughter of an ill-tempered curate and his never-healthy wife in Yorkshire, England. She and sisters Emily Jane (see next entry) and Anne (1820–1849), author of *The Tenant of Wildfell Hall* (1848), found emotional and creative release in writing poetry and fiction. Charlotte Brontë worked as a governess or teacher. Only one of her nearly two dozen manuscripts for novels saw publication in her lifetime — and then under the name Currer Bell.

Several writers have produced pastiches.

Original Work

Jane Eyre (1847)

Pastiches

Hilary Bailey, *Mrs. Rochester: A Sequel to Jane Eyre* (1997)
Kimberley A. Bennett, *Jane Rochester: A Novel Inspired by Charlotte Brontë's Jane Eyre* (2000)
Warwick Blanchett, *Mrs. Rochester: A Sequel to Jane Eyre* (2000)

Jasper Fforde, *The Eyre Affair: A Thursday Next Novel* (2001)
Elizabeth Newark, *Jane Eyre's Daughter* (2008)
Jean Rhys, *Wide Sargasso Sea* (1966)
Sharon Shinn, *Jenna Starborn* (2002)
Emma Tennant, *Adele: Jane Eyre's Hidden Story* (2000); *The French Dancer's Bastard: The Story of Adele from Jane Eyre* (2006); *Thornfield Hall: Jane Eyre's Hidden Story* (2007)

Posthumous Collaboration with Clare Boylan
Emma Brown (2003)

EMILY BRONTË
Heathcliff

Emily Jane Brontë (1818–1848) wrote only one novel, but it became a classic. *Wuthering Heights* came out in 1847 under the name Ellis Bell, the same year as Charlotte Brontë's *Jane Eyre* and Anne Brontë's *Agnes Grey* (as by Acton Bell) appeared.

Other writers have continued the story of lovers Heathcliff and Catherine Earnshaw.

Original Work
Wuthering Heights (1847)

Pastiches
Jeffrey Caine, *Heathcliff* (1987)
Maryse Conde, *Windward Heights* (1998)
Lin Haire-Sergeant, *H.: The Story of Heathcliff's Journey Back to Wuthering Heights* (1992) aka *Heathcliff: The Return to Wuthering Heights* (1992)
Rosemary Ellerbeck writing as Anna L'Estrange, *Return to Wuthering Heights* (1978)
Nicola Thorne, *Return to Wuthering Heights* (1998)
John Wheatcroft, *Catherine: Her Book* (1983)

GEORGETTE HEYER
Regency romances

Georgette Heyer (1902–1974) was a pioneer author of English historical romances from the Regency period. Married to a mining engineer, George Ronald Rougier, she lived in Tanganyika and Macedonia as well as England, where she was born.

Heyer wrote of the same time period as Jane Austen. But while Austen knew her setting firsthand, Heyer had to do some heavy research to give detail to her stories. She also wrote mystery novels and thrillers.

At least twice, Heyer learned that other novelists had used her characters, including their names, in their works. One episode was in 1950. Heyer said this, as related by biographer Jane Aiken Hodges in *The Private World of Georgette Heyer*: "[That writer owed me] what no self-respecting author should owe to another.... Cheek by jowl with some piece of what I should call special knowledge (all of which I can point out in my books) one finds an anachronism so blatant as to show that [she/they] know rather less about the period than the average schoolchild and certainly have never read enough contemporary literature to acquire the sudden bit of erudition that every now and then staggers the informed reader.... There is a certain salacity which I find revolting, no sense of period, not a vestige of wit, and no ability to make a character 'live.' There is a melodramatic bias, but the copying of names, the similarity of situations, the descriptions of characters have been enough to make one impartial reader at least detect the imitations." While she had ample proof of her priority, Heyer refused to bring lawsuit, according to Hodges.

The offending author has not been identified. Barbara Cartland wrote in the Heyer vein (far too many books to examine or list here), as did Clare Darcy (as listed). Another book here is science fiction, with a dose of Heyer language and relationship thrown in. Many readers found the Karen Joy Fowler book very Heyer-esque.

Pastiches

Clare Darcy, *Georgina* (1971)
Karen Joy Fowler, *The Jane Austen Book Club* (2005); *Letty* (1980)
Sharon Lee and Steve Miller, *Pilots Choice* (2001)

GRACE LIVINGSTON HILL

Queen of Christian romance

The daughter of Presbyterian minister Charles Montgomery Livingston, Grace Livingston Hill (1865–1947) grew up in Wellsville, New York. Her mother, Marcia Macdonald Livingston, was a publisher and writer of children's stories. Grace was home-schooled and attended Cincinnati Art School and Elmira Collegesoon took to the craft, specializing in romance with a Christian element. Her first book, *A Chautauqua Idyl*, came out in 1887. *Katherine's Yesterday and Other Christian Endeavor Stories* (1895) collected her earliest short stories. She married the Rev. Thomas Guthrie Franklin Hill in 1892. They had two daughters and lived in Swarthmore, Pennsylvania. Hill had a rigorous writing schedule with the

Philadelphia publisher J.B. Lippincott. She sometimes wrote as Marcia Macdonald and as Grace Livingston Hill Lutz. (Her second husband was Flavius Josephus Lutz.) The last novel she completed herself was *Where Two Ways Met* (1946). It, as its predecessors, had a happy ending.

After her death, daughter Ruth Livingston Hill completed the author's last, eightieth book.

Posthumous Collaboration

Ruth Livingston Hill, *Mary Arden* (1948)

Science Fiction

Isaac Asimov set the stage for pastiches by working with other writers in his lifetime. Douglas Adams, in comparison, had no expectation another writer someday would take up the tale of the Galaxy wanderer Arthur Dent. In how much detail L. Ron Hubbard outlined his Mission Earth series before his death is up for speculation; Robert Vaughn Young no doubt mustered most of the plots himself.

Douglas Adams
Thumbing

British science fiction writer Douglas Adams (1952–2001), creator of *The Hitchhiker's Guide to the Galaxy* as a radio series and later as a book series, was born in Cambridge and educated at Brentwood School, Essex, and St. John's College, Cambridge. Thanks to the success of the initial novel, Adams was the youngest writer to receive a Golden Pan award in 1984. He adapted the first and further books into a television series. Adams was living with his wife and family in California, working on a screenplay for a film version of Hitchhiker, when he died unexpectedly in 2001.

The writer's widow, Jane Belson, knowing Adams had planned another book to connect and resolve not only that sequence but the Dirk Gently Holistic Detective series as well, in 2008 endorsed writer Eoin Colfer (b. 1965) to write a sixth Hitchhiker book about the characters Arthur Dent, Trillian and Ford Prefect. Colfer explained to *The Guardian*, "People have said, quite rightly, that *Mostly Harmless* is a very bleak book. And it was a bleak book. I would love to finish Hitchhiker on a slightly more upbeat note, so five seems to be a wrong kind of number, six is a better kind of number." Colfer is author of the popular Artemis Fowl series for young adult readers.

Original Hitchhiker Works

The Hitchhiker's Guide to the Galaxy
(1979)
The Restaurant at the End of the Universe
(1980)

Life, the Universe and Everything (1982)
So Long, and Thanks for All the Fish
(1984)
Mostly Harmless (1992)

Pastiche

Eoin Colfer, And Another Thing... (2009)

ISAAC ASIMOV
Nightfall

Isaac Asimov (1920–1992) was "the pre-eminent popular-science writer of the day and for more than 40 years one of the best and best-known writers of science fiction," said *The New York Times* in a 1992 appreciation.

Asimov was born in the U.S.S.R. and emigrated to the United States at age three. He became a naturalized citizen. He received his Ph.D. in chemistry in 1948 from Columbia University and became a university professor, teaching at Boston University beginning in 1979. His first book was published in 1950 and he became a prolific writer of popular science and science fiction (and occasional mysteries) for adults and young readers. He won five Hugo awards (from fans) and three Nebula awards (from fellow writers) for his science fiction. His Foundation books set in a future galactic empire were singled out with a Hugo in 1966 for best all-time science fiction series. Asimov also wrote authoritative books on subjects as diverse as the Bible and the slide rule.

Asimov and Robert Silverberg thrice "collaborated" to produce novels based on Asimov short stories. Asimov provided story lines and Silverberg expanded the plots to novels. Two of the books appeared after Asimov's death, making them posthumous collaborations. Books in the Isaac Asimov's Robots in Time Series, written by William F. Wu, were based on Asimov's Laws of Robotics as outlined in several of his early novels, and appeared after Asimov's death.

"Nightfall," Asimov's well-known short story, tells of literal darkness coming to the planet Kalgash, a world that knows only light, and of the clash between science and religion. He sold it in 1941 to John W. Campbell, editor of *Astounding Science Fiction*. Three decades later, the Science Fiction Writers of America voted it the best science fiction short story ever written. Silverberg's expansion appeared in 1991.

"The Ugly Little Boy" was a short story issued in 1958 and *The Positronic Man* is based on "The Bicentennial Man" from 1976. Silverberg expanded both into novels. Born in 1935 in New York City, Silverberg has written more than 70 science fiction novels and also edited such periodicals as *Amazing* and *Fantastic*. He has his own Hugo, Nebula and other awards on the shelf.

Asimov's Laws of Robotics, and his massive Foundation Trilogy, inspired the bulk of the pastiches listed here, by various authors. Some of the series were authorized by Asimov before he died.

Original Foundation Works

Foundation (1951) Foundation Trilogy

Foundation and Empire (1952) Foundation Trilogy

Second Foundation (1953) Foundation Trilogy

Foundation's Edge (1982) Foundation novel

Foundation and Earth (1986) Foundation novel

Prelude to Foundation (1988) Foundation novel

Forward the Foundation (1993) Foundation novel

Foundation Pastiches

Greg Bear, *Foundation and Chaos: The Second Foundation Trilogy* (1999)

Gregory Benford, *Foundation's Fear: The Second Foundation Trilogy* (1998)

David Brin, *Foundation's Triumph: Second Foundation Trilogy* (2000)

Martin H. Greenberg, editor, *Foundation's Friends* (1989) includes stories by Ben Bova, Pamela Sargent, Robert Silverberg, Edward Wellen, Harry Turtledove, Connie Willis, George Alec Effinger, Mike Resnick, Barry N. Malzberg, Sheila Finch, Frederik Pohl, Poul Anderson, George Zebrowski, Robert Sheckley, Edward D. Hoch, Hal Clement, Harry Harrison, Orson Scott Card.

Original Robot Works

I, Robot (1950) short stories

The Complete Robot (1982) short stories

Robot Dreams (1986) short stories

Robot Visions (1990) short stories

The Caves of Steel (1954)

The Naked Sun (1957)

The Robots of Dawn (1983)

Robots and Empire (1985)

Robot Pastiches

Bruce Bethke, *Asimov's Robots and Aliens: Maverick* (1990)

Rob Chilson, *Isaac Asimov's Robot City: Refuge* (1989)

Arthur Byron Cover, *Isaac Asimov's Robot City: Prodigy* (1989)

Alexander C. Irvine, *Have Robot, Will Travel: The New Isaac Asimov's Robot Mystery* (2005)

Michael P. Kube-McDowell and Mike McQuay, *Isaac Asimov's Robot City* (2000)

Stephen Leigh, *Asimov's Robots and Aliens: Changeling* (1989)

Jerry Oltion, *Asimov's Robots and Aliens: Alliance* (1989); *Asimov's Robots and Aliens: Humanity* (1989)

Steve Perry & Gary A. Braunbeck, *Isaac Asimov's I-Bots: Time Was* (1998)

Cordell Scotten, *Asimov's Robots and Aliens: Renegade* (1989)

Robert Thurston, *Asimov's Robots and Aliens: Intruder* (1989)

Mark Tiedmann, *Mirage: The New Isaac Asimov's Robot Mystery* (2000); *Chimera: The New Isaac Asimov's Robot Mystery* (2001); *Aurora: The New Isaac Asimov's Robot Mystery* (2002)

William F. Wu, *Isaac Asimov's Robot City: Cyborg* (1988); *Isaac Asimov's Robot City:*

Perihelion (1988); *Isaac Asimov's Robots in Time Series: Predator* (1993); *Isaac Asimov's Robots in Time Series: Marauder* (1993); *Isaac Asimov's Robots in Time Series: Warrior* (1993); *Isaac Asimov's Robots in Time Series: Emperor* (1994); *Isaac Asimov's Robots in Time Series: Invader* (1994); *Isaac Asimov's Robots in Time Series: Dictator* (1994)

Posthumous Collaborations

Roger MacBride Allen, *Isaac Asimov's Caliban Trilogy: Caliban* (1993); *Isaac Asimov's Caliban Trilogy: Inferno* (1998); *Isaac Asimov's Caliban Trilogy: Utopia* (1999)
Robert Silverberg, *The Ugly Little Boy* (1992); *The Positronic Man* (1993)

ALFRED BESTER
Psychoshop

Manhattan-born Alfred Bester (1913–1987) wrote for radio (*Nick Carter, The Shadow, Nero Wolfe* and *Charlie Chan*) and television (*Sunday Showcase*) as well as magazines (*Astounding*), comic books (*Green Lantern* and *Superman*) and book publishers. He won the first Hugo Award, in 1953, for *The Demolished Man*.

Bester graduated from the University of Pennsylvania but never completed his studies at Columbia Law School. His first fiction work, "The Broken Axiom," appeared in *Thrilling Wonder Stories* in April 1939. From 1963 to 1971, he was editor of *Holiday* magazine.

Roger Zelazny completed the *Psychoshop* manuscript begun by Bester.

Posthumous Collaboration

Roger Zelazny, *Psychoshop* (1998)

PIERRE BOULLE
Apes

Born in Avignon, France, Pierre-François-Marie-Louis Boulle (1912–1994) — he shortened his name to Pierre Boulle for his fiction — trained as an engineer and worked on British rubber plantations in Malaya. He served in the French Army in Indochina during World War II. He was active in the resistance movement in China, Burma and French Indochina but was captured by Vichy France loyalists and imprisoned. He later was designated a chevalier by the Legion d'Honeur and received several medals. His experiences went into *My Own River Kwai* (1967), a non-fiction work, and into *The Bridge Over the River Kwai* (1952), an account of Allied POWs forced to build a railway. Turning to science fiction, Boulle wrote

Planet of the Apes in 1963. It was made into an Academy Award–winning film five years later.

There were several sequel films that inspired pastiche novels by mystery writer Michael Avallone (1924–1999), saga novelist John Jakes (b. 1932), science fiction writer Jerry Pournelle (b. 1922) and others.

Original Work

Planet of the Apes (1963)

Pastiches

Scott Allie and David Fabbri, *Planet of the Apes* (2001) film novelization
Benjamin Athens, *Leo's Logbook: A Captain's Days of Captivity* (2001)
Michael Avallone, *Beneath the Planet of the Apes* (1970) based on screenplay by Paul Dehn
George Alec Effinger, *Man the Fugitive* (1974); *Journey Into Terror* (1975); *Man the Hunted Animal* (1976); *Lord of the Apes* (1976)
David Gerrold, *Battle for the Planet of the Apes* (1973) film novelization
John Jakes, *Conquest of the Planet of the Apes* (1972) based on a screenplay by Paul Dehn
Jerry Pournelle, *Escape from the Planet of the Apes* (1973)
William T. Quick, *The Fall* (2002); *Colony* (2003)

ARTHUR C. CLARKE

Science fiction

British science fiction author Arthur C. Clarke (1917–2008) lived in his later years in Sri Lanka. Best known for *2001: A Space Odyssey*, which he wrote with film director Stanley Kubrick, Clarke had been a radar instructor for the Royal Air Force during World War II. His first fiction was for *Astounding Science Fiction* in 1946. *Rendezvous with Rama* (1973) won all the major science fiction writing awards. He was named Science Fiction Writers of America Grand Master in 1986 and was knighted in 1998.

Clarke turned over 100 pages of scribbled notes to his friend Frederick Pohl, who rendered them into Clarke's last novel, *The Last Theorem* (2008). The book, technically a work for hire, came out after Clarke's death, however, making it marginally a posthumous collaboration.

Posthumous Collaboration

Frederick Pohl, *The Last Theorem* (2008)

JO CLAYTON
Shadow

Science fiction and fantasy writer Jo Clayton (1939–1998) was born in California. She taught school for more than a decade before she moved to New Orleans to join the Sisters of Mount Carmel Catholic order. She settled in Portland, Oregon, in 1983.

She never completed the last book of a trilogy before her death to cancer. Kevin Andrew Murphy finished it.

Original Drum Works

Drum Warning (1996)   *Drum Calls* (1997)

Posthumous Collaboration

Kevin Andrew Murphy, *Drum Into Silence* (2002)

BRIAN DALEY
Gamma L.A.W.

Science fiction writer Brian Daley (1947–1996) was born in New Jersey. He wrote novels in the Star Wars universe, and adapted Star Wars to radio. He and his friend James Lucerno (b. 1947) wrote Robotech, Black Hole Travel Agency and Sentinels books together under the penname Jack McKinney.

After Daley's death, Lucerno edited the Gamma L.A.W. books for publication.

Posthumous Collaboration on Gamma L.A.W. Quartet

James Lucerno, *Smoke on the Water* (1997); *Screaming Across the Sky* (1998); *The Broken Country* (1998); *To Water's End* (1999)

PHILIP K. DICK
Blade Runner

Hugo Award–winning author Philip K. Dick (1928–1982) wrote innovative science fiction including *Do Androids Dream of Electric Sheep?*, the story of a futuristic bounty hunter who pursues rebellious androids. Dick probed social and political themes, and in this book examined the ethics of robotics.

The story became the basis of a popular motion picture, *Blade Runner*, and spawned several prose sequels including two by Kevin W. Jeter (b. 1950), a science fiction and horror writer known for his cyberpunk novels and entries in the Star Wars and Star Trek fiction series. Les Martin (b. 1934) has also written Indiana Jones novels for young readers based on that motion picture series and X-Files books derived from the popular television series.

Dick's fifth wife, Tessa B. Dick, completed the manuscript for *The Owl in Daylight*, based on a letter from Dick to his editor and agent, and planned a sequel, *The Owl at Twilight*.

Original Work

Do Androids Dream of Electric Sheep? (1968)

Pastiches

Kevin W. Jeter, *Edge of Human* (1995); *Replicant Night* (1996); *Eye and Talon* (2000)
Les Martin, *Blade Runner* (1982)

Posthumous Collaborations

Tessa B. Dick, *The Owl in Daylight* (2009); *The Owl in Twilight* (Announced)

ROBERT HEINLEIN

Stranger in a Strange Land

Robert Heinlein (1907–1988), a controversial and influential science fiction writer, wrote for mainstream periodicals such as *The Saturday Evening Post*. His heroes were often non-conformists; the main character of Hugo Award–winning cult-classic *Stranger in a Strange Land* (1961), Valentine Michael Smith, for example, brings a Martian free-love perspective to Earthen culture. (A year after his death, his widow, Virginia, reassembled Heinlein's full manuscript for re-publication by Ace/Putnam's.)

Heinlein's *Podkayne of Mars* (1963), about "Poddy" Fries and her brother Clark on a visit to Earth, likewise was republished by Baen Books with its original and revised endings in 1995, along with a third by Jim Baen.

Spider Robinson used Heinlein's outline for the 2006 novel *Variable Star*. It was sufficiently popular that Robinson contracted for two more sequels. John Varley and Joe Haldeman rewrote a Heinlein young adult novel.

Posthumous Restorations

Stranger in a Strange Land (1989)   *Podkayne of Mars* (1995)

Posthumous Collaborations

Spider Robinson, *Variable Star* (2006)   John Varley, *Rolling Thunder* (2008)

FRANK HERBERT
Dune

Dune by Frank Herbert (1920–1986) was one of the all-time best-selling science fiction novels. The Tacoma, Washington, native worked for a newspaper before joining the Navy Seabees during World War II. He sold an adventure story to *Esquire* in 1945 and a science fiction story to *Startling Stories* in 1947. He wrote his first novel, *The Dragon in the Sea*, in 1955. It took him six years to research and write *Dune*, which was serialized in *Analog* in 1963 and 1965. He had a hard time finding a book publisher until Chilton, which issued technical auto repair manuals, brought out the book. It won Nebula and Hugo awards, and gradually became a gigantic seller. A 1984 motion picture helped.

Herbert's son Brian and writer Kevin J. Anderson have added two trilogies based on the Dune story and started an open-ended series. They have completed two novels based on an outline by Frank Herbert, and they have written several short stories that were printed with various of the novels.

Original Dune Works

Dune (1965)   *God Emperor of Dune* (1981)
Dune Messiah (1969)   *Heretics of Dune* (1984)
Children of Dune (1976)   *Chapterhouse: Dune* (1985)

Posthumous Collaborations

Brian Herbert and Kevin J. Anderson, *Hunters of Dune* (2006); *Sandworms of Dune* (2007)

Dune Pastiches

Brian Herbert and Kevin J. Anderson, *House Atreides* (1999) Prelude to Dune; *House Harkonnen* (2000) Prelude to Dune; *House Corrino* (2001) Prelude to Dune; *The Butlerian Jihad* (2002) Legends of Dune; *The Machine Crusade* (2003) Legends of Dune; *The Battle of Corrin* (2004) Legends of Dune; *The Road to Dune* (2005) short stories; *Paul of Dune* (2008) Heroes of Dune; *The Winds of Dune* (2009)

CRAIG HINTON
Tardis tale

Craig Hinton (1964–2006) was a British writer with a fondness for the BBC-TV science fiction series *Doctor Who*, which began in 1963 and has continued, with brief lapses, since. Hinton was active with the Doctor Who Appreciation Society and wrote several non-fiction articles and reviews. He also taught math.

He wrote novels for Virgin Publishing's Missing Adventures series that continued the Doctor Who time travel tales beyond the television episodes. *The Crystal Bucephalus* was followed by seven more books in that and other series.

Hinton proposed a new adventure featuring the Sixth Doctor (the change of actors on the television show generated new doctors with different personalities) and began a manuscript. Editors rejected the premise. Hinton died of a heart attack. His friend Chris McKeon edited and completed *Time's Champion* and it was published by Telos Publishing to raise funds for the British Heart Foundation.

Posthumous Doctor Who collaboration

Chris McKeon, *Time's Champion* (2008)

L. RON HUBBARD

Mission Earth

L. Ron Hubbard (1911–1986) was a science fiction writer and founder of the Church of Scientology. His *Dianetics* outlined the doctrine of Scientology. His *Battlefield Earth* novel ran more than 700 pages. His ten-volume, 3,992-page *Mission Earth* series was at first a massive single manuscript. Robert Vaughn Young edited the material into ten books and wrote new introductory material. The first three were done under Hubbard's close supervision. The last seven were completed after his death.

Young wrote in 2000: "I forget what volumes had been approved when Hubbard died but I wasn't much past Book 3, if even that far. It meant the rest had to be done without him but we already had the format so the rest of the intros were done without his okay.... By the time I got to Book 6 or 7, I was running out of ideas for the robo-translator and the censor. How many original, new ways could the censor say Earth doesn't exist? Or the robo-translator saying how hard he worked to translate this into English, which doesn't officially exist. A few times I had to stick something in to break it up, which was fun, like talking about the speed of light and colors."

Original Mission Earth Works

The Invaders Plan (1985)   *The Enemy Within* (1986)
Black Genesis (1986)

Posthumous Mission Earth Collaborations

Robert Vaughn Young, *An Alien Affair* (1986); *Fortune of Fear* (1986); *Death Quest* (1987); *Voyage of Vengeance* (1987); *Disaster* (1987); *Villainy Victorious* (1987); *The Doomed Planet* (1987)

Posthumous Collaboration

Kevin J. Anderson, *Ai! Pedrito* (1998) based on a Hubbard Story

C.M. Kornbluth

Science fiction

American writer Cyril M. Kornbluth (1923–1958) wrote science fiction under several names. Best known for his short fiction, he got his start with *Super Science Stories* in 1940. His "The Meeting," completed by fellow writer Frederik Pohl (b. 1919) after Kornbluth's death, won a Hugo Award in 1972. Pohl finished several others of Kornbluth's manuscripts.

Posthumous Collaborations

Frederik Pohl, *The Wonder Effect* (1962) short stories; *Our Best: The Best of Frederik Pohl and C.M. Kornbluth* (1987); *His Share of Glory: The Complete Short Science Fiction of C.M. Kornbluth* (1997)

Walter M. Miller

More science fiction

Walter M. Miller, Jr. (1923–1996), a Florida native, studied at the University of Tennessee and the University of Texas. During World War II, he was an Army Air Corps tail gunner. He published science fiction stories in the 1950s, and won a Hugo Award for "The Darfsteller" in 1955. Three other stories from *The Magazine of Fantasy and Science Fiction* were assembled into the post-apocalyptic novel *A Canticle for Leibowitz* (1959). Miller took his own life in 1996.

Science fiction and fantasy writer Terry Bisson (b. 1942) completed Miller's last manuscript.

Original Work

A Canticle for Leibowitz (1959)

Posthumous Collaboration/Sequel

Terry Bisson, *Saint Leibowitz and the Wild Horse Woman* (1997)

PHILIP NOWLAN

Buck Rogers in the 25th century

"I, Anthony Rogers, am, so far as I know, the only man alive whose normal span of eighty-one years of life has been spread over a period of 573 years," relates the hero in the opening chapter of the novelette "Armageddon 2419 A.D." "To be precise, I lived the first twenty-nine years of my life between 1898 and 1927; the other fifty-two since 2419. The gap between these two, a period of nearly five hundred years, I spent in a state of suspended animation, free from the ravages of katabolic processes, and without any apparent effect on my physical or mental facilities."

Pennsylvania-born Philip Francis Nowlan (1888–1940) worked for several newspapers and collaborated with Dick Calkins on what Ron Goulart in *The Encyclopedia of American Comics from 1897 to the Present* (1990) calls "the first serious science fiction comic strip." "Buck Rogers" began as a newspaper strip in 1929, based on Nowlan's story from *Amazing Stories* for August 1928.

Buck awoke to a vastly new world of conflict and bold new science, of rocket ships, robots, ray guns and cruel conflict. "World domination was in the hands of Mongolians and the center of world power lay in inland China, with Americans one of the few races of mankind unsubdued — and it must be admitted in fairness to the truth, not worth the trouble of subduing in the eyes of the Han Airlords who ruled North America as titular tributaries of the Most Magnificent." Rogers quickly befriended a young woman, Wilma Deering, and in this story and the sequel, "Airlords of Han" (*Amazing Stories*, March 1929), challenged the future.

Rogers appeared in a twelve-episode motion picture serial starring Buster Crabbe and Constance Moore in 1939, a feature-length film in 1979 and radio (1932–47) and television (1951–52 and 1979–81) series as well as a handful of pastiche prose works by several writers.

Original Buck Rogers Works

Armageddon 2419 A.D. (1962) collects the story of that title and "The Airlords of Han, or Armageddon 2420"

Collaborations

Dick Calkins, *Story of Buck Rogers on the Planetoid Eros* (1931) juvenile; *Buck Rogers* (1933) juvenile; *Buck Rogers in the 25th Century* (1933) juvenile; *Buck Rogers in the City Below the Sea* (1933) juvenile; *Buck Rogers in the Dangerous Mission* (1934) reprints newspaper comics; *Buck Rogers on the Moons of Saturn* (1934) juvenile; *Buck Rogers in the City of Floating Globes* (1935) juvenile; *Buck Rogers in the Depth Men of Jupiter* (1935) juvenile; *Buck Rogers and the Doom Comet* (1935) juvenile; *Buck Rogers, 25th Century, Featuring Buddy and Allura, in "Strange Adventures of the Spider Ship"* (1935) juvenile; *Buck Rogers and the Planetoid Plot* (1936) juvenile; *Buck*

Rogers Book of Cartoon Strips (1937) reprints newspaper comics; *Buck Rogers, 25th Century A.D., in the Interplanetary War with Venus* (1938) juvenile; *Buck Rogers versus the Fiend of Space* (1940) juvenile; *Buck Rogers and the Overturned World* (1941) juvenile; *Buck Rogers and the Super-Dwarf of Space* (1943) juvenile; *Buck Rogers in the 25th Century* (1964–68) four volumes of newspaper comic reprints

Dick Calkins and Rick Yager, *The Collected Works of Buck Rogers in the 25th Century* (1969) newspaper comic reprints

Pastiches

Anonymous, *Buck Rogers and the Children of Hopetown* (1979) juvenile

Britton Bloom, *Matrix Cubed: Inner Plants* (1991)

C.M. Brennan, *Buck Rogers: The Genesis Web* (1992) first book in the Invaders of Charon series

Martin Caidin, *A Life in the Future* (1995)

John Eric Holmes with Larry Niven and Jerry Pournelle, *Mordred* (1980)

Abigail Irvine, M.S. Murdock, Flint Dille and Robert Sheckley, *Arrival* (1989)

William H. Keith, *Nomads of the Sky* (1992); *Warlords of Jupiter* (1993)

Jim Lawrence and Gray Morrow, *Buck Rogers in the 25th Century* (1981) reprints newspaper comics

Richard Lupoff, *Buck Rogers in the 25th Century* (1978)

M.S. Murdock, *Rebellion 2456: Martian Wars* (1989); *Hammers of Mars: Martian Wars* (1989); *Armageddon Off Vesta: Martian Wars* (1989); *Prime Squared: Inner Planets* (1990)

Richard S. McEnroe with Larry Niven and Jerry Pournelle, *Warrior's World* (1981)

John Miller, *First Power Play: Inner Plants* (1990)

Steven Schend, *War Against the Han: High Adventures Cliffhangers* (1993)

John Silversack with Larry Niven and Jerry Pournelle, *Rogers' Rangers* (1981)

Addison E. Steele (Richard A. Lupoff), *Buck Rogers in the 25th Century* (1978); *That Man on Beta* (1979)

GEORGE ORWELL

1984

George Orwell didn't live to see how accurate his futuristic novel *Nineteen Eighty-four* would be — or how controversial.

The author's real name was Eric Arthur Blair (1903–1950). He was born in India, the grandson of a plantation owner. His father was a civil servant. His mother took her children, including Eric, to England, where he was educated. He was a King's Scholar at Eton College. He joined the Indian Imperial Police in Burma in 1924 and served for three years. He returned to England and became a journalist and educator, though he is best remembered for writing fiction, for the novel mentioned and a second, *Animal Farm*, both required reading in high schools everywhere. *Nineteen Eighty-four* is a dystopian novel about Winston Smith, a disillusioned propagandist. It introduced Big Brother, newspeak, doublethink, groupthink and other concepts. *Animal Farm* is a democratic socialist's take on Europe and Josef Stalin on the eve of World War II, as personified in various barnyard creatures. Some have suggested the strong resemblance between the novel and a short story written by Russian historian Nikolay Kostomarov (1817–1885), "The Animal Riot," which describes a revolution instigated by farm animals, published in 1917, after his death.

Orwell's estate took exception to the 2002 publication of a takeoff by New York City native John Reed (b. 1969), *Snowball's Chance*. Hungarian writer Gyorgy Dalos (b. 1943) imagines a future that begins with the death of Big Brother in his book, *1985*.

Original Animal Farm Work
Animal Farm (1945)

Animal Farm Pastiches
Scott Bradfield, *Animal Planet* (1995)   John Reed, *Snowball's Chance* (2003)
Jane Doe, *Anarchist Farm* (1997)

Original 1984 Work
Nineteen Eighty-four (1949)

1984 Pastiche
Gyorgy Dalos, *1985* (1983)

H. BEAM PIPER

Fuzzy

H. Beam Piper (1904–1964) wrote space opera (melodramatic) and thoughtful science fiction novels and short stories. He first appeared in print with a short story in *Astounding Science Fiction* in 1947. The Fuzzy tales are about an odd specimen found on the planet Zarathustra.

The two pastiches were commissioned by Ace Books, which acquired Piper's rights after he committed suicide.

Selected Original Works
Little Fuzzy (1962)   *Fuzzies and Other People* (1984)
Fuzzy Sapiens (1964) aka *The Other
   Human Race*

Pastiches
Ardath Mayhar, *Golden Dream: A Fuzzy Odyssey* (1982)
William Tuning, *Fuzzy Bones* (1981)

ALEX RAYMOND

Outer space

Alex Raymond was an illustrator credited with writing the 1936 Grosset & Dunlap novel. Flash Gordon was born in a newspaper comic strip Jan. 7, 1934, and flourished there for decades. Gordon is a space adventurer often found in the company of Dr. Hans Zarkov and his love interest, Dale Arden. His nemesis, Ming the Merciless, is lord of the planet Mongo.

The space opera plots were lovingly rendered by Raymond (1909–1956), who also drew adventures of Rip Kirby, Jumgle Jim and Secret Agent X-9. Flash Gordon was made into a movie serial with Buster Crabbe and Jean Rogers. Only the earliest comic strip reprints are listed.

Several writers added to the Gordon opus.

Original Prose Novels

Flash Gordon in the Caverns of Mongo (1936)
Flash Gordon in the Ice Kingdom of Mongo (1967)
Flash Gordon in the Water World of Mongo (1971)

Pastiches

Carson Bingham (Bruce Cassidy), *The Witch Queen of Mongo* (1974); *The War of the Cybernauts* (1978)

David Hagberg, *Massacre in the 22nd Century* (1980); *War of the Citadels* (1980); *Crisis on Citadel II* (1980); *Forces from the Federation* (1981); *Citadels Under Attack* (1981); *Citadels on Earth* (1981)

Con Steffanson (Ron Goulart), *The Space Circus* (1969); *The Lion Men of Mongo* (1974); *The Plague of Sound* (1974)

Con Steffanson (Ron Goulart) and Bruce Bingham-Cassidy (Carson Bingham), *The Time Trap of Ming XIII* (1977)

ERIC FRANK RUSSELL

Space diplomacy

Hugo Award–winning British science fiction writer Eric Frank Russell's 1953 novella, "Design for Great-Day," is about an intergalactic troubleshooter, James Lawson, who tries to prevent a war between two alien races. Russell (1905–1978) wrote primarily for *Astounding Science Fiction* and *Weird Tales* under his own name and as Duncan H. Munro.

Alan Dean Foster (b. 1946), writer of science fiction and fantasy including Star Trek novelizations, Pip and Flinx novels and the Commonwealth series, expanded the story to novel length.

Posthumous Collaboration
Alan Dean Foster, *Design for Great-Day* (1995)

E.E. "DOC" SMITH
Lensmen

Edward Elmer Smith (1890–1965) had a Ph.D., thus he was familiarly known as "Doc" Smith. The specialist in doughnut and pastry "food" engineering crafted Skylark and Lensmen space operas for *Amazing Stories* and *Astounding Stories* beginning in the 1930s. Born in Wisconsin, he grew up in Idaho, where he attended the University of Idaho. He worked for the National Bureau of Standards in Washington, and earned his doctorate in chemical engineering from George Washington University. He worked for F.W. Stock & Sons and Dawn Doughnut Co., both food purveyors in Michigan. He wrote his first science fiction, *The Skylark of Space*, with his friend Lee Hawkins Garby.

Smith agreed William B. Ellern could write additional Lensmen episodes. After Smith's death, David Kyle completed three more authorized sequels in the Second-Stage Lensman Trilogy.

Original Lensmen Works

Triplanetary (1948)

First Lensman (1950)

Galactic Patrol (1950)

Gray Lensman (1951)

Second Stage Lensman (1963)

Children of the Lens (1954)

The Vortex Blaster (1960) aka *Masters of the Vortex* (1968)

Lensmen Pastiches

William B. Ellern, *New Lensmen* (1976); *Triplanetary Agent* (1978)

David Kyle, *The Dragon Lensmen* (1980); *Lensman from Rigel* (1981); *Z-Lensmen* (1983)

A.E. VAN VOGT
Slan

Alfred Elton van Vogt (1912–2000) was born in a Russian Mennonite settlement in Manitoba, Canada. His early writing adapted a system developed by John W. Gallishaw in *The Only Two Ways to Write a Short Story*. Van Vogt at first wrote confessionals, then switched to fiction and was active in science fiction's golden age in the pulp magazines. *Slan*, serialized in *Astounding Science Fiction* in 1940, told the story of a young superman on the run from humans.

Van Vogt left a partial manuscript and outline for a sequel, *Slan Hunter*. His widow, Lydia van Vogt, and Kevin J. Anderson completed it.

Original Work
Slan (1940)

Posthumous Collaboration
Lydia van Vogt and Kevin J. Anderson, *Slan Hunter* (2007)

JULES VERNE
Fogg

Jules Verne (1828–1905) explored water, air and space in his adventure novels *Journey to the Center of the Earth* (1864), *Twenty Thousand Leagues Under the Sea* (1870) and *Around the World in Eighty Days* (1873). Born in western France, Verne studied law but preferred to write, both for stage and page.

Among pastiche writers, K.J. Anderson has also written Star Wars Jedi Academy books and a Dune prequel.

Original Around the World Work
Around the World in Eighty Days (1872)

Around the World in Eighty Days Pastiche
Philip José Farmer, *Other Lot of Phileas Fogg* (1973)

Original Twenty Thousand Leagues Work
Twenty Thousand Leagues Under the Sea (1870)

Twenty Thousand Leagues Under the Sea Pastiches
K.J. Anderson, *Captain Nemo: The Fantastic History of a Dark Genius* (2007)
Xavier Joseph Carbajal, *Captain Nemo* (1996)
Robert Hillyer, *The Death of Captain Nemo* (1949)
Thomas F. Monteleone, *The Secret Sea* (1979)

Selected Other Original Work
The Mysterious Island (1874)

Pastiches
Mike Ashley and Eric Brown, editors, *The Mammoth Book of New Jules Verne Adventures* (2005)

Posthumous Collaboration
Michel Verne, *L'Eternal Adam* (1910)

KURT VONNEGUT
Kilgore Trout

Kurt Vonnegut, Jr. (1922–2007), had a dark sense of humor that is evident in his science fiction works, including *Slaughterhouse-Five* (1969), *Cat's Cradle* (1963) and *The Sirens of Titan* (1959). *God Bless You, Mr. Rosewater* (1965) was the first to include the character Kilgore Trout, a prolific but underappreciated science fiction writer somewhat based on science fiction writer Theodore Sturgeon.

Philip José Farmer pretended to be Kilgore Trout for a story that appeared in *The Magazine of Fantasy and Science Fiction* in December 1974 and January 1975. Many assumed Vonnegut wrote the tale. (Vonnegut didn't give permission for a sequel.) The book was eventually reprinted with Farmer's name.

Original Works in Which Kilgore Trout Appears

God Bless You, Mr. Rosewater (1965)	*Jailbird* (1979)
Slaughterhouse-Five (1969)	*Hocus Pocus* (1990)
Breakfast of Champions (1973)	*Timequake* (1997)

Pastiche
Philip José Farmer writing as Kilgore Trout, *Venus on the Half-Shell* (1975)

STANLEY G. WEINBAUM
Ganymede

Kentucky native Stanley G. Weinbaum (1902–1935) died of lung cancer within a year-and-a-half of the appearance of his first science fiction story, "A Martian Odyssey," in *Wonder Stories* for July 1934. He first studied chemical engineering and then English at the University of Wisconsin, but did not graduate.

Roger Sherman Hoar writing as Ralph Milne Farley completed a Weinbaum story, "Revolution of 1950," for *Amazing Stories'* October and November 1938 issues, but it hasn't been collected. Weinbaum's sister Helen finished his tenth interplanetary short story, "Tidal Moon," set on the planet Ganymede, originally printed in *Thrilling Wonder Stories* for December 1938.

Posthumous Collaboration
Helen Weinbaum, *Interplantary Odysseys* (2006) includes "Tidal Moon"

H.G. WELLS

Future and past

English writer Herbert George Wells (1866–1946) launched several streams of science fiction with his tales of time travel, moonwalking and science gone awry. Born in Kent, England, of low circumstances, Wells was a teacher before he turned his hand to writing. Many of his classic novels were filmed.

 Edison's Conquest of Mars was originally serialized in the *New York Journal* on the eve of Wells' publication of *The War of the Worlds* in 1898 and was an obvious pastiche, if not plagiarism, at the time.

Original Invisible Man Work
The Invisible Man (1897)

Invisible Man Pastiche
Dave Ulanski, *Legacy of the Invisible Man* (2003)

Original Island of Dr. Moreau Work
The Island of Dr. Moreau (1896)

Island of Dr. Moreau Pastiches
Brian Aldiss, *An Island Called Moreau* (1981) aka *Moreau's Other Island* (2002)
Ann Halam, *Dr. Franklin's Island* (2003)
Joseph Silva, *The Island of Dr. Moreau* (1977) screenplay adaptation

Original Time Machine Work
The Time Machine (1895)

Time Machine Pastiches
Karl Alexander, *Time After Time* (1979)
Stephen Baxter, *The Time Ships* (1995)
Richard Cowper, *The Hertford Manuscript* (1976)
Egon Friedell, *The Return of the Time Machine* (1946)
K.W. Jeter, *Morlock Night* (1979)
David J. Lake, *The Man Who Loved Morlocks* (1981)
Burt Libe, *Beyond the Time Machine* (2005); *Tangles in Time* (2005)
George Pal and Joe Morhaim, *Time Machine II* (1981)
Christopher Priest, *The Space Machine* (1976)
Ronald Wright, *A Scientific Romance* (1998)

Original War of the Worlds Work
The War of the Worlds (1898)

War of the Worlds Pastiches
Kevin J. Anderson, editor, *War of the Worlds: Global Dispatches* (1997)
Jeanne M. Dillard, *Resurrection* (1988)

Jean-Pierre Guillett, *La Cage de Londres* (2003) aka *The Cage of London*
Gabriel Mesta, *The Martian War* (2005)
Garrett P. Serviss, *Edison's Conquest of Mars* (1947)
George H. Smith, *The Second War of the Worlds* (1976)
Manly Wellman and Wade Wellman, *Sherlock Holmes' War of the Worlds* (1975)

JOHN WYNDHAM
Triffids

John Wyndham (1903–1969) was the penname John Wyndham Parkes Lucas Beynon Harris used on his post-apocalyptic tales, the best known of which is *Day of the Triffids*. Born in Warwickshire, England, the author and his brother, Vivian Beynon Harris, had disrupted and unhappy childhoods. Wyndham began to write in 1925, but only in the 1940s, when he worked for the government and served with the Royal Signal Corps, did he decide to write in a different style, and created the Triffids. Triffids are roaming, carnivorous plants that get out of hand. The main character, Bill Masen, is a Triffids expert desperate to find a way to inhibit the vegetations. The story became a 1962 motion picture.

Simon Clark told his story through the eyes of David Masen, son of the main character in Wyndham's book.

Original Work

Day of the Triffids (1951) aka *Revolt of the Triffids* (1951)

Pastiches

Simon Clark, *The Night of the Triffids* (2001)

ROGER ZELAZNY
Donnerjack

Roger Zelazny (1937–1995) won several Hugo and Nebula awards for his science fiction and fantasy. Born in Euclid, Ohio, he belonged to a creative writing club in high school. He studied Elizabethan and Jacobean drama at Columbia University and worked for the Social Security Administration after graduation. He became a fulltime writer in 1969 and soon established himself in science fiction's new wave. His Amber novels relate the adventures of Prince Corwin or his son, Merle.

Zelazny left two incomplete manuscripts that his companion, writer Jane Lindskold, finished. John Gregory Betancourt (b. 1963), who has written several

Star Trek novels, wrote four books in the prequel Roger Zelazny Dawn of Amber series authorized by the estate. The author's ...*And Call Me Conrad* was truncated for serialization in *The Magazine of Fantasy and Science Fiction* in 1965. That work was co-winner of the Hugo Award for Best Novel that year. Some, but not all, excisions for the magazine version were restored in the Ace Books edition. The title became *This Immortal*. A full version appeared in 2004.

Original Work

This Immortal (1966)

Posthumous Restoration

...And Call Me Conrad (2000)

Original Prince Corwin of Amber Works

Nine Princes in Amber (1970)   *The Hand of Oberon* (1976)
The Guns of Avalon (1972)   *The Courts of Chaos* (1978)
Sign of the Unicorn (1975)

Original Merle Works

Trumps of Doom (1985)   *Knight of Shadows* (1989)
Blood of Amber (1986)   *Prince of Chaos* (1991)
Sign of Chaos (1987)

Posthumous Collaborations, Roger Zelazny's Dawn of Amber Series

John Gregory Betancourt, *Nine Princes of Chaos* (2002); *Chaos and Amber* (2003); *To Rule in Amber* (2004); *Shadows of Amber* (2005)

Posthumous Collaborations

Jane Lindskold, *Donnerjack* (1997); *Lord Demon* (1999)

Westerns

Max Brand's entry in this section is a long one, as a slew of reissues of his pulp magazines stories for the first time (after initial periodical publication) appear *in the way he originally wrote them*. Editorial changes may be minor or they may be significant, and to the author's mind, unnecessary. Most writers aren't so fortunate as to warrant restorations; most have had to live with the results of editorial decisions. Other writers listed here have had the more usual pastiche experiences, from Budd Arthur picking up after his father to Loren Zane Grey (or, probably, a ghost writer) writing for his dad. Australian wordsmith Leonard F. Mears, one would think, turned out enough Larry and Stretch yarns to last a lifetime, but longtime fans wanted to pay one last tribute and that's how we've come to have two more Hopalong Cassidy novels on the bookshelf—sheer admiration (though the prose takes after the B-movie scripts more than Clarence E. Mulford's original lines). The case of Jonas Ward is interesting in that William R. Cox arguably turned in better renderings of the good-natured cowboy hero Buchanan than his originator, William Ard.

BURT ARTHUR

Canavan

Johnny "Red" Canavan, ex–Texas Ranger, faces ruthless saloon owner Nick Arveny, in the novel *Action at Truxton* (1965). Arveny's men have killed the sheriff and taken over the town. The novel is a later entry in the series started by Herber Shappiro (1899–1975) under the penname Burt Arthur. Shappiro changed his name legally to Herbert Arthur, Burt for short.

Shappiro was born in Texas and served in the military during World War I. He worked in New York and Chicago. He wrote Western pulp yarns and novels issued under his own name and various pseudonyms besides Burt Arthur. He also wrote screenplays and television scripts for *Cheyenne* and *Lawman*.

Herbert Arthur, Jr. (b. 1928), aka Budd Arthur, picked up the Canavan series after his father died.

Original Works

The Texan (1946)
Return of the Texan (1956)
Gunsmoke in Nevada (1957)

Walk Tall, Ride Tall (1963) written with Budd Arthur
Action at Truxton (1965) written with Budd Arthur

Posthumous Collaboration

Budd Arthur, *Canavan's Trail* (1980)

B.M. BOWER

Flying Chip

Bertha Muzzy Sinclair (1871–1940) was a rare female author of Western tales. Born in Minnesota, she and her family migrated to Montana. She taught in Grand Falls. She married Clayton J. Bower. She began to write stories about ranch life in 1900, under the name B.M. Bower. Because she used her initials, not all of her readers were aware of her gender. (A second marriage was to writer Bertrand W. Sinclair.)

Chip of the Flying U relates how hands Chip Bennett, Weary, Shorty and others cope with the arrival of ranch owner James G. Whitmore's sister, Della, who is a doctor. Several Chip stories appeared in periodicals and anthologies. Johnny Mack Brown played the hero in a 1949 film. Bower's friend Charles Russell illustrated some of her books.

Oscar J. Friend (1897–1963), a writer of pulp Westerns, science fiction, horror and crime stories, and later a writer of screenplays for Universal Studio and Walt Disney Productions, ghostwrote two Flying U novels after Bower's death, likely authorized by her estate.

Original Chip of the Flying U Works

Chip of the Flying U (1906)
The Happy Family (1910)
The Flying U Ranch (1914)
The Flying U's Last Stand (1915)

Dark Horse: A Story of the Flying U (1931)
The Flying U Strikes (1934)
Trouble Rides the Wind (1935)

Pastiches

Oscar Friend, *Border Vengeance* (1951); *Outlaw Moon* (1952)

MAX BRAND
Cowboys

Frederick Faust (1892–1944)— there's a biographical entry for him under his best-known penname, Max Brand, in the Classics (20th Century) section — has more than 300 Western novels and stories to his credit. His first sagebrush tale was published in *All-Story Weekly* in 1918. His first cowboy novel was *The Untamed* (1919).

During his lifetime, Dodd, Mead and other publishers condensed many of the pulp stories for book reprints. Post–1944 books, therefore, are indicated as *posthumous collaborations* here. Post–1992 books are *posthumous restorations*. When Golden West Literary Agency assumed responsibility for the author's writing output in 1992, it as often as possible provided Faust's original manuscripts to publishers for new editions. This list is for Westerns originally published as by Max Brand unless otherwise indicated, and in books published as by Max Brand.

William F. Nolan wrote a Max Brand pastiche, the eighth entry in the Powell's Army series, *Rio Renegade*. Nolan dedicated the book to Faust, wrote it in a Max Brand style and included Barry Silver as a villain. Other characters (the names are Faust pennames) include Sheriff Peter Henry Baxter and Col. Maxwell Schiller Brand.

Posthumous Collaborations

Silvertip's Search (1945) condensed "Silver's Search" by Max Brand, *Western Story Magazine*, Sept. 23, 1933

The Stolen Stallion (1945) condensed, *Western Story Magazine*, March 11, 1933

The Border Bandit (1947) includes title story, *Western Story Magazine*, Sept. 25, 1026; "The Border Bandit's Indian Brother," Oct. 2, 1926; and "The Border Bandit's Prize," Oct. 9, 1926

The False Rider (1947) condensed, *Western Story Magazine*, July 1, 1933

The Rescue of Broken Arrow (1948) condensed serial "The Horizon of Danger" by Peter Henry Morland, *Western Story Magazine*, Dec. 21, 1929, to Jan. 25, 1930

Flaming Irons (1948) condensed "The City in the Sky," *Western Story Magazine*, June 11, 1927 to July 16, 1927

Hired Guns (1948) condensed, *Western Story Magazine*, March 10, 1023, to April 2, 1923

Gunman's Legacy (1949) aka *Sixgun Legacy* (1950) condensed "Rancher's Legacy" by Peter Henry Morland, *Western Story Magazine*, Feb. 20, 1932, to March 30, 1926

The Bandit of the Black Hills (1949) by George Owen Baxter, *Western Story Magazine*, April 28, 1923, to June 2, 1923

Seven Trails (1949) condensed, "Seven Trails to Romance" by George Owen Baxter, *Western Story Magazine*, Sept. 1, 1923, to Oct. 6, 1923

Smuggler's Trail (1950) aka *Smoking Gun Trail* (1951) condensed "Scourge of the Rio Grande," *Argosy*, Oct. 20, 1934, to Nov. 24, 1934

Single Jack (1950) aka *Tenderfoot* (1967) condensed "Comanche," *Far West Illustrated*, December 1926 to April 1927

Sawdust and Sixguns (1950) condensed, *Far West Illustrated*, August 1927 to January 1928

The Galloping Broncos (1950) condensed from "Two Bronchos" by George Owen Baxter, *Western Story Magazine*, Nov. 9, 1929, to Dec. 14, 1929

The Hair-Trigger Kid (1951) condensed, "Duck Hawk's Master" by George Owen Baxter, *Western Story Magazine*, April 25, 1931, to March 31, 1931

Tragedy Trail (1951) condensed from serial by George Owen Baxter, *Western Story Magazine*, Feb. 25, 1928, to March 31, 1928

Border Guns (1952) condensed "The Brass Man" by George Owen Baxter, *Western Story Magazine*, June 23, 1928, to July 28, 1928

Strange Courage (1952) condensed "Daring Duval" by George Owen Baxter, *Western Story Magazine*, July 19, 1930, to Aug. 23, 1930

Outlaw Valley (1953) condensed, *Far West Illustrated*, April 1928 to August 1928

Smiling Desperado (1953) condensed "The Love of Danger," *Western Story Magazine*, Aug. 2, 1924, to Sept. 6, 1924

The Tenderfoot (1953) aka *Outlaw's Gold* (1976) condensed "Saddle and Sentiment," *Western Story Magazine*, April 19, 1924, to May 24, 1924

Outlaw's Code (1954) aka *Outlaw Code* (1968) condensed "The Lightning Runner" by John Frederick, *Western Story Magazine*, Jan. 9, 1932, to Feb. 13, 1932

The Gambler (1954) condensed *Western Story Magazine*, June 7, 1924, to July 12, 1924

The Invisible Outlaw (1954) condensed *Western Story Magazine*, Nov. 5, 1932, to Nov. 26, 1932

Speedy (1955) condensed, "Tramp Magic," *Western Story Magazine*, Nov. 2, 1931, to Dec. 26, 1931

Outlaw Breed (1955) condensed, "A Son of Danger," *Western Story Magazine*, April 17, 1926, to May 22, 1926

The Big Trail (1956) condensed, "The Trail to Manhood," *Western Story Magazine*, April 13, 1929, to May 18, 1929

Trail Partners (1956) condensed "All for One" by George Owen Baxter, *Western Story Magazine*, Oct. 1, 1932, to Oct. 22, 1932

Lucky Larribee (1957) condensed from serial by George Owen Baxter, *Western Story Magazine*, April 2, 1932, to May 7, 1932

Blood on the Trail (1957) condensed, "The Wolf and the Man" by George Owen Baxter, *Western Story Magazine*, March 4, 1933, to April 22, 1933

The White Cheyenne (1960) condensed from serial by Peter Henry Morland, *Western Story Magazine*, Dec. 12, 1925, to Jan. 20, 1926

The Long Chase (1960) condensed "Old Carver Ranch" by John Frederick, *Western Story Magazine*, Oct. 24, 1931, to Nov. 28, 1931

Tamer of the Wild (1962) condensed from serial by Peter Henry Morland, *Western Story Magazine*, Oct. 24, 1931, to Nov. 28, 1931

Mighty Lobo (1962) condensed from serial by George Owen Baxter, *Western Story Magazine*, July 23, 1932, to Aug. 13, 1932

The Stranger (1963) condensed *Western Story Magazine*, Jan. 12, 1929, to Feb. 9, 1929

Golden Lightning (1964) condensed *Western Story Magazine*, Aug. 22, 1931, to Sept. 26, 1931

The Gentle Gunman (1964) condensed from "Argentine" by George Owen Baxter, *Western Story Magazine*, May 31, 1924, to July 5, 1924

Torture Trail (1965) condensed "Torturous Trek," *Western Story Magazine*, Aug. 27, 1932, to Sept. 17, 1932

The Guns of Dorking Hollow (1965) condensed, "The Silver Struck," *Western Story Magazine*, Aug. 13, 1927, to Oct. 17, 1927

Ride the Wild Trail (1966) condensed "Dogs of the Captain," *Western Story Magazine*, Jan. 2, 1932, to Feb. 6, 1932

Larramee's Ranch (1966) condensed from serial by George Owen Baxter, *Western Story Magazine*, Sept. 13, 1924, to Oct. 18, 1924

Max Brand's Best Stories (1967) edited and rewritten by Robert Easton, includes "The King," *This Week*, Nov. 21, 1948; "Wine on the Desert," *This Week*, June 7, 1936; "Our Daily Bread," from *Wine on the Desert* (1940); "The Wolf Pack and the Kill," excerpt from "Harrigan," *Railroad Man's Magazine*, Nov. 2, 1918, to Nov. 30, 1918; "Internes Can't Take Money," *Cosmopolitan*, March 1936; "The Claws of the Tigress," excerpt by George Challis, *Argosy*, July 13, 1935; "The Silent Witness," *Black Mask Magazine*, March 1938; "The Kinsale" by Frederick Faust, *Saturday Evening Post*, June 27, 1936; "A Life for a Life" excerpt from "Calling Dr. Kildare," Argosy, March 25, 1939, to April 8, 1939; "The Luck of Pringle," Cosmopolitan, December 1937; "A Special Occasion" by Frederick Faust, *Harper's Magazine*, February 1934; and "The Sun Stood Still," *American Magazine*, December 1934

Rippon Rides Double (1968) condensed *Western Story Magazine*, Oct. 18, 1930, to Nov. 22, 1930

The Stingaree (1968) condensed, *Western Story Magazine*, June 7, 1930, to July 12, 1930

Thunder Moon (1969) condensed from George Owen Baxter serial, *Far West Illustrated*, April 1927 to August 1927

Trouble Kid (1970) condensed compilation of "Chip and the Cactus Man, *Western Story Magazine*, Jan. 10, 1931, and "Chip Traps a Sheriff," *Western Story Magazine*, Jan. 31, 1931

Ambush at Torture Canyon (1971) condensed compilation, "Spot Lester," *Western Story Magazine*, Oct. 17, 1931, "Nine Lives," *Western Story Magazine*, Oct. 31, 1931, and "Torture Canyon," *Western Story Magazine*, Nov. 14, 1931

Cheyenne Gold (1972) condensed "The Sacred Valley, *Argosy*, Aug. 10, 1935, to Sept. 14, 1935

Drifter's Vengeance (1973) condensed "Speedy — Deputy," *Western Story Magazine*, Feb. 13, 1932, "Seven-Day Lawman," *Western Story Magazine*, Feb. 27, 1932, and "Speedy's Mare," *Western Story Magazine*, March 12, 1932

The Granduca (1973), condensed, *Detective Fiction Weekly*, July 25, 1936, to Aug. 29, 1936

The Phantom Spy (1973) condensed "War for Sale," *Argosy*, April 23, 1937, to May 15, 1937

Dead Man's Treasure (1974) condensed "Perique" by Dennis Lawton, *Argosy*, Dec. 14, 1935, to Jan. 18, 1936

The Outlaw of Buffalo Flat (1974) condensed "The Mask of Ching Wo," *Railroad Man's Magazine*, August 1930 to February 1931

The Last Showdown (1975) condensed compilation of "The Duster, *Western Story Magazine*, Nov. 2, 1929, "Twisted Bars," *Western Story Magazine*, Nov. 16, 1929, and "Duster's Return," *Western Story Magazine*, Nov. 30, 1929

Rawhide Justice (1975) condensed compilation "Reata" by George Owen Baxter, *West-*

ern Story Magazine, Nov. 1, 1933, "Reata's Danger Trail" by Baxter, *Western Story Magazine*, Nov. 25, 1933, and "Reata's Desert Ride" by Baxter, *Western Story Magazine*, Dec. 9, 1933

Shotgun Law (1976), condensed compilation of "Hawks and Eagles" by George Owen Baxter, *Western Story Magazine*, Dec. 5, 1931, "Black Snake and Gun" by Baxter, *Western Story Magazine*, Dec. 19, 1931, and "Black Snake Joe" by Baxter, *Western Story Magazine*, Jan. 2, 1932

Bells of San Filipo (1977) condensed from serial by George Owen Baxter, *Western Story Magazine*, Nov. 6, 1926, to Dec. 11, 1926

Rider of the High Hills (1977) condensed compilation "Reata and the Hidden Gold" by George Owen Baxter, *Western Story Magazine*, Dec. 23, 1933, "Stolen Gold" by Baxter, *Western Story Magazine*, Jan. 6, 1934, and "Reata and the Overland Kid" by Baxter, *Western Story Magazine*, Jan. 20, 1934

The Reward (1977) condensed serial "Ronicky Doone's Reward," *Western Story Magazine*, July 15, 1922, to Aug. 19, 1922

Storm on the Range (1978) condensed and rewritten compilation "Treasure Well" by George Owen Baxter, *Western Story Magazine*, June 27, 1931, "Outlaw's Conscience" by Baxter, *Western Story Magazine*, July 11, 1931, and "Clean Courage" by Baxter, *Western Story Magazine*, July 25, 1931

Galloping Danger (1979) condensed and rewritten, *Western Story Magazine*, July 14, 1923, to Aug. 18, 1923

The Man from the Wilderness (1980) condensed and rewritten "Mountain Made" by George Owen Baxter, *Western Story Magazine*, Dec. 13, 1924, to Jan. 17, 1925

Max Brand's Western Stories (1981) edited by William F. Nolan, "Wine on the Desert," "Virginia Creeper," "Macdonald's Dream (rewritten "Sunset Wins"), "Partners," rewritten "Dust Across the Range" and "The Bells of San Carlos"

Wild Freedom (1981) condensed and rewritten "Wild Freedom" by George Owen Baxter, *Western Story Magazine*, Nov. 11, 1923, to Dec. 16, 1922

Thunder Moon's Challenge (1982) condensed and rewritten compilation "Red Wind and Thunder Moon by George Owen Baxter, *Western Story Magazine*, Aug. 27, 1927, "Thunder Moon — Pale Face" by Baxter, *Western Story Magazine*, Sept. 17, 1927, and "Thunder Moon — Squawman" by Baxter, *Western Story Magazine*, Sept. 24, 1927, to Oct. 22, 1927

Thunder Moon Strikes (1982) condensed and rewritten compilation of "Thunder Moon — Squawman" by George Owen Baxter, *Western Story Magazine*, Sept. 17, 1927, and "Thunder Moon Goes White" by Baxter, *Western Story Magazine*, Nov. 2, 1928

Lawless Land (1983) condensed and rewritten "Speedy's Crystal Game," *Western Story Magazine*, April 2, 1932, "Red Rock's Secret," *Western Story Magazine*, April 16, 1932, and "Speedy's Bargain," *Western Story Magazine*, May 14, 1932

Rogue Mustang (1984) condensed and rewritten compilation of "Paradise Al" by David Manning, *Western Story Magazine*, June 4, 1932, and "Paradise Al's Confession" by Manning, *Western Story Magazine*, July 16, 1932

Trouble in Timberline (1984) condensed and rewritten compilation of "The Quest," *West*, May 1933, "The Trail of the Eagle," *West*, July 1933, and "Outlaw Buster," *Complete Western Book Magazine*, August 1937

Max Brand's Best Western Stories Volume II (1985) edited by William F. Nolan, "The

Fear of Morgan the Fearless," rewritten "Dark Rosaleen," rewritten "Cayenne Char-lie, "The Golden Day," "Outcast" (rewritten "Outcast Breed")

Mountain Guns (1985) condensed and rewritten "Trouble's Messenger" by George Owen Baxter, *Western Story Magazine*, Sept. 6, 1930, to Oct. 11, 1930

The Gentle Desperado (1985) condensed and rewritten compilation of "The Terrible Tenderfoot" by George Owen Baxter, *Western Story Magazine*, July 2, 1927, "The Gentle Desperado" by Baxter, *Western Story Magazine*, July 16, 1927, and "Tiger, Tiger" by Baxter, *Western Story Magazine*, July 30, 1927

One Man Posse (1987) condensed and rewritten compilation "One Man Posse," *Mavericks*, September 1934, "Sleeper Pays a Debt," *Mavericks*, October 1934, "Satan's Gun Rider," *Mavericks*, November 1934, and "Sun and Sand" by Hugh Owen, *Western Story Magazine*, Feb. 16, 1935

Max Brand's Best Western Stories Volume III (1987) edited by William F. Nolan, rewrit-ten "Reata's Peril Trek," "Crazy Rhythm," "Dust Storm," "A Lucky Dog," "The Third Bullet," "Half a Partner" and "The Sun Stood Still"

The Nighthawk Trail (1987) condensed and rewritten compilation "Nighthawk Trail," *Western Story Magazine*, July 9, 1932, "Outlaws from Afar," *Western Story Maga-zine*, Aug. 20, 1932, and "Speedy's Desert Dance," *Western Story Magazine*, Jan. 18, 1933

Battle's End/The Three Crosses (1990) both edited stories

Chip Champions a Lady/Forgotten Treasure (1990) both edited stories

Coward of the Clan (1991) condensed and rewritten compilation of "Coward of the Clan" by Peter Henry Morland, *Western Story Magazine*, May 19, 1928, and "The Man from the Sky" by Morland, *Western Story Magazine*, June 2, 1928

Fugitives' Fire (1991), condensed and rewritten compilation of "Prairie Pawn" by Peter Henry Morland, *Western Story Magazine*, June 16, 1928, and "Fugitives' Fire" by Morland, *Western Story Magazine*, June 20, 1928

The Red Bandanna/Carcajou's Trail (1991) both edited stories

Outlaw Crew/The Best Bandit (1991) both edited stories

Range Jester/Black Thunder (1991) both edited stories

Posthumous Restorations

Valley of Jewels (1993) from *Western Story Magazine,* Aug. 2, 1926

The Cross Brand (1993) from *Short Stories,* Aug. 25, 1922

Dust Across the Range (1994) from *American Magazine*, November 1937 to February 1938

The Desert Pilot (1994) from *Western Story Magazine,* June 4, 1927

The Collected Stories of Max Brand (1994) edited by Robert and Jane Easton, "John Ovington Returns," *All-Story Weekly*, June 8, 1918, "Above the Law," *All-Story Weekly*, Aug. 31, 1918; "The Wedding Guest" by Frederick Faust, *Harper's Maga-zine*, January 1934; "A Special Occasion" by Faust, *Harper's Magazine*, February 1934; "Outcast Breed, *Star Western*, October 1934; "The Sun Stood Still," *Ameri-can Magazine*, December 1934; "Secret Agent Number One" ("The Strange Villa"), *Detective Fiction Weekly*, Jan. 5, 1935; "Claws of the Tigress" by George Challis, *Argosy*, July 13, 1935; "Internes Can't Take Money," *Cosmopolitan*, March 1936; "Fixed," *Colliers*, June 13, 1936, "Wine on the Desert" ("Wine in the Desert"), *This Week*, June 7, 1936; "Virginia Creeper," *Elks Magazine*, August 1937; "Pringle's

Luck," *Cosmopolitan*, December 1937; "The Silent Witness," *Black Mask Magazine*, March 1938; "Miniature," *Good Housekeeping*, September 1939; "Our Daily Bread," "Wine on the Desert" (1940), "Honor Bright," *Cosmopolitan*, November 1948; and "The King," *This Week*, Nov. 21, 1948

The Sacking of El Dorado (1994) includes "Bad-Eye: His Life and Letters, *All-Story Weekly*, Oct. 19, 1918; "The Ghost Rides Tonight!" (previously titled "The Ghost") *All-Story Weekly*, May 3, 1919; "A Sagebrush Cinderella," *All-Story Weekly*, July 10, 1920; "The Consuming Fire, *Argosy All-Story*, Nov. 27, 1920; "The Fear of Morgan the Fearless," *All-Story Weekly*, June 28, 1919; "The Sacking of El Dorado," *All-Story Weekly*, Oct. 11, 1919, restored

The Return of Free Range Lanning (1995) includes "The Black Muldoon by Peter Dawson, *Western Story Magazine*, Sept. 30, 1922; "Gunman's Bluff," *Star Western*, April 1924; "The Return of Free Range Lanning" (previously titled "When Iron Turns to Gold") by George Owen Baxter, *Western Story Magazine*, July 30, 1921, restored

Sixteen in Nome (1995) includes "Sixteen in Nome," *Western Story Magazine*, May 3, 1930; and "Battle's End," *Western Story Magazine*, May 10, 1930

Murder Me (1995) originally serialized in *Detective Fiction Weekly*, Sept. 21, 1935, to Nov. 2, 1935

Outlaws All: A Western Trio (1996) includes "Alex the Great: A Prologue to Sixteen in Nome" (previous title "Two Masters"), *Western Story Magazine*, April 5, 1930; "Riding into Peril" by John Frederick, *Western Story Magazine*, Nov. 19, 1921; and "Outlaws All: A Bull Hunter Story" (previously titled "Outlaws All"), *Western Story Magazine*, Sept. 10, 1921, restored

The Lightning Warrior (1996) includes "The Lightning Warrior" (originally titled "White Wolf") by George Owen Baxter, *Western Story Magazine*, Feb. 13, 1932, to March 19, 1932, restored

The Wolf Strain: A Western Trio (1996) includes "Bared Fangs" by George Owen Baxter, *Western Story Magazine*, May 10, 1924; "Gallows Gamble," *Star Western*, July 1934; and "The Wolf Strain: A Bull Hunter Story," *Western Story Magazine*, Sept. 24, 1921, restored

The One-Way Trail: A Western Trio (1996) includes "Forgotten Treasure" by George Owen Baxter, *Western Story Magazine*, Nov. 19, 1927; "The Man Who Forgot" (previously titled "The Man Who Forgot Christmas") by John Frederick, *Western Story Magazine*, Dec. 25, 1920; and "The One-Way Trail" by Baxter, *Western Story Magazine*, Feb. 4, 1922, restored

The Ghost Wagon and Other Stories (1996) edited by Jon Tuska, includes "The Ghost Wagon" (originally titled "The Cure of Silver Canon") by John Frederick, *Western Story Magazine*, Jan. 15, 1921; "Rodeo Ranch," *Western Story Magazine*, Sept. 1, 1923; "Slip Liddell" (previously "Senor Coyote"), *Argosy*, June 18, 1938 to June 25, 1938; and "A Matter of Honor" (originally "Jerico's 'Garrison Finish'"), *Western Story Magazine*, May 21, 1921

The Black Rider and Other Stories (1996) edited by Jon Tuska, includes "The Black Rider" by George Owen Baxter, *Western Story Magazine*, Jan. 3, 1925; "The Dream of Macdonald" (previously "'Sunset' Wins") by Baxter, *Western Story Magazine*, April 7, 1923; "Partners" by Frederick Faust, *American Magazine*, January 1938; and "The Power of Prayer" by John Frederick, *Western Story Magazine*, Dec. 23, 1922, restored

Bells of San Carlos and Other Stories (1996) edited by Jon Tuska includes, "Cayenne Charlie" by George Owen Baxter, *Western Story Magazine*, Feb. 22, 1930; "The Bells of San Carlos," *Argosy*, April 30, 1938; "Between One and Three" (previously "Mountain Madness") by George Owen Baxter, *Western Story Magazine*, Aug. 26, 1922; and "The Gift," *Western Story Magazine*, Dec. 24, 1921, restored

The Legend of Thunder Moon (1996) includes "The Legend of Thunder Moon" (originally titled "Thunder Moon") by George Owen Baxter, *Far West Illustrated*, April 1927 to August 1927, restored

Red Wind and Thunder Moon (1996) includes "Red Wind and Thunder Moon" by George Owen Baxter, *Western Story Magazine*, Aug. 27, 1927; and "Thunder Moon — Pale Face" by Baxter, *Western Story Magazine*, Sept. 17, 1927

Thunder Moon and the Sky People (1996) includes "Thunder Moon and the Sky People" (previously "Thunder Moon — Squawman") by George Owen Baxter, *Western Story Magazine*, Sept. 24, 1927 to Oct. 22, 1927, restored

Farewell, Thunder Moon (1996) includes "Farewell, Thunder Moon" (originally published as "Thunder Moon Goes White") by George Owen Baxter, *Western Story Magazine*, Nov. 3, 1928, restored

King Charlie (1997) includes "King Charlie and His Long Riders" by John Frederick, *Western Story Magazine*, May 6, 1922; "King Charlie — One Year Later" by Frederick, *Western Story Magazine*, May 27, 1922; "King Charlie's Hosts" by Frederick, *Western Story Magazine*, June 24, 1922; and "The Bill for Banditry" by Frederick, *Western Story Magazine*, Aug. 5, 1922, restored

Tales of the Wild West (1997) edited by William F. Nolan, includes "The Laughter of Slim Malone," *All-Story Weekly*, June 14, 1919; "The Champion," All-American Fiction, November 1937; "Master and Man," *Western Story Magazine*, Jan. 5, 1924; "Lake Tyndal," *All-American Fiction*, December 1937; "Two-Handed Man" by John Frederick, *Western Story Magazine*, Dec. 3, 1932; "Viva! Viva!," *Argosy*, Jan. 3, 1927; and "The Taming of Red Thunder," *Esquire*, September 1942, restored

The Stone That Shines (1997) includes "The Stone That Shines" (previously titled "Trail of the Stone-That-Shines") by George Henry Morland, *Western Story Magazine*, May 29, 1926 to July 3, 1926, restored

Men Beyond the Law: A Western Trio (1997) includes "Werewolf," *Western Story Magazine*, Dec. 18, 1926, "The Finding of Jeremy" (previously titled "His Back Against the Wall") by John Frederick, *Western Story Magazine*, March 12, 1921; "The Trail Up Old Arrowhead: A Bull Hunter Story (previously "Bull Hunter's Romance"), *Western Story Magazine*, Oct. 22, 1921, restored

Beyond the Outposts (1997) by Peter Henry Morland, *Western Story Magazine*, Jan. 24, 1925 to Feb. 28, 1925

The Fugitive's Mission: A Western Trio (1997) includes "The Fugitive's Mission," *Western Story Magazine*, Jan. 14, 1922; "The Strange Ride of Perry Woodstock (previously titled "Death Rides Behind"), *Dime Western*, March 1933; and "Reata: A Reata Story (previously "Reata") by George Owen Baxter, *Western Story Magazine*, Nov. 11, 1933, restored

Luck (1997) by John Frederick, *Argosy*, Aug. 9, 1919 to Sept. 13, 1919, restored

Crossroads (1997) by John Frederick, *Argosy*, Jan. 31, 1920 to March 6, 1920

Slumber Mountain: A Western Trio (1997) includes "The Outlaw Crew, *Western Story Magazine*, Feb. 20, 1932; "The Coward" (previously called "Under His Shirt"),

Western Story Magazine, Jan. 27, 1923; and "Slumber Mountain" by John Frederick, *Western Story Magazine*, July 8, 1922, restored

The Desert Pilot/Valley of Jewels (1997) from *Western Story Magazine*, June 4, 1927, and Aug. 21, 1926, respectively, restored

Two Sixes: A Western Trio (1997) includes "Winking Lights" by John Frederick, *Western Story Magazine*, Jan. 6, 1923; "The Best Bandit" by David Manning, *Western Story Magazine*, March 5, 1932; and "Two Sixes" by George Owen Baxter, *Western Story Magazine*, March 17, 1923, restored

The Sacking of El Dorado (1997) includes "Bad-Eye: His Life and Letters," *All-Story Weekly*, Oct. 19, 1918; "The Ghost Rides Tonight!" (originally published as "The Ghost"), *All-Story Weekly*, May 3, 1919; "A Sagebrush Cinderella," *All-Story Weekly*, July 10, 1920; "The Consuming Fire," *Argosy All-Story*, Nov. 27, 1920; "The Man Who Forgot" (previously "The Man Who Forgot Christmas"), *Western Story Magazine*, Dec. 25, 1920; "The Fear of Morgan the Fearless," *All-Story Weekly*, June 28, 1919; and "The Sacking of el Dorado," *All-Story Weekly*, Oct. 11, 1919, restored

The Abandoned Outlaw: A Western Trio (1997) includes "The Gold King Turns His Back" by John Frederick, *Western Story Magazine*, April 28, 1923; "The Three Crosses" by George Owen Baxter, *Western Story Magazine*, Jan. 23, 1932; and "The Abandoned Outlaw" by John Frederick, *Western Story Magazine*, March 26, 1923, restored

Safety McTee: A Western Trio (1998) includes "Little Sammy Green," *Western Story Magazine*, June 30, 1923; "Black Sheep" by George Owen Baxter, *Western Story Magazine*, July 28, 1923; and "Safety McTee," *Western Story Magazine*, Aug. 25, 1923, restored

In the Hills of Monterey (1998) by John Frederick, *Western Story Magazine*, Oct. 4, 1924 to Nov. 8, 1924, restored

The Rock of Kiever: A Western Trio (1998) includes "Range Jester," *Western Story Magazine*, May 28, 1932; "Slow Bill" by John Frederick, *Western Story Magazine*, Oct. 13, 1923; and "The Rock of Kiever," *Western Story Magazine*, Jan. 19, 1924, restored

Soft Metal: A Western Trio (1998) includes "The Red Bandanna" by George Owen Baxter, *Western Story Magazine*, Feb. 4, 1933; "His Name His Fortune," *Western Story Magazine*, June 9, 1923; and "Soft Metal" by Baxter, *Western Story Magazine*, Oct. 20, 1923, restored

Seven Faces (1998) from *Western Story Magazine*, Oct. 17, 1936 to Nov. 21, 1936, restored

The Lost Valley: A Western Trio (1998) includes "The Stage to Yellow Creek" (originally published as "Guardian Guns"), *Dime Western*, August 1933; "The Whisperer: A Reata Story" (previously "Reata's Danger Trail") by George Owen Baxter, *Western Story Magazine*, Nov. 25, 1933; and "The Lost Valley" (previously "The Emerald Trail") by John Frederick, *Western Story Magazine*, Feb. 25, 1922, restored

The One-Way Trail: A Western Trio (1998) includes "Forgotten Treasure" by George Owen Baxter, *Western Story Magazine*, Nov. 19, 1927; "Outcast Breed," *Star Western*, October 1934; and "The One-Way Trail" by Baxter, *Western Story Magazine*, Feb. 4, 1922, restored

Chinook (1998) by John Frederick, *Western Story Magazine*, July 13, 1929 to Aug. 10, 1929, restored

The Quest of Lee Garrison (1998) restored version of "Galloping Danger," *Western Story Magazine*, July 14, 1923 to Aug. 18, 1923

The Gauntlet: A Western Trio (1998) includes "The Blackness of McTee" (originally called "Black Thunder"), *Dime Western*, July 1933; "King of Rats: A Reata Story (previously "Reata's Desert Ride") by George Owen Baxter, *Western Story Magazine*, Dec. 9, 1933; and "The Gauntlet" by Baxter, *Western Story Magazine*, Nov. 12, 1921, restored

The Oath of Office: A Western Trio (1998) includes "The Fall and Rise of Newbold" (originally called "Chip and the Cactus Man"), *Western Story Magazine*, Jan. 10, 1931; "The Ivory Portrait" (previously "Chip Champions a Lady"), *Western Story Magazine*, Jan. 24, 1931; and "The Oath of Office" (previously "Chip Traps a Sheriff"), Western Story Magazine, Jan. 31, 1931, restored

The City in the Sky (1998) from *Western Story Magazine*, June 11, 1927 to July 16, 1927, restored

More Tales of the Wild West (1999) edited by William F. Nolan, includes "A Lucky Dog" by John Frederick, *Western Story Magazine*, Oct. 22, 1927; "Inverness" (originally called "Sleeper Turns Horse-Thief"), *Mavericks*, December 1934; "Crazy Rhythm," *Argosy*, March 2, 1935, "Death in Alkali Flat" (originally "Sun and Sand") by Hugh Owen, *Western Story Magazine*, Feb. 16, 1935; "Blondy" (previously "Bulldog"), *Collier's*, Feb. 23, 1924; and "A First Blooding," as restored by Joe R. Lansdale in *The New Frontier* (1989)

The Survival of Juan Oro (1999) is restored "The Survivor," *Western Story Magazine*, May 23, 1925 to June 27, 1925

Stolen Gold: A Western Trio (1999) includes "Sheriff Larrabee's Prisoner" by Martin Dexter, *Western Story Magazine*, Dec. 3, 1921; "A Shower of Silver" by John Frederick," *Western Story Magazine*, June 18, 1921; and "Stolen Gold: A Reata Story" (previously published as "Reata and the Hidden Gold") by George Owen Baxter, *Western Story Magazine*, Dec. 23, 1933, restored

The Geraldi Trail (1999) restores serial from *Western Story Magazine*, June 11, 1932 to July 2, 1932

Timber Line: A Western Trio (1999) includes "Above the Law," *All-Story Weekly*, Aug. 31, 1918; "One Man Posse," *Mavericks*, September 1934; and "Timber Line," *Western Story Magazine*, Nov. 24, 1923, restored

The Gold Trail: A Western Trio (1999) includes "Without a Penny in the World" by John Frederick, *Western Story Magazine*, Oct. 21, 1922; "Phil the Fiddler" by George Owen Baxter, *Western Story Magazine*, Dec. 30, 1922; and "The Gold Trail: A Reata Story" (originally published as "Stolen Gold") by Baxter, *Western Story Magazine*, Jan. 6, 1934, restored

Gunman's Goal: A James Geraldi Story (1999) serial originally published as "Three on a Trail," *Western Story Magazine*, May 12, 1928 to June 16, 1928, restored

The Overland Kid: A Western Trio (2000) includes "The Cabin in the Pines" by John Frederick, *Western Story Magazine*, Dec. 9, 1922; "Joe White's Brand" by George Owen Baxter, *Western Story Magazine*, Oct. 14, 1922; and "The Overland Kid" (previously "Reata and the Overland Kid"), *Western Story Magazine*, Jan. 20, 1934, restored

The Masterman (2000), serialized in *Argosy*, March 18, 1933, restored

The Outlaw Redeemer: A Western Duo (2000) includes "The Last Irving" (originally "Not the Fastest Horse") by John Frederick, *Western Story Magazine*, Nov. 7, 1925; and "The Outlaw Redeemer" (originally "The Man He Couldn't Get"), *Western Story Magazine*, Feb. 27, 1926, restored

The Peril Trek: A Western Trio (2000) includes "The Man Who Followed" by George Owen Baxter, *Western Story Magazine*, Dec. 10, 1921; "The Boy Who Found Christmas" by Baxter, *Western Story Magazine*, Dec. 22, 1923; and "The Peril Trek: A Reata Story" (originally "Reata's Peril Trek") by Baxter, *Western Story Magazine*, March 17, 1934, restored

The Bright Face of Danger: A James Geraldi Trio (2000) includes "The Golden Hours" (previously called "Gunman's Goal"), *Western Story Magazine*, July 14, 1928; "The Bright Face of Danger," *Western Story Magazine*, Aug. 18, 1928; and "Through Steel and Stone," *Western Story Magazine*, Sept. 19, 1928, restored

Don Diablo: A Western Trio (2001) includes "Mountain Raiders" by Peter Henry Morland, *Western Story Magazine*, April 23, 1932; "Rawhide Bound" by Morland, *Western Story Magazine*, May 21, 1932; and "The Trail of Death" (previously published as "Greaser Trail") by Morland, *Western Story Magazine*, April 9, 1932, restored

The Welding Quirt: A Western Trio (2001) includes "Lazy Tom Hooks Up with Skinny," *Western Story Magazine*, March 22, 1924; "Sleeper Pays a Debt," *Mavericks*, October 1934; and "The Welding Quirt," *Western Story Magazine*, April 12, 1924, restored

The Tyrant (2001) serial by George Challis, *Western Story Magazine*, Jan. 9, 1926 to Feb. 13, 1926, restored

The House of Gold: A James Geraldi Trio (2001) includes "The House of Gold," *Western Story Magazine*, Oct. 13, 1928; "The Return of Geraldi," *Western Story Magazine*, June 29, 1929; and "While Bullets Sang," *Western Story Magazine*, Aug. 17, 1929, restored

The Lone Rider (2002) serial previously published as "Fate's Honeymoon," *All-Story Weekly*, July 14, 1917 to Aug. 11, 1917

Smoking Guns: A James Geraldi Duo (2002) includes "Geraldi in the Haunted Hills," *Western Story Magazine*, Aug. 31, 1929; and "Smoking Guns," *Western Story Magazine*, Oct. 29, 1932, restored

Crusader (2002) includes "The Boy in the Wilderness" by George Owen Baxter, *Western Story Magazine*, July 19, 1924; "The Brute" by Baxter, *Western Story Magazine*, July 26, 1924; and "The Race" by Baxter, *Western Story Magazine*, Aug. 9, 1924, restored

Jokers Extra Wild: A Western Trio (2002) includes "Speedy — Deputy," *Western Story Magazine*, Feb. 13, 1932; "Satan's Gun Rider," *Mavericks*, November 1934; and "Jokers Extra Wild," *Short Stories*, Oct. 10, 1926, restored

Blue Kingdom (2003) restored serial "Blue Kingdom" by George Owen Baxter, originally published as "Strength of the Hills," *Western Story Magazine*, May 25, 1929 to June 29, 1929, restored

Flaming Fortune: A Western Trio (2003) includes "The Canon Coward," *Western Story Magazine*, Jan. 15, 1927; "A Wolf Among Dogs" by John Frederick, *Western Story Magazine*, July 5, 1924; and "Seven-Day Lawman," *Western Story Magazine*, Feb. 27, 1932, restored

The Runaways (2003) restores serial by George Owen Baxter, *Western Story Magazine*, Oct. 24, 1925 to Nov. 28, 1925

Peter Blue: A Western Trio (2003) includes "Speedy's Mare," *Western Story Magazine*, March 12, 1932; "His Fight for a Pardon" by George Owen Baxter, *Western Story Magazine*, July 27, 1925; and "Peter Blue, One-Gun Man," *Far West Illustrated*, June 1927, restored

The Golden Cat (2004) serial, *American Weekly*, July 13, 1930 to Oct. 16, 1930, restored

The Range Finder: A Western Trio (2004) includes "The Whisperer," *Argosy All-Story Weekly*, Aug. 21, 1920; "Flaming Fortune" by George Owen Baxter, *Western Story Magazine*, Feb. 19, 1927; and "The Range Finder" by Peter Henry Morland, *Western Story Magazine*, Nov. 14, 1925, restored

Mountain Storms (2004) restores serial "Wild Freedom" by George Owen Baxter, *Western Story Magazine*, Nov. 11, 1922 to Dec. 16, 1922

Hawks and Eagles: A Western Trio (2004) includes "Hawks and Eagles" by George Owen Baxter, *Western Story Magazine*, Dec. 5, 1931; "Black Snake and Gun" by Baxter, *Western Story Magazine*, Dec. 19, 1931; and "Black-Snake Joe" by Baxter, *Western Story Magazine*, Jan. 2, 1932, restored

Trouble's Messenger (2005) restored serial by George Owen Baxter, *Western Story Magazine*, Sept. 6, 1930 to Oct. 11, 1930

Bad Man's Gulch: A Western Trio (2005) includes "The Adopted Son," *All-Story Weekly*, Oct. 27, 1917; "Billy Angel, Trouble Lover" by George Owen Baxter, *Western Story Magazine*, Nov. 22, 1924; and "Bad Man's Gulch" by Baxter, *Western Story Magazine*, July 17, 1926, restored

Twisted Bars: A Western Trio (2005) includes "The Duster," *Western Story Magazine*, Nov. 2, 1929; "Twisted Bars," *Western Story Magazine*, Nov. 16, 1929; and "The Duster Returns," *Western Story Magazine*, Nov. 30, 1929, restored

The Crystal Game: A Western Trio (2005) aka *The Fugitive* (2007) includes "The Fugitive," *Western Story Magazine*, July 24, 1926; "Uncle Chris Turns North," *Western Story Magazine*, Dec. 8, 1923; and "Speedy's Crystal Game," *Western Story Magazine*, April 2, 1932, restored

Dogs of the Captain (2006) restored serial, *Western Story Magazine*, Jan. 2, 1932 to Feb. 6, 1932

Red Rock's Secret: A Western Trio (2006) includes "Cuttle's Hired Man," *Western Story Magazine*, March 1, 1924; "The Girl They Left Behind" by John Frederick, *Western Story Magazine*, June 21, 1924; and "Red Rock's Secret," *Western Story Magazine*, April 16, 1932, restored

Wheel of Fortune: A Western Trio (2006) includes "Chick's Fall," *Western Story Magazine*, Nov. 15, 1924; "Wheel of Fortune" (originally called "Fortune's Christmas"), *Western Story Magazine*, Dec. 20, 1924; and "Speedy's Bargain," *Western Story Magazine*, May 24, 1932, restored

Treasure Well: A Western Trio (2006) includes "Treasure Well" by George Owen Baxter, *Western Story Magazine*, June 27, 1931; "Outlaw's Conscience" by Baxter, *Western Story Magazine*, July 11, 1931; and "Clean Courage" by Baxter, *Western Story Magazine*, July 25, 1931, restored

Acres of Unrest (2007) restored serial, *Western Story Magazine*, June 12, 1926 to July 17, 1926

Rifle Pass: A Western Trio (2007) includes "The Nighthawk Trail," *Western Story Magazine*, July 9, 1932; "The Vamp's Bandit" by George Owen Baxter, *Western Story Magazine*, March 20, 1926; and "Rifle Pass," *Argosy*, Feb. 9, 1935, restored

Melody and Cordoba: A Western Trio (2007) includes "The Black Signal," *Western Story Magazine*, March 21, 1925, "Lew and Slim," *Western Story Magazine*, April 4, 1925, and "In the River Bottom's Grip," *Western Story Magazine*, April 11, 1925, restored

Outlaws from Afar: A Western Trio (2007) includes "The Law Dodger at Windy Creek,"

Western Story Magazine, Sept. 24, 1932; "The Trail of the Eagle," *West*, July 1933; and "Outlaws from Afar," *Western Story Magazine*, Aug. 20, 1932, restored
Rancher's Legacy (2008)
Nine Lives (2008)
The Good Badman: A Western Trio (2008)
The Love of Danger: A Western Trio (2008)
Rancher's Legacy (2008)
Silver Trail: A Western Story (2009)

Pastiche

William F. Nolan writing as Terence Duncan, *Rio Renegades* (1989)

RALPH COMPTON

Hit the Trail

Ralph Compton (1934–1998) was born in Alabama during the Great Depression. After a stint in the military, he later lived in Tennessee or traveled the highways as a songwriter or ad salesman. He became a publisher, record producer and songwriter before he began to write popular Western novels. His first was *The Goodnight Trail* in 1992.

Several writers wrote Compton pastiches under contract to Signet Books. There is also a series of "Ralph Compton Novels" written by several authors who presumably had the same Western sensibility as Compton.

Original Danny Duggin Work

Death Rides a Chestnut Mare (1999)

Danny Duggin Pastiches

Ralph W. Cotton, *The Shadow of a Noose* (2000); *Riders of Judgment* (2001); *Death Along the Cimarron* (2003)

Original Sundown Rider Series

North to Bitterroot (1996)   *Whiskey River* (1999)
Across the Rio Colorado (1997)   *Skeleton Lode* (1999)
The Winchester Run (1997)   *Demon's Pass* (2000)
Devil's Canyon (1998)

Sundown Rider Pastiches

Robert Vaughan, *Runaway Stage* (2002)
David Robbins, *Do or Die* (2003); *Nowhere, TX* (2004); *Bucked Out in Dodge* (2004); *West of Pecos* (2005)

Original Trail Drive Series

The Goodnight Trail (1992)
The Western Trail (1992)
The Chisholm Trail (1993)
The Bandera Trail (1993)
The California Trail (1993)
The Shawnee Trail (1994)
The Virginia City Trail (1994)

Dodge City Trail (1995)
The Oregon Trail (1995)
The Santa Fe Trail (1996)
The Old Spanish Trail (1998)
The Deadwood Trail (1999)
The Green River Trail (1999)

Trail Drive Pastiches

Robert Vaughan, *Ralph Compton's The Dakota Trail* (2001); *Ralph Compton's Alamosa Trail* (2002); *Ralph Compton's Bozeman Trail* (2002)

Dusty Richards, *Ralph Compton's The Abilene Trail* (2003); *Ralph Compton's Trail to Fort Smith* (2004); *Ralph Compton's The Ogallala Trail* (2005); *Ralph Compton's Trail to Cottonwood* (2007)

Jory Sherman, *Ralph Compton's The Ellsworth Trail* (2005)

Joseph A. West, *Ralph Compton's Tenderfoot Trail* (2007)

HAL DUNNING

White Wolf

Here's a case in which a writer died, the magazine publishing his stories was anxious for more and it hired other writers to produce pastiches. Few of those pastiches, if any, were ever bound between book covers. The pastiche title listed below is unexamined.

Detroit native Dunning (1880–1931), born Harold Wolcott Dunning, created the fictional character Jim-Twin Allen, alias White Wolfe, in 1927. An outlaw with a big grin, White Wolf often helps his lawman sheriff achieve justice. According to researcher Steve Holland, Dunning sold autos in New York state then abruptly went to France and became a writer. Dunning and his bride, Cicely D'Olier Wyatt, eventually came back to the United States and Dunning served in the military during World War I. The family later lived in Maine and Fairfield, Conn. Dunning contributed stories particularly to Street & Smith's *Complete Stories* magazine and *Wild West Weekly*. These stories were collected in several books.

At least three pulp writers wrote pastiches: Missourian Frederick C. Davis (1902–1977) author of "Operator 5" and other pulp stories; Washington-born Walker A. "Two-Gun" Tompkins (1849–1989), journalist and a prolific pulp writer of Rio Kid and other cowboys; and Paul S. Powers (1905–1971), a native Kansan and author of numerous Sonny Tabor and Kid Wolf tales under the name Ward M. Stevens.

Original Works

The Outlaw Sheriff (1928)
White Wolf's Law (1928)
White Wolf's Pack (1929)

The Wolf Deputy (1930)
White Wolf's Feud (1930)
White Wolf's Outlaw Legion (1933)

Pastiches as by Hal Dunning

Frederick C. Davis or Walker A. Tompkins or Paul S. Powers or all three, *The White Wolf Western Omnibus* (1951)

BRIAN WYNNE GARFIELD

Jeremy Six

Here's an inadvertent pastiche. Brian Garfield (b. 1939), crime novelist (*Death Wish*), Western writer and movie scripter, shaped a handful of oaters that Ace published in the 1960s under the Brian Wynne byline. The hero, Jeremy Six, was marshal of the town of Spanish Flat. The first book is more about the town; Six didn't get going strong until *Mr. Sixgun*.

Garfield didn't want to continue the series. Ace, believing it owned the series and the penname, commissioned Dudley Dean McGaughey (1906–1986) to write another book, *Gunslick Territory*. When it appeared in print, Garfield asserted his rights and asked that it not be reprinted.

Original Jeremy Six Series as by Brian Wynne

Range Justice (1960) aka *Justice at*
    Spanish Flat (1960)
Mr. Sixgun (1964)
The Night It Rained Bullets (1965)
The Bravos (1966)

The Proud Riders (1967)
A Badge for a Badman (1967)
Brand of the Gun (1968)
Gundown (1969)
Big Country, Big Men (1969)

Pastiche published as by Brian Wynne

Dudley Dean McGaughey, *Gunslick Territory* (1974)

ZANE GREY

Lassiter

The dentist from Ohio, Zane Grey (1872–1939), gave up his vocation after his Western novels began to sell. In a lengthy writing career, Grey's "themes were thoroughly American," said Jean Karr in *Zane Grey: Man of the West* (1949), "dealing with the rigors of frontier life and the heroic characters it produced; Indian massacres and the American Revolution; the vastness and promise of the West; the appeal of outdoor life; hunting and fishing; riding and roping; school days and baseball, the national sport."

In one of Grey's best-known novels, *Riders of the Purple Sage*, Jane Withersteen works to save her recently inherited Utah ranch, falls in love with hired cowhand Bern Venters, but is betrothed against her will to Elder Tull. Tull and the Mormon hierarchy terrorize Jane; the only one they fear is the dark, mysterious gunman, Lassiter. The book was criticized for what some took to be anti–Mormon elements, but biographer Frank Gruber in *Zane Grey* (1969) said the book nevertheless "was a magnificent epic story of a land, a people, a way of life. Read as entertainment alone, it is a powerful story against an awesome background, never depicted before and never again so well."

Lassiter appeared in a sequel by Grey and was revived in a series, purportedly by Grey's son Loren Zane Grey (1915–2007), telling stories of the gunman's hard living in the years before the events recorded in *Riders of the Purple Sage*.

Zane Grey's Western Magazine was a digest-size fiction magazine that began in 1946 and was revived in 1969. In its second run, its editors commissioned novelettes (as sequels to Grey works) from writers such as Bill Pronzini (b. 1943 in California) and Jeffrey Wallman (b. 1941 in Washington), publishing them under the name of Grey's real son, Romer Zane Grey (1910–1976). The stories were later packaged for paperback issue.

The pastiched heroes included Rich "Arizona" Ames, who has a reputation as a tough gunman, but nurses a secret hurt which can only be healed by a determined woman; Buckley Duane, driven to becoming an outlaw, pardoned through the efforts of Capt. Jim MacNelly of the Texas Rangers; Nevada Jim Lacy, wanted by both sides of the law; and Yaqui, a stoic Indian warrior.

There's a curious tagalong to the canon. In 1968 Ohio-born Willis Todhunter Ballard (1903–1980) wrote three books featuring a hard-nosed cowboy named Lassiter. Others also wrote entries and the series eventually numbered 31 titles, all issued in paperback. The books, observed David Pringle in *Imaginary People*, seemed "to have no connection with Zane Grey's work." Then the publisher, Leisure Books, which periodically re-issued the *Zane Grey's Western Magazine* pastiches, cover-blurbed two of the later Lassiter books in 1991 as "Zane Grey's Lassiter"—revisionist packaging without peer. (They are not included in this listing.)

Original Arizona Ames Work

Arizona Ames (1932)

Arizona Ames Pastiches

Bill Pronzini and Jeffrey Wallman writing as Romer Zane Grey, *Zane Grey's Arizona Ames: Gun Trouble on the Tonto Basin* (1980) three stories; *Zane Grey's Arizona Ames: King of the Outlaw Horde* (1980) three stories

Original Border Legion Work

The Border Legion (1916)

Border Legion Pastiche

Romer Zane Grey, *Zane Grey's Yaqui: Siege at Forlorn River* (1984) includes "The Heritage of the Legion"

Original Buck Duane Works

Lone Star Ranger (1915)   *The Last of the Duanes* (1983)

Buck Duane Pastiches

Romer Zane Grey, *Buck Duane: The Rider of Distant Trails* (1980) four stories; *Buck Duane: King of the Range* (1980); *Three Deaths for Buck Duane* (1986)

Original Burn Hudnall Work

The Thundering Herd (1925)

Burn Hudnall Pastiche

Romer Zane Grey, *Zane Grey's Yaqui: Siege at Forlorn River* (1984) includes "Riders of the Kiowa Trail"

Original Nevada Jim Lacy Work

Nevada (1928)

Nevada Jim Lacy Pastiche

Romer Zane Grey, *Nevada Jim Lacy: Beyond the Mogollon Rim* (1980) includes "Beyond the Mogollon Rim"

Original Lassiter Works

Riders of the Purple Sage (1912)   *The Rainbow Trail* (1915)

Lassiter Pastiches

Loren Zane Grey (first seven by Dudley Dean McGaughey), *Lassiter* (1985); *Ambush for Lassiter* (1985); *Lassiter's Gold* (1986); *Lassiter Tough* (1986); *The Lassiter Luck* (1986); *A Grave for Lassiter* (1987); *Mountain Manhunt* (1987); *Lassiter's Ride* (1988); *Lassiter on the Texas Trail* (1988); *Lassiter and the Great Horse Race* (1989); *Lassiter and the Golden Dragon* (1989); *Lassiter's Showdown* (1990); *Lassiter in the Comanche Stronghold* (1990)
Jack Slade, *Zane Grey's Brother Gun/Redgate Gold* (1991)

Original Laramie Nelson Work

Raiders of the Spanish Peaks (1938)

Laramie Nelson Pastiches
Romer Zane Grey, *Laramie Nelson: The Other Side of the Canyon* (1980) four stories; *Laramie Nelson: The Lawless Land* (1984) three stories

Original Chris Oliver Work
The Light of Western Stars (1914)

Chris Oliver Pastiche
Romer Zane Grey, *Nevada Jim Lacy: Beyond the Mogollon Rim* (1980) includes "The Call of the War Drums"

Original Al Slingerland Work
The U.P. Trail (1918) aka *The Roaring U.P. Trail* (1918)

Al Slingerland Pastiche
Romer Zane Grey, *Nevada Jim Lacy: Beyond the Mogollon Rim* (1980) includes "The Track of Blood"

Original Yaqui Work
Desert Gold (1913)
Zane Grey's Yaqui and Other Great Indian Stories (1976) edited by Loren Grey

Yaqui Pastiche
Romer Zane Grey, *Zane Grey's Yaqui: Siege at Forlorn River* (1984) includes "Siege at Forlorn River"

MARSHALL GROVER
Larry and Stretch

Larry Valentine and Stretch Emerson were featured in a long-running Australian series of short paperback Westerns. Typical plots are to be found in *Lone Star Firebrands* (the heroes become involved when Ash Hollow is transformed into a boom town), *Wheels Out of Jericho* (the duo rides shotgun for a hard-luck freight outfit) and *Feud at Mendoza* (The Ortega-Marvin feud in New Mexico won't permit Larry and Stretch to mind their own business for long). For its American version, Bantam changed the characters' names to Larry Vance and Streak Everett and the author became Marshall McCoy. Belmont's brief reprint series in the U.S. used the original character and author names.

The books were penned by Leonard F. Meares (1921–1993), part of his amazing 746-book output. Born in Sydney, He read Zane Grey, Clarence E. Mulford and William Colt Macdonald books at an early age, and also watched oater movies at the cinema. His first Western, *Trouble Town*, came into print in 1955. He introduced Larry and Stretch with his tenth book for Cleveland. He created other series, such as Big Jim Rand, and used other pennames over the years. He often produced two manuscripts a month, until his publisher, Horwitz, curtailed its English-language program in 1991. Meares died two years later.

In this listing, the first two books that team Larry and Stretch and Big Jim Rand are the prolific author's 400th and 500th published works, respectively, while the last two are his 600th and 700th titles. There were 417 Larry and Stretch tales in all.

American author Link Hullar and English author David Whitehead, longtime Meares fans, secured the permission of Meares' widow, Vida, to expand a short story into *Tin Star Trio*, and to turn story fragments into a second sequel. Meares had begun the works and, for copyright reasons with Horwitz, had been obliged to give the characters different names, Zack Holley and Curly Ryker.

Original Larry and Stretch Works (not all dates available)

Drift	*The Emerson Challenge*
Colorado Pursuit	*Texans Die Hard*
Born to Drift	*Texans Never Quit*
Cold Trail to Kirby	*Tall, Tough, and Texan*
Hell-Raisers	*Trail Dust*
Rawhide River Ambush (1958)	*Start Shooting, Texans*
Texans Are Trouble (1958)	*Texans Walk Proud*
Half-Cold Trail (1959)	*Texas Ghost Gun*
Ride Out, Texans (1959)	*Tall Riders*
Seventeen Guns (1959)	*North of Texas*
Texas Drifters (1959)	*We're from Texas*
Ride Reckless	*The Wayward Kind*
Greenback Fever	*Wild Trail to Denver*
Fast, Free and Texan	*Noon Train to Breslow*
The Feuders	*The Eyes of Texas*
The Four O'Clock Fracus	*Decoys from Hell*
Here Lies Andy McGraw	*Day of the Posse*
Seven for Banner Pass	*Now ... Texans*
Doom Trail	*Texan in My Sights*
First Kill	*Saludos, Texans*
Devil's Dinero	*Back in Texas*
Lone Star Valiant	*Defiant Texans*
Lone Star Hellions	*Bend of the River*
Lone Star Reckoning	*Bravados from Texas*
Lone Star Fury	*Close in for a Showdown*
Lone Star Reckless	*Follow the Texans*
Lone Star Vengeance	*Rogue Calibre*
Lone Star Firebrands	*Too Many Texans*
Lone Star Bodyguards	*Find Kell Wade*
Lone Star Lucky	*Ride Slow, Ride Wary*

Nobody Wants Reilly
This Range Is Mine
Rob a Bank in Kansas
Arizona Wild-Cat
Ride Out Shooting
Ride Wild to Glory
Border Storm
Draw, Aim, and Fire
Never Prod a Texan
The Fast Right Hand
Don't Count the Odds
Face the Gun
Decoys from Texas
A Bullet Is Faster
Gun Glory for Texans (1967)
Lone Star Rowdy (1967)
Many a Wild Mile (1967)
Trouble Trail Yonder (1967)
Two Tall Strangers (1967)
Boom Town Bravados (1967)
Legend of Bell Canyon (1967)
The Texans Came Shooting (1967)
Tombstone for a Fugitive (1967)
Too Tough for San Remo (1968)
Amarillo Ridge (1968)
The Bar G Bunch (1968)
High Spade (1968)
Kin to the Wild Wind (1968)
Wyoming Thunder (1968)
Big Day at Blue Creek (1968)
Wheels Out of Jericho (1968)
Calaboose Canyon (1969)
The Garrard Heritage (1969)
The Glory Wagon (1969)
Hot Sky Over Paraiso (1969)
Hour of Jeopardy (1969)
Turn and Fire (1969)
Three Trails to Modoc (1969)
Two for the Gallows (1969)
Feud at Mendoza (1969)
Trouble Is Our Shadow (1970)
All the Tall Men (1970)
The Big Dinero (1970)
Crisis in Babylon (1970)
The Freebooters (1970)
Gun Fury at Sun-Up (1970)
Guns Across the Rockies (1970)

Gunsmoke Challenge (1970)
Our Kind of Law (1970)
Saturday Night in Candle Rock (1970)
Texas Rampage (1970)
Born to Ramble (1970)
The Noose-Cheaters (1970)
They Won't Forget Sweeney (1971)
Montana Runaway (1972)
The Hellion Breed (1972)
Rampage at Rico Bend (1972)
Gunsmoke in Utopia (1973)
Hangrope for Beaumont (1973)
The Last Ambush (1973)
McCracken's Marauders (1973)
Mexican Jackpot (1973)
War Dance at Red Canyon (1973)
Cold-Eye Cordell (1973)
The Desperate Hours (1973)
Guns for the Ladies (1973)
Madigan's Day (1973)
Red Bandana (1973)
Who Killed Rice? (1973)
Dakota Red (1974)
Get Goin,' Greeley! (1974)
High Country Shootout (1974)
The Odds Against O'Shea (1974)
Doom Trail (1974)
Hijacker's Noon (1974)
Man on Pulpit Rock (1974)
The Predators (1974)
Saddletramp Justice (1974)
Tin Stars for Tall Texans (1974)
Damn Outlaws (1975)
They'll Hang Billy for Sure (1974)
Too Many Enemies (1974)
Delaney and the Drifters (1975)
Dollar Trail to Ramirez (1975)
The Last Challenge (1975)
Rescue Party (1975)
Winners and Losers (1975)
The Battle of Blunder Ridge (1976)
The Calaboose Gang (1976)
Colorado Belle (1976)
Kiss the Loot Goodbye (1976)
Outcasts of Sabado Creek (1976)
Dawson Died Twice (1976)
Follow That Train (1976)

Twenty Seven Rifles (1976)
The Bandit Trap (1976)
Before He Kills Again (1976)
Guns of the Valiant (1976)
Prelude to a Showdown (1976)
Raid a Painted Wagon (1976)
Suddenly a Hero (1976)
The Sundown Seven (1976)
Track of the Lawless (1976)
Three Days in Davisburg (1977)
8.10 from Verdugo (1977)
After the Payoff (1977)
Bullion Route (1977)
California Runaround (1977)
Dealer Takes Three (1977)
Everything Happens to Holley (1977)
Jokers Wild (1977)
Kansas Hex (1977)
Left Hand Luke (1977)
Lone Star Godfathers (1977)
Midnight Marauders (1977)
The Only Bank in Town (1977)
Royal Target (1977)
Beecher's Quest (1977)
Ghost of a Chance (1977)
Trouble Shooters Die Hard (1977)
Bullet for a Widow (1978)
Calaboose Express (1978)
Dinero Fever (1978)
Double Shuffle (1978)
Fogarty's War (1978)
Gold, Guns, and the Girl (1978)
Hammer's Horde (1978)
In Memory of Marty Malone (1978)
Mark of the Star (1978)
Nebraska Trackdown (1978)
The Rescuers Ride West (1978)
Wyoming Long Shot (1978)
Baker Street Breakout (1979)
Both Sides of Battle Creek (1979)
Dead Man's Share (1979)
The Doomed of Mesa Rico (1979)
Fort Dillon (1979)
High Stakeout (1979)
Keep Allison Alive (1979)
Pearson County Raiders (1979)
Run from the Buzzards (1979)

Phantom of Fortuna (1979)
Turn the Key on Emerson (1979)
The Women from Whitlock (1979)
Brady's Back in Town (1979)
In Pursuit of Quincey Budd (1979)
Posse Plus Two (1979)
The Seventh Guilty Man (1979)
They Came to Jurado (1979)
El Capitan's Enemies (1980)
Day of the Killers (1980)
Death Quest (1980)
Going Straight in Frizbee (1980)
Hackett's Gold (1980)
One More Showdown (1980)
Prey of the Rogue Riders (1980)
Ride Boldly in Dakota (1980)
Rough Night for the Guilty (1980)
Siege of Jericho (1980)
Vengeance in Spades (1980)
Wait for the Judge (1980)
Wrong Name on a Tombstone (1980)
Doc Rance of Rambeau (1980)
Gun Reckoning at Grundy's Grave (1980)
He's Valentine, I'm Emerson (1980)
Kid Light Fingers (1980)
The Lady Is a Target (1980)
Twenty Year Man (1980)
Lone Star Survivors (1980)
The Deadly Dollars (1981)
We Ride for Circle 6 (1981)
Load Every Rifle (1981)
Five Bullets for Judge Blake (1981)
Ride Out of Paradise (1981)
Lone Hand Emerson (1981)
Greel County Outcasts (1981)
Miss Lou and the Tall Men (1981)
Little Town, Big Trouble (1981)
Tin Star Shadow (1981)
Bravados of Bandera (1981)
Wild Widow of Wolf Creek (1981)
For the Hell of It (1981)
Ride Strong, Ride Free (1981)
Human Target (1981)
We Call Him Tex (1981)
Spanish Gold and Texas Guns (1981)
The Law Always Wins (1981)
Pursuit Party (1981)

Hide in Fear (1982)
Lucky Jake (1982)
Cormack Came Back (1982)
Cedro County Crisis (1982)
Latimer's Loot (1982)
Tame a Wild Town (1982)
Forgotten Enemy (1982)
The Last Witness (1982)
McEvoy's Mountain (1982)
Emerson's Hex (1982)
The Bullet in Mason's Back (1982)
Six-Gun Wedding (1982)
Colorado Woman (1982)
Young Bucks from Texas (1982)
Castle on Claw Creek (1982)
Pledge to a Doomed Man (1982)
Greenback Trail (1982)
The After-Midnight Gang (1982)
Bon Chance, Texans! (1982)
Two-Time Winner (1982)
The Cobb Creek Bunch (1982)
Howdy, Ladies (1983)
Debt to a Tin Star (1983)
Miracle at Dry Fork (1983)
Lady Luck and F. J. Beck (1983)
Peligro's Last Hour (1983)
Beauty and the Brigands (1983)
Wagon Number Three (1983)
Wrong Side of Glory Mountain (1983)
Claw Creek Crisis (1983)
The Piketown Flood (1983)
Calamity Is a Woman (1983)
Tanglefoot (1983)
Duffy's Dollars (1983)
The Saga of Sam Burdew (1983)
Texas Born, Chicago Bound (1983)
Shotgun Sharkey (1983)
Save a Bullet for Keehoe (1983)
Walking Tall, Striking Fear (1983)
Stakeout at Council Creek (1983)
The Dude Must Die (1983)
Terror Trail to Tortosa (1984)
Ventura Pass (1984)
The Tinhorn Murder Case (1984)
The Devil's Dozen (1984)
Emerson's Hideout (1984)
Heroes and Hellers (1984)

The Dinero Train (1984)
Day of the Plunderers (1984)
Ghost-Woman of Castillo (1984)
Kincaid's Last Ride (1984)
Defend Beacon Spring (1984)
Reunion in San Jose (1984)
The Only Way Is Up (1984)
Bandit Bait (1984)
Meet the McEgans (1984)
Wyoming Gun-Trap (1984)
Tandy's Legacy (1984)
Stay Away, Slade! (1984)
Destination Fort Ross (1985)
The Sound of Seeger's Guns (1985)
Montana Mail (1985)
The Best and the Worst (1985)
Five for the Shootout (1985)
Wild Night in Widow's Peak (1985)
The Domino Man (1985)
The Cannon Mound Gang (1985)
Billy Hull, R.I.P. (1985)
Sonora Wildcat (1985)
Trigger-Fast (1985)
Who's Gunning for Braid? (1985)
Night of the Guns (1985)
Gollan County Gallows (1985)
Run with the Loot (1985)
The President's Segundo (1985)
The Truth About Snake Ridge (1985)
Two Weeks in Wyoming (1985)
Whiskey Gulch (1985)
Terror's Long Memory (1985)
The Logantown Looters (1985)
Two Gentlemen from Texas (1986)
The Alibi Trail (1986)
Rough Route to Rodd County (1986)
Six Guilty Men (1986)
The Badge and Tully McGlynn (1986)
The Last Big Deal (1986)
The Trial of Slow Wolf (1986)
The Jubilo Stage (1986)
Plummer's Last Posse (1986)
Two Graves Waiting (1987)
Bandido Hunters (1987)
Fontaine's Sidekicks (1987)
Never Cheat a Texan (1987)
The Late Yuma Smith (1987)

One Mean Town (1987)
It Had to Be Ortega (1987)
Harrigan's Star (1987)
One Ticket to Sun Rock (1987)
Galatea McGee (1987)
Seven Killers East (1987)
Dynamite Demon (1988)
The Jonah Rock (1988)
McAllister's Victims (1988)
Queen of Spades (1988)
The Bridegroom's Bodyguards (1988)
Where the Money's Buried (1988)
Wyoming War-Fever (1988)
Four-Wheeled Target (1988)
Waiting for Wilkie's Wagon (1988)
Go West, Joe Best (1988)
Battle of Hogan's Hole (1988)
Feud-Breakers (1988)
Is Glennon Guilty? (1988)
Legend of Coyote Ford (1988)
Widow from Nowhere (1989)
The Second Chance Man (1989)
Hostage Hunters (1989)
Alias Ed Dacey (1989)
The Doomsday Gun (1989)
Beeby's Big Night (1989)
The Langan Legacy (1989)
Hackett's Bluff (1989)
Backtracking Little Red (1989)
The Selina Crisis (1989)
Wells Fargo Decoys (1989)
Wolf Creek or Bust (1989)
Friends of Barney Gregg (1989)
Runaway Ramsey (1989)
Battle Alley (1989)

High Card Killer (1989)
Revenge Is the Spur (1989)
The No Name Gang (1989)
Challenge the Legend (1989)
Slow Wolf and Dan Fox (1989)
The Lawman Wore Black (1989)
Uneasy Money (1989)
Terror for Sale (1989)
Rescue a Tall Texan (1989)
Spencer Started Something (1989)
Dakota Death-Trap (1989)
Whatever Became of Johnny Duke? (1989)
Once Upon a Gallows (1989)
The Gold Movers (1989)
Fortune Fever (1990)
Never Say Quit (1990)
In Cahoots (1990)
Banished from Bodie (1990)
Hold 'Em Back! (1990)
South to Sabine (1991)
Rough, Ready and Texan (1991)
Ruckus at Gila Wells (1991)
The Woman Hunt (1991)
The Wrong Victim (1991)
Bunko Trail (1991)
Bequest to a Texan (1991)
Right Royal Hassle (1991)
Moonlight and Gunsmoke (1991)
Wrangle Creek (1991)
Strangers Riding By (1991)
Conway's Chronicle (1991)
Vigil on Sundown Ridge (1992)
Eyes of a Killer (1992)
The Wildcat Run (1992)

Original Larry and Stretch and Big Jim Rand Works

San Baba Blockade (1970)
Last Stage to Delarno (1978)
Four Aces and the Knave (1979)

Reunion in Slade City (1983)
One Hell of a Showdown (1991)

Larry and Stretch and Big Jim Rand Pastiches

Link Hullar and David Whitehead, *The Star Trio* (1994); *A Quest of Heroes* (1996)

WILLIAM W. JOHNSTONE

Smoke Jensen

Missouri-born William W. Johnstone (1938–2004) wrote Westerns, adventure, science fiction and horror novels. He was one of the last of the pulpish, gritty authors agile in several genres, a master of multiple series. Johnstone, whose tradition is being carried on by "J.A. Johnstone," offered pure escape, violence, action, gunplay and a dose of conservative politics.

Johnstone, in a letter on his website, expressed pride in his series heroes, from terrorist fighter John Barrone in the Code Name books to Ben Raines in the futuristic Ashes tales or Smoke Jensen in the Western mountain man sagas. "I try to create the kinds of believable characters that we can all identify with, real people who face tough challenges," he said. "When one of my creations blasts an enemy into the middle of next week, you can be damn sure he had a good reason."

See Johnstone entry in the Action and Adventure section.

Original Smoke Jensen Works

The Last Mountain Man (1985)
Return of the Mountain Man (1986)
Trail of the Mountain Man (1987)
Revenge of the Mountain Man (1988)
Journey of the Mountain Man (1989)
Law of the Mountain Man (1989)
War of the Mountain Man (1990)
Code of the Mountain Man (1991)
Pursuit of the Mountain Man (1991)
Courage of the Mountain Man (1992)
Blood of the Mountain Man (1992)
Fury of the Mountain Man (1993)
Rage of the Mountain Man (1994)
Cunning of the Mountain Man (1994)
Power of the Mountain Man (1995)
Spirit of the Mountain Man (1996)

Ordeal of the Mountain Man (1996)
Triumph of the Mountain Man (1997)
Vengeance of the Mountain Man (1997)
Honor of the Mountain Man (1998)
Battle of the Mountain Man (1998)
Pride of the Mountain Man (1998)
Creed of the Mountain Man (1999)
Guns of the Mountain Man (1999)
Heart of the Mountain Man (2000)
Justice of the Mountain Man (2000)
Valor of the Mountain Man (2001)
Warpath of the Mountain Man (2002)
Trek of the Mountain Man (2002)
Quest of the Mountain Man (2003)
Ambush of the Mountain Man (2003)
Wrath of the Mountain Man (2004)

Smoke Jensen Pastiches

Fred Austin, *Destiny of the Mountain Man* (2005)
J.A. Johnstone, *Betrayal of the Mountain Man* (2006); *Rampage of the Mountain Man* (2007); *Violence of the Mountain Man* (2008)

Original Preacher Works

The First Mountain Man (1991)
Blood on the Divide (1992)

Absaroka Ambush (1993)
Forty Guns West (1993)

Cheyenne Challenge (1995)
Preacher and the Mt. Caesar (1995)
Blackfoot Messiah (1996)
Preacher (2002)

Preacher's Peace (2003)
Preacher's Justice (2004)
Preacher's Journey (2005)

Preacher Pastiches

Fred Austin, Preacher's Fortune (2006)

J.A. Johnstone, Preacher's Quest (2007); Preacher's Showdown (2008); Preacher's Pursuit (2009)

Original Last Gunfighter Works

The Drifter (2000)
Reprisal (2000)
Ghost Valley (2001)
The Forbidden (2001)
Showdown (2001)
Impostor (2002)
Rescue (2003)

The Burning (2003)
No Man's Land (2004)
Manhunt (2004)
Violent Sunday (2005)
Renegades (2005)
Savage Country (2006)
The Devil's Legion (2006)

Last Gunfighter Pastiches

J.A. Johnstone, Avenger (2007); Hell Town (2007); Ambush Alley (2008); Killing Ground (2008); Slaughter (2009)

Non-series Pastiches

J.A. Johnstone, Remember the Alamo (2007); Judgment Day (2008); Jacknife (2008); Six Ways from Sunday (2009)

KARL MAY

Shatterhand

Karl May (1842–1910) never saw the American West. But he crafted rousing frontier adventures about a rugged hero, Old Shatterhand, and his close friend Winnetou and a handful of other characters such as Old Firehand, Old Surehand and Sharpeye.

May was born in Holenstein-Ernstthal, Saxony, Germany, where, despite economic and social strife, he appeared destined for a career as an educator until he was convicted of theft and jailed (under false charges, he always claimed). Embittered, he thereafter swindled and conned his way through life and spent another term in jail. He encountered the American frontier while reading in prison. His first writing was a pair of American travel guides — based on atlases and other books and a good imagination — and a fiction trilogy, Winnetou, about a Cooperesque adventurer (modeled after May himself) and his blood brother, an Indian chief. May became a top-selling writer of his day in non–English-speaking countries. May visited the United States in 1908. He also wrote numerous Middle Eastern novels featuring the hero Kara Ben Nemsi.

Four motion pictures in the 1960s featured Lex Barker as Shatterhand and revived interest in the books. Stuart Granger appeared in another series of films about Old Surehand. New book translations still appear today. British writer B.J. Holmes (really Charles Langley Hayes), creator of the Reaper series, provided prose sequels.

Original Old Shatterhand Series

Winnetou (1893) translated into English in 1977
Old Surehand (1894) translated by Marlies Bugmann in 2007
Winnetou's Heritage (1910)
Winnetou the Apache Knight (2007)

Old Surehand: Quest (2007) translated by Marlies Bugmann
Winnetou II (2007) translated by Marlies Bugmann
Winnetou: The Treasure of Nugget Mountain (2007)

Pastiches

B.J. Holmes, *A Legend Called Shatterhand* (1990); *Shatterhand and the People* (1992)

JOHNSTON MCCULLEY
Zorro

Señor Zorro (The Fox) is the Robin Hood of the Old West in some sixty-five stories first published in *West, Argosy* and other pulp magazines and in a hardcover book. Johnston McCulley (1883–1958), a native of Illinois, wrote under his own and other names for the fiction magazines including *Detective Fiction Weekly*. His series characters included Thubway Tham, The Crimson Clown and The Mongoose. He was a *Police Gazette* reporter. Zorro's first appearance was in the story "The Curse of Capistrano" serialized in *All-Story Weekly* Aug. 9 to Sept. 6, 1919. Seventy-two more stories followed.

The hero was featured in motion pictures, in a Walt Disney television program (1957–59) and in a TV revival beginning in 1990 on The Family Channel. American and French graphic depictions of the hero have been reprinted. Several writers have turned in sequels in recent decades.

Original Zorro Works

The Mark of Zorro (1924)
The Further Adventures of Zorro (1926)
Zorro Vol. 1 (1991) short stories

Zorro Vol. 2 (1991) short stories
Zorro Vol. 3 (1991) short stories
Zorro: The Masters Edition (2000)

Zorro Pastiches

Isabel Allende, *Zorro: A Novel* (2005)

D.J. Arneson, *Zorro and the Pirate Raiders* (1986); *Zorro Rides Again* (1986)

David Bergantino, *Zorro and the Dragon Riders* (1999)

Scott Cienein, *The Legend of Zorro* (2005)

Sandra Curtis, *Zorro Unmasked* (1997)

Les Dean, *Zorro, the Gay Blade* (1981)

Mark Dunster, *Zorro* (1995)

Steve Frazee, *Walt Disney's Zorro* (1958)

Samantha Grey, *Mark of Zorro* (1990)

Frank Laurie, *The Mark of Zorro* (1998)

Don McGregor and Sidney Lima, *Zorro 1: Scars!* (2005) graphic novel

Don McGregor, Andy Mushynsky, John Nyberg, Mike Mahew and Hilary Barta, *Zorro: The Lady Wears Red* (1998) graphic novel

Nedaud and Marcello, *Zorro in Old California* (1986)

Jerome Preisler, *Zorro and the Jaguar Warriors* (1998)

Alex Toth, *Zorro the Classic Adventures* (1988) graphic novel; *Zorro the Classic Adventures* (1988) graphic novel

Diego Vega and Jan Adkins, *Young Zorro: The Iron Brand* (2007)

John Whitman, *Mask of Zorro* (1998); *Zorro and the Witch's Curse* (1999)

JON MESSMAN

Trailsman

Western author Jon Messman (1920–2004) used the penname Jon Sharpe for his long-running bullets-and-lust series about Skye Fargo, a scout and hunter in this adult series. The hero, in *Red River Revenge*, typically, agrees to take the luscious Folsom girls through dangerous Chippewa country into the Dakota Territory. But before the trek even begins, the girls are gone and Fargo's neck is headed for a noose. The Trailsman is one of a quartet of "adult" cowboy heroes (Gunsmith, written pseudonymously by Robert Randisi, Longarm by Tabor Evans and Slocum by Jake Logan — the last two house names masking dozens of writers) that has endured for three decades.

Messman wrote action adventures under his own name and had other pennames, including Alan Joseph, for two 1970s crime novels, and Claude Nicole. He wrote under the house names Nick Carter and Paul Richards. Early in his career he scripted stories for Fawcett comic books.

Messman or his publisher Signet may have from time to time hired ghostwriters (such as Will C. Knott) for the Trailsman books. But after Messman's death, all of the entries were written by other hands. "The quality of the books in The Trailsman series is very uneven," Craig Clarke wrote on the Somebody Dies blog, "but gems are hidden throughout, and these fast-paced sexy reads are always worth the small cover price. For a while, however, I may limit my own purchases to those written by James Reasoner — or perhaps David Robbins."

Original Trailsman Works

Seven Wagons West (1980)
The Hanging Trail (1980)
Mountain Man Kill (1980)
The Sundown Searchers (1980)
The River Raiders (1981)
Dakota Wild (1981)
Wolf Country (1981)
Six-Gun Drive (1981)
Dead Man's Saddle (1982)
Slave Hunter (1982)
Montana Maiden (1982)
Condor Pass (1982)
Blood Chase (1982)
Arrowhead Territory (1983)
The Stalking Horse (1983)
Savage Showdown (1983)
Ride the Wild Shadows (1983)
Cry the Cheyenne (1983)
Spoon River Stud (1983)
The Judas Killer (1983)
Whiskey Guns (1983)
Border Arrows (1983)
The Comstock Killers (1983)
Twisted Noose (1983)
Maverick Maiden (1984)
Warpaint and Rifles (1984)
Bloody Heritage (1984)
Hostage Trail (1984) by Will C. Knott
High Mountain Guns (1984)
White Savage (1984) by Will C. Knott
Six-Gun Sombreros (1984)
Apache Gold (1984) by Will C. Knott
Red River Revenge (1984)
Sharps Justice (1984)
Kiowa Kill (1984)
The Badge (1984) by Will C. Knott
Valley of Death (1985)
Tomahawk Revenge (1985)
Grizzly Man (1985) by Will C. Knott
The Lost Patrol (1985) by Will C. Knott
The Range Killers (1985)
The Renegade Command (1985)
Mesquite Manhunt (1985)

Scorpion Trail (1985) by Will C. Knott
Killer Caravan (1985)
Hell Town (1985) by Will C. Knott
Six-Gun Salvation (1985)
The White Hell Trail (1985)
Swamp Slayer (1986)
Blood Oath (1986) by Will C. Knott
Sioux Captive (1986)
Posse from Hell (1986) by Will C. Knott
Longhorn Guns (1986)
Killer Clan (1986) by Will C. Knott
Thief River Showdown (1986)
Guns of Hungry Horse (1986)
Fortune Riders (1986)
Slaughter Express (1986)
Thunderhawk (1986)
The Wayward Lassie (1986)
Bullet Caravan (1986)
Horsethief Crossing (1987)
Stagecoach to Hell (1987)
Fargo's Woman (1987)
River Kill (1987)
Treachery Pass (1987)
Manitoba Marauders (1987)
Trapper Rampage (1987)
Confederate Challenge (1987)
Hostage Arrows (1987)
Renegade Rebellion (1987)
Calico Trail (1987)
Santa Fe Slaughter (1988)
White Hell (1988)
Colorado Robber (1988)
Wildcat Wagon (1988)
Devil's Den (1988)
Minnesota Missionary (1988)
Smokey Hell Trail (1988)
Blood Pass (1988)
Twisted Trails (1988)
Mescalera Mask (1988)
Dead Man's Forest (1988)
Utah Slaughter (1988)
Call White Wolf (1989)
Texas Hell Country (1989)

Brothel Bullets (1989)
Mexican Massacre (1989)
Target Conestoga (1989)
Mesabi Huntdown (1989)
Cave of Death (1989)
Death's Caravan (1989)
The Texas Train (1989)
Desperate Dispatch (1989)
Cry Revenge (1989)
Buzzard's Gap (1989)
Queen's High Bid (1990)
Desperate Desperadoes (1990)
Camp St. Lucifer (1990)
Riverboat Gold (1990)
Shoshoni Spirits (1990)
The Coronado Killers (1990)
Secret Sixguns (1990)
Comanche Crossing (1990)
Black Hills Blood (1990)
Sierra Shootout (1990)
Gunsmoke Gulch (1990)
Pawnee Bargain (1990)
Lone Star Lightning (1991)
Counterfeit Cargo (1991)
Blood Canyon (1991)
The Doomsday Wagons (1991)
Southern Belles (1991)
The Tamarind Trail (1991)
Gold Mine Madness (1991)
Kansas Kill (1991)
Gun Valley (1991)
The Arizona Slaughter (1991)
Renegade Rifles (1991)
Wyoming Manhunt (1991)
Redwood Revenge (1992)
Gold Fever (1992)
Desert Death (1992)
Colorado Quarry (1992)
Blood Prairie (1992)
Coins of Death (1992)
Nevada Warpath (1992)
Snake River Butcher (1992)
The Silver Maria (1992)
Montana Fire Smoke (1992)
Beartown Bloodshed (1992)
The Kentucky Colts (1993)
Sage River Conspiracy (1993)

Cougar Dawn (1993)
Montana Mayhem (1993)
Texas Triggers (1993)
Moon Lake Massacre (1993)
Silver Fury (1993)
Buffalo Guns (1993)
The Killing Corridor (1993)
Tomahawk Justice (1993)
Golden Bullets (1993)
Deathblow Trail (1993)
Abilene Ambush (1993)
Cheyenne Crossfire (1993)
Nebraska Nightmare (1994)
Death Trails (1994)
California Quarry (1994)
Springfield Sharpshooters (1994)
Savage Guns (1994)
Crowhearts' Revenge (1994)
Prairie Fire (1994)
Saguaro Showdown (1994)
Ambush at Skull Pass (1994)
Oklahoma Ordeal (1994)
The Sawdust Trail (1994)
Ghost Ranch Massacre (1995)
Texas Terror (1995)
North Country Guns (1995)
The Tornado Trail (1995)
Rogue River Feud (1995)
Revenge at Lost Creek (1995)
Yukon Massacre (1995)
Nez Perce Nightmare (1995)
Dakota Death Horse (1995)
Colorado Carnage (1995)
Black Mesa Treachery (1995)
Kiowa Command (1996)
Socorro Slaughter (1996)
Utah Trackdown (1996)
Dead Man's River (1996)
Sutter's Secret (1996)
Washington Warpath (1996)
Death Valley Bloodbath (1996)
Betrayal at El Diablo (1996)
Curse of the Grizzly (1996)
Colorado Wolfpack (1996)
Apache Arrows (1996)
Sagebrush Skeleton (1996)
The Greenback Trail (1996)

Vengeance at Deadman's Rapids (1997)
Blood Canyon (1997)
Bayou Bloodbath (1997)
Rocky Mountain Nightmare (1997)
Bullet Hole Claim (1997)
Blue Sierra Renegades (1997)
Sioux War Cry (1997)
Mercy Manhunt (1997)
Missouri Massacre (1997)
Pecos Death (1997)
Target Gold (1997)
Bullets and Bridles (1997)
Durango Duel (1997)
Montana Stage (1998)
Fort Ravage Conspiracy (1998)
Kansas Courage (1998)
Utah Uprising (1998)
Blackgulch Gambler (1998)
Wyoming Wildcats (1998)
Sixguns by the Sea (1998)
Salmon River Rage (1998)
The Oraro Search (1998)
Silver Hooves (1998)
Leavenworth Express (1998)
Mountain Man Killers (1998)
Oregon Outrider (1999)
Chimney Rock Burial (1999)
Arizona Renegade (1999)
Timber Terror (1999)
The Bush League (1999)
Badlands Bloodbath (1999)
Sioux Stampede (1999)
Apache Wells (1999)
Texas Hellion (1999)
Duet for Six-Gun (1999)
High Sierra Horror (1999)
Dakota Deception (1999)
Pecos Belle Brigade (1999)
Arizona Silver Strike (1999)
Aztec Gold (2000)
Montana Gun Sharp (2000)
California Crusader (2000)
Colorado Diamond Dupe (2000)
Idaho Ghost Town (2000)
Texas Tinhorns (2000)
Prairie Firestorm (2000)
Nebraska Slaying Ground (2000)

Navajo Renegade (2000)
Wyoming War Cry (2000)
Manitoba Marauder (2000)
Flatwater Firebrand (2001)
Salt Lake Siren (2001)
Pacific Phantom (2001)
Missouri Mayhem (2001)
Flathead Fury (2001)
Apache Duel (2001)
Flathead Fury (2001)
Denver City Gold (2001)
Dakota Damnation (2001)
Cherokee Justice (2001)
Comanche Battle Cry (2001)
Frisco Filly (2001)
Texas Blood Money (2001)
Woodland Warriors (2001)
Wyoming Whirlwind (2001)
West Texas Uprising (2002)
Pacific Polecats (2002)
Bloody Brazos (2002)
Texas Death Storm (2002)
Seven Devils Slaughter (2002)
Six-Gun Justice (2002)
Silver City Slayer (2002)
Arizona Ambush (2002)
Utah Uproar (2002)
Kansas City Swindle (2002)
Dead Man's Hand (2002)
Nebraska Gunrunner (2002)
Montana Madman (2003)
High Country Horror (2003)
Colorado Cutthroats (2003)
Casino Carnage (2003)
Wyoming Wolf Pack (2003)
Blood Wedding (2003)
Desert Death Trap (2003)
Badlands Bloodbath (2003)
Arkansas Assault (2003)
New Mexico Nightmare (2003)
Snake River Ruins (2003)
Dakota Death Rattle (2003)
Six-Gun Scholar (2003)
California Casualties (2004)
New Mexico Nymph (2004)
Devil's Den (2004)
Colorado Corpse (2004)

St. Louis Sinners (2004)
Nevada Nemesis (2004)
Montana Massacre (2004)
Nebraska Nightmare (2004)

Ozarks Onslaught (2004)
The Skeleton Canyon (2004)
Hell's Bells (2004)
Mountain Manhunt (2004)

Trailsmen Pastiches

Death Valley Vengeance (2005)
Texas Tart (2005)
New Mexico Nightmare (2005)
Kansas Weapon Wolves (2005)
Colorado Claim Jumper (2005)
Dakota Prairie Pirates (2005)
Salt Lake Slaughter (2005)
Texas Terror Trail (2005)
The California Camel Corps (2005)
Gila River Dry-Gulchers (2005)
Renegade Raiders (2005)
Mountain Mavericks (2005)
The Cutting Kind (2006)
The San Francisco Showdown (2006)
Ozark Blood Feud (2006)
Oregon Outlaws (2006)
Oasis of Blood (2006)
Six-Gun Persuasion (2006)
South Texas Slaughter (2006)
Dead Man's Bounty (2006)
Dakota Danger (2006)
Idaho Blood Sport (2006)
Backwoods Bloodbath (2006)
High Plains Grifters (2006)
Black Rock Pass (2006)
Terror Trackdown (2007)
Death Valley Demons (2007)
Wyoming Wipeout (2007)
Desert Duel (2007)

The Nebraska Night Riders (2007)
Montana Marauders (2007)
Border Bravados (2007)
California Carnage (2007)
Alaskan Vengeance (2007)
Idaho Impact (2007)
The Shanghaied Six-Guns (2007)
Texas Timber War (2007)
North Country Cutthroats (2007)
Missouri Manhunt (2008)
Beyond Squaw Creek (2008)
The Mountain Mystery (2008)
Nevada Nemesis (2008)
Louisiana Laydown (2008)
Oregon Outrage (2008)
Flathead Fury (2008)
Apache Ambush (2008)
Wyoming Death Trap (2008)
California Crackdown (2008)
Seminole Showdown (2008)
Silver Mountain Slaughter (2008)
Idaho Gold Fever (2009)
Texas Triggers (2009)
Bayou Trackdown (2009)
Tucson Temptress (2009)
Northwoods Nightmare (2009)
Beartooth Incident (2009)
Black Hills Badman (2009)

CLARENCE E. MULFORD

Hopalong Cassidy and the Bar-20

The son of a boiler salesman, Illinois-born Clarence E(dward) Mulford (1883–1956) voraciously read dime novels and *Harper's Weekly* as a youngster. His knowledge of the West coming from studious research, Mulford was working as a Brooklyn City Hall clerk when he wrote the first of his popular Bar-20 Western tales in 1905 for *Outing Magazine*. The stories of cussing, tobacco-chewing William

"Hopalong" Cassidy and his pards Red Connor, Johnny Nelson, Tex Ewalt and Buck Peters gained a sufficient enough following that the writer could semi-retire to Maine in 1925.

"One does not talk with Mulford long," noted journalist Martin Sheridan in the *Boston Herald* in 1940, "before it dawns that this man is doing more in his books than finding an outlet for his creative impulses, or making a fortune. He has a profound understanding and appreciation of all the rugged elements that made up the men who were pioneers in this young country and made much of its early history."

"In a way, Mulford personifies two of the basic kinds of pulp Western writer," said Ron Goulart in *An Informal History of the Pulp Magazine* (1973). "The man who fantasizes at a distance about the cowboy life and the man who writes out of first-hand knowledge of the West. Mulford was able to fuse imagination with experience and research. Many other writers would be able to get by only one part of that trinity."

Mulford's quest for a broader audience — and higher income — through motion picture sales ultimately did him in, creatively. Actor William Boyd appeared as a sanitized Hopalong in the first of a string of sixty-six popular, low-budget motion pictures produced by Harry "Pop" Sherman. Mulford didn't like the movies. "Imagine, Hoppy wearing clothes like those Bill Boyd wears," he griped. "Why, it's nonsense. If Hoppy ever showed up in a saloon in duds like that they'd shoot him down on sight."

Mulford quit writing in 1941, grumbling that he paid more to Uncle Sam in taxes than he could keep. Eight years later, Boyd acquired rights and brought the old movies to television and recorded a new radio series (co-starring Andy Clyde as California Carlson), touching off a major merchandizing bonanza. Several of Mulford's early books were condensed for a younger audience but there was demand for more. Mulford wasn't interested; he also wasn't in the best of health. The publisher, Doubleday, commissioned four new novels from a writer active in the pulp magazines, Louis L'Amour.

North Dakota–born L'Amour (1908–88) went on to become one of the century's best-selling Western writers with his novels of the Sacketts and others. Wrote Robert Weinberg in his introduction to *The Louis L'Amour Companion*, "L'Amour worked hard to maintain historical truth in his novels. His descriptions of the time and place and people are meticulous and worked out to the last detail. But ... many other Western writers are equally careful. Louis L'Amour's secret was no secret at all. He wrote the type of Westerns that people wanted to read."

L'Amour was generally faithful to Mulford in his four books, but was directed to portray Cassidy more in the vein of the motion picture hero. "Now Dad hated rewriting, and he'd never liked to be told what to do. He had a lot of respect for Clarence Mulford and felt that he was doing his best to carry on his tradition," wrote Beau L'Amour in an afterword to the 1991 edition of *The Riders of West Fork*. "Doubleday had been Mulford's publisher since 1925 and I think that Dad was deeply disturbed by the thought of being involved in selling out the writer to a company that ought to have had more respect for his work.

"Unfortunately he was broke."

L'Amour never acknowledged the four Cassidy books, but after his death they have appeared, under his byline, in new hard- and soft-cover editions.

During the early 1950s when the television and radio shows were popular, a number of children's books appeared featuring the cowboy hero. Stories from a newspaper comic strip drawn by Dan Spiegle were twice collected in book form. All are listed here.

Closely modeled on the Bill Boyd movies were two hardcover novels that came out in 2005: *Hopalong Cassidy Rides Again* by Wild Ol' Dan Blasius, based on an original manuscript by Jerry Rosenthal, who owns the media rights to Cassidy, and *Follow Your Stars* by Susie Coffman.

Original Hopalong Cassidy Works

Bar-20: Being a record of certain happenings that occurred in the otherwise peaceful lives of one Hopalong Cassidy and his companions on the range (1907) aka *Hopalong Cassidy's Rustler's Roundup* (1950)

Hopalong Cassidy (1910)

Bar-20 Days (1911) *Hopalong Cassidy's Private War* (1950)

The Coming of Cassidy—And the Others (1913) aka *The Coming of Hopalong Cassidy* (1950)

The Man from Bar-20—A Story of the Cow Country (1918)

Johnny Nelson: How a one-time pupil of Hopalong Cassidy of the famous Bar-20 ranch in the Pecos valley performed an act of knight-errantry and what became of it (1920)

The Bar-20 Three: Relating a series of startling and strenuous adventures, in the cowtown of Mesquite, of the famous Bar-20 trio, Hopalong Cassidy, Red Connors and Johnny Nelson (1921) aka *Hopalong Cassidy Sees Red* (1950)

Tex: How Tex Ewalt, two-gun man, philosopher, poet and one-time companion to Hopalong Cassidy, turned a whole community upside down, and dealt retributive justice to several of Windsor's leading citizens for the sake of the girl he loved (1922) aka *Tex of Bar-20* (1922)

Hopalong Cassidy Returns (1924)

Hopalong Cassidy's Protege (1926) aka *Hopalong Cassidy's Saddle Mate* (1949)

The Bar-20 Rides Again (1926) aka *Hopalong Cassidy's Bar-20 Rides Again* (1950)

Mesquite Jenkins (1928)

Hopalong Cassidy and the Eagle's Brood (1931)

Mesquite Jenkins, Tumbleweed (1932)

Trail Dust: Hopalong Cassidy and the Bar-20 with the Trail Herd (1934) aka *Hopalong Cassidy with the Trail Herd* (1950)

Hopalong Cassidy Takes Cards (1937)

Hopalong Cassidy Serves a Writ (1941)

Pastiches

Elizabeth Beecher, *Hopalong Cassidy Stories* No. 1 (1953) juvenile

Wild Ol' Dan Blasius based on an original manuscript by Jerry Rosenthal, *Hopalong Cassidy Rides Again!* (2005)

Tex Burns (Louis L'Amour), *Hopalong Cassidy and the Rustlers of West Fork* (1951);

Hopalong Cassidy's Trail to Seven Pines (1951); *Hopalong Cassidy and the Riders of High Rock* (1951); *Hopalong Cassidy, Trouble Shooter* (1952)

Susie Coffman, *Follow Your Stars* (2005)

Edmond Collier, *Hopalong Cassidy Stories* No. 2 (1954) juvenile

Arthur Groom, *Hopalong Cassidy Stories* No. 5 (1957) juvenile

Charles Hitchcock, *Hopalong Cassidy Stories* No. 3 (1955) juvenile; *Hopalong Cassidy Stories* No. 4 (1956) juvenile; *Hopalong Cassidy Stories* No. 6 (1958) juvenile

Peter O'Donnell and J. McNamara, *Hopalong Cassidy* (1954) graphic story

Dan Spiegle and Royal King Cole, *Hopalong Cassidy Western Comic Annual* No. 1 (1952) newspaper comic strip reprint; *Hopalong Cassidy and the Five Men of Evil* (1991) newspaper comic strip reprint

CHARLES PORTIS

Rooster Cogburn

Arizona native Charles Portis (b. 1933) wrote a story of crusty one-eyed marshal Reuben "Rooster" Cogburn and the plucky tomboy Mattie Ross which was serialized in *The Saturday Evening Post* in 1968 and issued as a book the next year. John Wayne played the character in a motion picture and sequel (1969 and 1975). Portis, a Marine Corps veteran and graduate of the University of Arkansas, was a journalist for many years before writing fiction.

The second film inspired a novelization.

Original Work

True Grit (1968)

Pastiche

Martin Julien, *Rooster Cogburn* (1975) based on the screenplay

NORMAN MACLEOD RAINE

Sagebrush

Norman MacLeod Raine (1871–1954) was born in England, of Scots descent, and after his mother's death, came with his father to settle in Arkansas. He attended Oberlin College in Ohio, traveled the country, worked on ranches, supervised schools and reported and edited news for The Rocky Mountain News and other papers. He wrote short stories and novels for the pulp fiction magazines. A conscientious writer, he settled into a rhythm of two novels a year until his death.

Fellow Western writer Bill Gulick in *Sixty-Four Years as a Writer* (2006), recalled, "When Norman MacLeod Raine died ... he was still writing, being half-way through a novel with a Colorado setting, *High Grass Valley*. His long-time editor and friend at Random House, Harry Maule, sent the unfinished manuscript to another Colorado writer, Wayne Overholser, then in his fifties, and asked if he could finish it. He said he could and did," and Gulick said he couldn't tell where one writer ended and the other picked up.

Washington-born Overholser (1906–1996) was a Spur Award–winning author in his own right. Three times.

Posthumous collaboration published as by Norman MacLeod Raine
Wayne D. Overholser, *High Grass Valley* (1955)

LES SAVAGE, JR.
Sixguns

Les Savage, Jr. (1922–1958), was a busy writer of Westerns and novelizations of television programs. His first novel, *Treasure of the Brasada*, came out in 1947. He favored unusual plots and characters, sometimes prompting editors to rewrite his stories.

Savage's agent, August Lenniger, believing his last novel needed considerable revision, after Savage's death sent the author's outline — though not his first draft — to Dudley Dean McGaughey (1906–1986), who then wrote an entirely new draft.

Posthumous collaboration published as by Les Savage, Jr., and Dudley Dean
Dudley Dean McGaughey, *Gun Shy* (1959) aka *Table Rock* (1993)

OLIVER STRANGE
Sudden

They call James Green "Sudden," that's how quickly he can draw his sixshooter, in the Western series created by British author Oliver Strange (1871–1952). Strange worked in the editorial department of George Newnes Ltd. in London, and began to write the adventures in retirement. Raised by Indians, seeking revenge on men who abused his family, the cowboy Sudden becomes a deadly gunfighter (and later a special agent to the Arizona governor).

After Strange's death, during the Picadilly Cowboy paperback fever of the late 1960s, Frederick H. Christian (a pseudonym for Frederick Nolan) continued the series. *Western Magazine* in January 1981 published another adventure, "The Return of Sudden."

Original Sudden Westerns

The Range Robbers (1930)
The Law o' the Lariat (1931)
Marshal of Lawless (1933) aka *Lawless*
Sudden (1933)
Sudden—Outlawed (1935) aka *Outlawed* (1936)

Sudden—Goldseeker (1937)
Sudden Rides Again (1938)
Sudden Takes the Trail (1940)
Sudden Takes Charge (1940)
Sudden Makes War (1942)
Sudden Plays a Hand (1950)

Pastiches

Frederick Nolan writing as Frederick H. Christian, *Sudden Strikes Back* (1966); *Sudden—Troubleshooter* (1967); *Sudden at Bay* (1968); *Sudden—Apache Fighter* (1969); *Sudden—Dead or Alive* (1970)

Fran Striker

The Lone Ranger

The order of things was a little reversed with The Lone Ranger. Buffalo-born Fran Striker (1903–1962) created the character of the masked range rider and his companion Tonto for a radio show on WEBR, soon switching to WXYZ. Striker sold rights to the character to producer George W. Trendle but continued to script the radio program. *The Lone Ranger* ran 2,956 episodes from 1933 to 1954. Striker also wrote *Green Hornet* and *Challenge of the Yukon* scripts, and wrote scenarios for the television versions of *The Lone Ranger* and *Sergeant Preston of the Yukon*. He was also a comic strip writer.

But when it came to the book versions of *The Lone Ranger*, another comic strip writer, Massachusetts-born comic book scripter Gaylord Du Bois (1899–1993), wrote a pastiche, you might say, before Striker took over and wrote the rest of the Grosset & Dunlap series. "By Gaylord Dubois Based on the Famous Radio Adventure Series by Fran Striker," it said on the title page of the first edition. Striker apparently rewrote that novel; later editions bore his byline, not Du Bois's.

Recent pastiches have been tied to motion picture releases.

Original Works

The Lone Ranger and the Mystery Ranch (1938)
The Lone Ranger and the Gold Robbery (1939)
The Lone Ranger and the Outlaw Stronghold (1939)
The Lone Ranger and Tonto (1940)

The Lone Ranger at the Haunted Gulch (1941)
The Lone Ranger Traps the Smugglers (1941)
The Lone Ranger Rides Again (1943)
The Lone Ranger Rides North (1943)
The Lone Ranger and the Silver Bullet (1948)
The Lone Ranger on Powderhorn Trail (1949)
The Lone Ranger in Wild Horse Canyon (1950)
The Lone Ranger West of Maverick Pass (1951)
The Lone Ranger on Gunsight Mesa (1952)
The Lone Ranger and the Bitter Spring Feud (1953)
The Lone Ranger and the Code of the West (1954)
The Lone Ranger and Trouble on the Santa Fe (1955)
The Lone Ranger on Red Butte Trail (1956)

Big Little Books

The Lone Ranger and His Horse Silver (1935)
The Lone Ranger and the Vanishing Herd (1936)
The Lone Ranger and the Menace of Murder Valley (1938)
The Lone Ranger and the Lost Valley (1938)
The Lone Ranger and Dead Men's Mine (1939)
The Lone Ranger and the Black Shirt Highwayman (1939)
The Lone Ranger and the Red Renegades (1939)
The Lone Ranger Follows Through (1941)
The Lone Ranger and the Secret Weapon (1943)
The Lone Ranger on the Barbary Coast (1944)
The Lone Ranger and the Silver Bullet (1946)
The Lone Ranger and the Secret of Somber Cavern (1950)

Pastiches

Gaylord Du Bois, *The Lone Ranger* (1936)
Gary McCarthy, *The Legend of the Lone Ranger* (1981) movie novelization

British Annuals

The Lone Ranger (1958) juvenile
The Lone Ranger Adventure Stories (1959) juvenile
The Lone Ranger (1961) juvenile
The Lone Ranger Television Story Book
  (1964) juvenile
The Lone Ranger (1968) juvenile
The Lone Ranger (1969) juvenile
The Lone Ranger (1976) juvenile
The Lone Ranger (1977) juvenile

Graphic Novels

Comic Strip Showcase 1 Featuring The Lone Ranger (1990) reprints newspaper comic strips
Joe R. Lansdale, *The Lone Ranger and Tonto* (1995)
Brett Matthews and Sergio Cariello, *The Lone Ranger* (2007); *The Lone Ranger Vol. 2* (2008)

JONAS WARD

Buchanan

Through publishing momentum more than literary acclaim, Tom Buchanan, a wandering cowpoke who tries to keep his nose out of trouble, survived his creator's death.

New York–born William Ard (1922–1960), a graduate of Dartmouth College, wrote copy for the Buchanan Advertising Agency, scripts for Warner Brothers and mystery and Western novels under several pennames for paperback publishers including Fawcett.

At his death, Ard had just launched the Lou Largo private eye stories under his own name (see Mystery section) and the Buchanan oaters under the Jonas Ward (W. Ard, get it?) penname.

Tom Buchanan, a big, amiable drifter (played by Randolph Scott in a 1958 motion picture, *Buchanan Rides Alone*) rode the range another quarter century, thanks to science fiction writer Robert Silverberg, who completed Ard's last manuscript, and Brian Garfield, who wrote an entry when the publisher decided to continue the series.

"The way the book came to be written," Garfield said in a 1981 letter to the author, "was that I happened to be living in the Royalton Hotel in New York, across the street from Fawcett's then-offices, and Knox Burger (then editor of Fawcett Gold Medal books, nowadays an agent) asked me if I'd mind doing a Buchanan book quick-like because they had a hole in their publication schedule to fill. I needed money at the time (it was about 1966 or 1967) and grabbed the opportunity, then read Ard's Buchanan books, didn't think much of them, realized the only way to get through the job with sanity intact was to thrust tongue firmly into cheek, and did so. I'm not sure whether Ard intended his books to be funny. I hope mine was, at least a little. I had fun writing it. I know Bill Cox has fun writing them too. I'm not sure Ard had that much fun with them, though...."

"Buchanan is likeable as well as heroic; I think that sets him aside from the brooding gunfighter heroes of most Westerns of the post–World War II era; that may help account for his popularity," said Garfield, who was born New York City in 1939 and after writing a number of Western and mystery books went on to a career scripting movies.

William R. Cox (1901–1988) in his continuation of the series introduced a frequent companion for Buchanan, a champion black boxer named Coco Bean. Born in New Jersey, Cox began writing for the pulp fiction magazines. He served a term as president of Western Writers of America. His last books were in his own Western series featuring Cemetery Jones.

"Bill Ard died after doing a couple of Buchanans and left outlines with Knox Burger at Fawcett ... [after two other writers] I took over—and the series took off...," said Cox in a 1979 letter to the author. "They are fun to do.... The hero always triumphs and goes on to his next adventure. I think the inclusion of strong women characters have helped.

"These are simple stories with characters not too complex. If there are psychological undertones, a subtlety in the relationship between Buchanan and Coco Bean they have not interfered with enjoyment in the stories. A certain amount of historical research goes into each — this has not deterred the faithful. Buchanan is a peaceable Everyman who is forced into dramatic situations by force of circumstances."

Original Buchanan books by Jonas Ward

The Name's Buchanan (1956)
Buchanan Says No (1957)
One-Man Massacre (1958)

Buchanan Gets Mad (1958)
Buchanan's Revenge (1960)

Posthumous collaboration issued as by Jonas Ward

Robert Silverberg, *Buchanan on the Prod* (1960)

Pastiches issued as by Jonas Ward

William R. Cox, *Buchanan's War* (1971); *Trap for Buchanan* (1972); *Buchanan's Gamble* (1973); *Buchanan's Siege* (1973); *Buchanan on the Run* (1974); *Get Buchanan* (1974); *Buchanan Calls the Shots* (1975); *Buchanan's Big Showdown* (1976); *Buchanan's Texas Treasure* (1977); *Buchanan's Stolen Railway* (1978); *Buchanan's Manhunt* (1979); *Buchanan's Range War* (1980); *Buchanan's Big Fight* (1981); *Buchanan's Black Sheep* (1985); *Buchanan's Stage Line* (1986)
Brian Garfield, *Buchanan's Gun* (1968)

OWEN WISTER

The Virginian

Owen Wister's influential novel of a rugged cowboy's romance with a school marm provided the basis for a television series, *The Virginian* (1962–1970), later called *The Men From Shiloh* (1970–1971), that in turn prompted a paperback novel.

Wister (1860–1938) was born in Pennsylvania, educated in New Hampshire and graduated from Harvard University, where a classmate was Theodore Roosevelt, future Rough Rider. He worked in the financial world, and dabbled in writing. To recover from a nervous breakdown, he relocated to Wyoming, the first of many trips. Completing requirements for a law degree, he entered a Philadelphia practice. He continued writing stories for periodicals until 1897, when he attempted a novel, Lin McLean. *The Virginian* became a popular book instantly upon publication. It established in the main character, the rough Trampas, and others, many of the prototypes of Western fiction, including the drawdown.

Dudley Dean McGaughey (1906–1986) wrote Westerns and crime novels under his own name and as Dean Owen, Dudley Dean, Owen Evens, Lincoln Drew, Jackson Cole and Owen Dudley. He novelized stories from *Bonanza, The Rebel* and other television series.

Original work

The Virginian: A Horseman of the Plains (1902)

Pastiche

Dean Owen, *The Men from Shiloh: Lone Trail for the Virginian* (1971)

Bibliography

Ahlquist, Dale. "Who Is This Guy and Why Haven't I Heard of Him?" *American Chesterton Society Website.* <http://chesterton.org/discover/who.html> (Jan. 9, 2009).

Atkinson, Nathalie. "The Man who Really Has Played Sam Again." *National Post,* Feb. 20, 2009. <http://www.canada.com/entertainment/books/really+played+again/1312155/story.html> (March 4, 2009).

Auer, Tom. "Robert B. Parker Interview." *The Bloomsbury Review,* June 1991.

"Author Michael Crichton Dies from Cancer." *ET Online,* Nov. 5, 2008. <http://www.movieweb.com/news/NEJJXMMJNwxJOM> (Feb. 22, 2009).

Bertha M. Bower Papers, *University of Oklahoma Western History Collection.* <http://libraries.ou.edu/etc/westhist/bower/inventory.html> (Feb. 5, 2009).

Bibliography of Jane Austen Sequels. <http://www.pemberley.com/janeinfo/austeql.html> (viewed June 9, 2008).

"Billtry." *Literary News,* March 1895.

Blau, Eleanor. "Do Scarlett and Rhett Discover Love Anew? A Sequel Reveals All." *New York Times,* Sept. 25, 1991, C15.

Bradford, K. Tempest. "Blog for a Beer: Should a Series Die When the Author Does?" *Fantasy Magazine,* Sept. 19, 2008. <http://www.darkfantasy.org/fantasy/?p=932> (March 4, 2009).

Breen, Jon L. "The Ghost of Miss Truman." *Weekly Standard,* Nov. 18, 2002.

Cambridge History of English and American Literature, Vol. 14. Cambridge: University Press, 1907.

Cameron-McCarron, Shelley. "The Literary Scholar." *Canadian Geographic,* April 2008, 26.

Carpenter, Humphrey, and Mari Prichard. *The Oxford Companion to Children's Literature.* New York: Oxford University Press, 1984.

Carpenter, Leonard. Interview. *Hyborian Report* Vol. 1 No. 4 (1988).

Cary, Alice. "The Boxcar Children Roll On." *BookPage Website.* <http://www.bookpage.com/9705bp/children/theboxcarchildren.html> (June 18, 2008).

Cawthorn, James, and Michael Moorcock. *Fantasy: The 100 Best Books.* New York: Carroll & Graf, 1988.

Chandler, Raymond. "The Simple Art of Murder." *Atlantic Monthly,* December 1944.

Chevalier, Tracy, ed. *Twentieth-Century Children's Writers,* 3rd edition. Detroit: St. James Press, 1989.

Cronk, Lainey S. "Two New Novels Carry on the Walter Utt Legacy." *Pacific Union College News and Archives,* 2008. <http://www.puc.edu/news/archives/2008/two-new-novels-carry-on-the-walter-utt-legacy> (Feb. 23, 2009).

DeAndrea, William L. *Encyclopedia Mysteriosa.* New York: Prentice Hall General Reference, 1994.

Delbanco, Andrew. Review of *The Buccaneers*. *The New Republic*, October 1993.

Del Negro, Janice. Julius Lester Interview. *Booklist*, Feb. 15, 1995.

Demko, George J. "Strangers on Terrain: Foreign crime novelists trying to set their stories in America have too often been clueless." *January Magazine*, August 2004. <http://januarymagazine.com/features/stranterrain.html> (March 20, 2009).

Depkin, Friedrich. *Sherlock Holmes, Raffles, and Their Prototypes*. Fanlight House, 1949.

DeSilva, Bruce. "'New' Tolkien Splendidly Rewarding." *CNN Website*. <http://www.cnn.com/2007/SHOWBIZ/books/04/17/review.tolkien.ap/index.html> (April 17, 2007).

Donahue, Deirdre. "Getting Wind of a Few 'Scarlett' Sequel Secrets." *USA Today*, May 22, 1991.

_____. "'Valley of the Dolls' Sequel Is a Shadow of the Original." *USA Today*, June 21, 2001, D1.

Drake, David. *David Drake Website*. <http://david-drake.com/hunter.html> (July 6, 2008).

Drew, Bernard A. *Hopalong Cassidy: The Clarence E. Mulford Story*. Metuchen, N.J.: Scarecrow Press, 1991.

_____. "Introduction" in *Compliments of the Domino Lady*, edited by Rich Harvey. Bordentown, N.J.: Bold Venture Press, 2004.

Dyer, Carolyn Stewart, and Nancy Tillman Romalov, eds. *Rediscovering Nancy Drew*. Iowa City: University of Iowa Press, 1995.

Dyer, Richard. "Reopening the Baffling Case of E. Drood," *Boston Globe*, June 30, 1992, 25.

Edelman, David Louis. "My Introduction to the Reissue of Mervyn Peake's 'Titus Alone.'" *David Louis Edelman Website*. <http://www.davidlouisedelman.com/fantasy/titus-alone-introduction/> (Jan. 14, 2009).

Edgar Rice Burroughs Website. <http://www.tarzan.org/history_of_tarzan_part1.html> (Oct. 29, 2008).

Edwards, Anne. *The Road to Tara: The Life of Margaret Mitchell*. London: Hodder & Stoughton, 1983.

"1869 Novel Done at Last." *New York Daily News*, June 5, 2005, 26.

Ellsworth, Mary Ellen. *Gertrude Chandler Warner and the Boxcar Children*. Morton Grove, IL: Albert Whitman, 2002.

El-Sadek, Nafisa Abd. "A Critical Assessment of Aspects of Illustration and Translation in Children's Literature." *University of Edinburgh Department of Islamic & Middle Eastern Studies*, 2001. <http://members.tripod.com/netlangs-ivil/EDUNI/Paper2/2index.htm> (Feb. 13, 2009).

Epstein, Norrie. *The Friendly Dickens*. New York: Viking Penguin, 1998.

Eyles, Allen. *The World of Oz*. Tucson, AZ: HP Books, 1985.

"Fake Harry Potter Book Released in China." *USA Today*, July 5, 2002.

Fein, Esther B. "Heathcliff and Huck Going Way of Scarlett." *New York Times*, Feb. 5, 1992, C15.

Flood, Alison. "Eoin Colfer to Write Sixth Hitchhiker's Guide book." *Guardian*, Sept. 17, 2008.

"Further Adventures of Sherlock Holmes (& Friends)." *Reader's Advisor*. <http://sachem.suffolk.lib.ny.us.advisor/holmes.htm> (June 6, 2008).

Gardner, Martin. *The Annotated Casey at the Bat*. New York: Clarkson Potter, 1967.

Geist, Christopher D. "The Plantation Novel: Paperback Genre of the 1970s?" *Paperback Quarterly*, Spring 1980, 42.

Gilsdorf, Ethan. "Lore of the 'Rings' Is the Lure of 'Hurin.'" *Boston Globe*, April 26, 2007, E6.

Goulart, Ron. *An Informal History of the Pulp Magazine*. New York: Ace, 1973.

_____, ed. *The Encyclopedia of American Comics from 1897 to the Present*. New York: Facts on File, 1990.

Grant, Traci. "Heathcliff's Stormy Sequel." *Boston Globe*, July 29, 1992, 61.

Green, Joseph, and Jim Finch. *Sleuths, Sidekicks and Stooges*. Hants, England: Scholar Press, 1997.

Green, Roland. *The Barbarian Scroll* No. 15 (1991).

Greenwald, Marilyn S. *The Secret of the Hardy Boys*. Ohio University Press, 2004.

Gruber, Frank. *Zane Grey: A Biography*. New York: Walter J. Black, 1969.

Guiley, Rosemary Ellen. *The Complete Vampire Companion: Legend and Lore of the Living Dead*. New York: Macmillan, 1994.

Gulick, Bill. *Sixty-Four Years as a Writer*. Caldwell, Idaho: Caxton Press, 2006.

Gunn, Ian. "The Origins of Thomas the Tank Engine." <http://www.iglobal.com/Drew/origins.htm> (Feb. 16, 2009).

Guthmann, Edward. "Joe Gores' Novel about Sam Spade's Early Days." *San Francisco Chronicle*, Feb. 6, 2009.

Halberstadt, John. "Who Wrote Thomas Wolfe's Last Novels?" *New York Review of Books*, March 19, 1981.

Halliwell, Leslie. *The Filmgoer's Companion*, 4th edition. New York: Flare, 1975.

"Happily Snared in Web of Austen's 'Charlotte,'" *USA Today*, May 11, 2000, 6D.

Harbottle, Philip. "The British Imitators of Tarzan." *Paperback Parade* No. 23 (March 1991): 35.

_____. "The British Tarzans: A Bibliography." *Paperback Parade* No. 23 (March 1991): 41.

Hart, James D. *The Oxford Companion to American Literature*. New York: Oxford University Pres, 1956.

Hebert, Rosemary, ed. *The Oxford Companion to Crime & Mystery Writing*. New York: Oxford University Press, 1999.

Herron, Don, ed. *The Dark Barbarian: The Writings of Robert E. Howard: A Critical Anthology*. Rockville, Maryland: Wildside Press, 1984.

Hodges, Jane Aiken. *The Private World of Georgette Heyer*. London: Bodley Head, 1984.

Honan, Park. *Jane Austen: Her Life*. New York: Ballantine, 1987.

Horner, Shirley. "Little Toot." *New York Times*, Nov. 26, 1989.

Hubin, Allen J. *Crime Fiction, 1749–1980: A Comprehensive Bibliography*. New York: Garland, 1984.

_____. *1981–1985 Supplement to Crime Fiction 1749–1980*. New York: Garland, 1988.

Inge, M. Thomas. *Handbook of Popular American Literature*. Greenwood Press, 1988.

"Interview with the Writer Roland Green," *The Barbarian Scroll* No. 15 (1991).

Itzkoff, Dave. "Author Appeals Injunction Against Salinger Sequel," *New York Times*, July 24, 2009.

Johannsen, Albert. "The House of Beadle and Adams and Its Dime and Nickel Novels: The Story of a Vanished Literature." *Northern Illinois University Libraries Website*. <http://www.ulib.niu.edu/badndp/bibindex.html> (April 13, 2009).

Jordan, Tina. "Books: David Foster Wallace." *Entertainment Weekly*, March 13, 2009.

Kakutani, Michiko. "And Then What Happened? Read the Sequel." *New York Times*, June 5, 1992, C1.

Karr, Jean. *Zane Grey: Man of the West*. New York: Grosset & Dunlap, 1949.

Kay, Jennifer. "'Green Gables' Gets a Prequel." *Berkshire Eagle*, March 7, 2008.

Kellner, Tomas. "Stranger Than Fiction." *Forbes Website*, Oct. 28, 2002. <http://www.forbes.com/forbes/2002/1028/110_print.html> (Feb. 22, 2009).

Kelly, Susan. "The Captain's Courageous Wife Sets Sail." *USA Today*, Nov. 18, 1999, 7D.

King, David M. "James Bond After Ian Fleming — A Collection." *AB Bookman's Weekly*, April 5, 1993, 1441.

Kirkpatrick, David D. "Court Halts Book Based on 'Gone with the Wind,'" *New York Times*, April 21, 2002, B1.

Kittredge, William, and Steven M. Krauzer. *The Great American Detective*. New York: New American Library, 1978.

Klaw, Rick. "The Sincerest Form of Flattery." *The SF Site*. <http://www.sfsite.com/columns/geeks135.htm> (July 19, 2006).

Lane, Andrew. "Passing the Baton: The Phenomenon of 'Sequels by Other Hands' Is Investigated." *Million: The Magazine of Popular Fiction*, (January-February 1991): 44.

_____. "Return of Fu Manchu," *Million: The Magazine of Popular Fiction* No. 4 (July-August 1991): 19.

_____. "A Story for Which the World Is Not Yet Prepared." *Million: The Magazine of Popular Fiction* No. 2 (March-April 1991): 49.

"Lassie Collectibles and Memorabilia." <http://www.geocitie.com/collectlassie/books.htm> (June 16, 2008).

Leary, Stephen. "Who Is Writing Robert Ludlum's Books?" *The Leary Letter*. <http://blog.stephenleary.com/2006/07/who-is-writing-robert-ludlums-books.html> (Feb. 22, 2009).

Lehmann-Haupt, Christopher. "Mole, Badger and Mr. Toad, Redux." *Berkshire Eagle*, Oct. 21, 1994, C7 (reprinted from *New York Times*)

Lesher, Linda Parent. *The Best Novels of the Nineties*. Jefferson, N.C.: McFarland, 2000.

"Literary and Trade Notes." (Vanderpoole/Sand), *Publishers Weekly*, Sept. 24, 1887, 316. <http://books.google.com/books?id=InkWAAAAMAAJ&pg=PA316&lpg=PA316&dq=George+Sand+Manuscript+Lew&source=web&ots=DBzkoBFATE&sig=Wuy4AIoDR1hXaoxCIaKAIQ6s8BQ&hl=en&sa=X&oi=book_result&resnum=4&ct=result> (Jan. 8, 2009).

"Literary Sequels." *Romantic Times*. <http://www.romantictimes.com/forum/viewtopic.php?t=9607> (Oct. 17, 2008).

Little Toot Website. <http://www.littletoot.org/books.asp> (Feb. 21, 2009).

Lord, Glenn, ed. *The Last Celt: A Bio-bibliography of Robert Ervin Howard*. West Kingston, R.I.: Donald M. Grant, 1976.

Lovisi, Gary. *Sherlock Holmes: The Great Detective in Paperback*. Brooklyn, N.Y.: Gryphon Books, 1990.

"Ludlum Identity: How a Bestselling Author Was Bourne Again." *The Independent*, Aug. 1, 2007. <http://www.independent.co.uk/arts-entertainment/books/features/the-ludlum-identity-how-a-bestselling-author-was-bourne-again-459830.html> (Feb. 22, 2009).

Lupoff, Richard A. "Mister Burroughs and Me." *Paperback Parade* No. 10 (December 1988): 39.

Lynds, Gayle. "Remembering Robert Ludlum (1927–2001)." *Mystery Ink*. <http://www.mysteryinkonline.com/ludlumrip.htm> (June 10, 2003).

MacDonald, Jay Lee. "The Truth about True at First Light." *BookPage*. <http://www.bookpage.com/9907bp/patrick_hemingway.html> (Jan. 9, 2009).

Mackey, Margaret. *The Case of Peter Rabbit: Changing Conditions of Literature for Children*. Kindle, 2007.

"Marion Zimmer Bradley Biography." *AllSands*. <http://www.allsands.com/history/people/marionzimmerbr_zrp_gn.htm> (Feb. 21, 2009).

Maslin, Janet. "In 'Scarlett,' Only the Names Are the Same." *New York Times*, Sept. 27, 1991.

"Max Brand Bibliography." <http://www.maxbrandonline.com/bibliography.htm> (Oct. 16, 2008).

McCormick, Donald. *Who's Who in Spy Fiction*. London: Elm Tree Books, 1977.

McGrath, Charles. "Revisiting a Potboiler You Can't Improve." *New York Times*, Nov. 16, 2004, C1.

_____. "What Makes Him the Supersleuth?" *New York Times*, May 20, 2005, B27.

McHugh, Matt. "Ever Wonder What Happened to Scrooge? So Have These Authors:

Recent Literary Sequels to A Christmas Carol." <http://www.mattmchugh.com/what_happened_to_scrooge/index.html> (March 4, 2009).

McManus, Kelly. "Ghosts of SF Past." *Globe and Mail*, March 31, 2007, D27.

Medley, Mark. "The Curious Business of Editing Death Authors." *Weekend Post*, Dec. 6, 2008.

Mehegan, David. "Appeals Court Lifts Injunction on New 'Wind.'" *Boston Globe*, May 26, 2001, F1.

_____. "'Wind' Chill." *Boston Globe*, April 18, 2001, C1.

Memmott, Carol. "The Author and the Impaler: Kostova Spent 10 Years with Vlad/Dracula." *USA Today*, June 14, 2005, 6D.

Mendelsohn, Ink. "Oz — As We All Loved It." *American Collector's Journal*, (May 1985): 1.

Meyer, Karl E. "The Curious Incident of the Sleuth in the Meantime." *New York Times*, Jan. 19, 2000, 1.

Miller, John R. "Curious George Goes Hollywood." *Wall Street Journal*, Feb. 2, 2006.

Miller, Roger K. "Expert Spadework." *National Post*, Feb. 20, 2009. <http://www.canada.com/entertainment/books/Expert+spadework/1312139/story.html> (March 4, 2009).

Milner, Nina. "Duncan Campbell Scott." *Famous Poets and Poems*. <http://famouspoetsandpoems.com/poets/duncan_campbell_scott> (March 27, 2009).

"Modern Sequels." *State Library of Tasmania Website*. <http://www.statelibrary.tas.gov/au/whatdo/reading/modseq.a > (June 6, 2008).

Moon Shines Down: Publisher's Description, *Thomas Nelson Website*. <http://www.thomasnelson.com/consumer/product_detail.asp?sku=140031299X> (Feb. 25 2009).

"More Harry Potter News: Lawsuit Continues." *Chronicle SF Fantasy & Horror Monthly Trade Journal*, (October 2002): 6.

"Moscow Journal: 'War and Peace,' the Sequel: Scholars See Scarlett." *New York Times*, March 5, 1996.

Nevins, Francis M., Jr. "The World of William Ard." *The Armchair Detective*, Vol. 15 No. 2 (1982).

Newman, Kim. "The Return of Philip Marlowe." *Million: The Magazine of Popular Fiction* No. 4 (July-August 1991): 52.

Nielsen, Leon. *Robert E. Howard: A Collector's Descriptive Bibliography, with Biography*. Jefferson, N.C.: McFarland & Co., 2007.

Nolan, William F. "Max Brand: Pulp King." *Paperback Parade* No. 23 (March 1991): 9.

Nye, Jody Lynn. *Jody Lynn Nye Website*. <http://www.sff.net/people/JodyNye/faq.htm> (April 9, 2009).

Oakes, Keily. "Rewriting the Classic Novels." *BBC News Online*, Aug. 20, 2004. <http://news.bbc.co.uk/2/hi/entertainment/3583430.stm> (March 5, 2009).

"One Good Book Deserves Another: A Modern Spin on the Classics." *The Reader's Advisor*. <http://sachem.suffolk.lib.ny.us/advisor/sequels.htm> (June 30, 2008).

O'Rourke, Meghan. "*Ariel* Redux: The Latest Chapter in the Sylvia Plath Controversy." *Slate*, Dec. 7, 2004. <http://www.slate.com/id/2110754/> (Feb. 5, 2009).

_____. "Nancy Drew's Father." *New Yorker*, Nov. 8, 2004, 120.

Peary, Dan. *Guide for the Film Fanatic*. New York: Simon & Schuster, 1986.

Pederson, Jay P., ed. *St. James Guide to Crime & Mystery Writers*, fourth edition. Detroit: St. James Press, 1996.

Pepinster, Catherine. "Waugh Family Fury at 'Brideshead' Sequel." *Independent*, Aug. 17, 2003.

"'Peter Bell' — New Facts about Wordsworth's Poem." *New York Times*, 20 July 1901, BR9.

"Philadelphian: The Late Richard Powell's Classic Novel is Restored by Plexus Publishing, Inc." *Philly Future*, posted Nov. 15, 2006. <http://www.phillyfuture.org/node/4450> (Jan. 9, 2009).

Picker, Leonard. "Lord Peter Wimsey and Harriet Vane Redux." *Publishers Weekly*, Jan. 20, 2003.

Pierce, J. Kingston. "Killers, Cover-ups & Max Allan Collins." *January Magazine.* <http://www.januarymagazine.com/profiles/collins.html> (Jan. 9, 2009).

"Playboy of the Eastern World: 'The Tale of Genji.'" *Economist,* Dec. 20, 2008.

Plunkett, Terry. "Woodshed on the Moon: Thoreau Poems." Review, *Kennebec: A Portfolio of Maine Writing,* Vol. 16, p. 10.

Pomerantz, Dorothy. "Ghost Writers." *Forbes.* <http://www.forbes.com/2005/10/26/publishing-dead-authors_deadceleb05_cz_dp_1027authors.html> (Jan. 10, 2009).

Princess Nourmahal. Review, *New York Times,* Nov. 5, 1888.

Pringle, David. "Of Sequels and Prequels — and Sequels by Other Hands." *Million: The Magazine of Popular Fiction* (May-June 1992): 24.

Pronzini, Bill, and Marcia Muller. *1001 Midnights: The Aficionado's Guide to Mystery and Detective Fiction.* New York: Arbor House, 1986.

Rich, Motoko. "The Real Carver: Expansive or Minimal." *New York Times,* Oct. 17, 2007.

_____. "Rhett, Scarlett and Friends Prepare for Yet Another Encore." *New York Times,* May 16, 2007, B1.

Riding, Alan. "Victor Hugo Can't Rest in Peace, As a Sequel Makes Trouble." *New York Times,* May 29, 2001, B1.

"Robert Jordan (1948–2007)." *Locus* (October 2007): 10.

Robinson, Eleanor. "Once Upon a Time... A Happy Ending for the Unauthorised Sequel?" *New Zealand Postgraduate Law e-Journal* No. 4. <http://nzpostgraduatelawejournal.auckland.ac.nz/PDF%20Articles/Issue%204%20(2006)/EleanorONCE%20UPON%20A%20TIME.pdf> (17 October 2008).

Rothstein, Mervyn. "Isaac Asimov, Whose Thoughts and Books Traveled the Universe, Is Dead at 72." *New York Times,* April 7, 1992.

Salinger Case Appeal, <http://www.scribd.com/doc/17649921/Salinger-Case-Defendants-2ndCir-Brief-72309> (viewed July 25, 2009).

Salt Water Review and Charles Simmons Interview. *Powells Books Website.* <http://www.powells.com/biblio?show=TRADE%20PAPER:USED:9780671035679:5.95&page=readinggroupguide>

Sampson, Robert. *Yesterday's Faces Vol. 6: Violent Lives.* Bowling Green, Ohio: Bowling Green State University Popular Press, 1993.

"Sanderson Named Jordan's Collaborator." *Locus* (January 2008): 10.

Sandomir, Richard. "The Ludlum Conundrum: A Dead Novelist Provides New Thrills." *New York Times,* July 30, 2007.

Sawyer, Andy. "Fairy-Tale Horror." *Million: The Magazine of Popular Fiction* No. 4 (July-August 1991): 31.

Schwarzbaum, Lisa. "'Rebecca' Redux." *Entertainment Weekly,* Oct. 2, 1993, 67.

Shapiro, Laura. "Manderly Confidential." *New York Times Book Review,* Oct. 14, 2001, 31.

Sheridan, Martin. "Wrote Western Movies Before He Saw a Cowboy." *Boston Herald,* March 24, 1940.

"Sherlock Holmes Returns." *Harris County Public Library eBranch.* <http://www.hcpl.net/booklists/sherlock.htm> (June 6, 2008).

Silvey, Anita. *100 Best Books for Children.* Boston: Houghton Mifflin, 2004.

Simkin, John E. *The Whole Story: 3000 Years of Sequels & Sequences.* Victoria, Australia: Thorpe, 1998.

"Sir Arthur Conan Doyle & Sherlock Holmes (Canon and Pastiche)." Mysetrylist.com. <http://www.mysterylist.com/holmes.htm> (May 28, 2005).

Slavitt, Davir R. "You Can Go Holmes Again." *New York Review of Books,* Oct. 17, 1993.

Snider, Mike. "Son Navigates Shifting Sands to Extend the Legacy of 'Dune.'" *USA Today,* Oct. 14, 1999, 5D.

Sprague de Camp, L., ed. *The Blade of Conan.* New York: Ace, 1979.

Stanley, Alessandra. "Frankly My Dear, Russians Do Give a Damn." *New York Times*, May 12, 2008.

Steinbrunner, Chris, and Otto Penzler. *Encyclopedia of Mystery & Detection*. New York: McGraw Hill, 1976.

Stocking, Marion K. "Woodshed on the Moon." Review, *Beloit Poetry Journal*, summer 1992, 42.

Strock, Ian Randal. "Unpublished Michael Crichton Novel to Appear Later this Year." *SFScope*, April 6, 2009. <http://sfscope.com/2009/04/unpublished-michael-crichton -n.html> (April 9, 2009).

Suellentrop, Chris. "Dead Man Writing: How to Keep Writing your Late Father's Books." *Slate*, Feb. 20, 2003. <http://www.slate.com/id/2078980/> (Feb. 14, 2009).

Sultzberger, A.G. "Holden Caulfield, a Ripe 76, Heads to Court Again." *New York Times*, June 17, 2009.

Swanson, Jean, and Dean James. *By a Woman's Hand: A Guide to Mystery Fiction by Women*. New York: Berkley Prime Crime, 1994.

Thomas, Roy. "Thomas Talks." *Conan Saga* 73, Marvel Comics, April 1993.

"Trailsman by Jon Sharpe." *Somebody Dies*, Feb. 11, 2009. <http://somebodydies. blogspot.com/2009/02/trailsman-by-jon-sharpe-western-series.html> (March 22, 2009).

"Very European Hero." *The Economist*, Dec. 20, 2008.

Young, Robert Vaughn. "Mission Earth: The Rest of the Story." <http://www.lermanet. com/cos/MissionEarth.htm> (Feb. 12, 2009).

Walt Whitman Birthplace Association Website. <http://www.waltwhitman.org/AboutWhit man.asp> (Jan. 10, 2009).

"Was Bertha M. Clay Really Thomas W. Hanshew?" *New York Times*, June 7, 1914.

Webster, Jack. *Alistair MacLean: A Life*. London: Chapmans Publishers, 1991.

Weinberg, Robert, ed. *The Louis L'Amour Companion*. New York: Bantam, 1994.

Wheatley, Jane. "Last Writes." *The Times*, Aug. 25, 2007. <http://entertainment.timeson line.co.uk/tol/arts_and_entertainment/books/fiction/article2320620.ece> (March 19, 2009).

Whitehead, David. "David Whitehead Remembers Leonard Meares." *Black Horse Extra*. <http://blackhorsewesterns.com/> (June 22, 2008).

Wiley, David. "In Search of Perfection: Unfinished Literary Masterpieces." *About.com*. <http://classiclit.about.com/od/historyofbooks/a/aa_unfinished.htm> (Feb. 23, 2009).

Wilson, Budge. Interview. *Reuters*, March 19, 2008.

"Winnie-the-Pooh to Return." *Albany Times-Union*, January 10, 2009.

"Woman Writes Sequel to A Dream of Red Mansions." *Beijing Review*. <http://www.bj review.com.cn/books/txt/2006–12/11/content_93810.htm> (March 4, 2009).

"Women's Dime Novel Romance Series and Story Papers." *American Women's Dime Novel Project: Dime Novels for Women, 1870–1920*. <http://chnm.gmu.edu/dimenovels/ romance_series.html> (April 13, 2009).

Zipp, Yvonne. "Holmes, the Sequel, the Prequel, and Mrs., Too." *Christian Science Monitor*, May 10, 2005.

Index